Human and Machine Vision II

PERSPECTIVES IN COMPUTING, Vol. 13

(Formerly "Notes and Reports in Computer Science and Applied Mathematics")

W. Rheinboldt and D. Siewiorek, editors

Human and Machine Vision II

Azriel Rosenfeld, editor

Center for Automation Research
University of Maryland
College Park, Maryland

ACADEMIC PRESS, INC.
Harcourt Brace Jovanovich, Publishers

Boston Orlando San Diego
New York Austin London Sydney
Tokyo Toronto

Academic Press, Inc.
Orlando, Florida 32887

Library of Congress Cataloging in Publication Data
Human and machine vision II.

(Perspectives in computing ; 13)
Largely papers of the second Workshop on Human and Machine Vision, held in
Montréal, Canada, Aug. 1-3, 1984 in conjunction with the International Conference on
Pattern Recognition.
First appeared in the Aug., Sept., and Oct. issues of Computer vision, graphics and
image processing.
Includes bibliographies.
1. Visual perception—Congresses. 2. Computer vision—Congresses. 3. Image
processing—Congresses.

I. Rosenfeld, Azriel, Date   II. Workshop on Human and Machine Vision (2nd : 1984 :
Montréal, Québec) III. Title: Human and machine vision 2. IV. Series.
BF241.H86 1986   006.3'7   86-45928

ISBN 0-12-597345-4 (alk. paper)

9 8 7 6 5 4 3 2 1
Printed in USA

Contents

Preface

The second Workshop on Human and Machine Vision was held in Montreal, Canada on August 1–3, 1984, in conjunction with the International Conference on Pattern Recognition. This book contains eleven of the papers presented at the Workshop, together with three other papers (by M. Leyton, B. Smith, and G. Sperling) on related themes.

The Proceedings of the First Workshop, held in Denver, Colorado in 1980, were published in book form by Academic Press in 1983 (J. Beck, B. Hope, and A. Rosenfeld, eds., *Human and Machine Vision*.) The papers in the present volume first appeared in the August, September, and October 1985 issues of the journal *Computer Vision, Graphics and Image Processing*; they are collected here in book form to make them more widely available to students and researchers in both fields — visual perception and computer vision.

The workshops, and the publications resulting from them, serve an important purpose in enhancing communications between the two fields. Both groups can benefit substantially from exchanges of ideas. It is planned to continue to hold such workshops on a regular basis.

Azriel Rosenfeld

Contributors

Haruo Asada, *Artificial Intelligence Laboratory, Massachusetts Institute of Technology, Cambridge, Massachusetts 02139*

Jacob Beck, *Department of Psychology, University of Oregon, Eugene, Oregon 97403-1227*

Irving Biederman, *Department of Psychology, University of New York at Buffalo, Amherst, New York 14226*

Michael Brady, *Artificial Intelligence Laboratory, Massachusetts Institute of Technology, Cambridge, Massachusetts 02139*

Yoav Cohen, *Human Information Processing Laboratory, Psychology Department, New York University, New York, New York 10012*

Jerome A. Feldman, *University of Rochester, Rochester, New York 14627*

Ralph Norman Haber, *Department of Psychology, University of Illinois at Chicago, Chicago, Illinois 60680*

Donald D. Hoffman, *Natural Computation Group, Massachusetts Institute of Technology, Cambridge, Massachusetts 02139*

Takeo Kanade, *Department of Computer Science, Carnegie-Mellon University, Pittsburgh, Pennsylvania 15213*

Michael Landy, *Human Information Processing Laboratory, Psychology Department, New York University, New York, New York 10012*

S. Levy, *Schnurmacher Institute for Vision Research, State University of New York, State College of Optometry, New York, New York 10010*

Michael Leyton, *Department of Psychology and Social Relations, Harvard University, Cambridge, Massachusetts 02138*

M. Pavel, *Human Information Processing Laboratory, Psychology Department, New York University, New York, New York 10012*

Tomaso Poggio, *Artificial Intelligence Laboratory and Center for Biological Information Processing, Massachusetts Institute for Technology, Cambridge, Massachusetts 02139*

Jean Ponce, *Artificial Intelligence Laboratory, Massachusetts Institute of Technology, Cambridge, Massachusetts 02139*

Whitman Richards, *Natural Computation Group, Massachusetts Institute of Technology, Cambridge, Massachusetts 02139*

H.A. Sedgwick, *Schnurmacher Institute for Vision Research, State University of New York, State College of Optometry, New York, New York 10010*

Beverly J. Smith, *University of Victoria, Victoria, Canada*

David R. Smith, *Department of Computer Science, Carnegie-Mellon University, Pittsburgh, Pennsylvania 15213*

George Sperling, *Human Information Processing Laboratory, Psychology Department, New York University, New York, New York 10012*

Anne Treisman, *University of British Columbia, Vancouver, British Columbia, Canada*

Alan Yuille, *Artificial Intelligence Laboratory, Massachusetts Institute of Technology, Cambridge, Massachusetts 02139*

Steven W. Zucker, *Computer Vision and Robotics Laboratory, Department of Electrical Engineering, McGill University, Montreal, Quebec, Canada*

Perception of Transparency in Man and Machine*

Jacob Beck

University of Oregon, Eugene, Oregon 97403

Received October 31, 1984

The different tactics employed by human and machine vision systems in judging transparency are compared. Instead of luminance or reflectance (relative luminance), the human visual system uses lightness, a nonlinear function of reflectance, to estimate transparency. The representation of intensity information in terms of lightness restricts the operations that can be applied, and does not permit solving the equations describing the occurrence of transparency. Instead, the human visual system uses algorithms based on simple order and magnitude relations. One consequence of the human visual system not using a mathematically correct procedure is the occurrence of nonveridical perceptions of transparency. A second consequence is that the human visual system is not able to make accurate judgments of the degree of transparency. Figural cues are also important in the human perception of transparency. The tendency for the human visual system to see a simple organization leads to the perception of transparency even when the intensity pattern indicates transparency to be physically impossible. In contrast, given the luminances or reflectances, a machine vision system can apply the relevant equations for additive and subtractive color mixture to give veridical and quantitatively correct judgments of transparency. © 1985 Academic Press, Inc.

1. INTRODUCTION

This paper compares how a person judges transparency with how a machine judges transparency when programmed not to simulate human perception but to estimate transparency veridically. The case dealt with is of a diffusely reflecting achromatic object viewed in neutral illumination through a transparent medium that is nonselective for wavelength.

Transparency arises physically in two ways. Transparency can occur in looking through a fine wire mesh screen. If a person is far enough so that his eyes fail to accommodate for the wire mesh, the light from the wire mesh and from the holes blur on the retina. The retinal stimulus is a weighted average of the light intensity reflected from the wire mesh of the screen and the light transmitted by the holes in the screen from the object. Transparency occurring in this way is described as occurring through additive color mixture. Transparency also occurs when one looks through a transparent medium, such as a filter. When an object is viewed through a filter, part of the light is absorbed by the filter, and part of the light is transmitted by the filter, reflected by the object, and retransmitted by the filter. There are multiple reflections between the object and the filter before a ray emerges. The retinal stimulus is the result of the light reflected by the object and transmitted by the filter plus the surface reflectance from the filter. Transparency occurring in this way is described as occurring through subtractive color mixture.

*The writing of this paper was supported by AFOSR Contract F49620-83-C-0093 to the University of Oregon.

1

2. ADDITIVE COLOR MIXTURE

Metelli [1, 2] has proposed a model for the perception of transparency based on additive color mixture. Additive color mixture occurs when a device with open and closed sectors, called an episcotister, rotates rapidly in front of surfaces. Figure 1 depicts the retinal stimulus resulting when an episcotister rotates in front of surfaces A and B. Rotating the episcotister rapidly produces the perception of a transparent color (regions d and c) lying in front of surfaces A and B. The apparent reflectances of regions d and c is a weighted average, sometimes called Talbot's Law, of the light reflected from the background surfaces A and B and from the blades of the episcotister e. The apparent reflectances of regions d and c are equal to

$$d = \alpha a + (1 - \alpha)e \tag{1}$$

$$c = \alpha b + (1 - \alpha)e \tag{2}$$

where α is the proportion of light reflected from surface A (corresponding to the areal fraction occupied by the open sectors of the episcotister), $1 - \alpha$ is the proportion of light reflected from the blades of the episcotister (corresponding to the areal fraction occupied by the blade of the episcotister), a is the reflectance of surface A, b is the reflectance of surface B, and e is the reflectance of the episcotister blades.

The values of a, b, c, and d are given by the retinal stimulus and the visual system needs to solve for α and e. Solving Eq. (1) and (2) for α and e yields

$$\alpha = (d - c)/(a - b) \tag{3}$$

$$e = (ac - bd)/(a + c) - (b + d). \tag{4}$$

Alpha is the proportion of the apparent reflectances of d and c determined by the reflectances a and b and is an index of transparency. When the apparent reflectance (or luminance) of region d equals the apparent reflectance (or luminance) of region c, $\alpha = 0$ and the overlying surface composed of regions d and c is opaque. When the difference in apparent reflectance (or luminance) $d - c$ equals the difference in apparent reflectance (luminance) $a - b$, the overlying surface composed of regions d

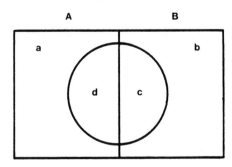

FIG. 1.   The retinal stimulus resulting from an episcotister rotating in front of two surfaces differing in reflectance. Capital letters A and B indicate the background surfaces. Lowercase letters indicate regions of differing intensity.

and c is perfectly transparent. Certain constraints follow from the physics of the situation. Since α is restricted to values between 0 and 1, Eq. (3) implies (i) if $a > b$, then $d > c$ and vice versa if $a < b$, and (ii) the absolute difference $|a - b|$ must be greater than the absolute difference $|d - c|$. Constraint (i) is a restriction on the order of the intensities and ensures that α is positive. Constraint (ii) is a restriction on the magnitudes of the intensities and ensures that α is less than 1. Since e is also restricted to values greater than or equal to 0 and less than or equal to 1, order and magnitude constraints can also be derived from Eq. (4). Eq. (4) implies (iii) if $(a + c) > (b + d)$ then $ac > bd$ and vice versa if $(a + c) < (b + d)$, and (iv) the absolute difference $|(a + c) - (b + d)|$ must be greater than the absolute difference $|ac - bd|$. Constraint (iii) ensures that e is nonnegative, and constraint (iv) ensures that e is less than 1. The four constraints are independent. Numerical values can be assigned to the reflectances a, b, c, and d in Eqs. (3) and (4) that satisfy three of the constraints but not the fourth.

Beck et al. [3] investigated how violations of constraints (i) through (iv) affect the perception of transparency. Figure 2a depicts the stimuli used. Capital letters identify surfaces and lowercase letters regions of differing reflectance. The stimuli were computer generated pictures of two overlapping squares, a top and bottom square on a larger background surface. Figure 2b shows a stimulus satisfying constraints (i) through (iv). The bottom square can be seen as transparent and overlying the top square and the background.

Metelli [1, 2] showed that violations of either constraints (i) or (ii) adversely affect the perception of transparency. Beck et al. [3] found that the perception of transparency varied inversely with the salience with which constraints (i) or (ii) are violated. The perception of transparency did not occur when either constraint (i) or constraint (ii) were violated strongly. Figure 3a shows a stimulus which strongly violates the order relation of constraint (i). The reflectance of region a is less than

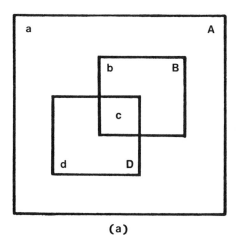
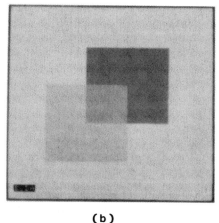

(a) (b)

FIG. 2. (a) Stimulus configuration. Capital letters indicate the surfaces depicted. Lowercase letters indicate regions of differing intensity. (b) Stimulus satisfying constraints (i) through (iv).

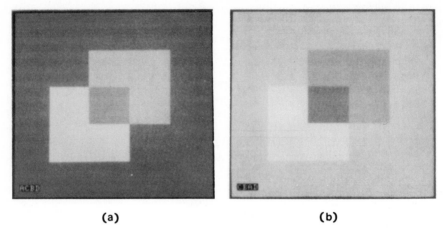

(a)   **(b)**

FIG. 3.   (a) Stimulus strongly violating constraint (i); (b) stimulus strongly violating constraint (ii).

that of region b, but the reflectance of region d which overlies a is greater than that of region c which overlies b. Figure 3b shows a stimulus which strongly violates the magnitude relation of constraint (ii). The reflectance difference between a and b is contained within the reflectance difference between c and d. Metelli did not investigate the effect of violating constraints (iii) and (iv) on transparency. Beck et al. [3] have shown that violations of constraints (iii) and (iv) do not adversely affect the perception of transparency. This has important consequences for the perception of transparency. It makes possible the nonveridical perception of transparency. That is, a pattern of intensities which physically cannot occur in an actual case of transparency will be seen as transparent. Before pursuing this further, I will turn to another question first.

3. SUBTRACTIVE COLOR MIXTURE

The perception of transparency often occurs in terms of subtractive color mixture rather than in terms of additive color mixture. Constraints (i) and (ii) were derived from a model which assumes additive color mixture. The question can be raised: Why do constraints (i) and (ii) predict the perception of transparency as well as they do since they appear to be ecologically unrepresentative?

The physical situation is depicted in Fig. 4a. Figure 4b illustrates the multiple reflections and transmittances that occur. Light is in part reflected from the front surface of the filter, and in part transmitted by the filter and reflected from the opaque surface behind the filter; the reflected light is in part transmitted and in part reflected back and so on. In Fig. 4, a is the reflectance of surface A, b is the reflectance of surface B, f is the reflectance of the filter F, and t is the transmittance of the filter. The apparent reflectances of regions d and c are equal to

$$d = f + (t^2a)/(1 - fa) \tag{5}$$

$$c = f + (t^2b)/(1 - fb). \tag{6}$$

The values of a, b, c, and d are given by the retinal stimulus and the visual system needs to solve for t and f.

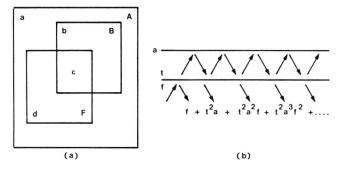

FIG. 4.   (a) Illustration of subtractive color mixture occurring with a filter. Capital letters A, B, and F indicate the background surfaces and the filter. Lowercase letters indicate regions of differing reflectance. (b) Illustration of the pattern of reflectance—a is the reflectance of surface A, f is the reflectance, and t the transmittance of filter F.

Solving Eqs. (5) and (6) for t and f yields

$$t = \sqrt{\frac{(c - bcd + bd^2 - d)(b - a - abc + a^2c)}{(b - a + abd - abc)^2}} \tag{7}$$

$$f = \frac{(bd - ac)}{(b + abd) - (a + abc)}. \tag{8}$$

Order and magnitude constraints for the perception of transparency with subtractive color mixture can be derived from Eqs. (7) and (8). Since the perception of transparency occurs when t is restricted to values between 0 and 1, Eq. (7) implies: (v) $(c - bcd + bd^2 - d)(b - a - abc + a^2c) > 0$ and (vi) $(b - a + abd - abc)^2 > (c - bcd + bd^2 - d)(b - a - abc + a^2c)$. Constraint (v) ensures that t is positive and constraint (vi) that it is less than 1. Since the reflectance of the filter, f, is also restricted to values greater than or equal to 0 and less than 1, Eq. (8) implies: (vii) if $bd > ac$, then $b + abd > a + abc$ and vice versa if $bd < ac$, and (viii) the absolute difference $|b + abd - a + abc|$ must be greater than the absolute difference $|bd - ac|$. Constraint (vii) ensures that f is positive and constraint (viii) ensures that f is less than 1. An additional constraint is that $t + f$ must be less than or equal to 1.

What is the relationship between the equations derived from the episcotister and filter models? Equations (1) and (2) are clearly not equal to Eqs. (5) and (6). The order and magnitude constraints defining the boundary conditions for solutions of the two sets of equations, however, appear to be closely related. Equations (5) and (6) of the filter model imply constraints (i) and (ii) derived from Eq. (3) of the episcotister model, and Eqs. (1) and (2) of the episcotister model imply constraints (v) and (vi) derived from Eq. (7) of the filter model. Although we have not been able to demonstrate it mathematically, a computer search of the solutions to Eqs. (5) and (6) of the filter model has failed to find any solutions that violate constraints (iii) and (iv) derived from Eq. (4). Similarly, a computer search of the solutions to Eqs. (1) and (2) of the episcotister model has failed to find any solutions that violate constraints (vii) and (viii) derived from Eq. (8) of the filter model. The variables were incremented by 0.02 within the bounds for each set of equations, and the calculations were carried out to four decimal places. Thus, transparency with subtractive color mixture entails the computationally simpler constraints (i) through (iv) derived from the equations for additive color mixture. Judgments of the degree of transparency based on Eq. (3) will not be quantitatively correct with subtractive color mixture. However, this is not important since, as will be shown, humans are not generally able to make quantitatively accurate judgments of transparency.

Constraints (i) and (ii) are ecologically valid indicators of transparency because the order and difference relations embodied by them are true for both additive and subtractive color mixture. If we translate constraints (i) and (ii) into words, one can see intuitively why they hold. Constraint (i) says: No matter how transparency is produced, the overlaying of a transparent surface cannot change the order of the lightness values. If in Fig. 2a region a is lighter than region b, then the area overlying region a, region d, must be lighter than the area overlying region b, region c. Constraint (ii) says: When lightness values are reduced by overlaying a transparent surface, the lightness difference within the transparent area (regions d and c) must be less than the lightness difference outside of the transparent area (regions a and b). The brain has internalized constraints (i) and (ii) for inferring transparency on the basis of the physical causes of transparency. If constraints (i) or (ii) are violated, the change in intensities in a pattern are not ascribed to transparency. Constraints (iii) and (iv) do not have a simple interpretation in terms of lightness and the visual system does not use them in judging transparency.

4. NONVERIDICAL PERCEPTION OF TRANSPARENCY

What are the consequences of the visual system not being sensitive to violations of constraints (iii) and (iv)? Equation (3) gives the degree of transparency for additive color mixture when Eq. (4) is satisfied. That is, when the values a, b, c, and d are such that constraints (i) through (iv) are satisfied. Since α and e in a physical instance of transparency are less than or equal to 1, constraints (i) through (iv) are automatically satisfied. However, since the visual system is not sensitive to violations of constraints (iii) and (iv), it is possible to choose reflectance values which produce a perception of transparency but which physically is impossible. If in Fig. 2a the reflectance of region a is 0.57, of region b 0.47, of region c 0.24 and of region d 0.33, constraints (i) and (ii) are satisfied ($\alpha = 0.90$), while constraints (iii) and (iv) are not ($e = -1.83$). Though constraints (iii) and (iv) are not satisfied, the bottom square was readily seen as transparent [3]. Substituting the values for a, b, c, and d in Eq. (3) gives a predicted transparency of 0.90. The mean of subjects' judgments of transparency was 0.46. The reason for the discrepancy between subjects' estimates of transparency and the predicted transparency from Eq. (3) is easily seen. Though the difference between reflectances d and c (0.90) is close to the difference between reflectances a and b (0.10) giving a transparency estimate of (0.90), the reflectance of region d (0.33) is not similar to the reflectance of region a (0.57) and the reflectance of region c (0.24) is not similar to the reflectance of region b (0.47). This can occur because constraints (iii) and (iv) are not satisfied. In a real physical instance of transparency, where constraints (iii) and (iv) are not violated, this would not be possible. When the difference between the reflectances d and c $(d - c)$ approaches the difference between the reflectances a and b $(a - b)$, then the reflectance of region d approaches the reflectance of region a, and the reflectance of region c approaches the reflectance of region b. Physically, Eq. (3) both sets conditions through constraints (i) and (ii) for the occurrence of transparency and tells how transparent a surface is with additive color mixture. Psychologically, Eq. (3) sets conditions through constraints (i) and (ii) on *whether* the perception of transparency occurs, but does not always accurately indicate *how* transparent a surface is seen to be. As in the example just given, to suppose that the visual system always uses Eq. (3) without modification to determine the degree of transparency can lead to an absurdity. Two questions need to be answered: Why is the human visual system not sensitive to violations of constraints (iii) and (iv)? How does the human visual system judge the degree of transparency?

5. REFLECTANCE VS LIGHTNESS

To answer these questions, we have to deal first with another question. Metelli's Eq. (3) describing the conditions for the perception of transparency assumes that perceived transparency is determined by reflectance values. Reflectances are physical values and not psychological values. The psychological dimension corresponding to reflectance is lightness. Lightness is the dimension of sensory experience which may be described as going from white through gray to black as reflectance goes from 100 to 0%. Physical differences are not the same as psychological differences. Several equations have been proposed as approximate expressions of the relation between lightness and reflectance (or relative luminance). For example, lightness has been proposed to grow as a logarithmic function of reflectance, and as a linear function of the cube root of reflectance. A minimal condition is that lightness is a negatively accelerated monotonic function of reflectance. Figure 5 illustrates such a relationship. Lightness on the y axis is related by a negatively accelerated function to reflectance on the x axis. A monotonic transformation preserves order. Thus, constraint (i) is satisfied in terms of lightness if it is satisfied in terms of reflectance. The satisfaction of constraint (ii), which involves differences, depends on particular values. Constraint (ii) can be satisfied in terms of reflectance values, but not in terms of lightness values and vice versa. For example, consider the absolute differences $|a - b|$ and $|d - c|$ in Fig. 5. In terms of reflectance, the difference $|a - b|$ is greater than the difference $|d - c|$ satisfying constraint (ii). In terms of lightness, the difference $|a' - b'|$ is smaller than the difference $|d' - c'|$ violating constraint (ii).

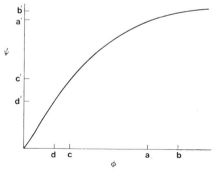

FIG. 5. Illustration of the relationship between lightness (ψ) and reflectance (ϕ).

The perception of transparency depends on checking whether constraints (i) and (ii) are satisfied. What is the nature of the representation on which this checking is done? Is it in terms of reflectance values or in terms of lightness values? Beck *et al.* [3] have shown that the stimulus representation for transparency judgments is, as might be expected, in terms of lightness values and not reflectance values. Why constraints (i) and (ii) and not (iii) and (iv) are psychologically relevant can now be understood. The constancy of lightness in a scene with an overall change in the illumination keeps the ratios of intensities in the scene the same. Thus it is important for the visual system to encode information about the ratios of intensities. If the sensory transformation is approximately logarithmic, this means that the visual system has to encode information about sensory differences. That is, in order to determine whether intensity ratios are the same, the visual system has evolved mechanisms for comparing lightness differences. The order of lightness values, their differences, and the relative sizes of lightness differences are encoded by the visual system because of their ecological importance. The visual system is thus equipped for determining whether constraints (i) and (ii) are satisfied. Constraints (iii) and (iv) involve operations of addition and multiplication. What is the sum of a light gray and a medium gray or the product of a light gray and a medium gray seems like a nonsensical question. It is an unnatural psychological thing to take sums and products of lightness values. They are not intuitively interpretable, I believe, because there is no adaptive need for the visual system to judge sums and products of lightnesses. Applying constraints (iii) and (iv) to lightness values is not possible because there has been no ecological reason for developing this ability.

6. PERCEPTION OF THE DEGREE OF TRANSPARENCY

What determines the perception of transparency? One possibility is that substituting lightness values for reflectances in Eq. (3) correctly predicts the perceived degree of transparency. The argument for this is that the estimate of transparency is based on the reduction of apparent contrast. The perception of the degree of transparency is assumed to be a function of the similarity of the lightnesses in regions d and c relative to the similarity of the lightnesses in regions a and b. If the lightnesses of regions d and c are equal, that is, if their contrast is zero, then the degree of perceived transparency is zero. As the lightness difference between regions d and c approaches the lightness difference between regions a and b, the perceived degree of transparency goes to 100%.[1] This equation, however, cannot be correct without further restriction. In Fig. 6b, the lightness difference between d and c is nearly equal to that between a and b. Substituting subjects' estimates of lightness values in Eq. (3) gives a predicted transparency of 0.96 when the rectangle is seen as transparent and overlying the square [3]. A transparency of 0.96 implies that the lightnesses of regions d and a should be similar, and the lightnesses of regions c and b should be similar. This is clearly not the case. The mean of subjects' transparency estimates was 0.38 [3]. Just as with reflectances, substituting lightness values in Eq. (3) can lead to an incorrect prediction of transparency.

Figure 6b does not correspond to a physically possible instance of transparency. In an actual physical instance of transparency, if the reflectance difference $d - c$ is

---

[1] Transparency judgments based on Eq. (3) and on lightness, of course, will not be quantitatively correct for either additive or subtractive color mixture.

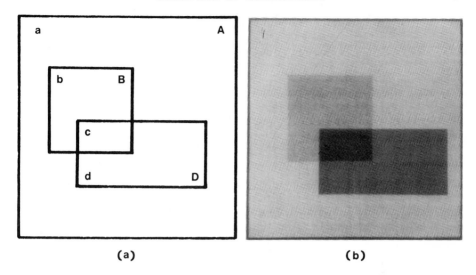

(a)   (b)

Fig. 6. (a) Stimulus configuration. Capital letters indicate the surfaces depicted. Lowercase letters indicate regions of differing intensity. (b) Stimulus violating constraint (iii).

close to the reflectance difference $a - b$ indicating high transparency, then the reflectance of region d would approach the reflectance of region a, and the reflectance of region c would approach the reflectance of region b. If the reflectances of regions d and a and of c and b approach each other, then the lightnesses of regions d and c would approach the lightnesses of regions a and b. The discrepancy between the predicted transparency of 0.96 and subjects' mean transparency judgment of 0.38 appears to be based on the fact that the lightness values of regions d and c differ from the lightness values of regions a and b. This occurs because the stimulus violates constraint (iii). One possibility is that in an actual instance of transparency where constraints (i) through (iv) are satisfied, perceived transparency is based on substituting lightness values in Eq. (3). That is, the perception of the degree of transparency is a function of the lightnesses of regions d and c relative to regions a and b. Only if application of Eq. (3) leads to contradiction, as it can in nonveridical instances of transparency, is the estimate modified. If Eq. (3) results in a high transparency (e.g., greater than 80 or 90%) and the lightnesses of regions d and a, and c and b are not similar (as they should be with high transparency), the estimate of transparency is adjusted downward. This is not a rational mathematical adjustment. The human visual system, when presented with conflicting information, produces a compromise. The estimated transparency is decreased by an arbitrary amount to resolve the contradiction. The adjustment is probably even nonlinear. A second possibility is that the perception of the degree of transparency is based on stimulus relations other than those that determine whether the perception of transparency occurs [3]. This is suggested by an initial study in which a correlation of only 0.55 was found between the means of 26 subjects' transparency estimates of 8 stimuli satisfying constraints (i) through (iv) and the transparency predicted by substituting lightness values in Eq. (3). There are 4 lightness contrasts in Fig. 6b. The contrasts between regions a and b, c and d, a and d, and c and b (see Fig. 6a for identification of the regions). Masin [4] has proposed that the perception of transparency is a weighted function of these lightness differences. Masin hypothesized that perceived transparency is less (a) the greater the lightness difference between the parts of a surface within the transparent area and the parts of the surface outside of the transparent area (d and a, and c and b), and (b) the smaller the lightness difference between the parts of different surfaces within the transparent area (d and c).

7. FIGURAL CUES

Transparency is indicated by both the alteration in image intensities, and the cues provided by the figural configuration. How do cues deriving from the pattern of intensities relate to figural information? Beck *et al.* [3] proposed that figural cues are primary. If the arrangement of contours strongly suggests transparency, then the order (constraint (i)) and magnitude relationships (constraint (ii)) are checked to see if they are consistent with the perception of transparency. If the figural cues for transparency are strong enough, then transparency may be seen even when the pattern of lightness relationships is implausible or even incorrect [3].

The importance of figural configuration is shown in the case of unbalanced transparency. The values of α and e in Eqs. (1) and (2) are assumed to be equal. This assumes that the transparent surface (regions d and c in Figs. 2a and 4a) have the same transparency and reflectance throughout. Metelli has called this "balanced transparency." It is of course possible for the values of α and of e in Eqs. (1) and (2) to differ. In a case of unbalanced transparency, there are four unknowns (α_1, α_2, e_1 and e_2) and two equations. The system is underdetermined and there is no unique solution. Ordinarily, the visual system appears to incorporate an assumption of balanced transparency. Constraints (i) and (ii) follow only from the assumption of balanced transparency. If either the transparency or reflectance of the transparent surface (regions d and c) differ, physical instances of transparency can occur in which constraints (i) and (ii) are violated.

Fig. 7. An example of partial transparency. The surface appears in part transparent and in part opaque.

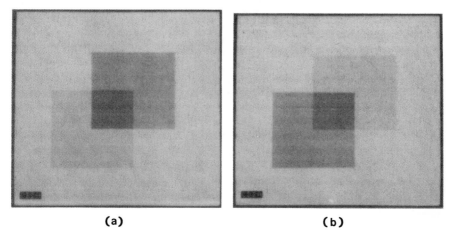

(a)   (b)

Fig. 8.   (a) The overlapping area is closer in lightness to the top square and there is a tendency to see the top square overlying the bottom square. (b) The overlapping area is closer in lightness to the bottom square and there is a tendency to see the bottom square overlying the top square.

Unbalanced transparency is highly unlikely. It is improbable for a change in transparency to occur just at a border. One can, however, produce the perception of unbalanced transparency when figural factors strongly suggest transparency. Figure 7 shows an example of unbalanced transparency. One perceives a surface that is in part opaque and in part transparent. Metelli has called this special kind of transparency "partial transparency." The perception of transparency in Fig. 7 simplifies the perceived shapes. Partial transparency is not ecologically representative and appears to occur because of a preference by the visual system for minimizing the complexity of the perceived shapes. It is an example of the operation of the Gestalt principle of Prägnanz. Of the many physical situations that are consistent with the prevailing stimulation, the visual system chooses the one that in some sense is simplest.

It should be pointed out that constraints (i) and (ii) and the figural configuration are not sufficient to uniquely determine the perception of transparency. For example, Figs. 8a and b show a stimulus which satisfies constraints (i) and (ii) when the bottom square is seen to overlie the top square and when the top square is seen to overlie the bottom square.[2] Auxiliary principles become necessary to predict whether the bottom square is seen as transparent and overlying the top square or the top square is seen as transparent and overlying the bottom square. One factor is that the overlapping area in the center is joined to the top or bottom square depending on which it differs least from in lightness. In Fig. 8a, the overlapping area differs least in lightness from the top square and there is a tendency to see the top square overlying the bottom square. In Fig. 8b, the overlapping area differs least in lightness from the

_____

[2] The derivation of Eq. (3) assumes that the overlying transparent regions are d and c and the underlying opaque regions are a and b. If the top square is seen to overlie the bottom square then regions b and d in Fig. 2 are interchanged.

bottom square and there is a tendency to see the bottom square overlying the top square [3].

8. HUMAN AND MACHINE JUDGMENTS OF TRANSPARENCY

There are four important differences between human and machine judgments of transparency. First, human vision, unlike machine vision, is constrained by the transformation of reflectance or luminance values into lightness values. Given the luminances or reflectances, a machine vision system can apply the equations for either additive or subtractive color mixture to give a quantitatively correct estimation of transparency. In contrast, the human vision system uses lightness values that yield perceptions of transparency that will not be quantitatively correct. This, however, appears not to be very important. The fact that one is able to make only approximately accurate estimates of transparency does not interfere with adaptive behavior.

Second, the representation of information in terms of lightness values restricts the operations that can be applied. Lightness values allow determining the order, the differences, and the relative sizes of the differences between lightness values. The limitation to these operations does not permit solving the equations underlying the occurrence of transparency. Instead, the visual system utilizes algorithms which are computationally simpler. To determine whether the images of overlying surfaces involve transparency, the visual system only checks whether the order and magnitude relations of constraints (i) and (ii) are satisfied. The use of simple order and magnitude algorithms reduces computation time and memory requirements at the expense of accuracy.

Third, a consequence of the human visual system not using a mathematically correct procedure is the occurrence of nonveridical perceptions of transparency. Such nonveridical perceptions of transparency can be avoided in machine vision. In machine vision, violations of constraints (iii) and (iv) would lead to the conclusion that a surface was not transparent. In human vision, violations of constraints (iii) and (iv) can lead to contradictory information about the degree of transparency. It is not yet understood how people make judgments of the degree of transparency.

Fourth, figural cues are primary in the human visual system. When the perception of transparency simplifies the shapes in a pattern, transparency will be seen, as in the case of partial transparency, even when it is highly implausible. The tendency for the visual system to seek a simple organization has evolved because it is adaptive for survival. It has no counterpart in machine vision.

REFERENCES

1. F. Metelli, Achromatic color conditions in the perception of transparency, in *Perception: Essays in Honor of J. J. Gibson* (R. B. MacLeod and H. L. Pick, Eds.), pp. 95–116, Cornell Univ. Press, Ithaca, New York, 1974.
2. F. Metelli, The perception of transparency, *Sci. Amer.* **230**, No. 4, 1974, 90–98.
3. J. Beck, K. Prazdny, and R. Ivry, The perception of transparency with achromatic colors, *Percept. Psychophys.* **35**, 1984, 407–422.
4. S. C. Masin, An experimental comparison of three- versus four-surface phenomenal transparency, *Percept. Psychophys.* **35**, 1984, 325–332.

Human Image Understanding: Recent Research and a Theory*

IRVING BIEDERMAN[†]

Department of Psychology, State University of New York at Buffalo, Amherst, NY 14226

Received July 11, 1985

The perceptual recognition of objects is conceptualized to be a process in which the image of the input is segmented at regions of deep concavity into simple volumetric components, such as blocks, cylinders, wedges, and cones. The fundamental assumption of the proposed theory, recognition-by-components (RBC), is that a modest set of components [N probably $\leq$ 36] can be derived from contrasts of five readily detectable properties of edges in a 2-dimensional image: curvature, collinearity, symmetry, parallelism, and cotermination. The detection of these properties is generally invariant over viewing position and image quality and consequently allows robust object perception when the image is projected from a novel viewpoint or degraded. RBC thus provides a principled account of the heretofore undecided relation between the classic principles of perceptual organization and pattern recognition: The constraints toward regularization (Pragnanz) characterize not the complete object but the object's components. Representational power derives from an allowance of free combinations of the components. A principle of componential recovery can account for the major phenomena of object recognition: If an arrangement of two or three primitive components can be recovered from the input, objects can be quickly recognized even when they are occluded, rotated in depth, novel, or extensively degraded. The results from experiments on the perception of briefly presented pictures by human observers provide empirical support for the theory. © 1985 Academic Press, Inc.

Any single object can project an infinity of image configurations to the retina. The orientation of the object to the viewer can vary continuously, each giving rise to a different 2D projection. The object can be occluded by other objects or texture fields, as when viewed behind foliage. The object can even be missing some of its parts or be a novel exemplar of its particular category. The object need not be presented as a full colored, textured image but instead can be a simplified line drawing. But it is only with rare exceptions that an image fails to be rapidly and readily classified, either as an instance of a familiar object category or as an instance that cannot be so classified (itself a form of classification).

A Do-It-Yourself Example

Consider the object shown in Fig. 1. We readily recognize it as one of those objects that cannot be classified into a familiar category. Despite its overall unfamiliarity, there is near unanimity in its descriptions. We parse—or segment—its parts at regions of deep concavity and describe those parts with common, simple volumetric terms, such as "a block," "a cylinder," "a funnel or truncated cone." We

---

*This research was supported by the Air Force Office of Scientific Research, Grant F4962083C0086. The contributions of my students Tom Blickle, Ginny Ju, Mary Lloyd, John Clapper, Robert Bennett, and Elizabeth Beiring are gratefully acknowledged. The manuscript profited through discussions with James R. Pomerantz, John Artim, and Brian Fisher.

[†]Requests for reprints should be addressed to Irving Biederman, Department of Psychology, State University of New York at Buffalo, 4230 Ridge Lea Road, Amherst, New York 14226.

13

Copyright © 1985 by Academic Press, Inc.
All rights of reproduction in any form reserved.
ISBN 0-12-597345-5

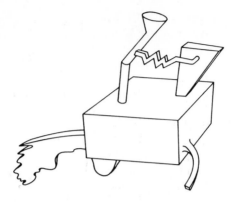

FIG. 1.   A do-it-yourself object. There is strong consensus in the segmentation loci of this configuration and in the description of its parts.

can look at the zigzag horizontal brace as a texture region or zoom in and interpret it as a series of connected blocks. The same is true of the mass at the lower left—we can see it as a texture area or zoom in and parse it into its various bumps.

Although we know that it is not a familiar object, after a while we can say what it resembles: "A New York City hot dog cart, with the large block being the central food storage and cooking area, the rounded part underneath as a wheel, the large arc on the right as a handle, the funnel as an orange juice squeezer and the various vertical pipes as vents or umbrella supports." It is not a *good* cart, but we can see how it might be related to one. It is like a ten-letter word with four wrong letters.

We readily conduct the same process for any object, familiar or unfamiliar, in our foveal field of view. The manner of segmentation and analysis into components does not appear to depend on our familiarity with the particular object being identified.

The naive realism that emerges in descriptions of nonsense objects may be reflecting the workings of a representational system by which objects are identified.

RECOGNITION: UNITS AND CATEGORIES

The number of categories into which we can classify objects would appear to rival the number of words that can be readily identified when listening to speech. Lexical access during speech perception can be successfully modeled as a process mediated by the identification of individual primitive elements, the phonemes, from a relatively small set of primitives [41]. We only need about 38 phonemes to code all the words in English, 15 in Hawaiian, 55 to represent virtually all the words in all the languages spoken on Earth. Because the set of primitives is so small and each phoneme specifiable by dichotomous (or trichotomous) contrasts (e.g., voiced vs unvoiced, nasal vs oral) on a handful of attributes, one need not make particularly fine discriminations in the speech stream. The representational power of the system derives from its permissiveness in allowing relatively free combinations of its primitives.

The hypothesis explored here is that a roughly analogous system may account for our capacities for object recognition. In the visual domain, however, the primitive elements would not be phonemes but a modest number of simple volumes such as cylinders, blocks, wedges, and cones. Objects are segmented, typically at regions of sharp concavity and the resultant parts matched against the best fitting primitive. The set of primitives derives from combinations of contrastive characteristics of the edges in a 2D image (e.g., straight vs curved, symmetrical vs asymmetrical) that define differences among a set of simple volumes (viz., those that tend to be symmetrical and lack sharp concavities). The particular properties of edges that are postulated to be relevant to the generation of the volumetric primitives have the desirable properties that they are invariant over changes in orientation and can be determined from just a few points on each edge. Consequently, they allow a primitive to be extracted with great tolerance for variations of viewpoint and noise.

Just as the relations among the phonemes are critical in lexical access—"fur" and "rough" have the same phonemes but are not the same words—the relations among the volumes are critical for object recognition: Two different arrangements of the same components could produce different objects. In both cases, the representational power derives from the enormous number of combinations that can arise from a modest number of primitives. The relations in speech are limited to left-to-right (sequential) orderings; in the visual domain a richer set of possible relations allows a far greater representational capacity from a comparable number of primitives. The matching of objects in recognition is hypothesized to be a process in which the perceptual input is matched against a representation that can be described by a few simple volumes in specified relations to each other.

THEORETICAL DOMAIN: PRIMAL ACCESS

Our theoretical goal is to account for the *initial categorization* of isolated objects. Often, but not always, this categorization will be at a *basic level*, for example, when we know that a given object is a typewriter, banana, or a giraffe [57]. Much of our knowledge about objects is organized at this level of categorization—the level at which there is typically some readily available name to describe that category [57]. The hypothesis explored here predicts that in certain cases subordinate categorizations can be made initially, so that we might know that a given object is a floor lamp, sports car, or dachshund, more rapidly than we know that it is a lamp, car, or dog (e.g., [31]).

The role of surface characteristics. There is a restriction on the scope of this approach of volumetric modeling that should be noted. The modeling has been limited to concrete entities of the kind typically designated by English *count* nouns. These are concrete objects that have specified boundaries and to which we can apply the indefinite article and number. For example, for a count noun such as CHAIR we can say "a chair" or "three chairs." By contrast, *mass* nouns are concrete entities to which the indefinite article or number cannot be applied, such as water, sand, or snow. So we cannot say "a water" or "three waters," unless we refer to a count noun shape as in "a drop of water," "a bucket of water," or a "grain of sand," each of which does have a simple volumetric description. We conjecture that mass nouns are identified primarily through surface characteristics such as texture and color, rather than through volumetric primitives.

Under restricted viewing conditions, as when an object is partially occluded, texture, color, and other cues (such as position in the scene and labels), may contribute to the identification of count nouns, as for example, when we identify a particular shirt in the laundry pile from just a bit of fabric. Such identifications are indirect, typically the result of inference over a limited set of possible objects. The goal of the present effort is to account for what can be called *primal access*: the first contact of a perceptual input from an isolated, unanticipated object to a representation in memory.

BASIC PHENOMENA OF OBJECT RECOGNITION

Independent of laboratory research, the phenomena of every-day object identification provide strong constraints on possible models of recognition. In addition to the fundemental phenomenon that objects can be recognized at all (not an altogether obvious conclusion), at least five facts are evident. Typically, an object can be recognized:

1. rapidly,
2. when viewed from novel orientations,
3. under moderate levels of visual noise,
4. when partially occluded,
5. when it is a new exemplar of a category.

Implications

The preceding five phenomena constrain theorizing about object interpretation in the following ways.

1. Access to the mental representation of an object should not be dependent on absolute judgments of quantitative detail, because such judgments are slow and error prone [43, 23]. For example, distinguishing among just several levels of the degree of curvature or length of an object typically requires more time than that required for the identification of the object itself. Consequently, such quantitative processing cannot be the controlling factor by which recognition is achieved.

2. The information that is the basis of recognition should be relatively invariant with respect to orientation and modest degradation.

3. Partial matches should be computable. A theory of object interpretation should have some principled means for computing a match for occluded, partial, or new exemplars of a given category. We should be able to account for the human's ability to identify, for example, a chair when it is partially occluded by other furniture, or when it is missing a leg, or when it is a new model.

RECOGNITION-BY-COMPONENTS

Our hypothesis, recognition-by-components (RBC), bears some relation to several prior conjectures for representing objects by parts or modules (e.g., [13, 24, 38, 40, 67]). RBC's contribution lies in its proposal for a particular vocabulary of components derived from perceptual mechanisms and its account of how an arrangement of these components can access a representation of an object in memory.

When an image of an object is painted across the retina, RBC assumes that a representation of the image is segmented—or parsed—into separate regions at points of deep concavity, particularly at cusps where there are discontinuities in curvature [28]. Such segmentation conforms well with human intuitions about the boundaries of object parts, as was demonstrated with the nonsense object in Fig. 1. The resultant parsed regions are then approximated by simple volumetric components that can be modeled by generalized cones [13, 38, 39]. A generalized cone is the volume swept out by a cross section moving along an axis (as illustrated in Fig. 5 below). (Marr [38, 39] showed that the contours generated by any smooth surface could be modeled by a generalized cone with a convex cross section.) The cross section is typically hypothesized to be at right angles to the axis. Secondary segmentation criteria (and criteria for determining the axis of a component) are those that afford descriptions of volumes that maximize symmetry, length, and constancy of the size and curvature of the cross section of the component. These secondary bases for segmentation and component identification are discussed below.

The primitive components are hypothesized to be simple, typically symmetrical volumes lacking sharp concavities, such as blocks, cylinders, spheres, and wedges. The fundamental perceptual assumption of RBC is that the components can be differentiated on the basis of perceptual properties in the 2D image that are readily detectable and relatively independent of viewing position and degradation. These perceptual properties include several that have traditionally been thought of as principles of perceptual organization, such as good continuation, symmetry, and Pragnanz. RBC thus provides a principled account of the relation between the classic phenomena of perceptual organization and pattern recognition: although objects can be highly complex and irregular, the units by which objects are identified are simple and regular. The constraints toward regularization (Pragnanz) are thus assumed to characterize not the complete object but the object's components.

By the preceding account, surface characteristics such as color and texture will typically have only secondary roles in primal access. This should not be interpreted as suggesting that the perception of surface characteristics *per se* is delayed relative to the perception of the components but merely that in most cases the surface characteristics are generally less efficient routes for accessing the classification of a count object. That is, we may know that a chair has a particular color and texture simultaneously with its volumetric description, but it is only the volumetric description that provides efficient access to the mental representation of CHAIR.[1]

Relations among the components. Although the components themselves are the focus of this article, as noted previously the arrangement of primitives is necessary for representing a particular object. Thus an arc *side-connected* to a cylinder can yield a cup as shown in Fig. 2. Different arrangements of the same components can readily lead to different objects, as when an arc is connected to the top of the cylinder to produce a pail in Fig. 2. Whether a component is attached to a long or short surface can also affect classification as with the arc producing either an attache case or a strongbox in Fig. 2.

The identical situation between primitives and their arrangement exists in the phonemic representation of words, where a given subset of phonemes can be rearranged to produce different words.

---

[1] There are, however, objects that would seem to require both a volumetric description and a texture region for an adequate representation, such as hairbrushes, typewriter keyboards, and corkscrews. It is unlikely that many of the individual bristles, keys, or coils are parsed and identified prior to the identification of the object. Instead those regions are represented through the statistical processing that characterizes their texture (e.g., [5, 32]), although we retain a capacity to zoom down and attend to the volumetric nature of the individual elements. The structural description that would serve as a representation of such objects would include a statistical specification of the texture field along with a specification of the larger volumetric components. These compound texture-componential objects have not been studied but it is possible that the characteristics of their identification would differ from objects that are readily defined solely by their arrangement of volumetric components.

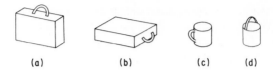

(a)   (b)   (c)   (d)

FIG. 2.   Different arrangements of the same components can produce different objects.

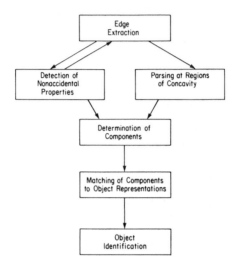

FIG. 3.   Presumed processing stages in object recognition.

The representation of an object would thus be a structural description that expressed the relations among the components [71, 74, 1]. A suggested (minimal) set of relations is described in Table 1, and would include specification of the relative sizes of the components and their points of attachment.

Stages of processing.   Figure 3 presents a schematic of the presumed subprocesses by which an object is recognized. An early edge extraction stage provides a line drawing description of the object. From this description, nonaccidental properties of the image, described below, are detected. Parsing is performed at concave regions simultaneously with a detection of nonaccidental properties. The nonaccidental properties of the parsed regions provide critical constraints on the identity of the components. Within the temporal and contextual constraints of primal access, the stages up to and including the identification of components are assumed to be bottom-up. A delay in the determination of an object's components should have a direct effect on the identification latency of the object. The arrangement of the components is then matched against a representation in memory. It is assumed that the matching of the components occurs in parallel, with unlimited capacity. Partial matches are possible with the degree of match assumed to be proportional to the similarity in the components between the image and the representation.[2] This stage model is presented to provide an overall theoretical context. The focus of this article is on the nature of the units of the representation.

A PERCEPTUAL BASIS FOR A COMPONENTIAL REPRESENTATION

Recent theoretical analyses of perceptual organization [12, 36, 72] suggest a perceptual basis for RBC. The central organizational principle is that certain properties of the 2D image are taken by the visual system as strong evidence that the 3D object contains those same properties. For example, if there is a straight line in the image, the visual system infers that the edge producing that line in the 3D world is also straight. Images that are symmetrical only under reflection, are interpreted as arising from objects with that property. The visual system ignores the possibility that the property in the image is merely a result of a (highly unlikely) accidental alignment of eye and a curved edge.

If the image is symmetrical, we assume that the object projecting that image is also symmetrical. The order of symmetry is also preserved: Images that are symmetrical under both rotation and reflection, such as a square or circle, are interpreted as arising from objects (or surfaces) that are symmetrical under both rotation and reflection. Although skew symmetry is often readily perceived as arising from a tilted symmetrical object or surface, there are cases where skew symmetry is not readily detected [75]. Parallelism and cotermination constitute the remaining nonaccidental relations. All five of these 2D *nonaccidental* properties and the associated 3D inferences are described in Fig. 4 (modified from [36]). Witkin and Tennenbaum [72] (see also [36]) argue that the evidence for organizational constraints is so strong and the leverage provided for inferring a 3D structure so powerful, that it poses a challenge to the effort in computer vision and perceptual psychology that ignored these constraints and assigned central importance to variation in local surface characteristics, such as luminance.

Psychological Evidence for the Rapid Use of Nonaccidental Relations

There is no doubt that images are interpreted in a manner consistent with the nonaccidental principles. But are these relations used quickly enough so as to provide a perceptual basis for the components that allow primal access? Although all the principles have not received experimental verification, the available evidence does suggest that the answer to the preceding question is "yes." There is strong evidence that the visual system quickly assumes and uses collinearity, curvature, symmetry, and cotermination. This evidence is of two sorts: (a) demonstrations, often compelling, showing that when a given 2D relation is produced by an accidental alignment of object and image, the visual system accepts the relation as existing in the 3D world, and (b) search tasks showing that when a target differs from distractors in a nonaccidental property, as when one is searching for a curved arc among straight segments, the detection of that target is facilitated compared to conditions where targets and background do not differ in such properties.

---

[2] Modeling the matching of an object image to a mental representation is a rich, relatively neglected problem area. Tversky's [66] contrast model provides a useful framework with which to consider this similarity problem in that it readily allows distinctive features (i.e., components) of the image to be considered separately from the distinctive components of the representation. This allows principled assessments of similarity for partial objects (components in the representation but not in the image) and novel objects (containing components in the image that are not in the representation). It may be possible to construct a dynamic model based on a parallel distributed process as a modification of the kind proposed by McClelland & Rumelhart [42] for word perception, with components playing the role of letters. One difficulty facing such an effort is that the neighbors for a given word are well specified and readily available from a dictionary; the set of neighbors for a given object is not.

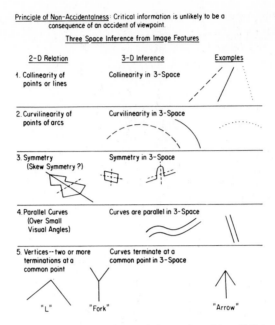

FIG. 4. Five nonaccidental relations (adapted from [36]).

Collinearity vs curvature. The demonstration of the collinearity or curvature relations is too obvious to be performed as an experiment. When looking at a straight segment, no observer would assume that it is an accidental image of a curve. That the contrast between straight and curved edges is readily available for perception was shown by Neisser [46]. He found that a search for a letter composed only of straight segments, such as a *Z*, could be performed faster when in a field of curved distractors, such as *C*, *G*, *O*, and *Q*, then when among other letters composed of straight segments such as *N*, *W*, *V*, and *M*.

Symmetry and parallelism. Many of the Ames demonstrations, such as the trapezoidal window and Ames room, derive from an assumption of symmetry that includes parallelism [30]. Palmer [49] showed that the subjective directionality of arrangements of equilateral triangles was based on the derivation of an axis of symmetry for the arrangement. King, Tangney, Meyer, and Biederman [34] demonstrated that a perceptual bias towards symmetry accounted for a number of shape constancy effects. Garner [23] Checkosky and Whitlock [19], and Pomerantz [54] provided ample evidence that not only can symmetrical shapes be quickly discriminated from asymmetrical stimuli, but the degree of symmetry was also a readily available perceptual distinction. Thus stimuli that were invariant under both reflection and 90° rotation could be rapidly discriminated from those that were only invariant under reflection [19].

Cotermination. The "peephole perception" demonstrations, such as the Ames chair [30] or the physical realization of the impossible triangle [51], are produced by accidental alignment of noncoterminous segments. The success of these demonstrations document the immediate and compelling impact of this relation.

The registration of cotermination is important for determining vertices, which provide information that can serve to distinguish the components. In fact, one theorist [12] has suggested that the major function of eye movements is to determine coterminous edges. With polyhedra (volumes produced by planar surfaces), the Y, arrow, and L vertices allow inference as to the identity of the volume in the image. For example, the silhouette of a brick contains a series of six vertices, which alternate between Ls and arrows, and an internal Y vertex, as illustrated in any of the straight edged cross-sectioned volumes in Fig. 6. The Y vertex is produced by the cotermination of three segments, with none of the angles greater than 180°. (An arrow vertex contains an angle that exceeds 180°.) This vertex is not present in components that have curved cross sections, such as cylinders, and thus can provide a distinctive cue for the cross-section edge. Perkins [52] has described a perceptual bias toward parallelism in the interpretation of this vertex.[3] (Chakraverty [18] has discussed the vertices formed by curved regions.) Whether the presence of this particular internal vertex can facilitate the identification of a brick vs a cylinder is not yet known but a recent study by Biederman and Blickle ([8], described below) demonstrated that deletion of vertices adversely affected object recognition more than the deletion of contours at midsegment.

An example of a non-coterminous vertex is the T, although there is a termination of one segment on another. Such vertices are important for determining occlusion and thus segmentation (along with concavities), in that the edge forming the (normally) vertical segment of the T cannot be closer to the viewer than the segment forming the top of the T. By this account, the T vertex might have a somewhat different status than the Y, arrow, and L vertices, in that the T's primary role would be in segmentation, rather than in establishing the identity of the volume.[4]

The high speed and accuracy of determining a given nonaccidental relation, e.g., whether some pattern is symmetrical, should be contrasted with performance in making absolute quantitative judgments of variations in a single, physical attribute, such as length of a segment or degree of tilt or curvature. For example, the judgment as to whether the length of a given segment is 10, 12, 14, 16, or 18 in is notoriously slow and error prone [43, 23, 5, 69, 70, 22]. Even these modest performance levels are challenged when the judgments have to be executed over the brief 100 ms intervals

---

[3] When such vertices formed the central angle in a polyhedron, Perkins [52] reported that the surfaces would almost always be interpreted as meeting at right angles, as long as none of the three angles was less than 90°. Indeed, such vertices cannot be projections of acute angles [33] but the human appears insensitive to the possibility that the vertices could have arisen from obtuse angles. If one of the angles in the central Y vertex was acute, then the polyhedra would be interpreted as irregular. Perkins found that subjects from rural areas of Botswana, where there was a lower incidence of exposure to carpentered (right-angled) environments, had an even stronger bias toward rectilinear interpretations than Westerners [53].

[4] The arrangement of vertices, particularly for polyhedra, offers constraints on "possible" interpretations of lines as convex, concave, or occluding, e.g., [60]. In general, the constraints take the form that a segment cannot change its interpretation, e.g., from concave to convex, unless it passes through a vertex. "Impossible" objects can be constructed from violations of this constraint [77] as well as from more general considerations [76, 60]. It is tempting to consider that the visual system captures these constraints in the way in which edges are grouped into objects, but the evidence would seem to argue against such an interpretation. The impossibility of most impossible objects is not immediately registered, but requires scrutiny and thought before the inconsistency is detected. What this means in the present context is that the visual system has a capacity for classifying vertices locally, but no perceptual routines for determining the global consistency of a set of vertices.

[21] that is sufficient for accurate object identification. Perhaps even more telling against a view of object recognition that would postulate the making of absolute judgments of fine quantitative detail is that the speed and accuracy of such judgments decline dramatically when they have to be made for multiple attributes [43, 23, 21]. In contrast, object recognition latencies are reduced by the presence of additional (redundant) components with complex objects ([9] described below).

COMPONENTS GENERATED FROM DIFFERENCES IN NONACCIDENTAL PROPERTIES AMONG GENERALIZED CONES

I have emphasized the particular set of nonaccidental properties shown in Fig. 4 because they may constitute a perceptual basis for the generation of the set of components. *Any* primitive that is hypothesized to be the basis of object recognition should be rapidly identifiable and invariant over viewpoint and noise. These characteristics would be attainable if differences among components were based on differences in nonaccidental properties. Although additional nonaccidental properties exist, there is empirical support for rapid perceptual access to the five described in Fig. 4. In addition, these five relations reflect intuitions about significant perceptual and cognitive differences among objects.

From variation over only two or three levels in the nonaccidental relations of four attributes of generalized cylinders, a set of 36 components can be generated. A

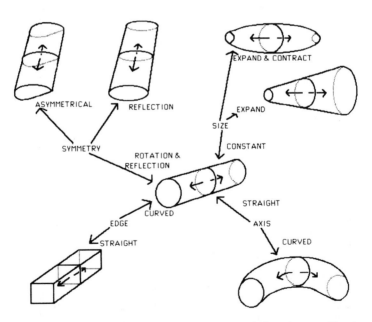

FIG. 5. Variations in generalized cones that can be detected through nonaccidental properties. Constant-sized cross sections have parallel sides; expanded or expanded and contracted cross sections have sides that are not parallel. Curved vs straight cross sections and axes are detectable through collinearity or curvature. The three values of cross-section symmetry (symmetrical under reflection and 90° rotation; reflection only; or asymmetrical) are detectable through the symmetry relation.

CROSS SECTION

Geon	Edge Straight S Curved C	Symmetry Rot & Ref ++ Ref + Asymm –	Size Constant ++ Expanded – Exp & Cont --	Axis Straight + Curved –
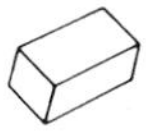	S	+ +	+ +	+
	C	+ +	+ +	+
	S	+	–	+
	S	+ +	+··	–
	C	+ +	–	+
	S	+	+··	+

FIG. 6. Proposed partial set of volumetric primitives (Geons) derived from differences in nonaccidental properties.

subset is illustrated in Fig. 5. Some of the generated volumes and their organization are shown in Fig. 6. Three of the attributes describe characteristics of the cross section: its shape, symmetry, and constancy of size as it is swept along the axis. The fourth attribute describes the shape of the axis:

1. Cross section
    A. Edges
        S Straight
        C Curved
    B. Symmetry
        + + Symmetrical: invariant under rotation and reflection
        + Symmetrical: invariant under reflection
        − Asymmetrical
    C. Constancy of size of cross section as it is swept along axis
        + Constant
        − Expanded
        − − Expanded and contracted
2. Axis
    D. Curvature
        + Straight
        − Curved.

The values of these four attributes are presented as contrastive differences in nonaccidental properties: straight vs curved, symmetrical vs asymmetrical, parallel vs nonparallel. Cross-section edges and curvature of the axis are distinguishable by collinearity or curvilinearity. The constant vs expanded size of the cross section would be detectable through parallelism; a constant cross section would produce a generalized cone with parallel sides (as with a cylinder or brick); an expanded cross section would produce edges that were not parallel (as with a cone or wedge), and a cross section that expanded and then contracted would produce an ellipsoid with nonparallel sides and an extrema of positive curvature (as with a lemon). As Hoffman and Richards [28] have noted, such extrema are invariant with viewpoint. The three levels of cross-section symmetry are equivalent to Garner's [23] distinction of the number of different stimuli produced by 90° rotations and reflections of a stimulus. Thus a square or circle would be invariant under 90° rotation and reflection; but a rectangle or ellipse would be invariant only under reflection, as 90° rotations would produce a second figure. Asymmetrical figures would produce eight different figures under increments of 90° rotation and reflection.

Negative Values

The plus values are those favored by perceptual biases and memory errors. No bias is assumed for straight and curved edges of the cross section. For symmetry, clear biases have been documented. For example, if an image *could* have arisen from a symmetrical object, then it is interpreted as symmetrical [34]. The same is apparently true of parallelism. If edges could be parallel, then they are typically interpreted as such, as with the trapezoidal room or window.

Curved axes.   Figure 7 shows three of the most negatively marked primitives with curved cross sections. Such volumes often resemble biological entities. An expansion and contraction of a rounded cross section with a straight axis produces an ellipsoid (lemon) (Fig. 7a); an expanded cross section with a curved axis produces a horn

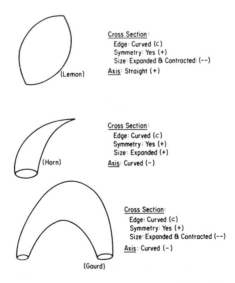

FIG. 7.   Three curved components with curved axes or expanded and/or contracted cross sections. These tend to resemble biological forms.

Geon	Edge Straight s Curved c	Symmetry Rot & Ref ++ Ref + Asymm −	Size Constant ++ Expanded − Exp & Cont −−	Axis Straight + Curved −
		CROSS SECTION		
	S	+	+ +	−
	C	+	+ +	−
	S	+ +	−	−
	C	+ +	−	−
	S	+	−	−
	C	+	−	−

FIG. 8.   Components with curved axis and straight or curved cross sections. Determining the shape of the cross section, particularly if straight, might require attention.

(Fig. 7b), and an expanded and contracted cross section with a rounded cross section produces a banana slug or gourd (Fig. 7c).

In contrast to the natural forms generated when both cross section and axis are curved, the components swept by a straight edged cross section traveling along a curved axis (e.g., the components on the first, third, and fifth rows of Fig. 8) appear somewhat less familiar and more difficult to apprehend than their curved counterparts. It is possible that this difficulty may merely be a consequence of unfamiliarity. Alternatively, the subjective difficulty might be produced by a conjunction-attention effect (CAE) of the kind discussed by Treisman (e.g., [63]). CAEs are described in the section on attentional effects. In the present case, given the presence in the image of curves and straight edges (for the rectilinear cross sections with curved axis), attention (or scrutiny) may be required to determine which kind of segment to assign to the axis and which to assign to the cross section. Curiously, the problem does not present itself when a curved cross section is run along a straight axis to produce a cylinder or cone. The issue as to the role of attention in determining components would appear to be empirically tractable using the paradigms created by Treisman and her colleagues [63, 62].

Asymmetrical cross sections.   There are an infinity of possible cross sections that could be asymmetrical. How does RBC represent this variation? RBC assumes that the differences in the departures from symmetry are not readily available and thus do not affect primal access. For example, the difference in the shape of the cross section for the two straight edged volumes in Fig. 9 might not be apparent sufficiently quickly to affect object recognition. This does not mean that an individual could not store the details of the volume produced by an asymmetrical cross section. But if such detail required additional time for its access, then the expectation is that it could not mediate rapid object perception. A second way in which

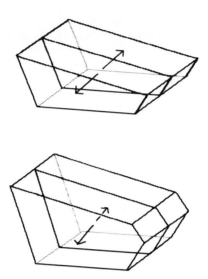

FIG. 9. Volumes with an asymmetrical, straight edged cross sections. Detection of differences between such volumes might require attention.

asymmetrical cross sections need not be individually represented is that they often produce volumes that resemble symmetrical, but truncated, wedges. This latter form of representing asymmetrical cross sections would be analogous to the schema-plus-correction phenomenon noted by Bartlett [73]. The implication of a schema-plus-correction representation would be that a single primitive category for asymmetrical cross sections and wedges might be sufficient. For both kinds of volumes, their similarity may be a function of the detection of a lack of parallelism in the volume. One would have to exert scrutiny to determine whether a lack of parallelism had originated in the cross section or in a size change of a symmetrical cross section. In this case, as with the components with curved axes described in the preceding section, a single primitive category for both wedges and asymmetrical straight edged volumes could be postulated that would allow a reduction in the number of primitive components. There is considerable evidence that asymmetrical patterns require more time for their identification than symmetrical patterns [19, 54]. Whether these effects have consequences for the time required for object identification is not yet known.

Conjunction-attentional effects. A single feature can be detected without any effect of the number of distracting items in the visual field. For example, the time for detecting a blue shape (a square or a circle) among a field of green distractor shapes is unaffected by the number of green shapes. However, if the target is defined by a *conjunction* of features, e.g., a blue square among distractors consisting of green squares and blue circles, so that both the color *and* the shape of each item must be determined to know if it is or is not the target, then target detection time increases linearly with the number of distractors [63]. These results have led to a theory of visual attention that assumes that the human can monitor all potential display positions simultaneously and with unlimited capacity for a single feature (e.g., something blue, or something curved). But when a target is defined by a *conjunction* of features, then a limited capacity attentional system that can only examine one display position at a time must be deployed [63].

The extent to which Treisman and Gelade's [63] demonstration of conjunction-attention effects may be applicable to the perception of volumes and objects has yet to be evaluated. In the extreme, in a given moment of attention, it may be the case that the values of the four attributes of the components are detected as independent features. In cases where the attributes, taken independently, can define different volumes, as with the shape of cross sections and axis, an act of attention might be required to determine the specific component generating those attributes: Am I looking at a component with a curved cross section and a straight cross section or is it a straight cross section and a curved axis? At the other extreme, it may be that an object recognition system has evolved to allow automatic determination of the components.

The more general issue is whether relational structures for the primitive components are defined automatically or whether a limited attentional capacity is required to build them from their individual edge attributes. It could be the case that some of the most positively marked volumes are detected automatically, but that the volumes with negatively marked attributes might require attention. That some limited capacity is involved in the perception of objects (but not necessarily their components) is documented by an effect of the number of irrelevant objects on perceptual search [6]. Reaction times and errors for detecting an object, e.g., a chair, increased linearly as a function of the number of nontarget objects in a 100 ms presentation of a clockface display [6]. Whether this effect arises from the necessity to use a limited capacity to construct a component from its attributes or whether the effect arises from the matching of an arrangement of components to a representation is not yet known.

Metric variation. For any given component type, there can be an infinite degree of metric variation in aspect ratio, degree of curvature (for curved components), and departure from parallelism (for nonparallel components). How should this quantitative variation be conceptualized? The discussion will concentrate on aspect ratio, probably the most important of the variations. But the issues will be generally applicable to the other metric variations as well. (Aspect ratio is a measure of the elongation of a component. It can be expressed as the width-to-height ratio of a bounding rectangle that would just enclose the component. It is somewhat unclear as to how to handle components with curved axis. The bounding rectangle could simply enclose the component, whatever its shape. Alternatively, two rectangles could be constructed.)

One possibility is to include specification of a range of aspect ratios in the structural description of the object. It seems plausible to assume that recognition can be indexed, in part, by aspect ratio in addition to a componential description. An object's aspect ratio would thus play a role similar to that played by word length in the tachistoscopic identification of words, where long words are rarely proffered when a short word is flashed. Consider an elongated object, such as a baseball bat with a (real) aspect ratio of 15 : 1. When the orientation of the object is orthgonal to the viewpoint, so that its aspect ratio is 15 : 1, recognition might be faster then when it is shown at an orientation where its length is only slightly larger than its diameter, so that the aspect ratio of its image is only 2 : 1. One need not have a particularly fine-tuned function for aspect ratio as large differences in aspect ratio between two components would, like parallelism, be preserved over a large proportion of arbitrary viewing angles.

Another way to incorporate variations in the aspect ratio of an object's image is to represent only qualitative differences, so that variations in aspect ratios exert an effect only when the relative size of the longest dimensions undergo reversal. Specifically, for each component and the complete object, three variations could be defined depending on whether the axis was much smaller, approximately equal to, or much longer than the longest dimension of the cross section. For example, for a component whose axis was longer than the diameter of the cross section (which would be true in most cases), only when the projection of the cross section became longer than the axis would there be an effect of the object's orientation, as when the bat was viewed almost from on end so that the diameter of the handle was greater than the projection of its length.

A close dependence of object recognition performance on the preservation of the aspect ratio of a component in the image would be inconsistent with the emphasis by RBC on dichotomous contrasts of nonaccidental relations. Fortunately, these issues on the role of aspect ratio are readily testable. Bartram's [4] experiments, described in the section on orientation variability, suggest that sensitivity to variations in aspect ratio need not be given heavy weight: Recognition speed is unaffected by variation in aspect ratio across different views of the same object.

Planar components.   A special case of aspect ratio needs to be considered: When the axis for a constant cross section is much smaller than the greatest extent of the cross section, a component may lose its volumetric character and appear *planar*, as the flipper of the penguin in Fig. 11, or the eye of the elephant in Fig. 12. Such shapes can be conceptualized in two ways. The first (and less favored) is to assume that these are just quantitative variations of the volumetric components, but with an axis length of zero. They would then have default values of a straight axis (+) and a constant cross section (+). Only the edge of the cross section and its symmetry could vary.

Alternatively, it might be that a flat shape is not related perceptually to the foreshortened projection of the volume that could have produced it. Using the same variation in cross-section edge and symmetry as with the volumetric components, seven *planar* components could be defined. For + + symmetry there would be the square and circle (with straight and curved edges, respectively), for + symmetry the rectangle, triangle, and ellipse. Asymmetrical (−) planar components would include trapezoids (straight edges), and drop shapes (curved edges). The addition of these seven planar components to the 36 volumetric components yields 43 components (a number close to the 55 phonemes required to represent all languages). [The triangle is here assumed to define a separate component, although a triangular cross section was not assumed to define a separate volume under the intuition that a prism (produced by a triangular cross section) is not quickly distinguishable from wedges.] My preference for assuming that planar components are not perceptually related to their foreshortened volumes is based on the extraordinary difficulty of recognizing objects from views that are parallel to the axis of the major components, as shown in Figs. 27 and 28.

Selection of axis.   Given that a volume is segmented from the object, how is an axis selected? Subjectively, it appears that an axis is selected that would maximize its length, the symmetry of the cross section, and the constancy of the size of the cross section. It may be that by having the axis correspond to the longest extent of the component, bilateral symmetry can be more readily detected as the sides would be closer. Typically, a single axis satisfies all three criteria, but sometimes these criteria are in opposition and two (or more) axes (and component types) are plausible [14]. Under these conditions, an axis will often be aligned to an external frame, such as the vertical [29].

RELATIONS OF RBC TO PRINCIPLES OF PERCEPTUAL ORGANIZATION

Textbook presentations of perception typically include a section of Gestalt organizational principles. This section is almost never linked to any other function of perception. RBC posits a specific role for these organizational phenomena in pattern recognition. Specifically, as suggested by the section on generating components through nonaccidental properties, the Gestalt principles (or better, nonaccidental relations) serve to determine the individual components, rather than the complete object. A complete object, such as a chair, can be highly complex and asymmetrical, but the components will be simple volumes. A consequence of this interpretation is that it is the components that will be stable under noise or perturbation. If the components can be recovered and object perception is based on the components, then the object will be recognizable.

This may be the reason why it is difficult to camouflage objects by moderate doses of random occluding noise, as when a car is viewed behind foliage. According to RBC, the components accessing the representation of an object can readily be recovered through routines of collinearity or curvature that restore contours [36]. *These mechanisms for contour restoration will not bridge cusps.* For visual noise to be effective, by these considerations, it must obliterate the concavity and interrupt the contours from one component at the precise point where they can be joined, through collinearity or constant curvature, with the contours of another component. The likelihood of this occurring by moderate random noise is, of course, extraordinarily low and it is a major reason why, according to RBC, objects are rarely rendered unidentifiable by noise. The consistency of RBC with this interpretation of perceptual organization should be noted. RBC holds that the (strong) loci of parsing is at cusps; the components are organized from the contours between cusps. In classical Gestalt demonstrations, good figures are organized from the contours between cusps. Experiments subjecting these conjectures to test are described in a later section.

A LIMITED NUMBER OF COMPONENTS?

The motivation behind the conjecture that there may be a limit to the number of primitive components derives from both empirical and computational considerations, in addition to the limited number of components that can be discriminated from differences in nonaccidental properties among generalized cones. People are not sensitive to continuous metric variations as evidenced by severe limitations in the human's capacity for making rapid and accurate *absolute* judgments of quantitative shape variations.[5] The errors made in the memory for shapes also document an insensitivity to metric variations. Computationally, a limit is suggested by estimates of the number of objects we might know and the capacity for RBC to readily represent a far greater number with a limited number of primitives.

Empirical support for a limit. Although the visual system is capable of discriminating extremely fine detail, I have been assuming that the number of volumetric primitives sufficient to model rapid human object recognition may be limited. It should be noted that the number of proposed primitives is greather than the three—cylinder, sphere, and cone—advocated by many how-to-draw books. Although these three may be sufficient for determining relative proportions of the parts of a figure and can furnish aid for perspective, they are not sufficient for the *rapid* identification of objects.[6] Similarly, Marr and Nishihara's [40] pipe-cleaner (viz., cylinder) representations of animals would also appear to posit an insufficient number of primitives. On the page, in the context of other labeled pipe-cleaner animals, it is certainly possible to arrive at an identification of a particular (labeled) animal, e.g., a giraffe. But the thesis proposed here would hold that the identifications of objects that were distinguished only by the aspect ratios of a single component type, would require more time than if the representation of the object preserved its componential identity. In modeling only animals, it is likely that Marr and Nishihara capitalized on the possibility that appendages, e.g., legs and neck, can often be modeled by the cylindrical forms of a pipe cleaner. By contrast, it is unlikely that a pipe-cleaner representation of a desk would have had any success. The lesson from Marr and Nishihara's demonstration, even limited for animals, may well be that a single component, varying only in aspect ratio (and arrangement with other components), is insufficient for primal access.

As noted earlier, one reason not to posit a representation system based on fine quantitative detail, e.g., many variations in degree of curvature, is that such *absolute judgments* are notoriously slow and error prone unless limited to the 7 ± 2 values argued by Miller [43]. Even this modest limit is challenged when the judgments have to be executed over a brief 100 ms interval [21] that is sufficient for accurate object identification. A further reduction in the capacity for absolute judgments of quantitative variations of a simple shape would derive from the necessity, for most objects, to make simultaneous absolute judgments for the several shapes that constitute the object's parts [43, 21]. This limitation on our capacities for making absolute judgments of physical variation, when combined with the dependence of such variation on orientation and noise, makes quantitative shape judgments a most implausible basis for object recognition. RBC's alternative is that the perceptual discriminations required to determine the primitive components can be made

---

[5]Absolute judgments are judgments made against a standard in memory, e.g., that shape A is 14 in in length. Such judgments are to be distinguished from *comparative judgments* in which both stimuli are available for simultaneous comparison, e.g., that shape A, lying alongside shape B, is longer than B. Comparative judgments appear limited only by the resolving power of the sensory system. Absolute judgments are limited, in addition, by memory for physical variation. That the memory limitations are severe is evidenced by the finding that comparative judgments can be made quickly and accurately for differences so fine that tens of thousands of levels can be discriminated. But accurate absolute judgments rarely exceed 7 ± 2 categories [43].

[6]Paul Cezanne is often incorrectly cited on this point. "Treat nature by the cylinder, the sphere, the cone, *everything in proper perspective so that each side of an object or plane is directed towards a central point*"(Italics mine, Cezanne [17]). Cezanne was referring to perspective, not the veridical representation of objects.

qualitatively, requiring the discrimination of only two or three viewpoint-independent levels of variation.[7]

Our memory for irregular shapes shows clear biases toward "regularization" (e.g., [78]). Amply documented in the classical shape memory literature was the tendency for errors in the reproduction and recognition of irregular shapes to be in a direction of "regularization," in which slight deviations from symmetrical or regular figures were omitted in attempts at reproduction. Alternatively, some irregularities were emphasized ("accentuation"), typically by the addition of a *regular* subpart. What is the significance of these memory biases? By the RBC hypothesis, these errors may have their origin in the mapping of the perceptual input onto a representational system based on regular primitives. The memory of a slight irregular form would be coded as the closest regularized neighbor of that form. If the irregularity was to be represented as well, an act that would presumably require additional time and capacity, then an additional code (sometimes a component) would be added, as with Bartlett's [73] schema with correction."

Computational Considerations

Are 36 components sufficient? Is there sufficient coding capacity in a set of 36 components to represent the basic level categorizations that we can make? Two estimates are needed to provide a response to this question: (a) the number of readily available perceptual categories, and (b) the number of possible objects that could be represented by 36 components. Obviously, the value for (b) would have to be greater than the value for (a) if 36 components are to prove sufficient.

How many readily distinguishable objects do people know? How might one arrive at a liberal estimate for this value? One estimate can be obtained from the lexicon. There are approximately 1,000 relatively common basic level object categories, such as chairs and elephants.[8] Assume that this estimate is too small by a factor of three, so we can discriminate approximately 3,000 basic level categories. As is discussed below, RBC holds that perception is based on the particular, subordinate level object rather than the basic level category so we need to estimate the mean number of instances per basic level category that would have readily distinguishable exemplars. Almost all natural categories, such as elephants or giraffes, have one or only a few instances with differing componential description. Dogs represent a rare exception for natural categories in that they have been bred to have considerable variation in their descriptions. Person-made categories vary in the number of allowable types,

---

[7] This limitation on our capacities for absolute judgments also occurs in the auditory domain [43]. It is possible that the limited number of phonemes derives more from this limitation for accessing memory for fine quantitative variation than it does from limits on the fineness of the commands to the speech musculature.

[8] This estimate was obtained from three sources: (a) Several linguists and cognitive psychologists provided guesses of 300 to 1,000 concrete noun object categories. (b) The six year old child can name most of the objects that he or she sees on television and has a vocabulary that is under 10,000 words. Perhaps 10%, at most, are concrete nouns. (c) Perhaps the most defensible estimate was obtained from a sample of Webster's 7th New Collegiate Dictionary. The author sampled 30 pages and counted the number of readily identifiable, unique concrete nouns that would not be subordinate to other nouns. Thus "wood thrush" was not counted because it could not be readily discriminated from a "sparrow." "Penguin" and "ostrich" and any doubtful entries were counted as separate noun categories. The mean number of nouns per page was 1.4, with a 1,200 page dictionary this is equivalent to 1,600 noun categories.

TABLE 1

Generative Power of 36 Components

36	First component, C_1
×	
36	Second component, C_2
×	
3	Size $[C_1 \gg C_2, C_2 \gg C_1, C_1 = C_2]$
×	
1.8	C_1 top or bottom (represented for 80% of the objects)
×	
2	Nature of join [end-to-end or end-to-side]
×	
2	Join at long or short surface of C_1
×	
2	Join at long or short surface of C_2
=	55,987 possible two component objects

With 3 components, ignoring relations:
55,987 × 36 = 2 million possible objects, equivalent to learning 304 new objects every day (approx. 20/waking hour) for 18 years.

but this number often tends to be greater than the natural categories. Cups, typewriters, and lamps have just a few (in the case of cups) to perhaps 15 or more (in the case of lamps) readily discernible exemplars. Let us assume (liberally) that the mean number of *types* is 10. This would yield an estimate of 30,000 readily discriminable objects (3,000 categories × 10 types/category). The second source for the estimate is the rate of learning new objects. Thirty thousand objects would require learning an average of 4.5 objects per day, every day for 18 years, the modal age of the subjects in the experiments described below.

Although the value of 4.5 objects learned per day seems reasonable for a child in that it approximates the maximum rates of word acquisition during the ages of 2–6 years [16, 44], it certainly overestimates the rate at which adults develop new object categories. The impressive visual recognition competence of a child of six, if it were based on 30,000 visual categories, would require the learning of 13.5 objects per day, or about one per waking hour. By the criterion of learning rate, 30,000 categories would appear to be a liberal estimate.

How many objects could be represented by 36 components? Calculations of this estimate are presented in Table 1. If we consider the number of possible objects that could be represented by just two components, with a conservative estimate of the number of readily discriminably different ways in which those components might combine, then over 55,000 objects can be generated. Five relations among pairs of components are considered: (a) Whether component *A* is above or below component *B*, a relation, by the author's estimate, that is defined for at least 80% of the objects. Thus giraffes, chairs, and typewriters have a top-down specified organization of their components but forks and knives do not. (b) Whether the connection between any pair of joined components is end-to-end (and of equal sized cross section at the join), as the upper and fore arms of a person, or end-to-side, producing one or two concavities, respectively [38]. Two concavity joins are far more common in that it is rare that two end-to-end joined components have equal sized cross sections. (c) Whether component *A* is much greater than, smaller than, or approximately equal to component *B*. (d) Whether each component is connected at its longer or shorter side. The difference between the attache case in Fig. 3a and the strongbox in Fig. 3b are produced by differences in relative lengths of the surfaces of a brick that is connected to the arch (handle). The handle on the shortest surface produces the strongbox; on a longer surface, the attache case. Similarly, among other differences, the cup and the pail in Figs. 3c and 3d, respectively, differ as to whether the handle is connected to the long surface of the cylinder (to produce a cup) or the short surface (to produce a pail). (Other than a sphere and a cube, all primitives will have at least a long and a short surface, ignoring the orientation of the surface. Other than a brick and a cylinder, which have two, most, such as a wedge, will have at least five distinguishably different surfaces, if we ignore left–right differences. That is, there will be a front, back, top, bottom, and side. Now, a second volume can be joined to the first at its top, bottom, front, back, or side. There are four degrees of freedom if the second volume is joined to the bottom of the first, then it cannot be joined at its top. Consequently, there are 20 possible combinations (joins) made between two five-surfaced primitives. The tabled estimate considers only two levels of this variation.)

If a third component is added to the two, then 2 million possible objects can be represented, even if we completely ignore the relations among this third volume and the other two! This would be equivalent to learning 304 objects/day every day for 18 years or 20 objects per hour for the 16 waking hours of every day for those 18 years.

The representational capacity is, of course, a multiplicative function of the number of primitives or relations, so slight increases in either have a dramatic effect on the representational capacity. For example, with 50 components, a value close to the number of phonemes, there are 108,000 two-component objects and 5.4 million possible three-component objects, again ignoring the relation between the third component and the other two. This would be equivalent to learning 960 objects/day every day for 18 years or an object a minute of the 16 waking hours of every day for those 18 years.[9] How many components would be required for the unambiguous identification of most objects? If only 1% of the possible combinations of components were actually used (i.e., 99% redundancy), and objects were distributed homogenously among combinations of components, *then only two or three components would be sufficient to unambiguously represent most objects.*

We do not yet know if there is a real limit to the number of components but the task to determine if one exists may ultimately prove similar to the task faced by the phonetician as he or she attempts to determine the set of phonemes that characterizes the linguistic corpus for a given community. The phonemes required to represent a large sample of words from the corpus are noted. At some point, an asymptote is reached and additional words can be represented according to the already existing phoneme set. The issues in vision are: (a) whether an asymptote will

[9] Fifty primitives does seem like a considerable number, given most psychological theories. But it would be approximately equivalent to the number of phonemes and well within the capacity of current recent chip technology. A recently announced VLSI chip [58], the PF474, can perform several thousand string comparisons per second with a ranked list of the 16 best matches that might have the potential to code tests for the discrimination among the components and perform the matching of component arrangements for object perception. (Each component can be represented by a single string.) It has already been applied in speech perception systems.

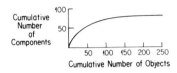

FIG. 10.   Predicted asymptote in the number of generated components from the segmentation of a large number of objects.

be reached as observers generate components from a large corpus of objects (Fig. 10), (b) whether there would be a strong consensus as to the members of this set, and (c) whether objects generated from these components would be identified as readily as their natural counterparts. A limit to the number of components would imply categorical effects such that quantitative variations in the contours of an object, e.g., degree of curvature, that did not alter a component's identity would have less of an effect on the identification of the object itself, compared to contour variations that did alter a component's identity.

EXPERIMENTAL SUPPORT FOR A COMPONENTIAL REPRESENTATION

According to the RBC hypothesis, the preferred input for accessing object recognition is that of the volumetric components. In most cases, only a few appropriately arranged volumes would be all that is required to uniquely specify an object. Rapid object recognition should then be possible. Neither the full complement of an object's components, nor its texture, nor its color, nor the full bounding contour (or envelope or outline) of the object need be present for rapid identification. The problem of recognizing tens of thousands of possible objects becomes, in each case, just a simple task of identifying the arrangement of a few from a limited set of components.

Overview of Experiments

Several object-naming reaction-time experiments have provided support for various aspects of the RBC hypothesis. In all experiments, subjects named briefly presented pictures of common objects (see Figs. 11, 12). That RBC may provide a sufficient account of object recognition was supported by experiments indicating that objects drawn with only two or three of their components could be accurately identified from a single 100 ms exposure. When shown with a complete complement of components, these simple line drawings were identified almost as rapidly as full colored, detailed, textured slides of the same objects. That RBC may provide a necessary account of object recognition was supported by a demonstration that degradation (contour deletion), if applied at the regions that are critical according to RBC, rendered an object unidentifiable. All the original experimental results reported here have received at least one, and often several, replications.

Perceiving Incomplete Objects

Biederman, Ju, and Clapper [9] (1985) studied the perception of briefly presented partial objects lacking some of their components. A prediction of RBC was that only two or three components would be sufficient for rapid identification of most objects. If there were enough time to determine the components and their relations, then

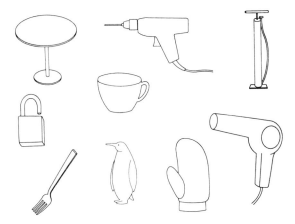

FIG. 11.   Nine of the experimental objects.

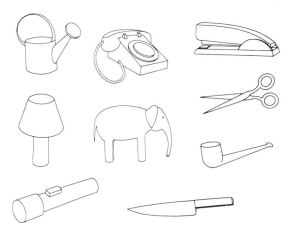

FIG. 12.   An additional set of nine of the experimental objects.

object identification should be possible. Complete objects would be maximally similar to their representation and should enjoy an identification speed advantage over their partial versions.

Stimuli.   The experimental objects were line drawings of 36 common objects, half of which are illustrated in Figs. 11 and 12. The depiction of the objects and their partition into components were done subjectively, according to generally easy agreement among at least three judges. The artists were unaware of the set of components described in this article. For the most part, the components corresponded to the parts of the object. Seventeen component types (ignoring aspect ratios) were sufficient to represent the 180 components comprising the complete versions of the 36 objects.

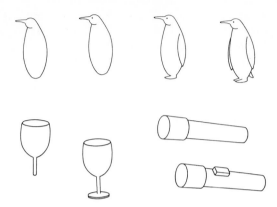

FIG. 13. Illustration of the partial and complete versions of two three-component objects (the wine glass and flashlight) and a nine-component object (the penguin).

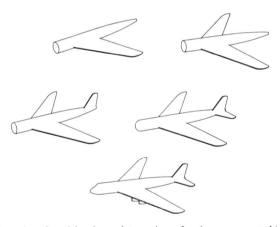

FIG. 14. Illustration of partial and complete versions of a nine component object (airplane).

The objects were shown either with their full complement of components, or partially, but never with less than two components. The first two components that were selected were the largest and most diagnostic components from the complete object and additional components were added in decreasing order of size or diagnosticity, as illustrated in Figs. 13 and 14. Additional components were added in decreasing order of size and/or diagnosticity, subject to the constraint that the additional component be connected to the existing components. For example, the airplane which required nine components to look complete, would have the fuselage and two wings when shown with three of the nine components. The objects were displayed in black line on a white background and averaged 4.5° in greatest extent.

The purpose of this experiment was to determine whether the first few components that would be available from an unoccluded view of a complete object would be sufficient for rapid identification of the object. In normal viewing, the largest and most diagnostic components are available for perception. We ordered the components by size and diagnosticity because our interest, as just noted, was on primal access in recognizing a complete object. Assuming that the largest and most diagnostic components would control this access, we studied the contribution of the nth largest and most diagnostic component, when added to the $n - 1$ already existing components, because this would more closely mimic the contribution of that component when looking at the complete object. (Another kind of experiment might explore the contribution of an "average" component by balancing the order of addition of the components. Such an experiment would be relevant to the recognition of an object that was occluded in such a way that only the displayed components would be available for viewing.)

Complexity. The objects shown in Figs. 11 and 12 illustrate the second major variable in the experiment. Objects differ in complexity, by RBC's definition, in the number of components that they require to look complete. As noted previously, it would seem plausible that partial objects would require more time for their identification than complete objects, so that a complete airplane of nine components, for example, might be more rapidly recognized than only a partial version of that airplane, with only three of its components. The prediction from RBC was that complex objects, by furnishing more diagnostic combinations of components, would be more rapidly identified than simple objects. This prediction is contrary to those models that assume that objects are recognized through a serial contour tracing process (e.g., [27, 68]).

General procedure. Trials were self paced. The depression of a key on the subject's terminal initiated a sequence of exposures from three projectors. First, the corners of a 500 ms fixation rectangle (6° wide) which corresponded to the corners of the object slide was shown. The fixation slide was immediately followed by a 100 ms exposure of a slide of an object that had varying numbers of its components present. The presentation of the object was immediately followed by a 500 ms pattern mask consisting of a random appearing arrangement of lines. The subject's task was to name the object as fast as possible into a microphone which triggered a voice key. The experimenter recorded errors. Prior to the experiment, the subjects read a list of the object names to be used in the experiment. (Subsequent experiments revealed that this procedure for name familiarization produced no effect. When subjects were not familiarized with the names of the experimental objects, results were virtually identical to when such familiarization was provided. This finding indicates that the results of these experiments were not a function of inference over a small set of objects.) Even with the name familiarization, all responses that indicated that the object was identified were considered correct. Thus "pistol," "revolver," "gun," and "handgun" were all acceptable as correct responses for the same object. RTs (reaction times) were recorded by a microcomputer which also controlled the projectors and provided speed and accuracy feedback on the subject's terminal after each trial.

Design. Objects were selected that required 2, 3, 6 or 9 components to look complete. There were nine objects for each of these complexity levels yielding a total set of 36 objects. The various combinations of the partial versions of these objects brought the total number of experimental trials (slides) to 99. Each of 48 subjects viewed all the experimental slides. In addition, two slides of other objects preceded

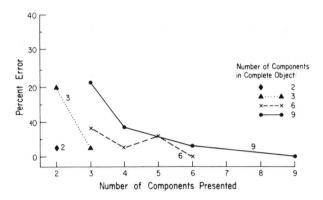

Fig. 15.   Mean per cent error as a function of the number of components in the displayed object (abscissa) and the number of components required for the object to appear complete (parameter). Each point is the mean for nine objects on the first occasion when a subject saw that particular object.

and followed each block of experimental trials as buffer slides for warm up. These were not included in the data analyses.

The various conditions are notated as follows: the digit in parenthesis indicates the number of displayed components and the digit preceding the parenthesis indicates the number of components required for the object to look complete. Thus the airplane shown with three of its nine components would be designated as 9(3). The combinations used were: 2(2), 3(2), 3(3), 6(3), 6(4), 6(5), 6(6), 9(3), 9(4), 9(6), and 9(9). The 11 conditions with nine objects each yielded 99 experimental trials that were organized into 2 blocks of 53 or 54 trials each (the 44 or 45 experimental slides plus two buffer slides at the beginning and end of each block). Four sequences of the slides were balanced by Latin square so that each slide had the same mean serial position.

Results.   Figure 15 shows the mean error rates as a function of the number of components actually displayed on a given trial for the conditions in which no familiarization was provided. Each function is the mean for the nine objects at a given complexity level.

Each subject saw all 99 slides but only the data that a subject viewed a particular object for the first time will be discussed here. These responses were unaffected by prior trials in which the subject might have viewed that object in partial or complete form. (The primary effect of including prior trials of an object was to improve the performance on those trials where the subjects viewed a partial object that had previously been experienced in a complete or more complete version.) For a given level of complexity, increasing numbers of components resulted in better performance but error rates were modest. When only three or four components for the complex objects (those with six or nine components to look complete) were present, subjects were almost 90% accurate (10% error rate). In general, the complete objects were named without error so it is necessary to look at the RTs to see if differences emerge for the complexity variable.

Mean correct RTs, shown in Fig. 16, provide the same general outcome as the errors, except that there was a slight tendency for the more complex objects, when complete, to have shorter RTs than the simple objects. This advantage for the complex objects was actually underestimated in that the complex objects had longer names (three and four syllables) and were less familiar than the simple objects. Oldfield [48] showed that object-naming RTs were longer for names that have more syllables or are infrequent. This effect of slightly shorter RTs for naming complex objects has been replicated and it seems safe to conclude, conservatively, that complex objects do not require more time for their identification than simple objects. This result is contrary to serial-contour tracing models of shape perception (e.g., [27, 68]). Such models would predict that complex objects would require more time to be seen as complete compared to simple objects, which have less contour to trace. The slight RT advantage enjoyed by the complex objects is an effect that would be expected if their additional components were affording a redundancy gain from more possible diagnostic matches to their representations in memory.

Line Drawings vs Colored Photography

The components that are postulated to be the critical units for recognition can be depicted by a line drawing. Color and texture would be secondary routes for recognition. From this perspective, Biederman and Ju [9] reasoned that naming RTs for objects shown as line drawings should closely approximate naming RTs for those objects when shown as colored photographic slides with complete detail, color, and texture. To our knowledge, no previous experiment had compared these different forms of representing objects on the speed and accuracy of basic-level object classification.[10]

General method.   The general procedure and design closely followed that described for the previous experiment. Thirty subjects viewed brief presentations of slides of line drawings and professionally photographed full colored slides of the same objects in the same orientation.

Line drawing and color photography versions of each of 29 objects yielded 58 experimental slides. Conditions of exposure, luminance, and masking were selected which would favor the colored slides, so RT correlates of this advantage could be explored. An earlier experiment had shown that the colored slides were more adversely affected by a mask (a colored slide of a complex collage of many colored shapes and textures), so the mask was omitted. (The effects of a number of variables on the difference between line drawings and colored slides are described in another report [9].

Results.   Mean correct naming times were 804 ms for the line drawings and 784 ms for the colored slides. Error rates averaged 2% for both conditions.

---

[10]An oft cited study, Ryan and Schwartz [59], did compare photography (black and white) against line and shaded drawings and cartoons. Subjects had to determine not the basic level categorization of an object but which one of four configurations of three objects (the positions of five double-throw electrical knife switches, the cycles of a steam valve, and the fingers of a hand) was being depicted. For two of the three objects, the cartoons had lower thresholds than the other modes. But stimulus sampling and drawings and procedural specifications make it difficult to interpret this experiment. For example, the determination of the switch positions was facilitated in the cartoons by filling in the handles so they contrasted with the background contacts. The cartoons did not have lower thresholds than the photographs for the hands, the stimulus example that is most frequently shown in secondary sources (e.g., [45, 56] 1984). Even without a mask, threshold presentation durations were an order of magnitude longer than was required in the present study.

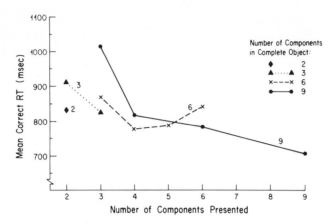

FIG. 16. Mean correct reaction time as a function of the number of components in the displayed object (abscissa) and the number of components required for the object to appear complete (parameter). Each point is the mean for nine objects on the first occasion when a subject saw that particular object.

An analysis of the individual stimuli indicated that the 20 ms naming RT advantage for the colored slides was not due to a contribution of color or lightness (and often texture) of these stimuli. This was determined by partitioning the slides into two sets: those whose color was diagnostic as to the objects' identity (e.g., mushroom, fork, camera, fish) and those objects whose color was not diagnostic to their identity (e.g., chair, hair dryer, pen, mitten). If color was responsible for the 20 ms advantage, those objects for which it was diagnostic should have had a greater advantage for the color slides over the line drawings. But the opposite was true. Objects ($N = 12$) whose color was *not* diagnostic enjoyed a 35 ms color advantage compared to a 33 ms color advantage for the color-diagnostic objects ($N = 17$). Thus, the slight advantage in naming speed for the colored slides was not a consequence of the diagnostic use of color and brightness but, in our opinion, likely derived from more accurate rendition of the components. For example, a number of the objects or parts, such as the hairdryer or front leg of the elephant, were drawn in silhouette so they appear planar.

The conclusion from these studies is that simple line drawings, when depicting the complete object, can be identified almost as quickly (within 20 ms) as a full-colored slide of that same object. That simple line drawings can be identified so rapidly as to approach the naming speed of fully detailed, textured, colored photographic slides supports the premise that the earliest access to a mental representation of an object can be modeled as a matching of a line-drawing representation of a few simple components. Such componential descriptions are thus *sufficient* for primal access.

The Perception of Degraded Objects

Evidence that a componential description may be *necessary* for object recognition (under conditions where contextual inference is not possible) derives from experiments on the perception of objects which have been degraded by deletion of their contour [8].

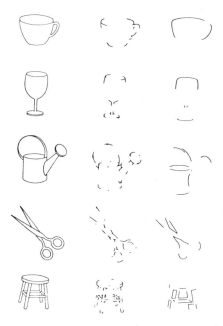

FIG. 17. Example of five stimulus objects in the experiment on the perception of degraded objects. The left column shows the original intact versions. The middle column shows the recoverable versions. The contours have been deleted in regions where they can be replaced through collinearity or smooth curvature. The right column shows the nonrecoverable versions. The contours have been deleted at regions of concavity so that collinearity or smooth curvature of the segments bridges the concavity. In addition, vertices have been altered, e.g., from Ys to Ls, and misleading symmetry and parallelism introduced.

RBC holds that parsing of an object into components is performed at regions of concavity. The nonaccidental relations of collinearity and curvilinearity allow *filling-in*: they extend broken contours that are collinear or smoothly curvilinear. In concert, the two assumptions of: (a) parsing at concavities, and (b) filling-in through collinearity or smooth curvature lead to a prediction as to what should be a particularly disruptive form of degradation. If contours were deleted at regions of concavity in such a manner that their endpoints, when extended through collinearity or curvilinearity, bridge the concavity, then the components would be lost and recognition should be impossible. The cup in the right column of the top row of Fig. 17 provides an example. The curve of the handle of the cup is drawn so that it is continuous with the curve of the cylinder forming the back rim of the cup. This form of degradation, in which the components cannot be recovered from the input through the nonaccidental properties, is referred to as *nonrecoverable degradation* and is illustrated for the objects in the right column of Fig. 17.

An equivalent amount of deleted contour in a midsection of a curve or line should prove to be less disruptive as the components could then be restored through collinearity or curvature. In this case the components should be *recoverable*. Example of recoverable forms of degradation are shown in the middle column of Fig. 17.

General method. Recoverable and nonrecoverable versions of 35 objects were prepared, yielding 70 experimental slides. In addition to the procedures for producing nonrecoverable versions described above, components were also camouflaged by contour deletion that produced symmetry, parallelism, and vertices that were not characteristic of the original object. For example, in Fig. 17, the watering can has false vertices suggested in the region of its spout and the stool has a number of *T* vertices transformed to *L* vertices. Symmetrical regions of the stool also suggest components where they would not be parsed in the original intact version. Even with these techniques, it was difficult to remove all the components and some remained in nominally nonrecoverable versions, as with the handle of the scissors.

The slides were arranged in two blocks, each with all 35 objects. Approximately half (17 or 18) of the slides in each version were recoverable and the other half were unrecoverable versions. Slides were displayed for 100, 200, or 750 ms. Four sequences were used in which the order of the blocks was balanced and half the subjects viewed each block in forward order; the other half in reverse order. These orders were balanced over slide durations so that each slide (a) had the same mean serial position, and (b) was presented with equal frequency at the three presentation durations. A separate group of six subjects viewed the slides at a 5 s exposure duration.

Prior to the experiment, all subjects were shown several examples of the various forms of degradation for several objects that were not used in the experiment. In addition, familiarization with the experimental objects was manipulated between subjects. Prior to the start of the experimental trials, different groups of six subjects: (a) viewed a three second slide of the intact version of the objects, e.g., the objects in the left column of Fig. 17, which they named, (b) were provided with the names of the objects on their terminal, or (c) were given no familiarization. As in the prior experiments, the subjects task was to name the objects.

A glance at the second and third columns in Fig. 15 is sufficient to reveal that one does not need an experiment to show that the nonrecoverable objects would be more difficult to identify than the recoverable versions. But we wanted to determine if the nonrecoverable versions would be identifiable at extremely long exposure durations (5 s) and whether the prior exposure to the intact version of the object would overcome the effects of the contour deletion. The effects of contour deletion in the recoverable condition was also of considerable interest when compared to the comparable conditions from the partial object experiments.

Results. The error data are shown in Fig. 18. Identifiability of the nonrecoverable stimuli was virtually impossible: The median error rate for those slides was 100%. Subjects rarely guessed wrong objects in this condition. Almost always they merely said that they "don't know." In those few cases where a nonrecoverable object was identified, it was for those instances where some of the components were not removed, as with the circular rings of the handles of the scissors. Even at 5 s, error rates for the nonrecoverable stimuli, especially in the *name* and *no familiarization* conditions, was extraordinarily high. Objects in the *recoverable* condition were named at high accuracy at the longer exposure durations.

As in the previous experiments, there was no effect of familiarizing the subjects with the names of the objects compared to the condition in which the subjects were provided with no information about the objects. There was some benefit, however, of providing intact versions of the pictures of the objects. Even with this familiarity,

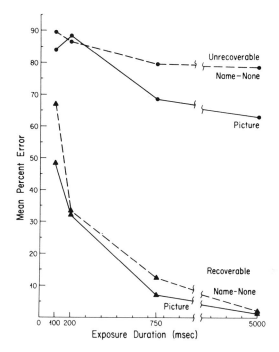

FIG. 18.   Mean percent errors in object naming as a function of exposure duration, nature of contour deletion (recoverable vs. nonrecoverable components), and prefamiliarization (none, name, or picture). No differences were apparent between the none and name pretraining conditions so they have been combined into one function.

performance in the *nonrecoverable* condition was extraordinarily poor, with error rates exceeding 60% when subjects had a full five seconds for deciphering the stimulus. As noted previously, even this value underestimated the difficulty of identifying objects in the nonrecoverable condition, in that identification was possible only when the contour deletion allowed some of the components to remain recoverable.

The emphasis on the poor performance in the nonrecoverable condition should not obscure the extensive interference that was evident at the brief exposure durations in the *recoverable* condition. The previous experiments had established that intact objects, without picture familiarization, could be identified at near perfect accuracy at 100 ms. At this exposure duration, error rates for the recoverable stimuli in the present experiment, whose contours could be restored through collinearity and curvature, were approximately 65%. The high error rates at 100 ms exposure duration suggests that these filling-in processes require both time (on the order of 200 ms) and an image—not merely a memory representation—to be successfully executed.

The dependence of componential recovery on the availability of contour and time was explored parametrically by Biederman and Blickle [8]. To produce the nonrecoverable versions of the objects it was necessary to delete or modify the vertices.

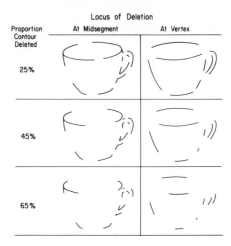

FIG. 19. Illustration for a single object of 25, 45, and 65% contour removal centered at either midsegment or vertex.

The recoverable versions of the objects tended to have their contours deleted in midsegment. It is possible that some of the interference in the nonrecoverable condition was a consequence of the removal of vertices, rather than the production of inappropriate components. The experiment also compared these two loci (vertex or midsegment) as sites of contour deletion. Contour deletion was performed either at the vertices or at midsegments for 18 objects, but without the accidental bridging of components through collinearity or curvature that was characteristic of the nonrecoverable condition. The percent contour removed was also varied with values of 25, 45, and 65% removal and the objects were shown for 100, 200, or 750 ms. Other aspects of the procedure were identical to the previous experiments with only name familiarization provided. Figure 19 shows an example for a single object.

The mean percent errors are shown in Fig. 20. At the briefest exposure duration and the most contour deletion (100 ms exposure duration and 65% contour deletion), removal of the vertices resulted in considerably higher error rates than the midsegment removal, 54 and 31% errors, respectively. With less contour deletion or longer exposures, the locus of the contour deletion had only a slight effect on naming accuracy. Both types of loci showed a consistent improvement with longer exposure durations, with error rates below 10% at the 750 ms duration. By contrast, the error rates in the nonrecoverable condition in the prior experiment exceeded 75%, even after 5 s. We conclude that the filling-in of contours, whether at midsegment or vertex, is a process that can be completed within 1 s. But the suggestion of a misleading component through collinearity or curvature that bridges a concavity produces an image that cannot index the original object, no matter how much time there is to view the image. Although accuracy was less affected by the locus of the contour deletion at the longer exposure durations and the lower deletion proportions, there was a consistent advantage on naming latencies of the midsegment removal, as shown in Fig. 21. (The lack of an effect at the 100 ms exposure duration with 65% deletion is likely a consequence of the high error rates for the vertex

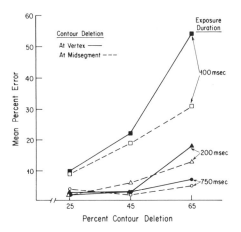

FIG. 20.   Mean percent object naming errors as a function of locus of contour removal (midsegment or vertex), percent removal, and exposure duration.

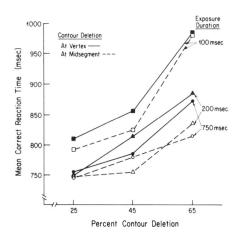

FIG. 21.   Mean correct object naming reaction time (ms) as a function of locus of contour removal (midsegment or vertex), percent removal, and exposure duration.

deletion stimuli.) This result shows that if contours are deleted at a vertex they can be restored, as long as there is no accidental filling-in, but the restoration will require more time than when the deletion is at midsegment. Overall, both the error and RT data document a striking dependence of object identification on what RBC assumes to be a prior and necessary stage of componential determination.

Perceiving degraded vs partial objects.   In the experiments with partial objects and contour deletion, objects were shown with less than their full amount of contour. With the partial objects, the missing contours were in the form of complete components that were missing; the components that were present were present in intact form. With the degraded objects, the deleted contour was distributed across all of the object's components. Biederman, Beiring, Ju, and Blickle [7] compared the effects of midsegment contour deletion, where the contours could be restored through collinearity or curvature, with the removal of whole components, when an equivalent amount of contour was deleted for each object. With partial objects, it is unlikely that the missing components are added imaginally, prior to recognition. Logically, one would have to know what object was being recognized to know what parts to add. Instead, indexing (addressing) a representation most likely proceeds in the absence of the parts. The two methods for removing contour are thus seen as affecting different stages. Deleting contour in midsegment affects processes prior to and including those involved in the determination of the components (Fig. 3). The removal of whole components (the partial object procedure) is assumed to affect the matching stage, reducing the number of common components between the image and the representation and increasing the number of distinctive components in the representation. Contour filling-in is typically regarded as a fast, low level process. The finding that partial complex objects—with only three of their components present—can be recognized more readily than objects whose contours can be restored through filling-in would document the efficiency of a few components for accessing a representation.

The procedure for this experiment closely followed the previous experiments. The stimuli were the 18 objects that required six or nine components to look complete in the partial object experiment. The three component versions of these objects were selected as the partial object stimuli. For each of these objects, contour was deleted in midsegment to produce a version that had the same amount of contour removed as the three component versions. For example, removing six of the nine components of the stool removed 45% of its contour. The degraded version of the stool also had 45% of its contour removed, except that the removal was distributed in midsegment throughout the object. Some sample stimuli are shown in Fig. 22. The mean deletion was 33% (S.D. 15.6; range 11.7–68.2%). Objects were presented for 65, 100, and 200 ms.

Results.   At the shortest (65 ms) exposure duration, removing components was less disruptive than deleting contours in midsegment, 24–39% errors, respectively (Fig. 23). This difference was reduced and even reversed at the longer exposure durations. The RTs (Fig. 24) show the interaction even more strongly. The result of this comparison provides additional support for the dependence of object recognition on componential identification. RBC posits that a sufficient input for recognition is a diagnostic subset of a few components (a partial object). If all of an object's components were degraded (but recoverable), recognition would be delayed while the contours were restored through the filling-in routines. Once the filling-in was completed, a better match to the object's representation would be possible than with a partial object that had only a few of its components. Longer exposure durations increase the likelihood that filling-in would be completed, at which point the image would provide a better match to the representation. The results indicate that the costs of identification speed and accuracy for contour deletion were greater than the costs from removing some of an object's components at the briefest exposure durations. A subjective demonstration of the processing time required for contour restoration is presented in the next section.

Contour deletion by occlusion.   The degraded recoverable objects in the right columns of Fig. 17 have the appearance of flat drawings of object with interrupted

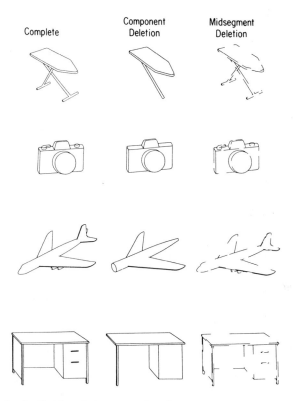

FIG. 22. Sample stimuli with equivalent proportion of contours removed either at midsegments or as whole components.

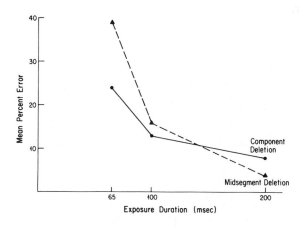

FIG. 23. Mean percent errors of object naming as a function of the nature of contour removal (deletion of midsegments or components) and exposure duration.

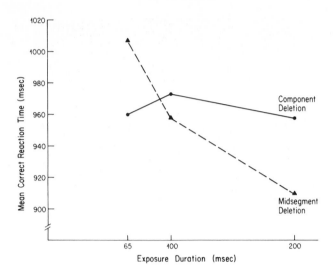

FIG. 24.   Mean correct reaction time (ms) in object naming as a function of the nature of contour removal (deletion at midsegments or components) and exposure duration.

contours. Biederman and Blickle [8] designed a demonstration of the dependence of object recognition on componential identification by aligning an occluding surface so that it appeared to produce the deletions. If the components were responsible for an identifiable volumetric representation of the object, we would expect that with the recoverable stimuli, the object would complete itself under the occluding surface and assume a three dimensional character. This effect should not occur in the nonrecoverable condition. This expectation was met as shown in Figs. 25 and 26. These stimuli also provide a demonstration of the time (and effort?) requirements for contour restoration through collinearity or curvature. We have not yet obtained

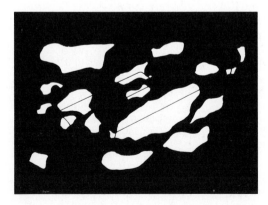

FIG. 25.   Nonrecoverable version of an object where the contour deletion is produced by an occluding surface.

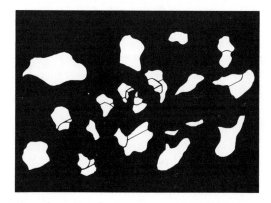

FIG. 26. Recoverable version of an object where the contour deletion is produced by an occluding surface. The object is the same as that shown in Fig. 25. The reader may note that the 3D percept in this figure does not occur instantaneously.

objective data on this effect, which may be complicated by masking effects from the presence of the occluding surface, but we invite the reader to share our subjective impressions. When looking at a nonrecoverable version of an object in Fig. 25, no object becomes apparent. In the recoverable version in Fig. 26, an object does pop into a 3D appearance, but most observers report a delay (our own estimate is approximately 500 ms) from the moment the stimulus is first fixated to when it appears as an identifiable 3D entity.

This demonstration of the effects of an occluding surface to produce contour interruption also provides a control for the possibility that the difficulty in the nonrecoverable condition was a consequence of inappropriate figure–ground groupings, as with the stool in Fig. 17. With the stool, the ground that was apparent through the rungs of the stool became figure in the nonrecoverable condition. (In general, however, only a few of the objects had holes in them where this could have been a factor.) This would not necessarily invalidate the RBC hypothesis but merely would complicate the interpretation of the effects of the nonrecoverable noise, in that some of the effect would derive from inappropriate grouping of contours into components and some of the effect would derive from inappropriate figure–group grouping. That the objects in the nonrecoverable condition remain unidentifiable when the contour interruption is attributable to an occluding surface suggests that figure–group grouping cannot be the primary cause of the interference from the nonrecoverable deletions.

SUMMARY AND IMPLICATIONS OF THE EXPERIMENTAL RESULTS

The sufficiency of a component representation for primal access to the mental representation of an object was supported by two results: (a) that partial objects with two or three components could be readily identified under brief exposures, and (b) comparable identification performance between the line drawings and color photography. The experiments with degraded stimuli established that the components are necessary for object perception. These results suggest an underlying principle by which objects are identified.

Componential Recovery Principle

The results and phenomena associated with the effects of degradation and partial objects can be understood as the workings of a single *principle of componential recovery*: If the components in their specified arrangement can be readily identified, object identification will be fast and accurate. In addition to those aspects of object perception for which experimental research was described above, the principle of componential recovery might encompass at least four additional phenomena in object perception: (a) that objects can be more readily recognized from some orientations than others (orientation variability), (b) objects can be recognized from orientations not previously experienced (object transfer), (c) articulated (or deformable) objects, with variable componential arrangements, can be recognized even when the specific configuration might not have been experienced previously (deformable object invariance), and (d) novel instances of a category can be rapidly classified (perceptual basis of basic level categories).

Orientation Variability

Objects can be more readily identified from some orientations compared to other orientations [50]. According to the RBC hypothesis, difficult views will be those in which the components extracted from the image are not the components (and their relations) in the representation of the object. Often such mismatches will arise from an "accident" of viewpoint where an image property is not correlated with the property in the 3D world. For example, when the viewpoint in the image is parallel to the major components of the object, the resultant foreshortening converts one or some of the components into surface components, such as disks and rectangles in Fig. 27, which are not included in the componential description of the object. In addition, as illustrated in Fig. 27, the surfaces may occlude otherwise diagnostic components. Consequently, the components extracted from the image will not readily match the mental representation of the object and identification will be much

FIG. 27.   A viewpoint parallel to the axes of the major components of a common object.

FIG. 28.   The same object as in Fig. 27, but with a viewpoint not parallel to the major components.

more difficult compared to an orientation, such as that shown in Fig. 28, which does convey the components. A second condition under which viewpoint affects identifiability of a specific object arises when the orientation is simply unfamiliar, as when a sofa is viewed from below or when the top-bottom relations among the components are perturbed as when a normally upright object is inverted.

Palmer, Rosch, and Chase [50] conducted an extensive study of the perceptability of various objects when presented at a number of different orientations. Generally, a three-quarters front view was most effective for recognition. Their subjects showed a clear preference for such views. Palmer *et al.* termed this effective and preferred orientation of the object its *canonical orientation*. The canonical orientation would be, from the perspective of RBC, a special case of the orientation that would maximize the match of the components in the image to the representation of the object.

An apparent exception to the preference for three-quarters frontal view preference was Palmer *et al.'s* [50] finding that frontal (facial) views enjoyed some favor in viewing animals. But there is evidence that routines for processing faces have evolved to differentially respond to cuteness [25, 26], age (e.g., [37]), and emotion and threats (e.g., [20, 65]). Faces may thus constitute a special stimulus case in that specific mechanisms have evolved to respond to biologically relevant quantitative variations and caution may be in order before results with face stimuli are considered as characteristic of the perception of objects in general.

Transfer Between Different Viewpoints

When an object is seen at one viewpoint or orientation it can often be recognized as the same object when subsequently seen at some other viewpoint, even though there can be extensive differences in the retinal projections of the two views. The componential recovery principle would hold that transfer between two viewpoints would be a function of the componential similarity between the views. This could be experimentally tested through priming studies with the degree of priming predicted to be a function of the similarity (viz., common minus distinctive components) of the two views. If two different views of an object contained the same components RBC would predict that, aside from effects attributable to variations in aspect ratio, there should be as much priming as when the object was presented at an identical view. An alternative possibility to componential recovery is that a presented object would be mentally rotated [61] to correspond to the original representation. But mental rotation rates appear to be too slow and effortful to account for the ease and speed in which transfer occurs between different orientations.

There may be a restriction on whether a similarity function for priming effects will be observed. Although unfamiliar objects (or nonsense objects) should reveal a componential similarity effect, the recognition of a familiar object, whatever its orientation, may be too rapid to allow an appreciable experimental priming effect. Such objects may have a representation for each orientation that provided a different componential description. Bartram's [3] results support this expectation that priming effects might not be found across different views of familiar objects. Bartram performed a series of studies in which subjects named 20 pictures of objects over eight blocks of trials. (In another experiment, Bartram [4] reported essentially the same results from a same–different name matching task in which pairs of pictures were presented.) In the *identical condition*, the pictures were identical across the trial blocks. In the *different view* condition, the same objects were depicted from one block to the next but in different orientations. In the *different exemplar* condition, different exemplars, e.g., different instances of a chair, were presented, all of which required the same response. Bartram found that the naming RTs for the *identical* and *different view* conditions were equivalent and both were shorter than control conditions, described below, for concept and response priming effects. Bartram theorized that observers automatically compute and access all possible 3D viewpoints when viewing a given object. Alternatively, it is possible that there was high componential similarity across the different views and the experiment was insufficiently sensitive to detect slight differences from one viewpoint to another. However, in four experiments with colored slides, we [11] failed to obtain any effect of variation in viewing angle and have thus replicated Bartram's basic effect (or lack of an effect). At this point, our inclination is to agree with Bartram's interpretation, with somewhat different language, but restrict its scope to familiar objects. It should be noted that both Bartram's and our results are inconsistent with a model that assigned heavy weight to the aspect ratio of the image of the object or postulated an underlying mental rotation function.

Different Exemplars Within An Object Class

Just as we might be able to gauge the transfer between two different views of the same object based on a componential based similarity metric, we might be able to predict transfer between different exemplars of a common object, such as two different instances of a lamp or chair.

Bartram [3] also included a *different exemplar* condition, in which different objects with the same name, e.g., different cars, were depicted from block to block. Under the assumption that different exemplars would be less likely to have common components, RBC would predict that this condition would be slower than the *identical* and *different view* conditions but faster than a *different object* control condition with a new set of objects that required different names for every trial block. This was confirmed by Bartram.

For both different views of the same object, as well as different exemplars (subordinates) within a basic level category, RBC predicts that transfer would be based on the overlap in the components between the two views. The strong prediction would be that the same similarity function that predicted transfer between different orientations of the same object would also predict the transfer between different exemplars with the same name.

The Perceptual Basis of Basic Level Categories

Consideration of the similarity relations among different exemplars with the same name raises the issue as to whether objects are most readily identified at a basic, as opposed to a subordinate or superordinate, level of description. The componential representations described here are representations of *specific*, subordinate objects, though their identification was always measured with a basic level name. Much of the research suggesting that objects are recognized at a basic level have used stimuli, often natural, in which the subordinate level had the same componential description as the basic level objects. Only small componential differences, color or texture, distinguished the subordinate level objects. Thus distinguishing Asian elephants from African elephants or Buicks from Oldsmobiles require fine discriminations for their verification. It is not at all surprising that with these cases basic level identification would be most rapid. On the other hand, many humanmade categories, such as lamps, or some natural categories, such as dogs (which have been bred by humans), have members that have componential descriptions that differ considerably from one exemplar to another, as with a pole lamp vs a ginger jar table lamp, for example. The same is true of objects that are different from a prototype, as penguins or sport cars. With such instances, which unconfound the similarity between basic level and subordinate level objects, perceptual access should be at the subordinate (or instance) level, a result supported by a recent report by Jolicoeur, Gluck, and Kosslyn [31].

It takes but a modest extension of the componential recovery principle to problems of the similarity of objects. Simply put, similar objects will be those that have a high degree of overlap in their components and in the relations among these components. A similarity measure reflecting common and distinctive components [66] may be adequate for describing the similarity among a pair of objects or between a given instance and its stored or expected representation, whatever their basic or subordinate level designation.

The Perception of Nonrigid Objects

Many objects and creatures, such as people and telephones, have articulated joints that allow extension, rotation, and even separation of their components. There are two ways in which such objects can be accommodated by RBC. One possibility is that independent structural descriptions are necessary for each sizable alteration in the arrangement of an object's components. For example, it may be necessary to establish a different structural description for Fig. 29a than 29d. If this were the case, then a priming paradigm might not reveal any priming between the two stimuli. Another possibility is that the relations among the components can include a

FIG. 29.   Four configurations of a nonrigid object.

range of possible values [40]. In the limit, with a relation that allowed complete freedom for movement, the relation might simply be JOINED. Even that might be relaxed in the case of objects with separable parts, as with the handset and base of a telephone. In that case, it might be either that the relation is NEARBY or else different structural descriptions are necessary for attached and separable configurations. Empirical research needs to be done to determine if less restrictive relations, such as JOIN or NEARBY, have measurable perceptual consequences. It may be the case that the less restrictive the relation, the more difficult the identifiability of the object. Just as there appear to be canonical views of rigid objects [50], there may be a canonical "configuration" for a nonrigid object. Thus, Fig. 29d might be more slowly identified as a woman than Fig. 29a.

CONCLUSION

To return to the analogy with speech perception made in the introduction of this article, the characterization of object perception that RBC provides bears close resemblance to many modern views of speech perception. In both cases, one has a modest set of primitives: In speech, the 55 or so phonemes that are sufficient to represent almost all the words of all the languages on earth; in object perception, perhaps, a limited number of simple components. The ease by which we are able to code tens of thousands of words or objects may derive less from a capacity for making exceedingly fine physical discriminations than it does from allowing free combination of a modest number of categorized primitives.

REFERENCES

1. D. Ballard and C. M. Brown, *Computer Vision*, Prentice–Hall, Englewood Cliffs, N.J., 1982.
2. H. G. Barrow and J. M. Tenenbaum, Interpreting line-drawings as three-dimensional surfaces, *Artif. Intell.* **17**, 1981, 75–116.
3. D. Bartram, The role of visual and semantic codes in object naming, *Cognit. Psychol.* **6**, 1974, 325–356.
4. D. Bartram, Levels of coding in picture–picture comparison tasks, *Mem. Cognit.* **4**, 1976, 593–602.
5. J. Beck, K. Prazdny, and A. Rosenfeld, A theory of textural segmentation, in *Human and Machine Vision* (J. Beck, B. Hope, and A. Rosenfeld, Eds.,) Academic Press, New York, 1983.
6. I. Biederman, On the semantics of a glance at a scene, in *Perceptual Organization*, (M. Kubovy and J. R. Pomerantz, Eds.), Erlbaum, Hillsdale, N.J., 1981.

7. I. Biederman, E. Beiring, G. Ju, and T. Blickle, A comparison of the perception of partial vs degraded objects, unpublished manuscript, State University of New York at Buffalo, 1985.

8. I. Biederman and T. Blickle, The perception of degraded objects, unpublished manuscript, State University of New York at Buffalo, 1985.

9. I. Biederman and G. Ju, A comparison of the perception of line drawings and colored photography, unpublished manuscript, State University of New York at Buffalo, 1985.

10. I. Biederman, G. Ju, and J. Clapper, The perception of partial objects, unpublished manuscript, State University of New York at Buffalo, 1985.

11. I. Biederman and M. Lloyd, Experimental studies of transfer across different object views and exemplars, unpublished manuscript, State University of New York at Buffalo, 1985.

12. T. O. Binford, Inferring surfaces from images, *Artif. Intell.* **17**, 1981, 205–244.

13. T. O. Binford, Visual perception by computer, *IEEE Systems Science and Cybernetics Conference*, Miami, December, 1971.

14. M. Brady, Criteria for the representations of shape, in *Human and Machine Vision* (J. Beck, B. Hope, and A. Rosenfeld, Eds.) Academic Press, New York, 1983.

15. R. A. Brooks, Symbolic reasoning among 3D models and 2D images, *Artif. Intell.* **17**, 1981, 205–244.

16. S. Cary, The child as word learner, in *Linguistic Theory and Psychological Reality*, (M. Halle, J. Bresnan, and G. A. Miller, Eds.), MIT Press, Cambridge, Mass., 1976.

17. P. Cezanne, Letter to Emile Bernard, in *Paul Cezanne's Letters* (J. Rewald, Ed.), (Translated by M. Kay), Cassirrer, London, 1904/1941.

18. I. Chakravarty, A generalized line and junction labeling scheme with applications to scene analysis, *IEEE Trans. Pattern Anal. Mech. Intell. PAMI-*, 1(2) April, 1979, 202–205.

19. S. F. Checkosky and D. Whitlock, Effects of pattern goodness on recognition time in a memory search task. *J. Exp. Psychol.* **100**, 1973, 341–348.

20. R. G. Coss, Delayed plasticity of an instinct: Recognition and avoidance of 2 facing eyes by the jewel fish, *Dev. Psychobiol.* **12**, 1979, 335–345.

21. H. Egeth and R. Pachella, Multidimensional stimulus identification, *Percept. Psychophys.* **5**, 1969, 341–346.

22. B. N. Fildes and T. J. Triggs, The effect of changes in curve geometry on magnitude estimates of road-like perspective curvature, *Percept. Psychophys.* **37**, 1985, 218–224.

23. W. R. Garner, *The Processing of Information and Structure*, Wiley, New York, 1974.

24. A. Guzman, Analysis of curved line drawings using context and global information, *Machine Intelligence* Vol. 6, Edinburgh Univ. Press, Edinburgh, 1971.

25. K. A. Hildebrandt, The role of physical appearance in infant and child development, in *Theory and Research in Behavioral Pediatrics*, Vol. 1. (H. E. Fitzgerald, E. Lester, and M. Youngman, Eds.), Plenum, New York, 1983.

26. K. A. Hildebrandt and H. E. Fitzgerald, The infant's physical attractiveness: Its effect on bonding and attachment, *Infant Mental Health J.* **4**, 1983, 3–12.

27. J. E. Hochberg, *Perception*, 2nd ed., Prentice–Hall, Englewood Cliffs, N.J., 1978.

28. D. D. Hoffman and W. Richards, Parts of recognition, *Cognition* **18**, 1985, 65–96.

29. G. W. Humphreys, Reference frames and shape perception, *Cognit. Psychol.* **15**, 1983, 151–196.

30 W. H. Ittleson, *The Ames Demonstrations in Perception*, Hafner, New York, 1952.

31. P. Jolicoeur, M. A. Gluck, and S. M. Kosslyn, Picture and names: Making the connection, *Cognit. Psychol.* **16**, 1984, 243–275.

32. B. Julesz, Textons, the elements of texture perception, and their interaction, *Nature* **290**, 1981, 91–97.

33. T. Kanade, Recovery of the three-dimensional shape of an object from a single view, *Artif. Intell.* **17**, 1981, 409–460.

34. M. King, G. E. Meyer, J. Tangney, and I. Biederman, Shape constancy and a perceptual bias towards symmetry, *Percept. Psychophys.* **19**, 1976, 129–136.

35. J. F. Kroll and M. C. Potter, Recognizing words, pictures, and concepts: A comparison of lexical, object, and reality decisions, *J. Verbal Learn. Verbal Behav.* **23**, 1984, 39–66.

36. D. Lowe, Perceptual organization and visual recognition, unpublished doctoral dissertation, Department of Computer Science, Stanford University, 1984.

37. L. S. Mark and J. T. Todd, Describing perception information about human growth in terms of geometric invariants, *Percept. Psychophys.* **37**, 1985, 249–256.

38. D. Marr, Analysis of occluding contour, *Proc. Roy. Soc. London B* **197**, 1977, 441–475.

39. D. Marr, *Vision*, Freeman, San Francisco, 1982.

40. D. Marr and H. K. Nishihara, Representation and recognition of three dimensional shapes, *Proc. Roy. Soc. London B* **200**, 1978, 269–294.

41. W. Marslen-Wilson, Optimal efficiency in human speech processing, unpublished manuscript, Max Planck Instit fur Psycholinguistik, Nijmegen, The Netherlands, 1980.

42. J. L. McClelland and D. E. Rumelhart, An interactive activation model of context effects in letter perception, Part I: An account of basic findings, *Psychol. Rev.* **42**, 1981, 375–407.

43. G. A. Miller, The magical number seven, plus or minus two: Some limits on our capacity for processing information, *Psychol. Rev.* **63**, 1956, 81–97.

44. G. A. Miller, *Spontaneous Apprentices: Children and Language*, Seabury, New York, 1977.

45. U. Neisser, *Cognitive Psychology*, Appleton, New York, 1967.

46. U. Neisser, Decision time without reaction time: Experiments in visual scanning, *Amer. J. Psychol.* **76**, 1963, 376–385.

47. R. C. Oldfield and A. Wingfield, Response latencies in naming objects, *Q. J. Exp. Psychol.* **17**, 1965, 273–281.

48. R. C. Oldfield, Things, words, and the brain, *Q. J. Exp. Psychol.* **18**, 1966, 340–353.

49. S. E. Palmer, What makes triangles point: Local and global effects in configurations of ambiguous triangles, *Cognit. Psychol.* **12**, 1980, 285–305.

50. S. Palmer, E. Rosch, and P. Chase, Canonical perspective and the perception of objects, *Attention & Performance IX*, (J. Long and A. Baddeley, Eds.), Erlbaum, Hillsdale, N.J., 1981.

51. L. S. Penrose and R. Penrose, Impossible objects: A special type of illusion, *Brit. J. Psychol.* **49**, 1958, 31–33.

52. D. N. Perkins, Why the human perceiver is a bad machine, in *Human and Machine Vision* (J. Beck, B. Hope, and A. Rosenfeld, Eds.), Academic Press, New York, 1983.

53. D. N. Perkins and J. Deregowski, A cross-cultural comparison of the use of a Gestalt perceptual strategy, *Perception* **12**, 1983.

54. J. R. Pomerantz, Pattern and speed of encoding, *Mem. Cognit.* **5**, 1978, 235–241.

55. J. R. Pomerantz, L. C. Sager, and R. J. Stoever, Perception of wholes and their component parts: Some configural superiority effects, J. Exp. Psychol.: Human Percept. Perform. **3**, 1977, 422–435.

56. I. Rock, *Perception*, Freeman, New York, 1984.

57. E. Rosch, C. B. Mervis, W. Gray, D. Johnson, and Boyes-Braem, Basic objects in natural categories, *Cognit. Psychol.* **8**, 1976, 382–439.

58. S. Rosenthal, The PF474, *Byte* **9**, 1984, 247–256.

59. T. Ryan and C. Schwartz, Speed of perception as a function of mode of representation, *Amer. J. Psychol.* **69**, 1956, 60–69.

60. K. Sugihara, An algebraic approach to shape-from-image problems, *Artif. Intell.* **23**, 1984, 59–95.

61. R. N. Shepard and J. Metzler, Mental rotation of three dimensional objects, *Science* (Washington, D.C.) **171**, 1971, 701–703.

62. A. Treisman, Perceptual grouping and attention in visual search for objects, *J. Exp. Psychol. Human Percept. Perform.* **8**, 1982, 194–214.

63. A. Treisman and G. Gelade, A feature integration theory of attention, *Cognit. Psychol.* **12**, 1980, 97–136.

65. R. Trivers, *Social Evolution*, Benjamin/Cummings, Menlo Park, 1985.

66. A. Tversky, Features of similarity, *Psychol. Rev.* **84**, 1977, 327–352.

67. B. Tversky and K. Hemenway, Objects, parts, and categories, J. Exp. Psychol. Gen. **113**, 1984, 169–193.

68. S. Ullman, *Visual Routines*, A.I. Memo No. 723, Artificial Intelligence Laboratory, MIT, Cambridge, Mass., 1983.

69. V. Virsu, Tendencies to eyemovements and misperception of curvature, direction and length, *Percept. Psychophys.* **9**, 1971, 65–72.

70. V. Virsu, Underestimation of curvature and task dependence in visual perception of form, *Percept. Psychophys.* **9**, 1971, 339–342.

71. P. A. Winston, Learning structural descriptions from examples, in *The Psychology of Computer Vision*, (P. H. Winston, Ed.), McGraw-Hill, 1975.

72. A. P. Witkin and J. M. Tennenbaum, On the role of structure in vision, in *Human and Machine Vision* (J. Beck, B. Hope, and A. Rosenfeld, Eds.), Academic Press, New York 1983.

73. F. C. Bartlett, *Remembering: A Study in Experimental and Social Psychology*, Cambridge Univ. Press, London/New York, 1932.

74. R. Nevatia and T. O. Binford, description and recognition of curved objects, *Artif. Intell.* 8, 77–98.

75. S. E. Palmer, The psychology of perceptual organization: A transformational approach, in *Human and Machine Vision* (J. Beck, B. Hope, and A. Rosenfeld, Eds.) Academic Press, New York, 1983.

76. K. Sugihara, Classification of impossible objects, *Perception* 11, 1982, 65–74.

77. D. Waltz, Understanding of line drawings of scenes with shadows, *The Psychology of Computer Vision* (P. H. Winston, Ed.), McGraw–Hill, New York, 1975.

78. R. S. Woodworth, *Experimental Psychology*, Holt, New York, 1938.

Describing Surfaces*

JEAN PONCE, ALAN YUILLE, AND HARUO ASADA

_nce Laboratory, Massachusetts Institute of Technology,
Cambridge, Massachusetts 20742

Received August 30, 1984

This paper continues our work on visual representations of 2-dimensional surfaces. The theoretical component of our work is a study of classes of surface curves as a source of constraint on the surface on which they lie, and as a basis for describing it. We analyze bounding contours, surface intersections, lines of curvature, and asymptotes. Our experimental work investigates whether the information suggested by our theoretical study can be computed reliably and efficiently. We demonstrate algorithms that compute lines of curvature of a (Gaussian smoothed) surface; determine planar patches and umbilic regions; extract axes of surfaces of revolution and tube surfaces. We report preliminary results on adapting the curvature primal sketch algorithms of Asada and Brady [1984] to detect and describe surface intersections. © 1985 Academic Press, Inc.

1. INTRODUCTION

Recent work in *image understanding* [3, 10, 39] has centered on the development of modules that compute 3-dimensional depth, or depth gradients. Such modules include: stereo [27, 28, 41]; shape from shading [33, 34] and photometric stereo [56, 57]; shape from contour [13, 54, 4, 5]; shape from motion [18, 51]; and shape from texture [52]. In applying vision to robotics, range finding and structured light have been investigated as techniques for recovering depth directly [1, 32, 9, 24, 25, 44, 45, 50]. Although the work referred to above is largely experimental, it is clear that robust, efficient, practical 3-dimensional vision systems will soon be available.

Several authors have suggested that the output of these "shape from" processes is a representation(s) that makes explicit the surface depth $z(x, y)$ or the local surface normal $n(x, y)$. Barrow and Tenenbaum [6] call such a representation an "intrinsic image," which emphasizes that the representation has the same format as an image. Just as applications of 2-dimensional vision depend upon the development of rich representations of shape (for example, Brady and Asada [11]), computed from an image, so will applications of 3-dimensional vision. This paper is concerned with the geometrical basis of such a representation. In particular, a set of curves are isolated that lie upon the surface and enjoy a global property, for example being planar. The structure of the representation is currently under development.

The representation that we are developing is based on the concepts of differential geometry, principally because it provides a hierarchy of increasingly stringent

*This report describes research done at the Artificial Intelligence Laboratory of the Massachusetts Institute of Technology. Support for the laboratory's Artificial Intelligence research is provided in part by the System Development Foundation, the Advanced Research Projects Agency of the Department of Defense under Office of Naval Research Contract N00014-80-C-0505, the Office of Naval Research under Contract N00014-77-C-0389, and the System Development Foundation. This work was done while Haruo Asada was a visiting scientist at MIT on leave from Toshiba Corporation, Japan, and while Jean Ponce was a visiting scientist on leave from INRIA, Paris, France.

58

surface descriptions. A surface may simply be doubly curved, but it may be ruled, even developable, even conical. Our aim is to find the most stringent descriptors for portions of a surface. If, for example, there is a region of umbilic points, that indicates that part of the surface is spherical, then it is made explicit, as is the center of the corresponding sphere (Fig. 1). If there is a portion of the surface that is part of a surface of revolution, it is described as such, and the axis is determined (see Figs. 1 and 19).

Similarly, if there is a line of curvature or an asymptote that is planar or whose associated curvature (principal curvature or geodesic curvature, respectively) is constant, then it is made explicit. For example, the asymptote that marks the smooth join of the bulb and the stem of the lightbulb in Fig. 1, as well as the surface intersections marked on the oil bottle in Fig. 21, are noted in the representation. We may associate a description with a curve that is a surface intersection; but only if it has an important property such as being planar. For example, a slice of a cylinder taken oblique to the axis of the cylinder produces a planar curve of intersection. On the other hand, the intersection of two cylinders is not a planar curve.

Figure 1 illustrates the representation we are aiming at. The stem of the lightbulb is determined to be cylindrical, because it is ruled and because it is a surface of revolution. We can compute the axis of the stem. The bulb is determined to be a portion of a sphere, because it is a connected region of umbilic points. The center of the sphere can be computed. Similarly, the center of the sphere that forms the threaded end can be determined. The stem is smoothly joined to the bulb. Moreover, the axis of the cylindrical stem passes through the centers of the spheres defined by the bulb and threaded end. This distinguishes the diameters of each that are collinear with the stem axis, showing that the lightbulb is a surface of revolution. The geometrical primitives can be computed by the algorithms described below. We are working on the inference engine.

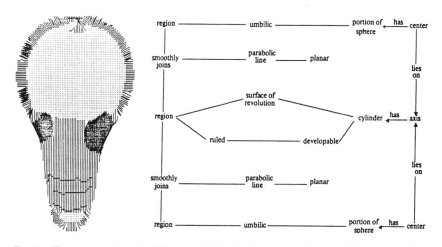

FIG. 1.   The representation of a lightbulb: (a) The dotted region consists of umbilic points, indicating that the bulb is spherical. The parallel lines are the meridians of the cylindrical stem. The parallels, which are also rulings, are not shown. The significant surface changes are shown. They indicate the smooth join between the bulb and the stem and between the stem and the threaded end. (b) The representation that we are working towards for the lightbulb.

In the next two sections we report recent theoretical developments and computational experiments. The theoretical component of our work is a study of classes of surface curves as a source of constraint on the surface on which they lie, and as a basis for describing it. We analyze bounding contours, surface intersections, lines of curvature, and asymptotes. Our experimental work investigates whether the information suggested by our theoretical study can be computed reliably and efficiently. We demonstrate algorithms that compute lines of curvature of a (Gaussian smoothed) surface; determine planar patches and umbilic regions; extract axes of surfaces of revolution and tube surfaces. We report preliminary results on adapting the curvature primal sketch algorithms of Asada and Brady [2] to detect and describe surface intersections. The experimental results appear to contradict statements by a number of authors to the effect that second differential quantities such as lines of curvature cannot be computed reliably.

2. SURFACE CURVES

2.1. Introduction

A surprising amount can be learned about a surface from certain curves that lie upon it. Our theoretical work is an investigation of classes of surface curves as a source of constraint on the geometry of the surface and as a basis for description of the surface. The curves that we have studied are: bounding contours [36, 35, 38, 6, 7, 8]; lines of curvature [46, 47, 14]; asymptotes [14]; and surface intersections [8].

We begin by discussing (extremal) bounding contours of a surface, where the surface normal turns smoothly away from the viewer. First, we recall that the surface normal can be determined from its (orthographic) projection. Then we present a new proof of a recent result due to Koenderinck [35] which states that the sign of the Gaussian curvature of the surface at points along the boundary curve is the same as the sign of the curvature of the projection of the boundary curve. We extend the result and show that, in general, points on the projection of an extremal boundary where the curvature is zero typically correspond to points on the surface that are locally flat (that is, where both principal curvatures are zero), or the boundary is locally aligned with a surface line of curvature whose curvature is zero. We suggest that these results may provide an alternative to line labelling for interpreting line drawings of curved objects.

The bounding contours of a surface are either extremal or mark discontinuities of some order $\mathscr{C}_n$. Depth discontinuities of type $\mathscr{C}_0$ typically occur at occluding boundaries. Most surface intersections are of type $\mathscr{C}_1$. Smooth joins are $\mathscr{C}_2$ discontinuities that can only be perceived if the curvature in a direction orthogonal to the join changes substantially. Asada and Brady [2] discuss the analogous situation for planar curves. A theorem of Joachimsthal [53, p. 68] implies that surfaces rarely intersect along their lines of curvature. For example, the intersection of the two cylinders in Fig. 2 is *not* a line of curvature of either surface.

The problem of detecting, localizing, and describing the discontinuities of a surface is analogous to computing the *primal sketch* representation for images [37, 30] and the *curvature primal sketch* representation of the significant changes of curvature along planar curves [2]. In Section 2.3, we show that Joachimsthal's theorem can, under certain circumstances, be undone by Gaussian smoothing. More

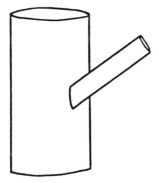

FIG. 2. The curve that is the intersection of the two cylinders is not a line of curvature of either cylinder.

precisely, we shall prove that although two surfaces rarely intersect along a line of curvature, the intersection generates a line of curvature of the surface that results from smoothing with a Gaussian distribution:

THEOREM. *Let $f(x, y, z)$ be a surface that is the cross product of a planar curve and a straight line. The lines of curvature of the convolution of f with a Gaussian distribution are in the plane of the curve and parallel to the generating line.*

The restriction that the straight line be orthogonal to the planar curve is severe and implies that the surface is cylindrical. We are investigating ways to weaken the assumption as part of our development of the *surface primal sketch* (e.g., Ponce and Brady [61]).

In Sections 2.4 and 2.5 we turn our attention to curves that lie in the interior of the visible portion of the surface, though they may intersect its boundaries. At each point of the surface, we define a set of *intrinsic directions* $\theta_i(x, y)$ in which the surface change locally appears to be intrinsically important, and we associate a descriptor $\delta_i(x, y)$ with each such direction. The set of intrinsic directions that we have investigated so far consists of the directions of principal curvature, the asymptotic directions (directions in which the normal curvature is zero), and the parabolic directions, across which the sign of the Gaussian curvature changes. The corresponding descriptors $\delta_i(x, y)$ are the principal curvatures, and, for the asymptotes, the geodesic curvature. Currently, no descriptor is associated with parabolic directions. We may find it necessary to investigate additional intrinsically important directions in due course, though the directions of principal curvature, and asymptotic and parabolic directions suffice for a broad class of analytic surfaces that includes surfaces of revolution, ruled and developable surfaces, and generalized cones.

The directions and descriptors are *local* statements about the surface. For example, the directions of principal curvature give the locally flattest coordinate system intrinsic to the surface. We aim to describe the *larger scale* structure of the surface. Whereas local surface structure is thoroughly discussed in differential geometry, larger scale structure is not. To determine the larger scale structure of the surface, we link the local directions to form smooth curves. These curves are the lines of curvature, asymptotes, and parabolic lines of the surface, and they are discussed in Sections 2.4 and 2.5. We propose that these smooth curves are only made explicit when they satisfy additional constraints. Currently, these constraints are that either (i) the descriptors δ_i in the directions θ_i are (nearly) constant along the curve, or (ii) the curve is (nearly) planar. The need for constraints on the surface curves is illustrated in Fig. 3, which shows the lines of curvature on an ellipsoid. Only three of the lines of curvature are planar, and they are the intersections of the symmetry planes of the ellipsoid with the surface. The surface is effectively described by these curves. We show how choosing a set of surface curves in this manner can automatically suggest a "natural parameterization" of a surface.

A surface curve is a geodesic if and only if its geodesic curvature is zero. Geodesics form a mathematically important class of curves. However, as we discuss below, there are situations in which, perversely, there are too many geodesics or too few. For the moment, we note that requiring planarity is less severe than requiring that the curve be a geodesic. A geodesic is planar if and only if it is a line of curvature. It follows that if the geodesic curvature is zero along a line of curvature then it is planar. However, planar lines of curvature are not necessarily geodesics, hence do not have zero geodesic curvature.

Section 2.4 is mostly given over to proving a theorem about generalized cones, a theorem that relates surface curves to a volumetric representation proposed by Marr [38]. Marr considered generalized cones [15, 16] with straight axes. He suggested that such a generalized cone is effectively represented by (i) those cross sections, called *skeletons*, for which the expansion function attains an extreme value; and (ii) the tracings, called *flutings*, for which the cross-section function attains an extremum. (A tracing is the space curve formed by a point of the cross-section contour as the cross section is drawn along the axis.) Figure 4 illustrates these terms. We prove the following theorem.

THEOREM.   *If the axis of a generalized cone is planar, and the eccentricity of the cone is zero, then* (i) *a cross section is a line of curvature if and only if the cross section is a skeleton; and* (ii) *a tracing is a line of curvature if the generalized cone is a tube surface (the expansion function is a constant), or the tracing is a fluting.*

The cone's eccentricity at a point is the angle between the tangent to the axis curve and the normal to the cross section through that point. It follows that the flutings

FIG. 3.   The lines of curvature of an ellipsoid. The only lines of curvature that are planar are the intersections of the surface with its planes of symmetry. Other lines of curvature do not seem to convey important information about the shape of the surface.

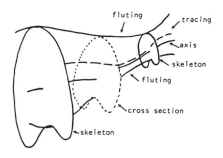

FIG. 4. A generalized cylinder is formed by drawing a uniformly-expanding planar cross section along a space curve.

and skeletons of a (planar axis) generalized cone are implied by both consideration of surface curves and by Marr's considerations of volumetric representations. Lines of curvature that satisfy a large scale constraint, such as being planar, provide a natural basis for describing a surface. As is illustrated by the ellipsoid shown in Fig. 2, and generalized cones more generally, there may only be a small number of lines of curvature that satisfy the large scale constraints. Coupled to a suitable scheme for surface interpolation (e.g., Terzopoulos [49]), they may provide a natural parameterization of the surface. Brady and Yuille [14] call such a parameterization a *curvature patch* representation.

As we shall show in Section 2.5, however, lines of curvature are a poor basis for describing many surfaces. In particular, ruled surfaces are seldom usefully described in terms of their lines of curvature, which typically fail to satisfy the large scale constraints. In such cases, the rulings are a better basis for description. The rulings of a developable surface are asymptotes, which are curves along which the normal curvature is zero. They are a useful basis for describing ruled surfaces. They are discussed in Section 2.4.

Section 3 reports some initial experiments on developing a *surface primal sketch* representation of significant surface changes. Significant surface changes are found as follows. First, the surface is filtered with a Gaussian distribution and its lines of curvature are found. These are projected into a plane and input to Asada and Brady's curvature primal sketch program. This isolates the significant curvature changes along the lines of curvature and describes each such change symbolically.

The final class of curves that we investigate are the parabolic curves. These are the smooth loci of parabolic points [31, pp. 197–202]. Koenderinck's theorem (re-proved in Sect. 2.2) suggests that parabolic points on extremal contours can be found. Figure 5 is reproduced from Hilbert and Cohn-Vossen [31, p. 197]. It shows the parabolic lines on the bust of the Apollo Belvidere. The footnote on page 198 of Hilbert and Cohn-Vossen has a familiar ring: "F. Klein used the parabolic curves for a peculiar investigation. To test his hypothesis that the artistic beauty of the face was based on certain mathematical relations, he had all the parabolic curves marked out on the Apollo Belvidere, a statue renowned for the high degree of classical beauty portrayed in its features. But the curves did not possess a particularly simple form, nor did they follow any general law that could be discerned."

FIG. 5.   Bust of the Apollo Belvidere with superimposed parabolic lines. (Reproduced from [31, p. 197].)

Consider, however, Fig. 6a, which shows the computed regions of positive (white) and negative (black) Gaussian curvature on the surface of a lightbulb. The parabolic curves are planar and they mark smooth joins between significant parts, such as the bulb and stem. This suggests that, just like directions of curvature, a parabolic curve needs to satisfy additional large scale constraints in order to be made explicit by the visual system. The cross product (Fig. 6b) of a straight line and a planar curve that is the smooth join of two curves whose (planar) curvatures have opposite signs (a

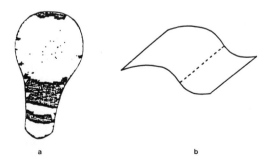

a   b

FIG. 6.   (a) The parabolic curves on a lightbulb are the transitions from elliptic regions (white) to hyperbolic regions (black). (b) The cross product of a planar curve with a smooth join and a straight line.

smooth join in the terminology of Asada and Brady [2]) is a simple surface that has a planar parabolic line. Asada and Brady point out that a smooth join is only perceivable if the difference between the curvatures of the flanking curves is sufficiently different. Few of the parabolic curves on the Apollo Belvidere have extended planar components. Those that do, such as the line on the forehead, are crossed by curves that do not have perceivable smooth joins. Two exceptions are the smooth join between the mouth and chin, and the smooth join between the nostril and the rest of the nose.

In general, it does not appear that the Gaussian curvature is a useful descriptor for a surface. The reason seems to be connected with the fact that the Gaussian curvature is a divergence expression [22, p. 196]. This means that its Euler–Lagrange equation vanishes. A divergence term can be added to any variational problem, for example, surface interpolation [27, 49, 12], without changing the resulting surface. Representations based on Gaussian curvature typically suppress spatial structure.

We omit analysis of certain classes of surface curve, particularly geodesics. There are at once too many geodesics, yet, in many cases, too few. There are too many since there is a geodesic through every point on a surface in every direction. The geodesics on a cylinder, for example, are all the helices ($R\cos\theta$, $R\sin\theta$, $k\theta$), where R is the radius of the cylinder. On the other hand, only those meridians of a surface of revolution that are extrema of the surface width (skeletons, if it is thought of as a generalized cone) are geodesics. We have, moreover, proposed that to be made explicit, a surface curve must satisfy certain strong constraints. In particular, we would require a geodesic to be planar. However, if a geodesic is planar then it is a line of curvature [53, p. 103].

2.2. Bounding Contours

Barrow and Tenenbaum [7] propose that there are two distinct types of contour that bound a surface, which they call *extremal* and *discontinuity*. At an extremal boundary, the surface normal turns away smoothly from the viewer. A discontinuity boundary marks the abrupt termination of a smooth surface, perhaps to intersect another surface (see Barrow and Tenenbaum [7, Fig. 3.1]). Since a discontinuity boundary could be produced by the edge of a ribbon that is oriented in an arbitrary direction, it is difficult to infer a great deal about the flanking smooth surface solely from the image of a discontinuity boundary. Brady and Yuille [13], Barnard and Pentland [5], and Barrow and Tenenbaum [7] offer some suggestions.

Extremal boundaries are a rich source of information. First, suppose that a surface $f(x, y, z) = 0$ is orthographically projected onto a plane whose normal is **k**. Suppose that the surface has an extremal boundary, then its boundary rim curve contains **k** and lies in the tangent plane of the surface. That is, $\mathbf{k} \cdot \nabla f = 0$, which can be written $\mathbf{k} \cdot \mathbf{n} = 0$, where **n** is the local surface normal.

Let the boundary curve $r(s)$ lying on the surface have tangent vector $\mathbf{T}(s) = d\mathbf{r}/ds$. Now **n** is orthogonal to both **k** and **T**, from which it follows that **n** is parallel to $\mathbf{k} \times \mathbf{T}$. The image of the boundary curve is

$$\mathbf{r}_P(s_P) = \mathbf{k} \times (\mathbf{r} \times \mathbf{k}),$$

whose tangent is

$$\mathbf{T}_P = \frac{d\mathbf{r}_P}{ds_P} = \mathbf{k} \times (\mathbf{T} \times \mathbf{k}) \frac{ds}{ds_P}. \tag{1}$$

That is, the image of the tangent to the boundary curve is parallel to the tangent to the image of the boundary curve. In fact, it is easy to see that

$$\frac{ds}{ds_P} = \left\{ 1 - (\mathbf{T} \cdot \mathbf{k})^2 \right\}^{-1/2}. \tag{2}$$

Since the unit surface normal $\mathbf{n}$ is parallel to $\mathbf{k} \times \mathbf{T}$, it follows from Eqs. (1) and (2) that it is parallel to $\mathbf{k} \times \mathbf{T}_P$ and so the surface normal at an extremal boundary can be determined from the image if the (orthographic) viewing direction is known. This result is due to Barrow and Tenenbaum [6].

An arbitrary curve parameterized by arclength s and lying on the surface satisfies (see, e.g., [42, p. 103]):

$$\kappa(s)\mathbf{N}(s) = \kappa_n(s)\mathbf{n}(s) + \kappa_g(s)\mathbf{n} \times \mathbf{T}(s), \tag{3}$$

where $\mathbf{T}$ and $\mathbf{N}$ are the unit tangent and unit normal to the curve (in the moving trihedron of the curve); κ is the curvature $|d\mathbf{T}/ds|$ of the curve; κ_n is the normal curvature of the curve, defined as the curvature of the curve that is the intersection of the surface and the plane that contains $\mathbf{n}$ and $\mathbf{T}$; and κ_g is called the geodesic curvature (Fig. 7).

From now on, we restrict attention to the extremal boundary curve. Since $\mathbf{k} \cdot \mathbf{n} = 0$, Eq. (3) implies

$$\kappa \mathbf{N} \cdot \mathbf{k} = \kappa_g [\mathbf{k}, \mathbf{n}, \mathbf{T}],$$

where [...] indicates the triple scalar product. Since $\mathbf{k} \cdot \mathbf{n} = 0$ (and $\mathbf{n} \cdot \mathbf{T} = 0$), the

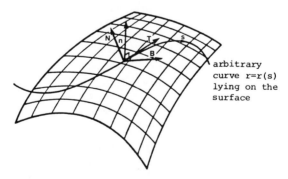

arbitrary
curve r=r(s)
lying on the
surface

FIG. 7.   A curve lying on a surface. The vectors $\mathbf{T}, \mathbf{N}, \mathbf{B}$ are the moving trihedron of the curve, whose curvature is κ. The surface normal is $\mathbf{n}$.

triple scalar product is zero if and only if $\mathbf{k}$ coincides with $\mathbf{T}$. Similarly, $\mathbf{k} \cdot \mathbf{N}$ is zero if and only if $\mathbf{k}$ lies in the rectifying plane spanned by the tangent $\mathbf{T}$ and the binormal $\mathbf{B}$. It follows from general position arguments that if $\mathbf{k}$ has a component out of the rectifying plane then

$$\kappa = 0 \quad \text{if and only if} \quad \kappa_g = 0. \tag{4}$$

Squaring Eq. (3) yields

$$\kappa^2 = \kappa_n^2 + \kappa_g^2. \tag{5}$$

It follows that if $\kappa = 0$ then $\kappa_n = \kappa_g = 0$, and if $\kappa_g = 0$, then by Eq. (4), in general, $\kappa = 0$, and $\kappa_n = 0$. It is easy to show (see Appendix A) that

$$\kappa_P^2 = \frac{\left\{ 1 - (\mathbf{T} \cdot \mathbf{k})^2 - (\mathbf{N} \cdot \mathbf{k})^2 \right\}}{\left\{ 1 - (\mathbf{T} \cdot \mathbf{k})^2 \right\}^3} \kappa^2, \tag{6}$$

where κ_P is the curvature of the projected curve $\mathbf{r}_P(s_P)$. It follows that, in general,

$$\kappa_P = 0 \quad \text{if and only if} \quad \kappa = 0. \tag{7}$$

We can now present a new proof of a recent result due to Koenderinck [35] that relates the curvature κ_P of the projection of the boundary curve to the Gaussian curvature κ_G of the surface. The key is to choose an appropriate parameterization of the surface at a point on the boundary curve (Fig. 8). Define the radial curve at a point on the boundary to be the (normal) intersection of the surface with the plane that contains the surface normal $\mathbf{n}$ and the view vector $\mathbf{k}$. Let the radial curve be parameterized by u, and denote points along the radial curve by $\mathbf{r}_r(u)$. Using s and u to parameterize the surface in the neighborhood of a point on the boundary, we

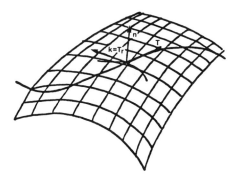

FIG. 8. The rim and radial coordinate frame. The radial curve is the intersection of the surface and the plane that contains the view vector and the surface normal. The boundary curve defines the other parameter.

find the first and second fundamental forms of the surface:

$$
\mathbf{G} = \begin{pmatrix} 1 & \mathbf{T} \cdot \mathbf{T}_r \\ \mathbf{T} \cdot \mathbf{T}_r & 1 \end{pmatrix}
$$

$$
\mathbf{D} = \begin{pmatrix} \kappa_r \mathbf{n} \cdot \mathbf{N}_r & \mathbf{n} \cdot \dfrac{\partial^2 \mathbf{r}}{\partial s\, \partial u} \\ \mathbf{n} \cdot \dfrac{\partial^2 \mathbf{r}}{\partial s\, \partial u} & \kappa \mathbf{n} \cdot \mathbf{N} \end{pmatrix},
$$

(8)

where κ_r is the curvature of the radial curve. In order for the boundary rim to be visible, κ_r must be positive.

Note that, in general, $\mathbf{T} \cdot \mathbf{T}_r \neq 0$. Since the tangent $\mathbf{T}_r$ to the radial curve $\mathbf{r}_r$ lies in the plane spanned by both $\mathbf{k}$ and $\mathbf{n}$ (remembering that we are considering a boundary curve), and is in the surface tangent plane, we have

$$
\mathbf{T}_r = \mathbf{k} \qquad \text{and} \qquad \mathbf{N}_r = \mathbf{n}.
$$

(9)

It follows that $\mathbf{T}_r$ is constant along the boundary curve, so that

$$
0 = \frac{\partial \mathbf{T}_r}{\partial s}
$$

$$
= \frac{\partial^2 \mathbf{r}}{\partial u\, \partial s}.
$$

The second fundamental form reduces by Eqs. (9) and (10) to

$$
\mathbf{D} = \begin{pmatrix} \kappa_r & 0 \\ 0 & \kappa \mathbf{n} \cdot \mathbf{N} \end{pmatrix}.
$$

(11)

Since

$$
\mathbf{n} = \frac{\mathbf{k} \times \mathbf{T}}{\left\{ 1 - (\mathbf{k} \cdot \mathbf{T})^2 \right\}^{1/2}},
$$

we find

$$
\mathbf{n} \cdot \mathbf{N} = \frac{[\mathbf{k}, \mathbf{T}, \mathbf{N}]}{\left\{ 1 - (\mathbf{k} \cdot \mathbf{T})^2 \right\}^{1/2}}
$$

$$
= \frac{\left\{ 1 - (\mathbf{k} - \mathbf{T})^2 - (\mathbf{k} \cdot \mathbf{N})^2 \right\}^{1/2}}{\left\{ 1 - (\mathbf{k} \cdot \mathbf{T})^2 \right\}^{1/2}}.
$$

The Gaussian curvature κ_G of the surface at points along extremal boundaries is given by [26, p. 112]:

$$\kappa_G = \frac{|\mathbf{D}|}{|\mathbf{G}|}$$

$$= \frac{\kappa_r \kappa \mathbf{n} \cdot \mathbf{N}}{1 - (\mathbf{T} \cdot \mathbf{k})^2}$$

$$= \kappa_r \kappa \frac{\left\{ 1 - (\mathbf{k} \cdot \mathbf{T})^2 - (\mathbf{k} \cdot \mathbf{N})^2 \right\}^{1/2}}{\left\{ 1 - (\mathbf{k} \cdot \mathbf{T})^2 \right\}^{3/2}}. \tag{12}$$

It finally follows from Eq. (6) that

$$|\kappa_G| = |\kappa_r \kappa_P|. \tag{13}$$

Since κ_r is always positive, *the sign of the Gaussian curvature of the surface at points along the boundary curve is the same as the sign of the curvature of the projection of the boundary curve* [35].

We can prove a slight extension to Koenderinck's result. If κ_P is zero, then the Gaussian curvature κ_G is zero. Also, recall from Eq. (6) that if κ_P is zero then (in general) the curvature κ of the boundary curve is also zero. It follows from Eq. (5) that the normal curvature κ_n of the boundary curve is also zero. Denote the principal curvatures at the surface point by κ_1, κ_2. The Gaussian curvature $\kappa_G = \kappa_1 \kappa_2$ is zero, and so at least one of κ_1, κ_2 is zero. But, by Euler's theorem,

$$\kappa_n = \kappa_1 \cos^2 \theta + \kappa_2 \sin^2 \theta,$$

and so $\kappa_1 = \kappa_2 = 0$ or θ is zero or $\pi/2$. That is, points on the projection of an extremal boundary where the curvature κ_P is zero typically correspond to surface points that are locally flat, that is, where both principal curvatures are zero, or the boundary is locally aligned with a surface line of curvature whose curvature is zero.

We have assumed that it is possible to determine which bounding contours are extremal and which mark discontinuities. This is a reasonable assumption in the case of dense surface data such as that used in the experiments reported in the next section. It is much more difficult in the case of line drawings such as that shown in Fig. 9. Barrow and Tenenbaum [7] propose that line labelling can suffice to make the distinction. We suggest that the results derived in this section hint at a more general approach that is based on an analysis of the surfaces meeting at a corner. For example, if the smooth contour curves are all extremal then the Gaussian curvature would be positive along the curve with positive curvature and negative along the curves with negative curvature. This would imply that the surface changes the sign of its Gaussian curvature. But there are no surface markings or other evidence that it does. A more parsimonious assumption is that the surface has the same (positive) Gaussian curvature everywhere, and hence that the contour curves with negative curvature are discontinuities. This is, in fact, what is perceived.

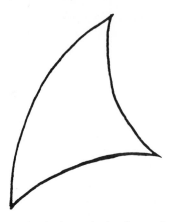

FIG. 9.   A line drawing that is perceived as the curved surface of a sail.

We can derive further results about the relationships between surface curves and the surface. For example, the sign of the normal curvature along the boundary rim can be determined from its projection [58].

2.3. Surface Intersections

In this section, we prove the following theorem, which suggests that we can find surface intersections at a given scale of Gaussian smoothing by inspecting the lines of curvature. We noted earlier that it undoes Joachimstal's theorem.

THEOREM 1.   *The Gaussian convolution of a cylindrical surface is cylindrical. In more detail, let $f(x, y, z)$ be a surface that is the cross product of a planar curve and a straight line. The lines of curvature of the convolution of f with a Gaussian are in the plane of the curve and parallel to the generating line.*

We begin with a lemma, whose proof is simple and is omitted.

LEMMA.   *Let $\mathbf{r}(x, y) = x\mathbf{i} + y\mathbf{j} + f(x)\mathbf{k}$ be a cross product surface consisting of parallel instances of a curve $f(x)$ in the x–z plane. The principal curvatures and directions of $\mathbf{r}(x, y)$ are zero in the y direction and the curvature of f in the x–z plane.*

Proof of Theorem 1.   We assume that the surface has the form of the lemma. Since the Gaussian is separable, the convolution of the surface is

$$G_\sigma(r) * f(x) = G_\sigma(y) * (G_\sigma(x) * f(x)).$$

By the derivative theorem for convolutions, it follows that

$$\{G_\sigma(r) * f(x)\}^{(n)} = G_\sigma(y) * \{G_\sigma(x) * f(x)\}^{(n)}.$$

Convolution with a constant is simply multiplication by a constant, and so the principal curvatures of $G_\sigma(r) * f(x)$ are the same as the principal curvatures of $G_\sigma(x) * f(x)$, which are given by the lemma.

The lemma can be extended straightforwardly to show that the Gaussian convolution of a surface of the form $z = f(x)(A + By)$ is a similar surface $z = (G_\sigma * f(x))(A + By)$ but the lines of curvature are not preserved.

2.4. Lines of Curvature

Brady and Yuille [14] argue that, in many cases, the lines of curvature give a natural parameterization of a surface. One practical advantage is that a computer-aided design (CAD) patch representation based on lines of curvature avoids problems of local flattening of the surface. Stevens [46, 47] has studied drawings consisting of a repeated pattern of "parallel" planar curves and the curved surfaces they suggest. He proposes that the given curves are often interpreted as lines of curvature of the perceived surface.

In Section 2.1 we noted that a line of curvature has to satisfy additional constraint if it is to be made explicit. For example, only the planar lines of curvature of the ellipsoid shown in Fig. 2 are useful for describing the surface.

Consider a surface of revolution. Suppose that the axis is aligned with the z axis. The surface is formed by rotating the (one-parameter) curve $p(u)\mathbf{i} + z(u)\mathbf{k}$ about $\mathbf{k}$. The surface is

$$\mathbf{r}(u, \theta) = p(u)\cos\theta\mathbf{i} + p(u)\sin\theta\mathbf{j} + z(u)\mathbf{k}.$$

The principal curvatures (see, e.g., [42, p. 86] are the meridians and the parallels, all of which are planar. In addition, the parallels are circular, so the curvature along any one of them is constant. The curvature along a parallel is $\mathbf{n}^T\mathbf{r}^*/p(u)$, where $\mathbf{r}^* = (\cos\theta, \sin\theta, 0)^T$. The foreshortening of the expected curvature $p(u)$ exemplifies Meusnier's theorem [53]. On the other hand, the asymptotes on a surface of revolution are, in general, complex space curves and the geodesic curvature is a complex function of position along the asymptote.

Surfaces of revolution are essentially 1-dimensional in that their shape is completely determined by a planar curve. It is reasonable to ask whether lines of curvature are more generally useful. The theorem stated in Section 2.1 shows that they are. We first prove the theorem for the straight axis case originally studied by Marr [38], relegating the more general case to Appendix B.

THEOREM 2. *If the axis of a generalized cone is straight, and the axis is normal to the cross section, then* (i) *a cross section is a line of curvature if and only if it is a skeleton;* (ii) *a tracing is a line of curvature if and only if it is a fluting.*

Proof. To fix notation, we begin by analyzing a planar cross section (Fig. 10). The curve is $(f(s), g(s))$, where s denotes arc length, and so its *radial distance* from

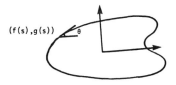

FIG. 10. A planar cross-section curve.

the origin is given by

$$d^2(s) = f^2 + g^2. \tag{14}$$

Differentiating Eq. (14) with respect to arc length gives

$$\dot{d} = \frac{f\dot{f} + g\dot{g}}{d}. \tag{15}$$

Thus the radial distance attains an extremum where the numerator of Eq. (15) is zero. Now consider the orientation θ of the tangent to the curve.

$$\tan \theta = \frac{\dot{g}}{\dot{f}},$$

$$\sec^2 \theta \dot{\theta} = \frac{\dot{f}\ddot{g} - \dot{g}\ddot{f}}{\dot{f}^2},$$

$$\cos^2 \theta = \frac{\dot{f}^2}{\dot{f}^2 + \dot{g}^2}, \tag{16}$$

$$\dot{\theta} = \frac{\dot{f}\ddot{g} - \dot{g}\ddot{f}}{l^2},$$

where $l^2(s) = \dot{f}^2 + \dot{g}^2$. Notice that $\dot{\theta}$ is the curvature of the cross-section curve.

We are now ready to prove Theorem 2. Suppose, without loss of generality, that the straight axis of the cone is $\mathbf{k}$. Let the cross section be $f(s)\mathbf{i} + g(s)\mathbf{j}$, as above. Suppose the expansion function is $h(z)$, and assume that the eccentricity of the cone is zero, that is, the axis is normal to the cross section. The generalized cone is

$$\mathbf{r}(s, z) = h(z)f(s)\mathbf{i} + h(z)g(s)\mathbf{j} + z\mathbf{k}.$$

To save on notation, we suppress parameters. We find

$$\frac{\partial \mathbf{r}}{\partial s} = [h\dot{f}, h\dot{g}, 0]^T$$

$$\frac{\partial \mathbf{r}}{\partial z} = [\dot{h}f, \dot{h}g, 1]^T,$$

(where $[\dots]^T$ denotes the vector that is the transpose of the given row vector) and so the first fundamental form of the surface is (using the notation introduced above)

$$\mathbf{G} = \begin{pmatrix} h^2 l^2 & h\dot{h}d\dot{d} \\ h\dot{h}d\dot{d} & 1 + \dot{h}^2 d^2 \end{pmatrix}.$$

The surface unit normal $\mathbf{n}$ is parallel to $\mathbf{h} = [h\dot{g}, -h\dot{f}, h\dot{h}(\dot{f}g - f\dot{g})]^T$. The second fundamental form of the surface is

$$\mathbf{D} = \begin{pmatrix} \dfrac{1}{|\mathbf{h}|} h^2(\dot{f}\ddot{g} - \ddot{f}\dot{g}) & 0 \\ 0 & \dfrac{1}{|\mathbf{h}|} h\dot{h}(\dot{f}g - fg) \end{pmatrix}.$$

The principal directions of curvature are the eigenvectors of the matrix $\mathbf{G}^{-1}\mathbf{D}$, and this matrix is diagonal if and only if

$$\frac{dh}{dz}\frac{dd}{ds} = 0,$$

from which the result follows.

2.5. Asymptotes

We begin with an example that illustrates that lines of curvature are not always the best basis for describing a surface. Consider a helicoid of a single blade (Fig. 11), which can be parameterized as follows

$$\mathbf{r}(l,\theta) = [\,l\cos\theta, l\sin\theta, m\theta\,]^T,$$

where m and l are assumed positive. Denoting $\sqrt{l^2 + m^2}$ by d, and m/l by $\tan\psi$, we find

$$\mathbf{r}_l = [\cos\theta, \sin\theta, 0]^T$$

$$\mathbf{r}_\theta = [-l\sin\theta, l\cos\theta, m]^T$$

$$\mathbf{n} = [\sin\theta\sin\psi, -\cos\theta\sin\psi, \cos\psi]^T.$$

$$\mathbf{G} = \begin{pmatrix} 1 & 0 \\ 0 & d^2 \end{pmatrix}$$

$$\mathbf{D} = \begin{pmatrix} 0 & -\dfrac{m}{d} \\ -\dfrac{m}{d} & 0 \end{pmatrix}.$$

The principal directions of curvature are given by $\dot{l} = \pm d\dot{\theta}$, and the principal curvatures are $\pm m/d^2$. Since the parameter l varies in the principal directions, so does m, hence so does the principal curvature. It is easy to show that the lines of curvature are not planar.

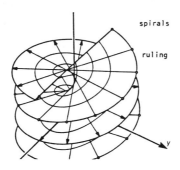

spirals

ruling

y

FIG. 11.   The helicoid of a single blade. (Reproduced from [23, Fig. 2-27, p. 94].)

Notice that the diagonal of **D** is zero. It follows that the normal curvature in the directions of the tangent vectors $\mathbf{r}_l, \mathbf{r}_\theta$ is zero. These are the asymptotes, and they correspond to the rulings and spirals that make up the helicoid. The geodesic curvature along the spirals is simply the curvature of the spiral considered as a curve. The geodesic curvature of the ruling is zero. (It is a curious fact that the lines of curvature cut the asymptotes at a constant angle of $\pi/4$.)

In general, ruled surfaces are poorly described by their lines of curvature. Examples such as the helicoid and the surface $z = kxy$ suggest that the asymptotes may be a better basis for description. The asymptotic direction can be found from Euler's theorem if the principal curvatures have opposite signs, that is, the Gaussian curvature is negative. Note that a given ruled surface may be generated by more than one set of rulings. Also, it is possible for a ruled surface to admit a significantly different description. For example, the hyperboloid $x^2 + y^2 - z^2 = 1$ is both a ruled surface and a surface of revolution.

In general, a ruled surface can be parameterized in the form

$$\mathbf{r}(s, t) = \mathbf{u}(s) + t\mathbf{w}(s),$$

where **u** is a curve called the directrix, and $\mathbf{w}(s)$ is the set of rulings. The theory of ruled surfaces emphasizes a unique curve, called the line of striction, that lies in the surface and is orthogonal to the $\mathbf{w}'$. It is not clear what role, if any, it plays in perception.

The normal to a ruled surface is parallel to

$$\mathbf{u}' \times \mathbf{w} + t\mathbf{w}' \times \mathbf{w},$$

and varies with t along the ruling. The normal direction is constant along a ruling if and only if $\mathbf{n} \cdot \mathbf{u}'$ is constant, which is if and only if the triple scalar product $[\mathbf{u}', \mathbf{w}', \mathbf{w}]$ is zero. Along such rulings, the determinant of the second fundamental form **D** is zero, and this in turn implies that the Gaussian curvature κ_G is zero. If this condition holds for all rulings on a ruled surface, the surface is called developable and the Gaussian curvature is everywhere zero. Informally, a surface is developable if it can be rolled out flat onto a plane. For such surfaces the rulings are both asymptotes and lines of curvature. For developable surfaces, the descriptive bases of Sections 2.4 and 2.5 coincide.

This section has advanced a number of mathematical methods for isolating curves that embody important information about a surface. Now we turn to their computation.

3. COMPUTATIONAL EXPERIMENTS

In this section we report on a number of computational experiments that investigate whether the surface curves and regions proposed by our theoretical analysis can be computed reliably and efficiently. The input to our programs are mostly (dense) depth maps obtained by the structured light systems at MIT [17] and INRIA [25]. Both systems are accurate to about 0.5 mm. The objects that we have worked with include: a bottle, an egg, a sphere, a styrofoam cup, a lightbulb, and a pen (all surfaces of revolution); a telephone handset (surface intersections and an approximately ruled surface); a coffee mug with a handle, a plastic container, a hammer, and a Renault part [25] (complex surfaces with surface intersections). We have also conducted experiments with artificial data to which controlled amounts of noise have been added.

3.1. Gaussian Smoothing

Depth maps generated by structured light systems are noisy, as are image surfaces. In recent years, Gaussian smoothing filters have been extensively investigated for early processing of images. For example, Marr and Hildreth [40] suggest Laplacian of a Gaussian filters $\nabla^2 G_\sigma$ for edge finding. These filters are closely approximated by difference-of-Gaussian (DOG) filters that can be efficiently implemented. Poggio and Torre [43] and Canny [21] have suggested directional edge finders whose first step is Gaussian smoothing.

Witkin [55] has proposed *scale-space filtering* in which a (1-dimensional) signal is filtered at a variety of spatial scales to produce a hierarchical description. Witkin suggests that it is possible to automatically determine a discrete set of "natural scales" at which to describe a signal symbolically. Witkin's scale-space representation is a ternary tree of zero crossings of G_σ''. He did not attempt to *interpret* the multiple descriptions in terms of primitive events. Asada and Brady [2] have shown how scale-space filtering can be used to generate a symbolic description of the significant curvature changes along a planar contour.

Yuille and Poggio [59] have provided some theoretical underpinning for the scale-space representation. They have shown that the contour of zero crossings of second derivatives ("fingerprint") may preserve enough information to reconstruct the original signal to within a constant scale factor. They also show [60] that a Gaussian filter is essentially unique in having the property that zero crossings are not introduced as one moves to coarser scales.

In view of this background with images, the first processing stage of our program is Gaussian smoothing. Initially, we applied the Gaussian filter at every surface point $z(x, y)$. This is unsatisfactory as it smooths across the depth discontinuities that are the bounding contours of an object (Fig. 12b). This is an advantage in edge

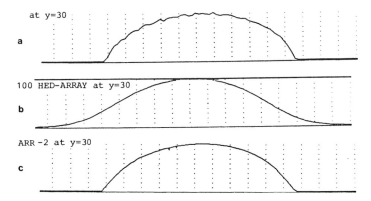

FIG. 12. (a) Raw data from a cross section of an oil bottle after scanning using the INRIA system. (b) Smoothing across surface boundaries with a Gaussian mask that is applied everywhere. (c) Gaussian smoothing using repeated averaging and computational molecules.

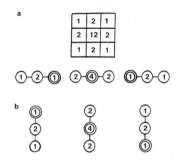

FIG. 13.   Gaussian smoothing: (a) the 3×3 mask that is repeatedly applied to approximate Gaussian filtering; (b) the computational molecules whose sum is the mask shown in (a).

detection; but a disadvantage in smoothing within a given region. In our experimental data, the depth discontinuities are sharp and easy to find before smoothing. It is difficult to prevent smoothing across discontinuities with a straightforward implementation of Gaussians using convolution masks. It is particularly difficult when the distance between opposite sides of a surface is roughly the same size as the footprint of the convolution mask as it typically is in our data.

We appeal to the central-limit theorem and implement Gaussian filtering using repeated averaging with the 3×3 mask shown in Fig. 13a (see Burt [19, 20]). Iterating n times approximately corresponds to filtering with a Gaussian whose standard deviation is proportional to $\sqrt{n}$. To prevent smoothing across previously marked depth discontinuities, we use the technique of computational molecules proposed by Terzopoulos [48] in his application of finite-element techniques to surface reconstruction. In more detail, the mask shown in Fig. 13a is viewed as the sum of the four molecules shown in Fig. 13b. To apply the filter to a surface point, only those molecules that do not overlap the set of points marked as discontinuities are used. Figure 12c shows the result of Gaussian smoothing using repeated averaging and computational molecules.

3.2. Lines of Curvature

Suppose that the (Gaussian smoothed) surface is given in vector form as $z(x, y)$. Its first and second derivatives can be estimated using the facet model [29]. We derived the finite difference operators shown in Fig. 14 by least squares fitting a

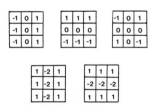

FIG. 14.   Operators used to estimate first and second derivatives of the Gaussian smoothed surface.

quadratic to a 3×3 facet of the surface. Although these operators are sensitive to noise in raw image or surface data, they perform well after Gaussian smoothing.

From these estimates we can compute the fundamental forms of the surface [42, 26]. The first fundamental form is

$$
\mathbf{G} = \begin{pmatrix} \mathbf{z}_x^2 & \mathbf{z}_x \cdot \mathbf{z}_y \\ \mathbf{z}_x \cdot \mathbf{z}_y & \mathbf{z}_y^2 \end{pmatrix}
$$

$$
= \begin{pmatrix} 1 + p^2 & pq \\ pq & 1 + q^2 \end{pmatrix}
$$

$$
= \begin{pmatrix} g_{11} & g_{12} \\ g_{12} & g_{22} \end{pmatrix}
$$

where p is the z component of $\mathbf{z}_x$ and q is the z component of $\mathbf{z}_y$. Similarly, the second fundamental form is

$$
\mathbf{D} = \begin{pmatrix} \mathbf{n} \cdot \mathbf{z}_{xx} & \mathbf{n} \cdot \mathbf{z}_{xy} \\ \mathbf{n} \cdot \mathbf{z}_{xy} & \mathbf{n} \cdot \mathbf{z}_{yy} \end{pmatrix}
$$

$$
= \begin{pmatrix} d_{11} & d_{12} \\ d_{12} & d_{22} \end{pmatrix}
$$

where $\mathbf{n}$ is the unit surface normal. The (tangent) principal directions are the solutions of the quadratic equation [26]

$$
(d_{12}g_{22} - d_{22}g_{12})\left(\frac{dy}{dx}\right)^2 + (d_{11}g_{22} - d_{22}g_{11})\frac{dy}{dx} + (d_{11}g_{12} - d_{12}g_{11}) = 0.
$$

Suppose that $\lambda = dy/dx$ is a tangent principal direction. Then the unit vector lying in the surface tangent plane in the principal direction is parallel to

$$
\mathbf{t} = [1, \lambda, p + q\lambda]'.
$$

By Euler's theorem, the surface tangent vectors $\mathbf{t}_{max}$ and $\mathbf{t}_{min}$ in the principal directions are orthogonal. Of course, their (orthographic) projections onto the plane $z = 0$ are not orthogonal, as Fig. 15 shows.

The surface curvatures in the principal directions are the roots of the quadratic [26, p. 112]:

$$
|\mathbf{G}|\kappa^2 - (g_{11}d_{22} + g_{22}d_{11} - 2g_{12}d_{12})\kappa + |\mathbf{D}| = 0. \tag{17}
$$

The curvature values can be used to extract planar patches of a surface and regions that consist entirely of umbilic points. To find planar patches, for example, we have adopted the simple approach to requiring the absolute values of both principal curvatures to be below a small threshold. Figure 16a shows the planar patches found by this technique for a Renault part used in experiments by Faugeras and his colleagues at INRIA. Faugeras et. al. [24, 25] have investigated a variety of

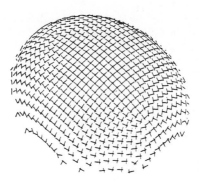

FIG. 15.   The orthographic projections of the principal directions of curvature for an ellipsoid.

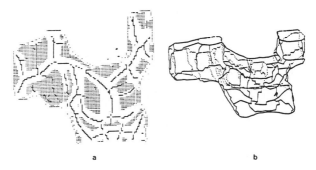

a   b

FIG. 16.   (a) Planar patches on the Renault part found by simply requiring the absolute values of both principal curvatures to be below a threshold. (b) The planar patches on the same part found by the INRIA group. (Reproduced from [25, p. 432].)

techniques that exploit special properties of planes. Figure 16b shows the planes computed by the INRIA group for the Renault part. It is the opinion of Jean Ponce, who has worked both an INRIA and at MIT, that the two methods are equally effective.

A point is umbilic if its principal curvatures are equal. The principal curvatures define a best fitting ellipsoid in the local neighborhood of a surface point. In the case of an umbilic point, the ellipsoid is a sphere. To determine umbilic points, we simply require that

$$\frac{|\kappa_1| - |\kappa_2|}{\max(|\kappa_1|, |\kappa_2|)}$$

is less than a threshold, where κ_1 and κ_2 are the solutions to Eq. (17). Figure 1 shows a region of umbilic points found for the lightbulb. It is well known (e.g., do Carmo [23, p. 147, Proposition 4]) that if all the points of a connected surface are umbilic, then the surface is either contained in a sphere or in a plane. Since the curvatures are non-zero, the connected region that is the bulb of the lightbulb is a portion of a sphere.

In order to extract the lines of curvature, the directions at the individual surface points need to be linked. This is more difficult than linking zero crossings to form an edge, for example, since the principal directions form a dense set. Figure 17 shows that lines of curvature cannot be extracted by simply choosing the 8-connected neighbor with the nearest direction after projection onto $z = 0$.

Instead, linking is based on the vectors $\mathbf{t}_{max}(x, y)$ in the surface tangent plane. Initially, each point (x, y) can potentially link to its 8-connected neighbors. As the program proceeds, neighbors become inhibited as they are linked to other points. The program conducts a breadth-first search. At each iteration, the point (x, y) for which a *closeness* evaluation function is minimized is chosen. If its minimizing neighbor is part of a growing line of curvature, (x, y) extends it, otherwise a new line of curvature is started. In either case, neighbors that are not minimizing inhibit their link to (x, y). The closeness function that is currently used is the sum of three dot products involving principal vectors at neighboring points in the surface tangent plane,

$$
\begin{aligned}
c(x_1, y_1, x_2, y_2) = {} & \mathbf{t}(x_1, y_1) \cdot \mathbf{t}(x_2, y_2) \\
& + \mathbf{t}(x_1, y_1) \cdot \mathbf{r}(x_1, y_1, x_2, y_2) \\
& + \mathbf{t}(x_2, y_2) \cdot \mathbf{r}(x_1, y_1, x_2, y_2),
\end{aligned}
$$

where $\mathbf{r}(x_1, y_1, x_2, y_2) = \mathbf{r}(x_1, y_1) - \mathbf{r}(x_2, y_2)$. Other evaluation functions could have used the curvature values as well as their directions, but we have not found this to be necessary. Figure 18 shows the lines of curvature found by the algorithm for a coffee cup and an oil bottle. The program gives similarly good results on all our test objects. Note that because of discretization it is possible for all the neighbors of a point to become inhibited before it is selected. Hence some points may not lie on the lines of curvature computed by the program.

FIG. 17. A swirling pattern of principal directions shows that lines of curvature cannot be extracted by simply choosing the 8-connected neighbor with the nearest direction after projection onto $z = 0$. The direction closest to the point marked A is at the point marked B, but C is more consistent with global judgments.

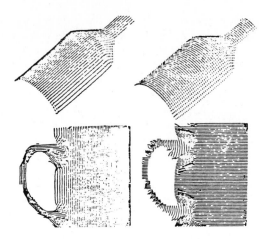

FIG. 18.　Linked lines of curvature found for an oil bottle and a coffee mug.

3.3. Using Lines of Curvature

Earlier, we showed that lines of curvature that are planar, or along which the principal curvature is constant, are important for describing surfaces. Given a linked list of surfaces points forming a line of curvature, we can determine the best fitting plane. If the set is $\{(x_i, y_i, a_i)|\ 1 \leq i \leq n\}$, then the least-squares fitting plane $ax + by + cz + d = 0$ is determined from a solution of

$$\begin{pmatrix} \text{var}(x) & \text{cov}(x, y) & \text{cov}(x, z) \\ \text{cov}(x, y) & \text{var}(y) & \text{cov}(y, z) \\ \text{cov}(x, z) & \text{cov}(y, z) & \text{var}(z) \end{pmatrix} \begin{pmatrix} a \\ b \\ c \end{pmatrix} = 0,$$

where $\text{var}(x)$ is the variance of the x_is, and $\text{cov}(x, y)$ the covariance of the x_i and y_i. We can determine whether a given population of points is planar by examining

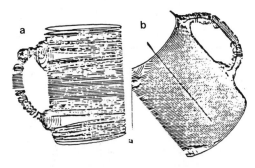

FIG. 19.　(a) The best fitting circles to the parallels of the cup. (b) The axis that is the locus of the centers of the best fitting circles shown in (a).

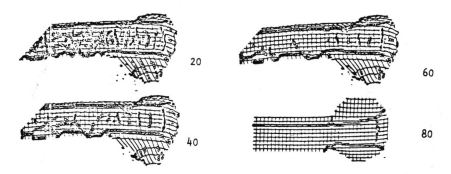

FIG. 20. Significant surface discontinuities found by the curvature primal sketch program at multiple scales. The input to the program is the lines of curvature computed at each scale. The scales shown are 20, 40, 60, and 80.

the condition number of the covariance matrix (compare Brady and Asada [11, pp. 341–342]). Similarly, we can compute the best fitting circle to a line of curvature and determine whether the population lies on that circle. Figure 19a shows the best fitting circles computed for the lines of curvature that are the parallels of a cup. Figure 19b shows the axis that is the locus of the centers of the circles in Fig. 19a.

We need to determine the significant discontinuities in a surface. The result would be a *surface primal sketch* analogous to Marr's [37] intensity change *primal sketch* (for image surfaces) and Asada and Brady's [2] *curvature primal sketch* for significant curvature changes along planar contours. In each case, the problem is to *detect* all significant changes, *localize* those changes as accurately as possible, and to *symbolically describe* the change. Yuille and Poggio [59, 60] have proved that, in principle, scale-space filtering enables a discontinuity to be accurately localized. Canny [21] uses the smallest scale at which a given intensity change can be detected to most accurately localize it. Figure 20 shows the surface intersections of a telephone handset found by a program described below after the surface has first been smoothed at a variety of scales. The increasing localization of the surface intersection flanking the elongated portion of the surface can be clearly seen.

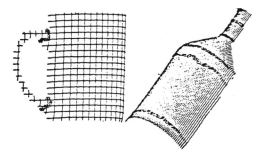

FIG. 21. Surface intersections found by the curvature primal sketch program applied to lines of curvature after they have been projected into their best fitting plane.

Canny's [21] claim that signal to noise increases proportional to the scale of the filter can also be seen. We are currently working to integrate these separate descriptions to yield a single description.

Earlier, we noted a theorem by Joachimsthal that shows that surfaces rarely intersect along their lines of curvature. We also showed that Gaussian smoothing overcomes this problem. So long as the curvature of the curve of intersection is small compared to the Gaussian filter, the lines of curvature of the smoothed surface lie parallel and perpendicular to the locus of curvature maxima of the smoothed surface. Asada and Brady [2] filter a planar contour at multiple scales to detect, localize, and describe the significant changes in curvature. As an initial experiment, we have applied the curvature primal sketch program to lines of curvature after they have been projected into their best fitting plane. The results encourage us to extend the Asada and Brady program to two dimensions. Figures 20 and 21 show some of the surface intersections found by this method.

APPENDIX A

We derive Eq. (6):

$$
\kappa_P^2 = \left(\frac{d\mathbf{T}_P}{ds_P} \right)^2
$$

$$
= \left(\frac{ds}{ds_P} \right)^2 \left(\frac{d}{ds} \frac{\mathbf{k} \times (\mathbf{T} \times \mathbf{k})}{ds \left\{ 1 - (\mathbf{T} \cdot \mathbf{k})^2 \right\}^{1/2}} \right)^2
$$

$$
= \left(\frac{ds}{ds_P} \right)^2 \frac{\left\{ 1 - (\mathbf{T} \cdot \mathbf{k})^2 - (\mathbf{N} \cdot \mathbf{k})^2 \right\}}{\left\{ 1 - (\mathbf{T} \cdot \mathbf{k})^2 \right\}^2} \kappa^2
$$

and the result follows from Eq. (2).

APPENDIX B: THE GENERALIZED CONE THEOREM

We prove a more general form of the theorem proved in Section 2.3. We relax the condition of the theorem to planar axes. As before, we assume that the eccentricity of the generalized cone is zero, so that the tangent to the axis curve is normal to the cross section. Without this assumption, the proof becomes quite complex.

THEOREM. *If the axis of a generalized cone is planar, and the eccentricity of the cone is zero, then* (i) *a cross section is a line of curvature if either the generalized cone is a surface of revolution or the cross section is an extremum; and* (ii) *a tracing is a line of curvature if the generalized cone is a tube surface (the expansion function is a constant), or the tracing is a fluting.*

Proof. Denote the Frenet–Serret moving trihedron of the axis curve by $(\mathbf{T}, \mathbf{N}, \mathbf{B})$. Since the axis is planar it has zero torsion, which simplifies the Frenet–Serret formulae

$$
\frac{d\mathbf{T}}{dt} = \kappa \mathbf{N} \qquad \text{and} \qquad \frac{d\mathbf{N}}{dt} = -\kappa \mathbf{T}. \tag{B.1}
$$

Note that the binormal **B** is constant, being the unit normal to the plane of the axis. Since the eccentricity of the cone is assumed to be zero, the tangent **T** to the axis is normal to the cross section, which has **N** and **B** as a basis. Let the axis of the cone be $\mathbf{a}(t)$, where t is arc length, and let the expansion function be $h(t)$. As in Section 2.3, suppose that the cross-section is given by $f(s)\mathbf{N} + g(s)\mathbf{B}$. The generalized cone is defined to be

$$\mathbf{r}(s,t) = \mathbf{a}(t) + h(t)\{f(s)\mathbf{N} + g(s)\mathbf{B}\}. \tag{B.2}$$

The analysis proceeds as in Section 2.3. The first fundamental form is

$$\mathbf{G} = \begin{pmatrix} h^2 l^2 & h\dot{h}d\dot{d} \\ h\dot{h}d\dot{d} & h^2 d^2 + (1 - \kappa h f)^2 \end{pmatrix}.$$

As expected, this reduces to the expression in Section 2.3 in the case $\kappa = 0$. The second fundamental form hints at the complexity of the most general case, when the axis is not restricted to lie in a plane,

$$\mathbf{D} = \begin{pmatrix} \dfrac{1}{|\mathbf{n}|}d_{11} & \dfrac{1}{|\mathbf{n}|}d_{12} \\ \dfrac{1}{|\mathbf{n}|}d_{12} & \dfrac{1}{|\mathbf{n}|}d_{22} \end{pmatrix},$$

where

$$\begin{aligned}
d_{11} &= h^2(\dot{f}\ddot{g} - \ddot{f}\dot{g})(1 - \kappa h f) \\
d_{12} &= -\kappa h^2 \dot{f}h(\dot{f}g - f\dot{g}) \\
d_{22} &= h\ddot{h}(\dot{f}g - f\dot{g})(1 - \kappa h f). \\
&\quad - (1 - \kappa h f)^2 h\kappa\dot{g} \\
&\quad - f h\dot{h}(\dot{f}g - f\dot{g})(\dot{\kappa}h + 2\kappa\dot{h}).
\end{aligned} \tag{B.3}$$

We establish the result as before.

ACKNOWLEDGMENTS

We thank several people who have commented on the ideas presented in this paper, particularly Brian Barsky, Tom Binford, Jean-Daniel Boissonat, Philippe Brou, Olivier Faugeras, Eric Grimson, Berthold Horn, Joe Mundy, Tommy Poggio, Demetri Terzopoulos, and Shimon Ullman. We are indebted to Olivier Faugeras and the INRIA group for giving us access to their ranging system. More especially, we appreciate the exchange of ideas, results, and personnel with INRIA. Steve Bagley, Margaret Fleck, and Eric Grimson made valuable comments on drafts of this paper.

REFERENCES

1. G. J. Agin, *Representation and Description of Curved Objects*, Stanford University AIM-73, 1972.
2. H. Asada and M. Brady, *The Curvature Primal Sketch*, MIT Artificial Intelligence Laboratory, AIM-758, 1984.

3. D. H. Ballard and C. M. Brown, *Computer Vision*, Prentice-Hall, Englewood Cliffs, N.J., 1982.
4. S. Barnard, Interpreting perspective images, *Artif. Intell.* **21**, No. 4, 1983, 435–462.
5. S. Barnard and A. P. Pentland, Three-dimensional shape from line drawings, in *Proc. 8th Intl. Joint Conf. Artif. Intell.*, Karlsruehe, 1983, pp. 1061–1063.
6. H. G. Barrow and J. M. Tenenbaum, Recovering intrinsic scene characteristics from images, in *Computer Vision Systems* (E. M. Riseman and A. Hanson, Eds.), pp. 3–26, Academic Press, New York, 1978.
7. H. G. Barrow and J. M. Tenenbaum, Interpreting line drawings as three-dimensional surfaces, *Artif. Intell.* **17**, 1981, 75–116.
8. T. O. Binford, Inferring surfaces from images, *Artif. Intell.* **17**, 1982, 205–245.
9. R. C. Bolles, P. Horaud, and M. J. Hannah, 3DPO: A three-dimensional parts orientation system, in *First International Symposium on Robotics Research* (M. Brady and R. Paul, Eds.), pp. 413–424, MIT Press, Cambridge, Mass., 1984.
10. M. Brady, Computational approaches to image understanding, *Comput. Surveys* **14**, 1982, 3–71.
11. M. Brady and H. Asada, Smoothed local symmetries and their implementation, *Int. J. Robotics Res.* **3**, No. 3, 1984.
12. M. Brady and B. K. P. Horn, Rotationally symmetric operators for surface interpolation, *Comput. Vision Graphics Image Process.* **22**, 1983, 70–95.
13. M. Brady and A. Yuille, An extremum principle for shape from contour, *IEEE Pattern. Anal. Mach. Intell.* **PAMI-6**, 1984, 288–301.
14. M. Brady and A. Yuille, *Representing Three-Dimensional Shape*, Romansy Conf., Udine, Italy, 1984.
15. R. A. Brooks, Symbolic reasoning among 3D models and 2D images, *Artif. Intell.* **17**, 1981, 285–348.
16. R. A. Brooks and T. O. Binford, Representing and reasoning about partially specified scenes, in *Proc. Image Understanding Workshop* (L. S. Baumann, Ed.), Science Applications, Inc., pp. 95–103.
17. P. Brou, Finding the orientation of objects in vector maps, *Intl. J. Robotics Res.* **3**, No. 4, 1984.
18. A. Bruss and B. K. P. Horn, Passive navigation, *Comput. Vision Graphics Image Process.* **21**, 1983, 3–20.
19. P. J. Burt, Fast filter transforms for image processing, *Comput. Graphics Image Process.* **16**, 1981, 20–51.
20. P. J. Burt, Fast algorithms for estimating local image properties, *Comput. Graphics Image Process.* **21**, 1983, 368–382.
21. J. F. Canny, *Finding Edges and Lines in Images*, Artificial Intelligence Lab. TR-720, MIT, Cambridge, Mass., 1983.
22. R. Courant and D. Hilbert, *Methods of Mathematical Physics*, Wiley–Interscience, New York, 1953.
23. M. P. do Carmo, *Differential Geometry of Curves and Surfaces*, Prentice–Hall, Englewood Cliffs, N.J., 1976.
24. O. D. Faugeras, *et al.*, Towards a flexible vision system, in *Robot Vision* (A. Pugh, Ed.), IFS, U.K.
25. O. D. Faugeras, *et al.*, Object representation, identification, and positioning from range data, in *First International Symposium on Robotics Research* (M. Brady and R. Paul, Eds.), pp. 425–446, MIT Press, Cambridge, Mass., 1984.
26. I. D. Faux and M. J. Pratt, *Computational Geometry for Design and Manufacture*, Ellis Horwood, Chichester, 1979.
27. W. E. L. Grimson, *From Images to Surfaces: A Computational Study of the Human Early Visual System*, MIT Press, Cambridge, Mass., 1981.
28. W. E. L. Grimson, *Computational Experiments with a Feature Based Stereo Algorithm*, Artificial Intelligence Laboratory, AIM-762, MIT, Cambridge, Mass., 1984.
29. R. M. Haralick, Edge and region analysis for digital image data, *Comput. Graphics Image Process.* **12**, 1980, 60–73.
30. R. M. Haralick, L. T. Watson, and T. J. Laffey, The topographic primal sketch, *Int. J. Robotics Res.* **2**, 1983, 50–71.
31. D. Hilbert and S. Cohn-Vossen, *Geometry and the Imagination*, Chelsea, New York, 1952.
32. S. W. Holland, L. Rossol, and M. R. Ward, CONSIGHT 1: A vision controlled robot system for transferring parts from belt conveyors, in *Computer Vision and Sensor Based Robots* (G. Dodd and L. Rossol, Eds.), Plenum, New York, 1979.
33. K. Ikeuchi and B. K. P. Horn, Numerical shape from shading and occluding boundaries, *Artif. Intell.* **17**, 1981, 141–185.
34. K. Ikeuchi, B. K. P. Horn, *et al.*, Picking up an object from a pile of objects, in *First International*

Symposium on Robotics Research (M. Brady and R. Paul, Eds.), pp. 139–162, MIT Press, Cambridge, Mass., 1984.

35. J. J. Koenderinck, *What Tells Us the Contour about Solid Shape?*, Dept. Medical and Physiol. Physics, Univ. Utrecht, Netherlands, 1984.

36. J. J. Koenderinck and A. J. van Doorn, The shape of smooth objects and the way contours end, *Perception* **11**, 1982, 129–137.

37. D. Marr, Early processing of visual information, *Philos. Trans. Roy. Soc. London B* **275**, 1976, 843–524.

38. D. Marr, Analysis of occluding contour, *Proc. R. Soc. London B* **197**, 1977, 441–475.

39. D. Marr, *Vision*, Freeman, San Francisco, 1982.

40. D. Marr and E. C. Hildreth, Theory of edge detection, *Proc. Roy. Soc. London B* **207**, 1980, 187–217.

41. J. Mayhew, Stereopsis, in *Physical and Biological Processing of Images*, (O. J. Braddick and A. C. Sleigh, Eds.), pp. 204–216, Springer-Verlag, New York, 1983.

42. R. S. Millman and G. D. Parker, *Elements of Differential Geometry*, Prentice–Hall, Englewood Cliffs, N.J., 1977.

43. T. Poggio and V. Torre, *Ill-Posed Problems and Regularization Analysis in Early Vision*, Artificial Intelligence Laboratory, AIM-773, MIT, Cambridge, Mass., 1984.

44. G. Porter and J. Mundy, Non-contact profile sensor system for visual inspections, in *Robot Vision* (A. Rosenfeld, Ed.), Proc. Soc. Photo-Opt. Instrum. Eng., pp. 67–76, 1982.

45. G. B. Porter and J. L. Mundy, A model-driven visual inspection module, *First International Symposium on Robotics Research* (M. Brady and R. Paul, Eds.), pp. 371–388, MIT Press, Cambridge, Mass., 1984.

46. K. A. Stevens, The visual interpretation of surface contours, *Artif. Intell.* **17**, 1982, 47–73.

47. K. A. Stevens, The line of curvature constraint and the interpretation of 3D shape from parallel surface contours, in *Proc. 8th Intl. Joint Conf. Artif. Intell.*, Karlsruehe, pp. 1057–1061, 1983.

48. D. Terzopoulos, The role of constraints and discontinuities in visible-surface reconstruction, in *Proc. 7th Intl. Joint Conf. Artif. Intell.*, Karlsruehe, pp. 1073–1077, 1983.

49. D. Terzopoulos, *The Computation of Visible Surface Representations*, Artif. Intell. Lab., MIT, Cambridge, Mass., 1984.

50. S. Tsuji and M. Asada, Understanding of three-dimensional motion in time-varying imagery, in *First International Symposium on Robotics Research* (M. Brady and R. Paul, Eds.), pp. 465–474, MIT Press, Cambridge, Mass., 1984.

51. S. Ullman, *The Interpretation of Visual Motion*, MIT Press, Cambridge, Mass., 1978.

52. F. Vilnrotter, R. Nevatia, and K. E. Price, Structural analysis of natural textures, in *Proc. Image Understanding Workshop* (L. S. Baumann, Ed.), pp. 61–68, 1981.

53. C. E. Weatherburn, *Differential Geometry of Three Dimensions*, Cambridge Univ. Press, Cambridge, U.K., 1927.

54. A. Witkin, Recovering surface shape and orientation from texture, *Artif. Intell.* **17**, 1981, 17–47.

55. A. Witkin, Scale-space filtering, in *Proc. 7th Int. Joint Conf. Artif. Intell.*, Karlsruehe, pp. 1019–1021, 1983.

56. R. J. Woodham, Photometric method for determining surface orientation from multiple images, *Opt. Eng.* **19**, 1980, 139–144.

57. R. J. Woodham, Analysing images of curved surfaces, *Artif. Intell.* **17**, 1981, 117–140.

58. A. L. Yuille and M. Brady, Surface information from boundary projections, MIT Artificial Intelligence Lab, forthcoming.

59. A. L. Yuille and T. Poggio, *Fingerprints Theorems for Zero-Crossings*, Artificial Intelligence Laboratory AIM-730, MIT, Cambridge, Mass., 1983.

60. A. L. Yuille and T. Poggio, *Scaling Theorems for Zero Crossings*, Artificial Intelligence Laboratory AIM-722, MIT, Cambridge, Mass., 1983.

61. J. Ponce and M. Brady, *Toward a surface primal sketch*, "Three dimensional vision", (T. Karade Ed.), Academic Press, 1985.

Connectionist Models and Parallelism in High Level Vision

Jerome A. Feldman

University of Rochester, Rochester, New York 14627

Received February 8, 1985

Students of human and machine vision share the belief that massively parallel processing characterizes early vision. For higher levels of visual organization, considerably less is known and there is much less agreement about the best computational view of the processing. This paper lays out a computational framework in which all levels of vision can be naturally carried out in highly parallel fashion. One key is the representation of all visual information needed for high level processing as discrete parameter values which can be represented by units. Two problems that appear to require sequential attention are described and their solutions within the basically parallel structure are presented. Some simple program results are included. © 1985 Academic Press, Inc.

1. INTRODUCTION

The human brain is an information processing system, but one that is quite different from conventional computers. The basic computing elements operate in the millisecond range and are about a million times slower than current electronic devices. Since reaction times for a wide range of tasks are a few hundred milliseconds [30], the system must solve hard recognition problems in about a hundred computational time steps. The same time constraints suggest that only simple signals can be sent from one neuron to another. The human information processing system is also adaptable, context-sensitive, error-tolerant, etc., in ways that far outstrip our current computational devices and formalisms.

Students of human and machine vision share the belief that massively parallel processing characterizes early vision. Computational, psychophysical, and biological findings agree on the extensive distribution of computation both in spatial organization and along dimensions such as ocularity, size (spatial frequency) and color. For higher levels of visual organization, considerably less is known and there is much less agreement about the best computational view of the processing. But the 100-step argument suggests that, at least for simple tasks, people can do visual recognition tasks much too fast for the processing to be serial. This paper attempts to lay out a computational framework in which all levels of vision can be naturally carried out in highly parallel fashion. In addition to the timing constraint, a biologically plausible model must meet a number of additional computational requirements. The limited number of computational units, their restricted connectivity and very low rate of communication all impose severe constraints which the model attempts to satisfy.

The rest of this introduction informally outlines a proposed model of vision which supports the idea of parallel processing. Section 2 contains a brief review of the connectionist computational model used in the technical sections of the paper. Section 3 describes in some detail the parallel algorithms for high-level visual recognition and how they satisfy a variety of constraints. The final section points out

86

some limitations on parallel processing in vision and lays out a connectionist model of sequential visual attention.

The central problem of vision is taken to be the identification and location of objects in the environment. The critical step in this process is the linking of incoming visual information to stored object descriptions; this is called *indexing* from the analogy of identifying a book from index terms. A system must also identify situations and use this information to guide action. Following the standard usage in computer vision, we divide the problem of visual recognition into three conceptual levels: low, intermediate, and high. Low level (or early) vision is characterized by the local nature of its computations. This corresponds to Marr's primal sketch and to anatomical structures from the retina through at least primary visual cortex. Typical low-level operations include image filtering, isolated feature detection, and some local relaxation or consistency calculations. There is no conceptual difficulty in designing massively parallel algorithms for these tasks and several existing systems do various of these tasks in parallel.

Intermediate level vision (ILV) has two major goals: segmentation and the calculation of invariants. The role of ILV is to reduce the incoming visual information to a form that will be effective for the recognition step of high-level vision. One requirement is that the ILV encoding capture the intrinsic properties of objects independent of the particular viewing conditions in the current instance [7]. Recognition also requires that the individual objects in a scene be separated so that they can be individually matched. Segmentation and calculating invariants are mutually interacting computations, depending also on context effects from high-level vision, among other things. Much of the current research in computer vision is concerned with ILV calculations; the development is far too rich to survey here. The computational character of these problems is much more complex than that of early vision; there are unsolved problems in the stability and efficiency of networks for ILV. But the general idea of parallel algorithms for ILV is well understood and a number of partial implementations have been carried out.

The research on parallel algorithms in computer vision has progressed to the point where some general principles are becoming apparent. There appear to be three computational paradigms that are easily adapted to massive parallelism: local calculations, neighborhood function, and Hough techniques. Successful applications have been based on combinations of the three computational principles. Calculations that are strictly localized to one area of an image are obviously easy to compute in parallel up to the number of desired results. These include filters and edge detection in early vision and local calculations of, for example, the brightness equation in intermediate level vision.

The second major class of parallel computation is in neighborhood interactions or relaxation [17]. Relaxation in low-level vision has been quite successful, e.g., in smoothing edge and optic flow fields. In a massively parallel system, one can have continuous interactions among strictly local calculations and neighborhood relations. The same idea can be carried over to intermediate level vision as was recognized early by Barrow and Tenenbaum [7] and is embodied in the smoothness constraint of the MIT school [29]. The intrinsic image diagram (Fig. 1.1) of Barrow and Tenenbaum continues to be a good characterization of parallel computation in intermediate vision. Notice that the local interactions include not only neighbors in the same plane, but also calculations of other invariants (planes) at the same point in the image.

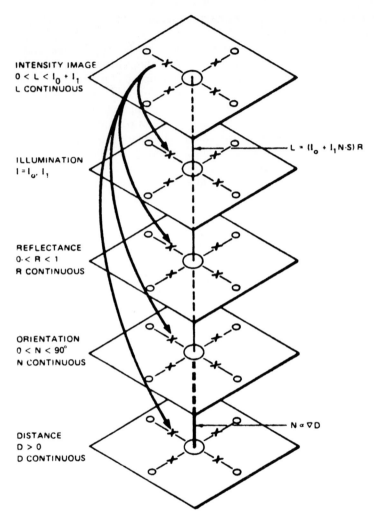

FIG. 1.1. A parallel computational model for recovering intrinsic images. (Used by permission of the authors.)

The third of the computational principles is less straightforward but is the key to much of the progress that has been made to date. This principle derives from Hough techniques [3], which in turn can be traced back to histograms. The idea is simply to count and compare things; the hard part is knowing what to count. Hough techniques and their parallel realizations are particularly good for computing global parameters from plentiful, but noisy local measurements. Typical applications include calculating lines from edge data, illumination angle from surface patches, or rigid body motion from local flow vectors. In each case, the answer can be characterized by a small number of parameters; counting the data consistent with each possible answer is an effective solution technique. In a parallel network, all of

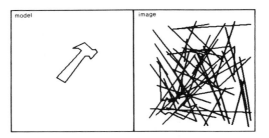

FIG. 1.2.   Recognizing a known object.

the relevant counts can be accumulated simultaneously. The example Hough calculations given above are in early and intermediate vision, but the technique applies to indexing and high level vision as well.

The idea behind applying Hough techniques to recognition is simple. Each visual feature computed in the intermediate stage votes for the objects most consistent with that feature. As an introductory example, we will consider the problem of recognizing a known object that has been transformed and hidden by noise (Fig. 1.2). The key constraint here is that the shape of the target is assumed to be known except for possible changes in position, rotation, and scale. Under these conditions, the system need only solve for four parameters: rotation and scale and translation in x and y. The sequential algorithm for finding the masked object compares every line in the image with every line in the model. A given image line will match with a fixed model line only for a particular choice of the four parameters. Many choices of parameters get votes, but the (normally unique) choice of parameters that gets a plurality of votes is the correct transform. We will describe the parallel implementation of this scheme in Section 2, after the definitions of our formalism. Of course, the example is greatly oversimplified and the remainder of the paper is concerned with extending parallel recognition techniques to more realistic examples.

2. CONNECTIONIST MODELS

2.1. Background and Overview

Computer science is just beginning to look seriously at parallel computation; it may turn out that conventional programs can be automatically translated into massively parallel networks meeting the hundred-time-step constraint. But no one has yet given the slightest indication of how this might be brought about. An obvious alternative is to start with a computational formalism that has a clear mapping to parallel implementation and attempt to build functional models of intelligent behavior in those terms. If this approach is on the right track, it should prove possible to construct better (clearer, more predictive) models in the parallel formalism than in conventional computer languages. A number of workers in psychology and artificial intelligence are finding these advantages in connectionist models and this paper has definitely required such treatment.

The term "connectionist" comes from a shared assumption of most massively-parallel computational formalisms. This feature arises from the observation that in the psychological quantum of 1/10 s only a small number (~ 6) of bits of information can be sent from one neuron to another by spike frequency. This means that the conventional computer mechanism of passing complex symbolic structures cannot be used directly and that the burden of computation must lie on the *connection* structure of the network. There has been a great deal of recent work on the properties of such systems [2, 11] and on their applications.

There is currently a growing interest in both the abstract properties of connectionist models and in their application to particular problems in the behavioral and brain sciences. The Winter 1985 issue of *Cognitive Science* is dedicated to this work. To a large extent, applications-oriented efforts such as the current paper use a representation where a single unit represents each item of interest such as a concept, a line segment, and so forth, and are called *localist* models. Another line of work [15] starts from the assumption that concepts are captured by a "pattern of activity" in a large group of units. Most of this work is concerned with general properties of connectionist networks, particularly learning in one form or another [1]. There are a number of positions between the extreme distributed approach and the "grandmother cell" approach to connectionist models. Some of these intermediate representations such as coarse–fine coding play an important role in this paper and are good candidates for describing physiological reality.

2.2. Units and Networks

As part of our effort to lay out a generally useful framework for connectionist theories, we have developed a standard model of the individual unit. These units have a very large number of incoming and outgoing connections and communicate with the rest of the network by transmitting a simple value. A unit transmits the same value to all units to which it is connected. The output value is closely related to the unit's potential and is best described as a level of activation. A unit's potential reflects the amount of activation it has been receiving from other units. All inputs are weighed and combined in a manner specified by the *site functions* and the *potential function* in order to update a unit's potential. A more technical description follows.

A network consists of a large number of units connected to a large number of other units via links. The units are computational entities defined by

$\{q\}$: a small set of states (fewer than 10)

p : a continuous value called potential

v : an output value, approximately 10 discrete values

i : a vector of inputs $i_1, i_2, \ldots, i_n$ (this is elaborated below)

together with functions that define the values of potential, state, and output at time $t + 1$, based on the values at time t:

$$p_{t+1} \leftarrow \mathbf{P}(i_t, p_t, q_t)$$
$$q_{t+1} \leftarrow \mathbf{Q}(i_t, p_t, q_t)$$
$$v_{t+1} \leftarrow \mathbf{V}(i_t, p_t, q_t).$$

A unit need not treat all inputs uniformly. Units receive inputs via links (or connections) and each incoming link has an associated *weight*. A weight may have a

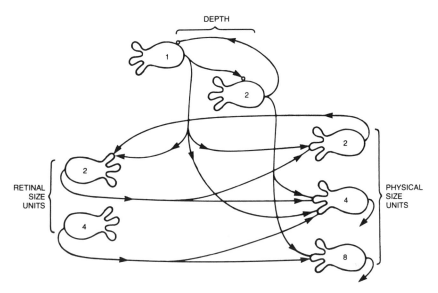

FIG. 2.1.   Relations among depth, retinotopic size, and physical size. (Taken from *Behav. Brain Sci.* **8,**
No. 2, June 1985.)

negative value. A unit weighs each input using the weight on the appropriate link.
Furthermore, a unit may have more than one "input site" and incoming links are
connected to specific sites. Each site has an associated site-function. These functions
carry out local computations based on the input values at the site, and it is the result
of this computation that is processed by the functions **P**, **Q**, and **V**. The notion of
sites is useful in defining interesting unit behavior such as OR-of-AND units where
the unit responds to the maximum activation at any of its sites and each site is
conjunctive. An example of this is shown in Fig. 2.1 where a unit representing a
physical size of 4 can be activated by either retinotopic size = 4 AND depth = 1
OR retinotopic size = 2 and depth = 2. This computational exercise is not, of
course, intended as a serious model of size constancy. There are several additional
basic computational points that arise from the network of Fig. 2.1.

First notice that there is a separate unit dedicated to each possible value of each of
the three parameters: depth, retinotopic size, and physical size; this unit/value (or
place coding) representation is central to all of our models. In this network, as in
many others, a consistent state should have only one active value for each parameter.
We assume that such networks have mutually inhibitory connections (shown only for
depth) among the competing values for each parameter. This mutual inhibition or
winner-take-all construction is used in many models and appears frequently in this
paper.

Assume for simplicity that the system is viewing a small circle centered on and
orthogonal to the line of sight. Then the network of Fig. 2.1 specifies a fixed relation
among retinotopic size, depth, and physical size. One way to view this is that a given
value of depth specifies a *mapping* from retinotopic to physical size; such mappings
will be used frequently in the model. The network actually does something computa-

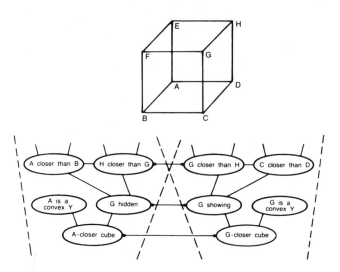

FIG. 2.2.   The Necker cube. (Taken from *Behav. Brain Sci.* **8**, No. 2, June 1985.)

tionally much more powerful; it embodies the mutual constraints among the three parameters. If, for example, the physical size of an object (e.g., a person) were known, this would determine the depth value. The computational notion of a network embodying mutual constraints is the fundamental paradigm of connectionist models. The behavior of such systems is characterized by states where a coalition of mutually reinforcing units becomes stable and suppresses its rivals. The two alternative readings of the Necker cube in Fig. 2.2 can be nicely interpreted as alternative stable coalitions. Notice that the flip between readings requires the simultaneous reinterpretation of perceptual features at many levels.

The stable coalition mechanism also has implications for the "grandmother cell" issue. Even the 3-unit loop capturing a size–depth relationship could be viewed as a "pattern of activity" of the three units. More generally, in any connectionist network there will always be many active units forming one or more coalitions. This does not suggest that one can usefully characterize the network in terms of diffuse system states instead of units with particular functions. On the other hand, a unit will participate in several coalitions and need not have a simple response pattern. There are both biological and computational advantages to using the simultaneous activity of multiple units to code some information of interest. Notice also that a coalition is not a particular anatomical structure, but a temporarily mutually reinforcing set of units, in the spirit of Hebb's cell assemblies [18a].

Another use of these networks is in the parallel realization of Hough transform techniques [4]. Figure 2.3a depicts the well-known scheme whereby edges (on the left) each "vote for" the slope (θ) and distance (ρ) of the line most consistent with the edge. Figure 2.3b shows how a simple network can carry out these calculations in a fully parallel fashion. The networks for the generalized Hough techniques used in Fig. 1.2 are more complex, but follow the same principles [6]. The idea of computing the best fit in a discrete parameter space is central to this paper and appears to be a key to parallelism in intermediate and high level vision.

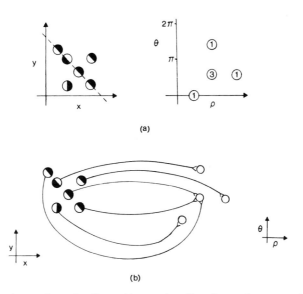

FIG. 2.3. Hough transform for lines: (a) counting θ and ρ values suggested by edges; (b) connectionist network for the calculation.

The 100 billion units that comprise the human brain also impose constraints on our models. For example, suppose we wanted to represent 10 values each of ten low-level visual features such as position, orientation, hue, contrast, motion, etc. Having a separate unit for each vector of values would require 10^{10} units which is clearly too many. Suppose instead we had units which were precise in only one dimension. Then we would need only 10×10 units but it would take the simultaneous activity of ten units to specify a full vector of values. There are a range of intermediate constructions [13, 14, 11]. One of these techniques (coarse–fine coding) appears close to the coding used in primary visual cortex, where units are broadly tuned in several dimensions and fine-tuned in one stimulus dimension.

2.3. Memory and Change

In the previous section, we saw how fixed connectionist networks could be designed to compute functions and relations quite efficiently. These fixed networks could have a certain amount of built-in flexibility by explicitly incorporating *parameters*. One can view the depth networks of Fig. 2.1 as computing the physical size of objects from the retinotopic size, parametrized by depth.

But there are also a number of situations where it does not seem plausible to assume the existence of either fixed or parametrized links. Obvious, though artificial, examples are the paired-associate tasks with nonsense syllables used by psychologists. A closely related real task is learning someone's name or the Hebrew word for apple. One cannot assume that all the required connections are pre-established, and it is known that they do not grow rapidly enough [8b]. What does seem plausible is that there is a built-in network, something like a telephone switching network, which can be configured to capture the required link between two units. We refer to this as establishing a "dynamic connection" in the uniform network. We are assuming (as is commonly done) that the weight of synaptic connections cannot change rapidly enough to do this, so that all dynamic connections are based on changes in the potential (p) and state (q) of individual units. The other basic constraints that we impose on possible solutions are that units broadcast their outputs and that there is no central controller available to set up the dynamic connections. These assumptions differ from those in the switching literature, and the results there do not carry over in any obvious way. The assumption is that only one dynamic connection is made at a time, but that several (e.g., 7 ± 2) must be sustainable without cross talk.

A sample task is to make arbitrary dynamic connections between two sets of units labelled $A \ldots Z$ and $a \ldots z$, respectively. These could be words in different languages, paired associates, words and images, and so on. Figure 2.3 depicts the situation for three units on each side.

The problem is how to establish, for example, the link $B-c$ without also linking, e.g., $B-b$, since the network is originally uniform. More precisely, we require an algorithm which, given the simultaneous activation of B and c, will establish p and q values in the units of our network such that (for some time) activating B will stimulate c but not a or b. For the most part we have considered symmetric networks where the "dynamic connection" $B-c$ will also have the activation of c stimulate B and not A or C. It should be clear that primitive units without any internal state (memory) will not be usable in such tasks.

The basic solution to the dynamic link problem in connectionist networks relies upon mutual inhibition between the alternative inter-units. For notational convenience, we represent this situation as an array of units, with the understanding that the array is a winner-take-all network. If the only active link were $B-c$, then only the three starred units would be active. Uniform dynamic link networks like those described above are an essential part of our model of how visual objects are linked to locations.

The network of Fig. 2.3 uses a separate intermediate unit dedicated to each possible pairing. The starred unit for $B-c$ is in two winner-take-all networks, the column which is "inputs to c," and the "outputs from B" net which is drawn in explicitly. When $B-c$ is active, it blocks all other uses of both B and c, which is the desired effect. The fact that our solution requires N^2 intermediate nodes to connect $2N$ units makes it impractical for linking up sets of 10^5 units like an educated person's vocabulary. There are, however, more complex interconnection networks which require about $4N^{3/2}$ units [10]. That paper also gives detailed descriptions of the unit computations required and some examples.

2.4. Random Interconnection Networks

There are both anatomical [8a] and computational reasons for looking carefully at random interconnection schemes. One possibility is to use random interconnection networks (in place of the uniform networks above) to dynamically connect arbitrary pairs of units from two distinct layers. As before, each unit is postulated to have links to some large number of intermediate units, whose role is strictly a linking one. In any random connection scheme there will be some finite probability that the required path is simply not present. The remarkable fact is that this failure probability can be made vanishingly small for networks of quite moderate size [10].

The idea is to have k (two or more) layers of intermediate units so that there is a tree of B^{k+1} links across the network, where B is the outgoing number of branches from each unit. This result has been known for some time and has been used as the basis of a proposed highly parallel computer [8c].

It is premature to speculate on the degree to which the association cortices of animals are more like the uniform or random networks (if either) but we can say something about the computational advantages of each. Uniform networks appear to be most useful for maintaining many simultaneous dynamic links which are easily turned on and off. They could only be expected to occur in well-structured stable domains because of the strong consistency requirements. In general, we would like t ι view uniform dynamic links as a mechanism roughly equivalent to modifiable o conjunctive connections where the number of possibilities is too great to wire up directly.

Random interconnection networks are not as stable and predictable as uniform ones, but have some other advantages. The lower requirements on the number and precision of wiring of intermediate units are clearly important. But the most interesting property of the random networks is the relative ease with which they could be made permanent. Suppose that instead of rapid change we wanted relatively long term linkage of units from the two layers. Our model specifies that this must be done by changing connection weights w_j. The point to be made here is that the random networks already have some units biased towards linking any particular pair from the two layers. By selectively strengthening the active inputs (on command) of the most appropriate units, the network can relatively quickly forge a reliable link between the pair. The details of how we propose that this comes about are given in Feldman [10]. Of course, once this has happened, the network will not be able to represent competing dynamic links, but its ability to capture new pairings will remain intact until a large fraction of the nodes are used up (cf. [8c]).

The fact that random (as opposed to uniform) interconnection networks could be readily specialized suggests that random networks may play an important role in permanent change and memory. After enough training, the originally random interconnection network would become one in which there was essentially a hard-wired connection between particular pairs of units from the two spaces.

The problem with this scheme as a proto-model of long term memory is that most of our knowledge is structured much more richly than paired associates. It is technically true that one can reduce any relational structure to one involving only pairings, and Fahlman [8c] suggests that the best current hardware approach is along these lines. But the intuitive, psychological, and physiological [38] notions of conceptual structures involve the direct use of more complex connection patterns. It turns out that the results on random interconnection layers extend nicely to the more general case.

The proposed solution to recruiting units to capture new associations depends on the properties of randomly connected graph structures. It turns out that a random graph of N nodes each connected to about $\sqrt{N}$ others has very useful statistical properties. (Think of N as about 1,000,000 and $\sqrt{N}$ as 1,000 for neural networks.) If some small number of nodes (say 30) are chosen at random, the important question is the probability of there being a small network that includes the chosen nodes and is sufficiently well connected to form a *stable coalition* (as defined in Section 2.2). If there is such a sub-network, it could be recruited to represent the new concept whose features are represented by the originally chosen nodes. For random networks of the type described above, the probability of there being a binding sub-network is quite high and the dynamics of recruiting the concept structure also appear to be feasible [10]. Notice that the concept would be represented by a few dozen units, providing another example intermediate between unit/value and diffuse representations.

This is the basic mechanism that we believe supports associative learning and appears to be close to what Wickelgren [38] had in mind. If random chunking networks can be made to support short-term associations through coalitions, the usual weight-changing algorithms would enable the associations to be made permanent [34a, 10]. Such mechanisms are postulated to underlie the grouping of an object instance with its properties and the structuring of a complex scene into a "situation" network. More generally, the technical notions of uniform and random dynamic links are essential to all local connectionist models, the current model of vision and space being the most comprehensive effort to date.

3. PARALLEL VISUAL RECOGNITION

The central problem addressed by this paper is how a visual system can recognize objects and situations with a delay of less than 100 times the speed of its basic computing units. The technical mechanisms presented in the previous section will enable us to look at this problem in more detail. We have already seen how a system built along the lines suggested in Section 2 could be made to recognize a fixed, 2-dimensional object in a very cluttered scene. Many of the same ideas will carry over to more complex vision problems, but there are also a number of new techniques needed.

One major addition to the notions examined above is the introduction of hierarchical object descriptions. Outline figures can be described directly in terms of their component lines, but this becomes infeasible in more realistic visual environments. Sabbah [32] has developed a connectionist system that demonstrates how the concepts of Section 2 can be used to recognize objects in a fairly complex domain, that of origami objects. Origami-world was introduced by Kanade [20] and shown to be an interesting task domain, especially for studying the role of skewed symmetries for determining the orientation of planes in space. Sabbah's work explores the use of connectionist networks to build fast and reliable solutions to this problem.

Figure 3.1 shows the behavior of the program when given a line drawing depiction of an origami chair. The crossed lines are an indication of where the program has deduced the presence of a plane in space. Figure 3.2 presents a hierarchical description scheme used in the system. The need for a hierarchical description should be clear; a single L-joint in the image could correspond to a huge range of appearance possibilities for the chair. The program includes intermediate level networks that compute more complex joints and ones that compute parallelograms in the image. These features can then be combined to provide effective indexing for objects like the origami chair. Sabbah's program actually does rather more than this. It incorporates "top-down" links from a 2-dimensional shape to the L-joints that could give rise to that shape (in a fixed position). This enables the system to be somewhat noise resistant and helps deal with the problems of occlusion. The program also uses T-joints as explicit occlusion cues. This enables it to deal correctly with scenes containing a modest amount of occlusion. The treatment of more general scenes with occlusion is one of the unsolved problems discussed in Section 4.

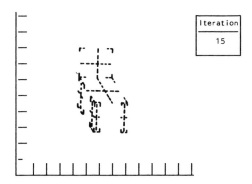

FIG. 3.1.   Origami chair behavior. (Used by permission of the author.)

Sabbah's origami world system used hierarchical descriptions and three dimensions, but in one way was less sophisticated than Ballard's object finder. The origami program did not explicitly compute the viewing transform and actually had to incorporate separate networks for the different appearance possibilities of objects like the origami chair. We have been working recently on a more general connectionist vision system design that is conceptually adequate to deal with a significant range of natural scenes. This is much more complex and is not completely implementable, but a description of it should help provide insight into the problem and our proposed solutions. The proposed parallel vision model and its relation to behavioral and biological findings have been described in detail elsewhere [9]. For our purposes, all that is required is an overview of how the system functionality is divided among four representational frames (Fig. 3.3).

The representation of information in the first frame is intended to model the view of the world that changes with each eye movement. The second frame must deal with the phenomena surrounding what has been called "the illusion of a stable visual world." A static observer has the experience of (and can perform as if he held) a much more uniform visual scene than the first foveal-periphery frame is processing at each fixation. One can think of the second frame as associated with the position of

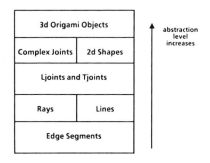

FIG. 3.2.   The origami world hierarchy—levels and hierarchy in the origami world. (Used by permission of the author.)

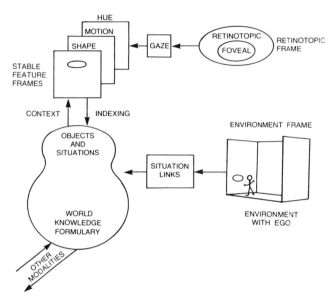

F<small>IG</small>. 3.3.   Four frames, major structures and links. (Taken from *Behav. Brain Sci.* **8**, No. 2, June 1985.)

the observer's head; this is an oversimplification, but conveys the right kind of relation between the two frames. Of course, neither of these frames is like a photographic image of the world. Light striking the retina is already transformed, and the layers of the retina, the thalamus, and the visual cortex all compute complex functions. The crucial difference between these two frames is that the first one is totally updated with each saccade and the second is not. The current model also assumes that the first (*retinotopic*) *frame* computes proximal stimulus features and the second captures distal (constancy, intrinsic) features as well as being stable; it is therefore called the *stable feature frame*.

The third and fourth representational frames are both multi-modal and thus unlikely to be the same as the first two. The third representation is not primarily geometrical and will be described in the next paragraph. The fourth, or *environmental frame*, is intended to model an animal's representation of the space around it at a given moment. It captures the information that enables one to locate quickly the source of a stimulus from sound, wind, smell, or verbal cue, as well as maintaining the relative location of visual phenomena not currently in view. For a variety of reasons, the model proposes a single allocentric environmental frame which gets mapped, by *situation links*, to the current situation and the observer's place in it.

The final representational frame to be considered is the observer's general knowledge of the world, including items not dealing with either vision or space. We follow the conventional wisdom in assuming that this knowledge is captured in propositional (relational) form, modeled in our case by a kind of semantic network. One class of knowledge encoded will be the visual appearance of objects encoded as a collection of relationships among primitive parts. These descriptions have much of the character of Minsky's conceptual frames [24] and of the object-centered frames of, for example, Ballard [3] and Hinton [13]. Since the other three representations are geometrically organized, we will refer to the collection of semantic knowledge as the *world knowledge formulary*, to emphasize its nature as a collection of conceptual relations. The formulary will carry much of the burden for integrating information from the other three frames and is far from adequately worked out in this paper. But all we need for now is the notion that the network representation is likely to be quite different from that of the retinotopic, feature, or environmental frame. All of this indicates that even a provisional model of vision and space will require at least four representational frames.

The central problem is linking visual feature information with the knowledge of how objects in the world can appear. The problem of going from a set of visual features to the description of a situation will be called the *indexing problem*, by analogy with looking up something in an index. The small world we will consider in detail has exactly six distinct visual features each with 10 possible values. Assume for now that any object in the small world can be characterized by some particular set of values for the six features. This would mean that each object has a distinct 6-digit visual code (not unlike a zip code). If the system could always reliably extract the values for the visual features, it would not be hard to identify which objects were in which places in the current environment. No additional problems would arise if some objects had multiple codes among the $10^6 = 1,000,000$ available. But the system, as specified, would totally break down if two objects needed to share the same code, i.e., looked identical relative to our set of features and values. We will have to address the question of ambiguous feature sets later.

The six particular visual features which we have chosen are intended to elucidate the major scientific problems in intermediate level vision and would not be the best choice for a practical computer vision system. We assume for now that the best value at each position of the current view is continuously maintained by parameter network computations [3] which will be elaborated below. Some of the parametrizations are turning out to be rather subtle. For example, it appears that natural textures can be well characterized by fractal parameters [27]. Features such as size and shape, which cover several units, are assumed to be represented by a single unit at the center of the region covered. Of course, the problem of breaking up the feature space into meaningful regions is a central one and the model will have to address it in detail.

The six visual features used in indexing are the following: lightness, hue, texture, shape, motion, and size. Obviously enough, ten values of these features (even in logarithmic scales) is not enough to characterize visual appearance in the real world; but the small world is rich enough to exhibit most of the required problems. The model assumes that the six features are continuously represented in six parallel 10×10 arrays which are intended to map the currently visible external world. There is also assumed to be a (10 valued logarithmic) depth map maintained as part of the same structure (Fig. 3.3). The depth map is needed for calculating constancy features such as object size and is also used directly in mapping the environment. The depth map is assumed to be calculated cooperatively with the six features planes, using binocular and other cues. These seven parallel arrays, along with some auxiliary structure, comprise the *stable feature frame* which is one of the four cornerstones of the model.

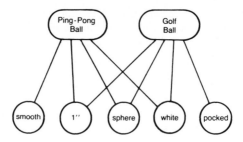

FIG. 3.4.   Ping-pong and golf balls. (Taken from *Behav. Brain Sci.* **8**, No. 2, June 1985.)

Our first notion of appearance models was that each object could be characterized by one or more sets of feature values. For objects that are sufficiently simple, this is not a bad approximation. You can probably name an object that is an approximately 1.5 in. white sphere and uniformly pock-marked even before seeing it hook into the rough. But for complex objects like a horse or Harvard Square, the single feature set is not even the right kind of visual information. Our way of handling the appearance models for complex objects and situations is taken from current AI practice. We assume that the appearance of a complex object is represented (as part of one's world knowledge) as a network of nodes representing the "appearance possibilities" or simpler components and relationships among them (Figs. 3.4, 3.5). There are several unsolved technical questions about the number of separate views maintained, and how much flexibility should be encoded in a description, but the general idea of hierarchical network is all we need at the moment.

Recall that the naive version of indexing was to use the 6-digit visual feature code to look up the name of the object with that description. Complex objects are assumed to be composed of parts, each part being either another complex object or a *visual element* that can be indexed by the 6-digit code. Now recall that all of our structures are assumed to be parallel and continuously active. This means that "indexing" can be continuously in progress between different areas of the feature frame and networks of visual appearance knowledge in the world knowledge formulary. The crude version of this idea is to assume that each set of visual features (for a point in the 10 × 10 feature frame map) picks out (indexes) the visual element which is appropriate. If this were to happen, it is not hard to see that a complex visible object would have many of its visual elements selected simultaneously and should therefore be recognizable. Recognition of an object or situation is modeled as a mutually reinforcing coalition of active nodes in the world knowledge frame. The mutual excitation of feature and model networks also involves top-down, *context*, links from visual elements to the feature units that are appropriate.

In order to make these notions more precise and eliminate the ghosts from our machine, we must describe all of this in considerably more detail, using the technical definitions of Section 2. The various components of both the feature frame and world knowledge frame will be elaborated in terms of the "units" of Section 2. Obviously enough, we will need separate units for each of the 100 spatial positions in each of the seven separate maps. In fact, it is also important to follow the unit/value principle and require a separate unit for each value of each cell in the maps above,

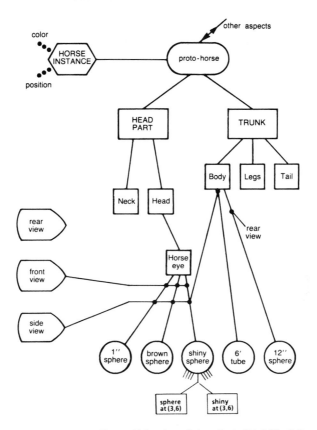

FIG. 3.5. General view of horse. (Taken from *Behav. Brain Sci.* **8**, No. 2, June 1985.)

giving a total of 7000 units. Following the connectionist dogma, we assume that visual elements are units which are connected to the appropriate set of visual-feature-value units. For example, Fig. 3.4 shows how golf and ping pong ball descriptions in the world knowledge frame might be connected (indexed) by visual features. Having a separate unit for each feature value and for each visual element allows the system to simultaneously maintain several possible interpretations of the scene. This essential information processing requirement is unachievable in conventional computational schemes.

It is easy to see how to make connections do the same job as the index codes. Each code for a visual element is mapped into a conjunction of links from units representing the appropriate value of each feature. A visual element with multiple codes has several disjunctive "dendrites," one for each code. Visual elements that are part of a complex object are also linked into a network for representing the appearance of the object (Fig. 3.5).

Complex objects (and situations) are represented as networks (in the world knowledge formulary) of nodes describing visual elements or other complex objects. There are tremendous problems of several different kinds in these semantic network models; these are discussed by Shastri and Feldman [34]. Our goal here is just to provide a plausible (though crude) model of how network representation of visual appearance could fit in the 4-frames paradigm.

The basic idea is that each visual element of a complex object is represented by a node that corresponds to a particular set of feature values as computed in the feature frame. Since indexing from features to elements occurs in parallel, there will usually be several simultaneously active element nodes for a complex object currently in view. This simultaneous activation of subparts will tend to cause the correct complex objects to be activated, independent of the details of how the relationships among the subparts are modelled. When we consider the details of complex object representations, a number of difficult technical problems arise. This is discussed in detail in Hrechanyk and Ballard [16] and we will be content here with a loose discussion, based on the example of representing the visual appearance of horses. Recall that the world knowledge formulary visual appearance models are far from complete—they are more like a verbal description of something not currently in view.

Obviously enough, the side and bottom views of a horse have relatively little in common. Even within the side view, the horse could appear in a variety of orientations and scale configurations and the relative positions of its subparts could also differ considerably. We must also account for the fact that there could be several distinguishable horses in a scene and that some of these may be partially occluded. Our current solution, depicted in Fig. 3.5, involves instance nodes, separate subnetworks for different views and cross-referenced structural descriptions. The prototype horse has a general hierarchical description where, e.g., the trunk is composed of a body, legs, and a tail. What visual elements might be involved in recognizing a horse will depend on whether it is a front, side, or other view. Thus the matching process would select together a prototype and a view which best matched the active visual elements. As always, there is assumed to be mutual inhibition among competing object descriptions and view nodes.

4. LIMITS ON PARALLELISM

The main issue addressed in this paper is how much of all this could be done in parallel with reasonable amounts of hardware (of the scale of the brain). There appear to be two separate places in the system where parallelism breaks down. The first problem that may require sequential processing is the abstraction of visual features from their spatial location in the intrinsic image or stable feature frame. The basic problem is combinatorial. Suppose one wanted to use collections of feature values to index into world knowledge. Even with as few as six features having ten values each, one gets 10^6 separate primitives. If we had a separate unit for each point in a 1000^2 image (typical of the retina or moderate resolution images), it would take 10^{12} units, which is more than our limit for the entire system. Realistic numbers for features and values clearly preclude this computational solution.

The fact that there are not enough units to denote one to each collection of features at each point in the visual field is a classic problem for parallel models. One common form of the question is to ask how a system can avoid detecting a red square when a red circle and a blue square are simultaneously present [11]. Our solution to this problem involves conjunctive connections (Section 2.2) and spatial coherence. The idea is to employ spatially invariant units to detect collection (here pairs) of specific feature values, i.e., a pocked sphere. There is assumed to be only one "pocked sphere" unit, but the activity of its inputs is conjoined so that two active inputs must be from the same point in space. The number of units required for this coding is rather modest. For the small world of six ten-valued features, there would be 15×10^2 or 1500 feature-pair units as opposed to the 100,000,000 that would be needed to encode a feature vector at every position in the 10×10 field. There are a variety of other ways to reduce the number of required units to a feasible number, but they all share the problem of vulnerability to confusion (crosstalk).

One abstract way to envision the crosstalk problem is to notice that any encoding of the space of feature vectors causes some sharing of codes. The system will not be able to distinguish two inputs that map to the same code. As a concrete example, the simultaneous appearance of an orange and a flying ping-pong ball might activate golf-ball in the network of Fig. 3.4. People do form such illusory conjunctions under certain conditions [36], but the problem does not arise in normal vision. This is partly explainable by mutual inhibition by other percepts, but there are good reasons to believe that sequential processing is used to avoid crosstalk. If the system could restrict input so that it came from only a small area of the field, the problem of potential crosstalk would be greatly reduced. This idea of sequentially focussing attention appears to be universally applicable to connectionist networks and fits quite nicely with the psychologist's notion of covert attention [31]. There are a number of open issues [9], but it does seem that sequential attention is the best known solution to the problem of crosstalk in a parallel system of bounded size.

The other place where parallelism in higher level vision appears to break down is related, but more subtle. Consider the recognition network for horses in Fig. 3.5. Also assume that the visual feature sets are represented independently of their position, as shown in that figure. A network like Fig. 3.5 would respond positively to an image in which the features of a horse were all present, but were totally scrambled in position and relative orientation, because the features have been abstracted from their spatial location. The relational information among features has been lost in the parallel indexing process. This problem of illusory conjunctions and misguided recognition does arise in special situations [37, 35] but not in normal vision.

There is one solution to this scrambled image problem that will occur immediately to any vision researcher—junction features. One could add to our mechanisms recognizers for junctions of features analogous to the L- and T-joints of blocks world vision. An image would have to match not only the individual features but also the junctions to be recognized. This does help considerably, but some confusions still can arise, particularly in scenes with occlusion. The only general solution we have found to this problem again requires sequential processing.

Even with sequential processing allowed, verifying the structural relations constituting something like a horse is not a trivial problem in connectionist modelling. A program recently developed by Plaut [28] points out some of the difficulties in this task and how they may be overcome. Because our simulator was so slow, the simulation is carried out in a pico world where visual input is confined to a hexagonal grid of ten cells (Fig. 4.1). Figure 4.1a depicts a toy train that is composed of a large and a small shiny red cylinder and two small dull brown spheres. The individual visual features are idealizations and their computation was not part of the program. Figure 4.1b shows how the individual features are combined (in parallel) to form feature collections which, in turn, index possible models of simple toys. A

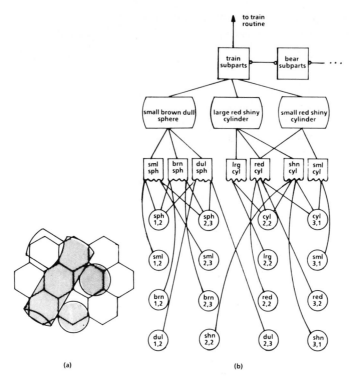

FIG. 4.1.   (a) Possible feature input. (b) Organization of portion of SIM for analyzing such input.

technical point is that the program employs feature-pair units (such as sml. sph. for small sphere) that force the two feature values to come from the same spatial position for the unit to become active. In such a network a small brown dull sphere anywhere in the image will cause the appropriate unit to be activated. As we mentioned before, if enough of the parts of the toy train are activated, the "train" node will be effectively indexed. But this is not the end of the recognition process.

For one thing, the train in Fig. 4.1 is translated and rotated. As we discussed earlier, there are good ways to compute image to model transforms in connectionist networks; Fig. 4.2 depicts such a network for our pico world. The idea here is to use the position and orientation of some major part of the object, here the train body, to determine the transform. By focussing attention on the large red shiny cylinder and exploiting the top-down connections back to spatial location units, the system can determine (i.e., activate) the parameters of the viewing transform. This obviously must be done sequentially for each object in the scene, but is only preliminary to the main process of the model verification.

Recall that the central problem was verifying the relationships among the component parts of an object such as a toy train. Notice that junctions alone will not distinguish the toy train from an object with the smokestack and one of the wheels switched. Our solution to the structure mapping problem involves sequentially verifying that each part is in the appropriate relation to its neighbors. The connectionist implementation of this scheme is suggested by Fig. 4.3.

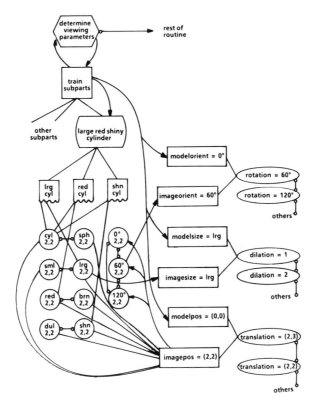

FIG. 4.2. Determination of viewing transform parameters.

The verification process begins with the principal part used to compute the viewing transform as in [22, 16]. Each subpart is checked in turn, using a connectionist routine [34] to select a particular part, compute where it should be and then focus attention on the appropriate part of space. For each part, its relative position in the model and the current viewing transform combine to determine its expected position in the image. In Fig. 4.3, the train top is one unit to the upper right of the body in the model, and the viewing transform is a rotation of 60° and a translation of (2, 2). The network shown combines these values to activate the position (3, 1) as the expected location of the top. By allowing input only from this location (i.e., attending only to it), the program is able to test for the presence of the right primitive in the right place. The details of this process and its extension to more complex problems is discussed in [16, 28].

Obviously enough, the current program is very primitive, but it does show a number of things. Parallel indexing from intrinsic features appears to be feasible and extendible to large problems. The parallel computations of a viewing transform from model to image is feasible at least for unoccluded objects with an identifiable orientation. Relational information lost in the parallel indexing process can be regained by sequentially attending to parts of a figure and the rest of the mechanism

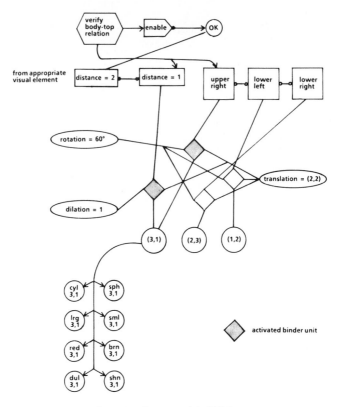

FIG. 4.3.   Structure of the VTM.

continues to be fully parallel. The major open questions involve extending these ideas to realistic domains, including occlusion and relating these algorithms to the intriguingly similar results on human eye-movements and attention.

Although the application of connectionist models to vision is at a very early stage, the results have been quite encouraging. It appears that low, intermediate, and high level visual processing can all be expressed well in the formalism, often better than in any other known way. The computational limitations that seem to be inherent and the natural solution to them map nicely onto what is known from brain and behavioral studies. Our current efforts include extending the ideas to harder problems, carrying out more detailed simulations (using a parallel computer) and working closely with colleagues in other disciplines to test specific hypotheses on natural vision.

REFERENCES

1. D. H. Ackley, G. E. Hinton and T. J. Sejnowski, A learning algorithm for Boltzmann machines, *Cognit. Sci.* **9**, 1985, Jan.–Mar., 147–169.
2. S. Amari and M. A. Arbib (Eds.), *Competition and Cooperation in Neural Nets*, Lecture Notes in Biomathematics (S. Levin Ed.), Vol. 45, Springer-Verlag, Berlin, 1982.
3. D. H. Ballard, Parameter networks, *Artif. Intell.* **22**, 1984, 235–267.

4. D. H. Ballard and C. M. Brown, *Computer Vision*, Prentice-Hall, Englewood Cliffs, N.J., 1982.
5. D. H. Ballard, G. E. Hinton, and T. J. Sejnowski, Parallel visual computation, *Nature* (*London*) **306**, No. 5938, 1983, 21–26.
6. D. H. Ballard, A. Bandyopadhyay, J. Sullins, and H. Tanaka, A connectionist polyhedral model of extrapersonal space, in *Proceedings, IEEE Workshop on Computer Vision: Representation and Control*, Annapolis, Md., 1984, pp. 18–24.
7. H. G. Barrow and J. M. Tenenbaum, Recovering intrinsic scene characteristics from images, in *Computer Vision Systems* (A. R. Hanson and E. M. Riseman, Eds.), Academic Press, New York, 1978.
8. C. M. Brown, Computer vision and natural constraints, *Science* (*Washington, D.C.*) **24**, No. 4655, 1984, 1299–1305.
8a. P. A. Buser and A. Roguel-Buser (Eds.), *Cerebral Correlates of Conscious Experience*, North-Holland, Amsterdam, 1978.
8b. C. W. Cotman, M. Nieto-Sampedro, and E. W. Harris, Synapse replacement in the nervous system of adult vertebrates, *Physiol. Rev.* **61**, No. 3, 1981, 684–738.
8c. S. E. Fahlman, The Hashnet interconnection scheme, Computer Science Dept, Carnegie–Mellon U., June 1980.
9. J. A. Feldman, Four frames suffice: A provisional model of vision and space, *Behav. Brain Sci.* June 1985, in press.
10. J. A. Feldman, Dynamic connections in neural networks, *Biol. Cybern.* **46**, 1982, 27–39.
11. J. A. Feldman and D. H. Ballard, Connectionist models and their properties, *Cognit. Sci.* **6**, 1982, 205–254.
12. J. A. Feldman and L. Shastri, Evidential inference in activation networks, *Proceedings*, Cognitive Science Conf., Boulder, Colo. June 1984.
13. G. E. Hinton, A parallel computation that assigns canonical object-based frames of reference, in *Proceedings, 7th IJCAI*, Vancouver, B.C., August 1981, pp. 683–685.
14. G. E. Hinton, Shape representation in parallel systems, in *Proceedings, 7th IJCAI*, Vancouver, B.C., August 1981, pp. 1088–1096.
15. G. E. Hinton and J. A. Anderson (Eds.), *Parallel Models of Associative Memory*, Erlbaum, Hillsdale, N.J., 1981.
16. L. M. Hrechanyk and D. H. Ballard, Viewframes: A connectionist model of form perception, *Proceedings*, CVPR, Washington, D.C. June 1983.
17. R. A. Hummel and S. W. Zucker, On the foundations of relaxation labeling processes, *IEEE Trans. Pattern Anal. Mach. Intell.* **PAMI-5**, 1983, 267–287.
18. P. Jolicoeur and S. M. Kosslyn, Coordinate systems in the long-term memory representation of three-dimensional shapes, *Cognit. Psych.* **15**, 1982, 301–345.
18a. P. W. Jusczyk and R. M. Klein (Eds.), *The Nature of Thought: Essays in Honour of D. O. Hebb*, Erlbaum, Hillsdale, N.J., 1980.
19. M. A. Just and P. A. Carpenter, Eye fixations and cognitive processes, *Cognit. Psych.* **8**, 1976, 410–480.
20. T. Kanade, *A Theory of Origami World*, TR CMU-CS-78-144, Dept. of Computer Science, Carnegie–Mellon Univ., 1978.
21. D. C. Marr, *Vision*, Freeman, San Francisco, 1982.
22. D. C. Marr, and H. K. Nishihara, Representation and recognition of the spatial organization of three-dimensional shapes, *Proc. R. Soc. London, B* **200**, 1978, 269–294.
23. M. Minsky, K-Lines: A theory of memory, *Cognit. Sci.* **4**, No. 2, 1980, 117–133.
24. M. Minsky, A framework for representing knowledge, in *Psychology of Vision* (P. Winston, Ed.), McGraw-Hill, New York, 1975.
25. Minsky, M. and S. Papert, *Perceptrons*, MIT Press, Cambridge, Mass., 1972.
26. S. E. Palmer, E. Rosch, and P. Chase, Canonical perspective and the perception of objects, in *Attention and Performance IX* (J. Long and A. Baddeley, Eds.), Erlbaum, Hillsdale, N.J. 1981.
27. A. P. Pentland, Shading into texture, in *Proceedings, AAAI-84*, 1984, pp. 269–273.
28. D. C. Plaut, *Visual Recognition of Simple Objects by a Connection Network*, TR143, Computer Science Dept., Univ. of Rochester, August 1984.
29. T. Poggio and V. Torre, Ill-posed problems and regularization analysis in early vision, in *Proceedings, DARPA Image Understanding Workshop*, October 1984, pp. 257–263.
30. M. I. Posner, *Chronometric Explorations of Mind*, Erlbaum, Hillsdale, N.J., 1978.

31. M. I. Posner and Y. Cohen, Components of visual orienting, in *Attention and Performance X* (H. Bouma and D. Bouwhis, Eds.), Erlbaum, Hillsdale, N.J., 1984.

32. D. Sabbah, Computing with connections in visual recognition of Origami objects, *Cognit. Sci.* (Special Issue on Connectionist Models), Winter 1985.

33. D. Sabbah, Design of a highly parallel visual recognition system, *Proceedings, 7th IJCAI*, Vancouver, B.C., August 1981.

34. L. Shastri and J. A. Feldman, Semantic networks and neural nets, TR131, Computer Science Dept., Univ. of Rochester, June 1984.

34a. R. S. Sutton and A. G. Barto, Toward a modern theory of adaptive networks: Expectation and prediction, *Psychol. Rev.* **88**, No. 2, 1981, 135–170.

35. P. Thompson, Margaret Thatcher: A new illusion, *Perception* **9**, 1980, 483–282.

36. A. M. Treisman, The role of attention in object perception, *Proceedings*, The Royal Society International Symposium on Physical and Biological Processing of Images, London, September 1982.

37. A. M. Treisman and G. Gelade, A feature-integration theory of attention, *Cognit. Psych.* **12**, 1980, 97–136.

38. W. A. Wickelgren, Chunking and consolidation: A theoretical synthesis of semantic networks, configuring in conditioning, S–R versus cognitive learning, normal forgetting, the amnesic syndrome, and the hippocampal arousal system, *Psychol. Rev.* **86**, No. 1, 1979, 44–60.

Toward a Theory of the Perceived Spatial Layout of Scenes

RALPH NORMAN HABER

Department of Psychology, University of Illinois at Chicago, Chicago, Illinois 60680

Received January 7, 1985

When normally sighted people observe a natural scene, their perceptions include seeing the supporting ground surface and the arrangements of the objects on that surface: where each object is in relation to the others, to the ground surface, and to the observer. This is defined as the perceived layout of a scene. Most current perceptual theories do not consider perceived layout, preferring to focus on the much narrower concern of perceived radial distance of objects from the observer, ignoring concern for the relationships among the objects of the scene, and among the observer in relation to the objects. In contrast, current cognitive theories have focused on cognitive maps as a spatial representation of scenes previously seen, maps which include explicit representation of spatial layout. However, cognitive theories have paid little theoretical attention to the spatial relationships in scenes currently on view, so they can tell us little about perceived layout, only remembered layout. Perceived layout has been missing from perceptual theories, and needs to be studied in its own right. In addition, to understand spatial cognition, cognitive maps, or any kind of representation of knowledge about the layout of space, we must study the properties of perceived layout—the perception of the arrangements of objects in a scene currently on view. To provide an example of the assessment of perceived layout, experimental data are presented on the psychophysical measurement of the perceived layout of a natural scene containing 13 objects arranged on a large flat lawn. Subjects are asked to draw a map of the scene, to estimate the absolute interobject distances between every pair of objects in feet, and to compare the relative magnitudes of every possible triplet of interobject distances. The matrices of the interobject distances derived from each of these three measures produce highly reliable and consistent 2-dimensional constructions of the scene through a multi-dimensional scaling analysis. These constructions resemble the physical layout of the actual scene quite closely. However, subjects tend to underestimate the distances between objects when the direction of the distances are parallel to their line of sight, compared to directions perpendicular to their line of sight. Not only does this tend to produce perceived layouts of the scene that are slightly more ellipical than in actuality, but more important, it means that subjects' perceived layouts change when they move to new viewing positions. These analyses and others are used to examine the usefulness and validity of these measures as indices of perceived layout. Following the psychophysical descriptions of the measures, a theoretical analysis of some of the properties of the perceived layout of space is provided, along with a consideration of some of the variables that are expected to affect these properties. The paper concludes with a return to the theoretical issues concerning the contents of a proper theory of space perception. © 1985 Academic Press, Inc.

1. INTRODUCTION

Perceived layout concerns the perception of the locations of the objects in the scene: their placement with respect to the ground surface; to one another; to the boundaries of the scene; and to the observer. My assumption is that whenever observers look at a scene, their perception of that scene always includes perceiving the arrangements among the objects that make up the scene, whatever else they may choose to notice or describe. The topic of my paper is an examination of the

109

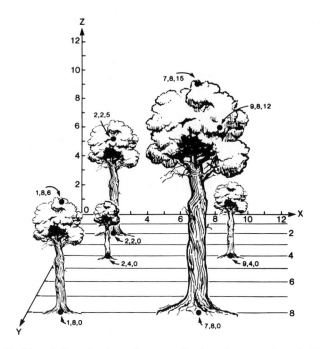

FIG. 1. A Euclidean 3-dimensional coordinate specification of a scene. Several XYZ coordinate locations are indicated.

properties of perceived layout. I have restricted my consideration to vision alone, since normally sighted persons receive virtually all of their information about the locations of objects in a scene through vision. Audition may make a negligible contribution, but rarely does any information come from smell, taste, or even touch.

Before we can analyse perceived layout, it is necessary to define physical layout. The easiest way to describe the physical location of objects in a natural scene is to posit a 3-dimensional Euclidean coordinate system, with an arbitrary origin placed either in the middle of the scene, or off along one edge. The basic supporting ground surface is then defined as a plane, on which are attached the objects of the scene, each intersecting the ground surface at defined XYZ coordinates. For ease of analysis, the ground can be assumed to be flat and level (i.e., the Z coordinate values are all constant throughout the XY plane of the scene), and the intersection of each object with the plane of the ground occurs at a single XY location, as if the objects were skinny saplings growing in a flat forest. The Z axis then provides a description of the heights of each object (see Fig. 1).

These simplifying assumptions are convenient ways to keep the geometry manageable, but they are not necessary. Euclidean coordinates can completely specify a scene even if the ground is uneven and not level, and if the objects have some mass so that their intersections with the ground cover some substantial area. Further, scenes can have free floating objects such as birds or clouds, or objects that are only attached to other objects, such as a swing hanging from a branch. A Euclidean 3-dimensional space can locate all of these, fixing each part of each surface of each object. Finally, objects can be located while in motion, by integrating the three dimensions over time, creating a fourth dimension. I call this geometrical description the *physical layout of a scene.*

The above description is sufficient to provide a physical definition of a scene in terms of the locations of its ground and all of its objects. Human beings are often among the objects in a scene, so they also have *XYZt* locations (even a different one for the left big toe from the pupil of the right eye). As an object in a scene, a person has no special location properties different from any other potentially moving object. The scene exists and can be described by the *XYZt* intersections and vertices of objects and ground whether a person is present or not, and whether anyone is looking at the scene or not.

I have chosen to use a Cartesian coordinate system based on Euclidean geometry, though other choices are possible. Specifically, I have chosen not to use a polar coordinate system, which inevitably places the observer at the origin, since I want to be able to test empirically questions regarding the position of the observer in the perceived layout of a scene. Another alternative is a city block metric [2, 108] which has some special properties for scenes lacking line of sight viewing and direct routes of travel between objects. Some experiments have even tested the usefulness of one metric vs. another (e.g., [78]). My concern is not with the particular metric chosen, but with a contrast between physical and perceived layout using the same metric, whichever one it is.

I assume that when observers look at a scene, part of their perception includes seeing the locations of the objects in relation to each other, to the ground, and to themselves. But while we can use the same geometrical measuring sticks to describe perceived layout, we cannot assume the same measurement scales, nor even that there is a necessary relationship between appearance and physical reality. Consequently, we must contrast the above physical description of the layout of the scene with a perceptual description of what observers see while looking. The latter is what I call the *perceived layout of a scene.* My concern is with the specification of perceived layout, its measurement, and its psychophysical relationships to physical layout.

The Theoretical Importance of Perceived Layout

There are convincing reasons why we need to know about perceived layout, and include it in our theories of visual perception. The following are a few examples:

1. The visual world around us is 3-dimensional, and is scattered with objects. Unless we are museum inmates, we rarely interact with 2-dimensional scenes, and virtually never encounter 1-dimensional scenes. Yet the major dependent variable in perceptual research on space perception is the estimated distance of an object from the observer—a 1-dimensional judgment of radial distance extending away from the observer (or a 2-dimensional judgment when displayed in polar coordinates). So while we can clearly ask observers in the laboratory to judge objects along a single dimension of radial distance, such a task taps into only a small part of space perception. Further, since the general finding from this research is that the perception of radial distance is not very accurate [38, 27, 91, 131, 40]), most of the focus of attention has been on the mismatch between perceived and objective radial distance,

without considering that radial distance is but one aspect of spatial perception, and perhaps not even a very important aspect.

2. One of the thorniest theoretical tangles of the past 150 years concerns how we perceive the intrinsic properties of space, independent of our position of observation (as well as other momentary variations in illumination, sun angle, shadow, and the like). A 1-dimensional representation of perception prevents addressing this question meaningfully, since the observer is inevitably and perhaps necessarily placed at the origin of the scaled representation. With a two or more dimension conceptualization, we both can ask theoretically, and measure empirically, whether the observer's position effects perception; and whether the perceived location of objects are anchored with respect to the observer's position, or to some other perhaps natural anchor in the scene itself. If the observer is not necessarily the center of his perceptual world, then the "problem" of explaining how he perceives the intrinsic properties of visual scenes suddenly becomes far more tractable. We can also ask whether conditions of observation systematically affect perceived layout, such as sun angle, visibility, and illumination; or whether there are affects of prior familiarity with the scene or with the objects found in the scene; or effects of position of observation, such as whether a scene looks the same when viewed while in its middle, or at its edge, or viewed from a balcony or an airplane.

3. Perceived layout must be an important component of the information we use to guide our locomotion through a scene, avoiding collisions and maintaining our intended route. Simply knowing the distances to various objects is not sufficient: we have to know the direction of the objects, the arrangements among them, and the potential paths between them. Without a description of what an observer sees, we have been hampered in our study of visually guided movements. Strelow [113] makes this point explicitly in his excellent review of theory contrasting visually guided locomotion to more cognitively guided processes in blind travelers. After considering the perceptual models underlying visual guidance, he notes that none of them include any specification of layout among objects, and concludes that a theory of visual guidance cannot be developed without such specification. One reason for this demand concerns the updating process needed as a traveler moves through a scene. Without a perceived layout, every aspect of the representation has to be altered with every step, a process demanding an incredible memory loading. A perceived layout of a scene, partially or totally independent of the position of the observer, requires little alteration or updating during the course of travel.

4. There is no reason why perceived spatial layout should exactly match the true physical layout, any more than why judged radial distance should exactly match physical radial distance. Until we measure perceived layout, we can never learn anything about the variables that affect its accuracy. For example, does a road or fence though a scene tend to perceptually repel objects on either side; are objects near to each other seen as farther apart than they really are; are objects located at the edge of a scene pulled into the scene perceptually; do tall or otherwise prominent objects cause objects nearby to them to be seen as farther away; are objects arranged in perceivable patterns, as in a row, seen as closer together; and so forth. These questions form part of what can become a new Gestalt psychology of 3-dimensional scenes, unlike the present version which is limited to flat patterns and designs. One experiment that addresses such questions about layout is by Kosslyn et al. [78],

although only in terms of remembered layout. Their 10 objects were distributed in a 17 foot square scene, bisected by an opaque barrier perpendicular to the line of sight, and a transparent barrier parallel to the line of sight. Objects separated by the opaque barrier were remembered as farther apart than they really were, and this was true for the transparent barrier for children as well.

5. The recent research on cognitive maps and spatial abilities frequently employ 2- and even 3-dimensional scenes. This work shows that observers are often able to reconstruct maps of scenes from memory, with the accuracy of these cognitive maps varying as a function of familiarity, observation conditions, relevance of the scene to the observer, etc. It is shortsighted for memory researchers to ask questions about 2- and 3-dimensional *memorial* representations of scenes, when we know next to nothing about 2- and 3-dimensional *perception* of comparable scenes. Cognitive maps, drawn or constructed from memory or imagination after viewing a scene, are not equivalent to responses made while the scene is in front of an attentive observer. What is missing from this memory work is any evidence of how much the systematic error effects found are due to changes introduced by memory variables, and how much is due to initial "errors" made while actually looking at the scene. I return to this below.

6. It is an unusual scene that can be viewed clearly in its entirety in a single glance, without eye, head, or body movements. For most natural scenes, observers move about continuously, and with the changing directions of gaze, only a few parts of the scene are simultaneously viewable. While theorists in both the Helmholtzian tradition (e.g., [49]) and the Gibsonian tradition (e.g., [121, 122]) have considered the perceptual effects of this normal viewing activity, only Hochberg (e.g., [65]) has explicitly shown that without a perceived layout (which he calls landmarks in this context), perceiving a single scene from multiple views is impossible. Hochberg has not provided any metric or independent definition of a landmark or perceived layout. His work, important as it is, depends on such specification.

7. A substantial literature exists on visual direction, though nearly all of it is based on data collected from observing flat displays arranged perpendicularly to the line of sight (see [93], for a review). In the natural world, direction of gaze varies in all three dimensions of space: aximuth, elevation, and distance into the scene. Further, direction of gaze changes constantly, so that there is no common direction of radial distance from observer to all of the objects. Does an observer use changes in the sense of visual direction to get information about where objects are located in a scene, or do perceived object locations, acquired from information contributing to all of space perception, account for how we perceive visual direction of gaze? Such a question can only be answered in the context of looking at 3-dimensional scenes, and measuring perceived layout of the objects in the scene. We must know more about the perceptual consequences of observers shifting their gaze from one object to another in a scene.

8. The development of environmental psychology as a dicipline (e.g., see [72, 73]) has increased the focus on the perception of natural scenes as an area of legitimate study. Further, we have had some models of the perception of scenes themselves (see [7, 125], for two quite different examples), models that suggest rule governed processes determining what our perception of such scenes must be like. But ultimately, such models and theories of scenes depend on data concerning the

perceived layout of scenes. Without the data, we lack the raw materials with which to generate better theories, and to provide critical tests and support for them.

9. In the same vein, recent developments in artificial intelligence, and especially in computer vision models and programs, require data about perceived layout, since perceived layout is or should be an important aspect of perception being modelled (e.g., see [26, 92, 10]). Without the empirical data on the way scenes are perceived, modellers have no reference points against which to construct and validate their programs.

10. Finally, if for no other reason, we need to examine 3-dimensional spatial layout because most observers introspectively feel that they see objects located in three dimensions, and what they see is accurately perceived.

Current Status of a Theory of Perceived Layout

Perceived layout of scenes (as perception rather than memory or cognition) is rarely discussed by any current (or ancient) perceptual theory. It has had little empirical attention: there is virtually no research that measures perceived layout, or that attempts to infer what observers know about the arrangements of objects in a scene while it is on view. These statements come as a shock to most theorists and researchers I have talked to, and they often claim that lots of work has been published on perceived layout. However, when asked for the references, nearly all of them turn out to be on radial distance, or remembered layout.

The reasons perceived layout has been ignored can be traced to the underlying concerns of current perceptual theories, especially theories stemming from Helmholtz's stress on inference or computation, and those stemming from Gibson's direct perception. A brief review of each theory illustrates this point.

The study of space perception from the time of Helmholtz has been primarily the study of depth, or more technically distance perception. The question usually asked, and the measure most often taken, is perceived egocentric or radial *distance* of objects from the observer. The Helmholtzian list of cues are shorthand descriptions of sources of information about the perceived distance of objects. Further, since perceived size, orientation, and shape are assumed to depend on knowledge of distance, egocentric distance assumes a central position in a complete account of spatial perception. Unfortunately, it has turned out that understanding how egocentric distance perception occurs is usually the only theoretical interest. Distance perception, narrowly defined, has become equated with spatial perception, broadly defined. Most experiments concerned with spatial perception study egocentric distance (or how egocentric distance perception is used to perceive the size, orientation, or shape of objects), and concentrate on psychophysical functions relating perceived radial distance to true radial distance under a variety of stimulus, instructional, and knowledge conditions. Typically, Stevens power functions [111, 91] are used to indicate the fidelity of the judgments, with the majority of studies yielding exponents less than unity, resulting especially from underestimation of the larger of the distances being judged (see [91, 115, 40] for reviews).

The shape of these radial distance functions has become a major theoretical focus in its own right. It is generally argued that radial distance perception is not particularly veridical, especially given the underestimation of far distances (and frequently overestimation of near distances as well) implied by the less than unity exponents. The theoretical questions revolve around how to account for this inaccuracy of radial distance perception (e.g., [40]), or how to explain it away. But these explanations do not consider other aspects of spatial perception, even at a minimal level. For example, I know of no data that contrasts Stevens' functions for radial distances between observer and objects with distances between two objects that are equidistant from the observer. Since the latter interobject distances are perpendicular to the line of sight, the factors usually invoked to explain non-unity exponents for radial distance would not apply for these horizontal distances. The narrow thrust of these efforts to treat radial distance as the only important dependent variable carries theorists even farther away from more general questions concerning spatial perception, so that research still says little about the perceived relationships among the objects themselves: what I have been calling the perceived layout of space.

Further, the Helmholtzian emphasis places the observer in the center of the scene, so that perception always is egocentric, by definition. Galileo and Kepler freed astronomy from an egocentric view, and we at least need to ask the modern equivalent of whether we are at the center of our perceptions of scenes, or can we describe the perception of scenes as having properties independent of the presence of our observations.

Figure 2 illustrates this contrast. When observers at the edge of a scene are asked to report their perception of the radial distance of each object from themselves, without regard to their direction of gaze, or the relation of the objects to one another, then their judgments can be scaled in one dimension without stress. That one dimension is usually called radial distance, as shown in the top of Fig. 2. In this kind of 1-dimensional graph, it makes little sense to have the zero point of the scale of radial distance at any place other than the location of the observer. Further, if the observer is placed somewhere else on the 1-dimensional scale, the interobject distances all have to be adjusted. From Descartes, in the 17th century, right up to the present, perceived radial distance has been the dependent variable, with cues to distance being the independent variables.

In contrast, if observers are asked to perceive objects as occupying different positions in a scene, then at least two dimensions are needed to represent this perception, as shown in the bottom of Fig. 2. Further, while the observer can be placed at the origin in such a representation, there is no requirement to do so, and nothing changes in any of the scenic relationships if the origin's position is placed in different locations in the representation, or even left out altogether. I have used only two dimensions in this illustration. Whether two are sufficient to represent what observers see depends on whether their judgments also reflect differences in height or elevation of objects above the ground plane of the scene, on the levelness and evenness of the ground, and on the nature of the metrics of perceived spatial location.

Consequently, preoccupation with the inference or computation process for the perception of the third dimension of physical space has kept theorists following a Helmholtzian tradition from carrying their analyses beyond the level of distance perception. They simply have not asked questions about layout, even about distances between objects that do not involve the observer as an anchor point. I can see no theoretical reason why such theorists cannot extend their vision to perceived layout —they simply have not done so.

The reason why the Gibsonians have not done so is quite different, and stems from strong theoretical convictions. Not only has Gibson opposed theories of

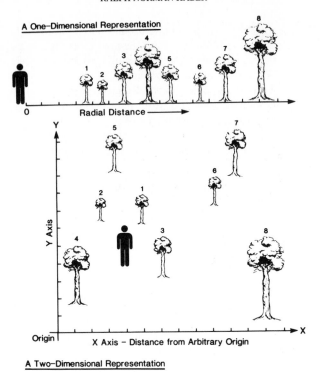

A One–Dimensional Representation

Radial Distance ⟶

A Two–Dimensional Representation

FIG. 2.   Top: Eight objects located in a 1-dimensional scene of radial distance, with the observer located at the zero point on the scale of distance. Bottom: Eight objects located in a 2-dimensional scene, with the observer in the scene.

perception that require inference processes, but he has opposed one that require any representation or construction transcending the information contained in the patterning of light reaching the eye over time. For Gibson, the location of each object is perceived because the light reaching the eye provides the information about its position—there is no need to invoke a perceived layout beyond that. Strelow [113] has examined this aspect of Gibsonian theory in some detail, showing why Gibson's reliance on direct perception provides him with no vehicle to discuss perceived layout. As Strelow points out, Gibson's careful distinction between perception and conception has left him with little theoretical support for understanding how scenes no longer on view are remembered. It has also deflected his interest from questions about layout questions in general.

What does it take to get perceived layout into a theory of perception? For a Helmholtzian, it is only a matter of carrying the theory and research a single step further—integrating what is known about egocentric distance with the remaining dimensions of visual space. For a Gibsonian, the shift in attention is more subtle, but is probably best obtained by starting to ask questions about perceptual memory: how do we remember what scenes look like that are not presently providing visual stimulation to the eyes? Developing the theoretical machinery to deal with such conceptual questions may make it possible for theories of direct perception to encompass perceived layout as well.

The study of perceived layout may be approached empirically, without making an initial commitment to either of these theoretical positions. I shall provide an example of one such study below.

Perceived Layout and Remembered Layout

While perceptual theories have virtually ignored perceived layout, more general cognitive theory has begun to include it under the rubric of cognitive maps, or spatial cognition. A number of recent volumes (e.g., [99, 100, 59, 98, 19]) attest to the interest shown in how we represent the spatial arrangements of the objects in scenes we have encountered. Almost without exception, however, this research is concerned with the representations of scenes *previously* perceived (and occasionally even fantasized), but not with the concurrent perception of scenes. This distinction between perceiving and remembering is not even appreciated in most of the research on spatial cognition. The operational definition for perception is the physical presence of the scene visible to the eyes. To describe the events internal to the observer as perception, there must be a scene on view before the eyes; if the scene is not presently physically visible, then those internal events are post-perceptual, and referred to as memory, imagery, or fantasy. Using this distinction, the research on cognitive maps has been memory research, since invariably, subjects are asked to make responses concerning the layout of scenes that are not presently on view.

While there are many theoretical differences between perceiving and remembering, this operational definition of the conditions under which observation occurs is critical in the study of spatial layout. The research on spatial cognition has already identified a number of variables that affect cognitive maps: familiarity of the scene; the frequency and conditions of original observation; the interplay between visual information, other sensory information, and nonsensory knowledge about the scene; the relevance of the scene to the subject; the cognitive developmental level of the observer; and the conditions of testing and the response measures used. Generally, the cognitive maps produced by the subject, or constructed from the subject's responses, are evaluated against a physical description such as a geographer's map of the original scene, with the similarity between the two being interpreted as a measure of the accuracy of a cognitive map. The failure to distinguish between perception and memory means that this research is incapable of determining which kinds of inaccuracies result from perceptual processes that occur during the viewing of the scene; and which inaccuracies in the cognitive maps result from memorial processes.

For example, Kosslyn *et al.* [78] found that fences tended to repel objects, so that observers remembered objects separated by fences as farther apart then they really were. This might be only an effect of memory, so that if an observer's perceived layout had been assessed while looking at a scene, the presence of the fence could have made no difference. Or it is possible that the distortion produced by barriers is perceptual in origin. Kosslyn *et al.* do not provide an answer. Bradley and Vido [9] do have a more direct test of the differences between perceived versus remembered space, though they only tested radial distances and not perceived layout. They asked subjects to make magnitude estimates of the radial distance of 15 objects from themselves that ranged from 20 feet to 14 miles, either while looking at the objects, or from their memory of the scene. When the preceptual judgments were plotted against the actual distances the average exponent of the resulting Stevens functions averaged 0.8, compared to 0.6 for the same functions based on memory. This result is consistent with other evidence of a reduction in the exponent of the power functions of sensory magnitudes estimated from memory (e.g., [79, 95]). Bradley and Vido also asked their subjects to draw a map of the locations of the objects, but unfortunately this was only done from memory and not while directly viewing the scene.

Consequently, it is at least theoretically possible that the *perceived* layout of space is highly accurate, and that all discrepancies between the physical layout and subjects' cognitive maps are due to changes that occur during retention or retrieval. In contrast, it is also possible that even while the scene is on view, an observer's perceived layout is distorted in just the ways the spatial cognition research suggests. Without the measurement of perceived layout, based on current observation of a scene on view, we can never learn where between the two extremes the answer lies.

There are contexts in which a perceived layout, in the way I have been discussing, never properly exists. Much of the research on cognitive maps has used scenes which are never completely on view at any one time. I may have a reasonable cognitive map of the town in which I live, even though there is no place that I can stand and see all of the town in a single glance, or even a succession of glances without walking considerable distances. Clearly, by my definition, such a map is based on memory. There has never been a single percept of the scene itself. One of the critical components of research on spatial cognition of scenes larger than single views is understanding what is perceived in each of the single views, and how those views are integrated and combined into a single representation that is remembered. Hochberg and Brooks [65] have begun to address this kind of question, in the context of the perceptual processes involved in integrating successive scenes of motion picture sequences when there is only partial overlap, or no overlap at all between successive series of frames.

There is yet another sense in which a remembered spatial layout may not have perceived spatial layout as an antecedent. When normally sighted observers are given verbal or conceptual information about a scene they have never seen, such as being told directions of a route to follow, then they presumably develop some kind of cognitive map of the scene (or at least the route), in the absence of ever having seen it before. By definition, there has been no perceived layout, since there had been no physical layout providing stimulation to the eyes, but there certainly is some variety of conceptual layout, which may or may not have similar properties to the other types of layout already described. Some recent work has contrasted cognitive maps acquired by reading a route map as compared to navigating the route itself (e.g., [117]), but again, this work has not included assessment of perceived layout directly.

Since different variables may affect our cognitive maps in these different conditions, we need to know how accurate perceived layout is, and the variables affecting it, in order to pull apart the variables that affect remembered and constructed layouts.

The absence of relevant research on perceived spatial layout, as well as absence of theoretical descriptions of such perceptions, poses some severe problems for my paper. I have little theory to guide me, and I have little data to limit me. Therefore, as a next step, I will describe some research I have done with Rick Toye on measurement of perceived layout of scenes (see also [119, 120, 57] for more details).

2. MEASURING PERCEIVED LAYOUT FROM RESPONSES ABOUT A SCENE

The most obvious way to assess the location of objects perceivers see in a scene is to have them draw a map of the scene. This procedure has been used extensively in the spatial cognition research concerned with memory for scenes. I had three concerns about this method. First, drawn maps are explicitly 2-dimensional (we have not considered asking our subjects to drawn 3- or 4-dimensional maps!), and thereby prevent us from asking questions about the number of dimensions contained in a perceived layout of space. Second, the findings of Tversky [124] suggest that the perception of maps may contain some inherent distortions that arise from Gestalt-like organizational processes. She did not study the production of maps in her research, but there is some chance that the same processes may affect the accuracy with which maps are drawn as well as perceived. And third, how do we separate out differences in map drawing abilities or differences in spatial understanding of maps that might have nothing to do with differences in perceived layout. Some people translate between 3-dimensional scenes and 2-dimensional maps of scenes easily, whereas others do not seem to know one end of a map from the other. The spatial cognition research that has used drawn maps as the dependent variable (see [99] for many examples) has found that the response maps are convenient to score, amenable to analysis, but that the individual differences are difficult to interpret and produce lots of noise in the results. Some of these individual differences can be reduced if the map drawer is given many opportunities to draw the map, each followed by feedback (see [112] for an example).

To avoid the limitations imposed by only using maps as responses, we also wanted data based on a very different response indicator. We choose one in which we asked subjects to estimate the distances between every pair of objects in the scene, including themselves as one of the objects. We asked them to do this in two different ways: first as an absolute distance in feet; and second, as a relative judgment between subsets of distances. While these interobject distance estimates are not themselves a layout of space, when we submit the matrix of all the estimates to a multi-dimensional scaling program, that program constructs an n-dimensional arrangement of the objects that satisfies all of the interobject distance estimates made by the observer. This n-dimensional construction can then be evaluated as a measure of an observer's perceived layout of the scene, through a psychophysical comparison between the constructed layout and the geometrical description of the actual scene. Since we have constructions based on three different kinds of input data (absolute distance estimates, relative distance judgments, and distances between points drawn on a map), we can also examine the resulting perceived layouts in terms of the properties of the input data themselves, such as their stability, consistency, scaling characteristics, and the like. Four different kinds of tests are used for this evaluation process.

First, do the interobject distance estimates produced by the observers bear a lawful relationship to the actual distances in the scene? As a minimum, there should be a monotonic relation between estimated interobject distance and real distance, but more than that, the scalar properties between true and estimated distance should be predictable. This test is traditionally made by examining Stevens functions.

Second, are the distance estimates produced by an observer internally consistent with themselves, so that the regression equation can locate each object without stressing any of the interobject distance estimates? Consistency does not imply anything about accuracy: to be consistent, an observer has to provide distance estimates that are derived from some possible n-dimensional space. It does not necessarily have to be the one being observed.

Third, is the n-dimensional space constructed from the multiple regression analysis lawfully related to the real scene? Do the number of dimensions required to satisfy the interobject distance judgments match the number the observer attended to in the real scene, and is the accuracy of object locations as good as performance measures and perceptual intuitions predict?

Finally, how sensitive is the perceived layout of space constructed by the scaling program to the viewing position of the observer? When the physical layout of space is defined in terms of the geometrical arrangements among the locations of objects, that layout does not change if the observer moves to a new viewing position. But what about perceived layout? To be a useful measure, the constructions either should not change with observer position changes, or, if we find different scaled constructions depending on viewer position, then we should be able to account for the ways in which position produces changes in perceived layout. For example, if far space is foreshortened in relation to near space, making scenes appear more ellipical then they really are, then the axes of the ellipse should rotate with the change in the observer's viewing position.

The research to be reported here depends in part on the usefulness of multi-dimensional scaling to describe the underlying perception by the observer. The above tests are designed to provide information on that usefulness. There is also a large existing literature that has used multi-dimensional scaling productively, most of it stemming from Shepard's [107] and Kruskal's [80, 81] methods (see also Arbie and Boorman [1]). These have been reviewed by Indow [70] for their application to perceptual research, and more recently by Ward and Russell [129], who reviewed some of the multi-dimensional scaling applications to psychological representations of spatial environments. None of this work included studies of perceived layout of objects. The most direct application of multi-dimensional scaling is by Kosslyn et al. [78]. They asked subjects (preschool children and adults) to rank order from memory the relative distances among the locations of 10 toys. These rankings were then submitted to a Kruskal multi-dimensional scaling procedure. The 2-dimensional solution was used to describe the remembered spatial positions of the objects, and the analyses showed rather good matches to the actual space. However, from the point of view of the present paper, Kosslyn et al.'s research is not about perception. Had they collected the same data from observers while they were actually looking at the scene of toys, then I would have an appropriate paper to reference on perceived layout.

3. EXPERIMENTAL PROCEDURE TO MEASURE PRECEIVED LAYOUT

To demonstrate the appropriate evidence on each of these four evaluations just described, we have run several experiments, of which one has been fully analysed. In this one, Toye [119] tested 8 subjects on a visually rich scene. Figure 3 is a

FIG. 3.   Photograph of the stake scene used by Toye [119], showing the location of the 13 stakes, and the ground, and the boundary areas beyond the scene. The camera is elevated and behind the scene more than were the subjects, whose positions can be seen by the sets of chairs on the side of the scene.

photograph of the scene taken from one of the subject's viewing positions (though slightly higher to show the layout better). The scene was an open grassy field 250 ft on a side, in which Toye planted 13 identically sized metal stakes, in an area spaaning a diameter of about 70 ft in the center of the field. Each stake was about an inch in diameter, and three feet tall. It was capped with a flag displaying an easily read large letter drawn on it. Figure 4 is a survey map of the arrangement of the planting of the 13 stakes. Toye had his observers sit next to one of the outermost stakes (either stake I or F), and except for having to remain seated, the subject was free to make eye, head, and body movements while looking at the scene of stakes. The perimeter of the field had tall buildings on two sides, and low buildings and trees on the other two. While the 13 objects are all the same size and shape, the viewing conditions provide extensive visual information about the objects' locations.

The subjects made all their responses twice, once before lunch and once after. One half of the subjects viewed the scene from the same viewing position for each set of responses (either stake I or stake F both times), whereas the other half of the subjects shifted 90° from stake I to F or vice versa (about 50 ft around the circumference of the scene) before they repeated their responses. This manipulation give us a check on the reliability of judgments for the non-movers, against which we can assess the effects of observer position for those subjects who moved.

Each subject produced three response measures, always in the same order. The first measure required the subject to *draw a map* of the scene while observing it. The subject was given an 8 by 10 white paper on a clip board, with a G indicated in the center (representing stake G). The subject was told to indicate his or her own

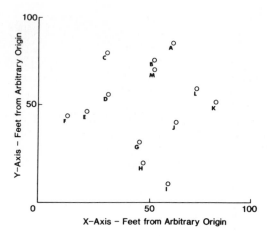

FIG. 4.   A survey map drawn of the stake scene, as viewed from above. The X and Y axes are in feet. The subjects sat either next to stake F or stake I while making their responses.

location near the bottom of the paper with a dot, putting the letter of the adjacent stake next to the dot, and then to place each of the remaining objects where they belonged, each indicated as a dot with an adjacent letter. The drawn map measure takes about 5 min.

The second measure is *relative distance* judgments among triplets of objects. On a response sheet are printed all possible triplets among the 13 objects (286 in all) in random order. For each triplet (e.g., *BDH*), the subject had to indicate which of the three interobject distances (*BD*, *BH*, or *DH*) was the largest. This test takes about 45 min with 13 objects.

The third measure asks the subject to estimate the *absolute distance* between all 78 pairings of the 13 objects. These 78 interobject distances are printed as letter pairs in three columns on a response form in random order. While looking at the scene, the subject writes down an estimate of the distance in feet between the two stakes with those letters. No anchor values are provided, either as to the absolute size of the stakes, or to any of the distances in the scene. The absolute distance estimates take about 20 min to complete with 13 objects.

The three response measures provided us with three different kinds of inputs to the multi-dimensional scaling analysis. We had no preconceptions as to which one would be the best (in terms of the evaluation criteria just described), or easiest to interpret. As it turned out, all three measures produced quite similar constructions, each of which met the evaluation criteria similarly. This increased our confidence that we were tapping the same underlying perceived layout of space with these responses.

The drawn map is already a 2-dimensional construction of the scene of stakes. However, since each subject was free to fill up as much of the paper as wished, the sizes of the drawn maps differed from one another. To facilitate comparison of the drawn maps with the scaled constructions based on the distance estimates, in which the axes of the scaled solutions were in standard deviation units (based on the standard deviation of the actual 78 interobject distances), we also submitted the

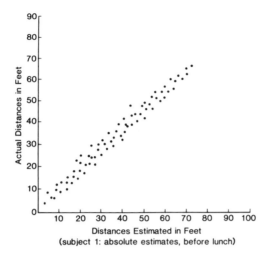

FIG. 5.   A plot of the estimated absolute distance estimates as a function of the acutal distances in feet for each of the 78 interobject distances for Subject 1, based on his first set of observations (before lunch). The plots of the other 7 subjects are very similar.

maps to the scaling routine. To do this, we measured each of the 78 interobject distances between the 13 dots drawn on a map to the nearest millimeter, and used this matrix of 78 scores as an input to the multi-dimensional scaling analysis. To scale the absolute distance judgments, we used the matrix of the 78 interobject distance estimates in feet as the input to the scaling program. With the relative distance judgments, we started by counting the number of times a subject selected each of the 78 interobject distances as the largest. This matrix of 78 frequencies was then used as an input to the scaling routine. Each of these inputs yields scaled outputs of 13 points in an n-dimensional space. We also applied Procustean rotations to the points to examine their relationships to the actual distribution of the points of the physical scene.

All multi-dimensional scaling analyses were carried out on the data from each subject separately.

4. RESULTS OF EMPIRICAL MEASUREMENTS OF PERCEIVED LAYOUT

The four kinds of evaluations of the subjects' responses, and the multi-dimensional scaled solutions based on them, are described below.

The Lawfulness of Distance Estimation Responses

Traditional analyses of the accuracy of distance judgments plot judged distance against true distance and examine the slope, intercept, and linearity of the resulting (Stevens) function. Figure 5 presents one such function, based on absolute distance estimates, for one subject tested on the stakes scene, using her first set of responses. Similar functions were computed for the relative distance judgments (counting the number of times each interobject distance was chosen as the largest in relation to all others), and for the interobject distances taken from the drawn maps (measured to the nearest millimeter). All of the functions resemble Fig. 5. The functions are close to straight lines (the average exponents were about 1.00), the slopes of the lines also average about 1.00, and the intercepts would be about zero if the functions were extended through the origin. The zero intercept is consistent with a ratio scaling of the estimates, the unity exponent with an equal interval scaling of the estimates, and the unity slope implies that the subjects have an accurate sense of the absolute magnitude of distances in feet. If these eight subjects are typical, then observers can make absolute distance judgments of interobject distances in the stake scene with the same properties as real distances possess. Similar data were found for the scaling of the relative distance and the drawn map distances, though for these, interpretation of the slope has little perceptual meaning. Of course, this is only one scene, and poorer performance on these three response measures might be found for scenes very much larger (or perhaps even very much smaller) than this one. The literature is also full of poorer indices when measures are taken from more impoverished scenes.

In sum, all three types of distance judgments possess lawful relationships to the real distances being judged, certainly as strong if not stronger than have been previously reported in the literature (see [91] for a review). Consequently, we have substantial confidence that our subjects' responses followed systematic psychophysical functions.

The Consistency of the Estimated Interobject Distances

When a matrix of numbers, such as the interobject distance estimates generated by our subjects, is subjected to multi-dimensional scaling, the regression process attempts to locate each object in an n-dimensional Euclidean space in such a way that its location simultaneously satisfies all of the judged distances between it and every other object. Only if these estimated interobject distances are consistent with one another can they be used to satisfactorily estimate what a perceived layout of space might look like.

We examined the degree of consistency of the absolute and relative distance estimates, by assessing the amount of variance explained by the solution (goodness of fit), the scalar properties of the judgments, and the stability of the output values over time.

The goodness of fit between the scaled solutions and the input data is specified in terms of the proportion of variance explained among the estimates, or R^2. This correlation is based on the 78 distance pairs, one member of each pair from the subjects' distance estimates and the other from the distance taken from the scaled solution. Figure 6 presents R^2 values for the 8 subjects for absolute distance and relative distance judgments of the stake scene, taken from their first set of responses, computed for 1-, 2-, and 3-dimensional solutions. Not suprisingly, the amount of variance explained by a 1-dimensional solution was quite low, since it attempts to reconcile all of the interobject distances estimates as if the objects had been arranged in a single straight row stretching away from the subject. The 2-dimensional solutions had a mean $R^2 = 0.92$ (ranging from 0.78 to 1.00 among the eight subjects). Addition of a third dimension added no further explanatory power. The R^2 values were slightly though significantly higher for the absolute as compared to the relative distance judgments for the two (or more) dimension solutions. In Kruskal's [80] classifications of R^2 values taken from a number of different kinds of scaling problems, he treats values in this range for the two dimension solutions as

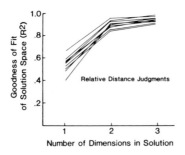

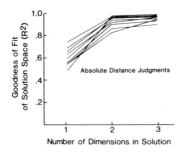

FIG. 6. Plots of the amount of goodness of fit (R^2) in the scaled solutions of the multi-dimensional scalings for 1-, 2-, and 3-dimensional solutions for each of the eight subjects, based on their first set of observations (before lunch), for the absolute distance estimates and the relative distance comparisons. No graph for the drawn map scaling is presented because R^2 must be 1.0 (less our error in measuring the interobject distances on the maps in millimeters) for two or more dimensions.

excellent fits, showing a remarkable internal consistency between the input values and the solution space.

The scalar properties of the subjects' judgments provides another assessment of the consistency of the representation. Multi-dimensional regression procedures require that the scalar properties of the entries be specified: the numbers can be treated as ordinal, interval, or ratio. For the relative distance judgments, this is an easy specification, since only ordinal properties were required of the subject (pick the largest of three interobject distances, irrespective of their absolute magnitudes). But the absolute distance judgments could have any one of the three properties. The R^2 values in Figure 6 are based on only an ordinal assumption, since this permits all of the scaled solutions to be run at the same level of assumption, and because ordinal numbers demand the fewest presuppositions about their underlying properties. Recomputation of the scalings with interval and with ratio assumptions produced no change in the R^2 measure for the absolute distance estimates, whereas the R^2 values for the relative distance estimates dropped. Since adding more restrictive assumptions did not decrease the goodness of fit between the solution space and the subjects' absolute distance judgments, this result is consistent with the conclusion that the subjects' absolute distance estimates have ratio scale properties: the difference between equal-sized intervals are equal, and the scale of distances has a true zero point.

FIG. 7.   Data from 4 subjects who did not shift positions, showing the overlap between the position of each object estimated by the scaling program based on data taken before and then again after lunch. The dots represent the before lunch location and the asterisk the after lunch location, with the dotted line indicating the direction and amount of discrepancy. Data are from the subjects' absolute distance estimations.

The stability of the scaled solutions over time is our final measure of consistency. Four subjects completed the same set of three measures twice from the same viewing position, separated in time by a lunch break. Figure 7 provides an example of a visual comparison of the before and after lunch solutions based on the absolute distance judgments of each of these four subjects. We computed, for each subject, the discrepancy between the XY coordinates of the first and second location of each object, as estimated by the multi-dimensional regression analysis, and averaged these across all 13 objects. We used as a metric for the X and Y axes the standard deviation of the 78 actual interobject distances, so that the average discrepancy measure is also in standard deviation units. We adapted a metric related to one proposed by Kruskal [80] in which

$$D = \frac{\sqrt{\left(x_i' - x_i''\right)^2 + \left(y_i' - y_i''\right)^2}}{k}$$

where D is the average discrepancy between first and second location of the 13 objects, $x'y'$ is the coordinate of the ith object on the first testing and $x''y''$ is the coordinate of the same object determined from the second testing, and k is the number of objects. If the underlying 2-dimensional object locations generated by the observers' judgments are the same on both observation occasions, then $D = 0.00$. When $D = 1.00$, then the average discrepancy is equal to one standard deviation of the distribution of all 78 actual interobject distances, which for this scene was 15.7 ft. The average D values over the four subjects who did not shift position is 0.23, 0.18, and 0.23 for absolute, relative, and map responses, respectively. These correspond to an average error of about 3.6, 2.8, and 3.6 ft in matching the location of the objects in the two perceived layouts. These also seem to be quite small values.

In sum, the 2-dimensional layouts of a scene constructed from the interobject distance responses of the subjects were highly consistent with their responses and highly stable over time. This conclusion provides further confidence that the subjects' interobject distances judgments reflect an underlying perceived layout of space, one possessing the properties found in the scaled solutions from the multiple regression analysis.

The Accuracy of the Constructed Layout of Space

There is no theoretical demand that the perceived layout of a scene must exactly match the actual arrangements among the objects. However, if the match is not very good, then there should be a systematic relationship describing the mismatches. The accuracy analyses are independent of the lawfulness and the consistency analyses just reported, since while both lawfulness and consistency are necessary for accuracy, the converse is not true. Several analyses examine the amount of accuracy.

One analysis concerns the number of dimensions in the constructed space. In the present case, the observers were asked to estimate distances between the objects, all of which were the same height, growing out of a ground plane which was approximately level and even. Consequently, a 2-dimensional solution should be found. The R^2 analysis of consistency provides an estimate of the number of dimensions needed in the scaled solutions to account for a particular proportion of variance. The proportion of variance explained is low for one dimensional solutions, reaches a high asymptote (mean $R^2 = 0.92$) when two dimensions are used, and increases only trivially further for three or more dimensions. When we plotted the 3-dimensional solutions, all of the the object locations lay on a single 2-dimensional plane, showing that there was no further variance accounted for by a third dimension. There is no statistical requirement that two dimensions would suffice, since 12 degrees of freedom exist in the scaling of 13 objects. That we found R^2 approaching 1.00 with only two dimensions lends credibility to the equation of the solution space with what the observer perceives when looking at the scene.

Another component of accuracy concerns the match between the locations of objects in the constructed layout and their locations in the actual scene. To

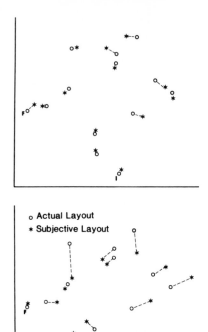

FIG. 8. Examples from 2 subjects of the overlap between the acutal positions of each object and the positions indicated by the 2-dimensional solution based on the absolute distance estimates. The first shows a very high degree of overlap ($D = 0.15$), while the second is an example of the very poor overlap ($D = 0.40$).

determine this, the 48 2-dimensional solutions (eight subjects by three measures by two observation opportunities) were each rotated and fit to the coordinate map of the true scene, using a Procrustean factor rotation. Each of these represents the best fit possible between the object locations in the real scene and the object locations in the scene constructed from the particular set of the subject's responses. Being Procrustean, while the entire constructed scene can be shrunk or expanded, it cannot be elongated, or changed in shape.

Figure 8 shows two examples of a visual comparison made by placing a template of the real scene over a constructed scene. The first of these is an example of a very good fit, and the second of a very poor one. The remaining 46 fall in between these extremes. The same D measure can be used to describe the average discrepancy between the constructed and the actual scene. The mean D values are 0.24, 0.22, and 0.32 for the absolute, relative and map distances, respectively, which correspond to average discrepancies of 3.8, 3.5, and 5.0 feet, respectively. An analysis of variance showed that the three response measures produce different accuracies, with the two distance measures best and equivalent, and the drawn maps slightly but significantly less accurate than either of the others. There are no differences as a function of replication, shifting position, or view of the scene.

I was surprised that the drawn maps resembled the actual scene less accurately than the constructions based on the two distance estimates, even given my reservations about the map measure. From the subject's point of view, it is the most direct measure, the fastest to produce, and does not require specific attention to subcomponents of the scene.

Some readers may wonder why we used an average D measure, taken over all 13 objects, rather than examine the discrepancy in locating each object separately. Such an object by object analysis is not interpretable because of the nature of the rotation process to find the best fit. The entire solution space is rescaled to minimize discrepancies, preserving only the relative positions of the objects along either axis. Consequently, the amount of mismatch for any single object cannot be determined. This problem was not appreciated by Kosslyn, Pick and Fariello [78], who tried to use a similar overlap analysis. Without a procedure to constrain the location of most of the objects, we cannot examine how accurate the subject is in placing single points. One such constraint procedure that can work presents subjects with drawn maps, already containing 12 points, and requires them only to mark in the location of the thirteenth. Across many subjects, the error in locating each point can be represented by the distribution of marks, which would provide a measure of both the magnitude and the direction of the errors in locating each object in the space. I do not yet have any data analysed with this method.

Even an average discrepancy measure provides impressive evidence of accuracy. The subject's distance estimates, whether absolute distance, relative distance, or even distances between points on a drawn map, all can be used to generate a 2-dimensional layout that not only resembles the actual scene, but resembles it closely enough that the average discrepancy between the actual and the constructed locations of objects is only a quarter standard deviation of all of the interobject distances. While there is no necessity that the constructed layout resemble the actual layout, the great similarity between the two found in this experiment further increases confidence in the use of the constructed scaled solutions as a measure of perceived layout of space.

The Dependence of Observer's Position on Perceived Layout

If viewing position affects the perceived layout, then when subjects move, their first and second constructed layouts should be less similar to each other, when compared to differences between the first and second constructed layouts of subjects who made their observations from the same viewing position. The group of subjects who did not move already provided evidence for reliability of spatial perception over time, as shown in Fig. 7. If the D values for those subjects who moved are as low as those from subjects who merely repeated their judgments from the same viewing position, then moving is irrelevant, and we can argue that the scene appears to look the same to the subjects regardless of the position from which they view it.

Figure 9 shows visually the discrepancies between the two sets of absolute distance estimates for the four subjects who moved. Using the same D measure as used for the data in Fig. 7, the means are 0.36, 0.26, and 0.47, for the absolute distance, relative distance, and drawn maps, respectively. While these values are still quite low, when the D values underlying Figs. 7 and 9 are contrasted (see Table 1), they

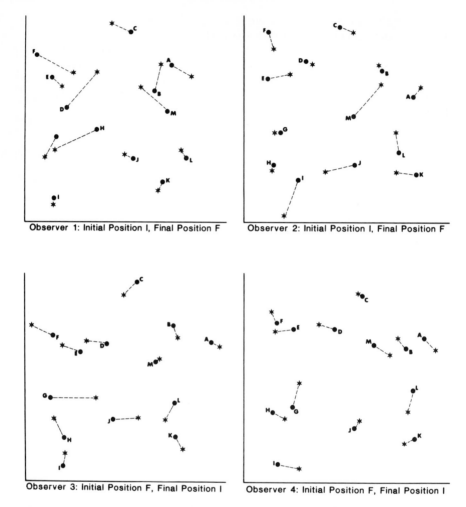

FIG. 9.　Data from the four subjects show shifted position between their first and second observations, showing the overlap between the position of each object estimated from data taken before and again after lunch. The dots indicate the before lunch location and the asterisks the after lunch locations, with the dotted line indicating the direction and amount of discrepancy. Data are based on absolute distance.

show larger discrepancies for the movers: for each of the three response measures, the D for the movers was significantly larger (averaging about a 2 ft decrepancy increase over that of the non-movers). Therefore, viewing the scene twice from the same place yields more similar versions of the scene than if the observer views it from two different positions. This suggests that perceived layout is dependent of viewing position.

　　The D analysis does not indicate the nature of dependence. To do this, we examined differences in the estimates of interobject distances as a function of

TABLE 1

The Mean, over Four Subjects, of the Average Discrepancy between
the First and Second Measurements, in D Units

	Absolute distance	Relative distance	Drawn map
Subjects who stayed	0.23	0.18	0.22
Subjects who moved	0.36	0.26	0.47
Difference	0.13	0.08	0.25
Corresponding difference in feet	2.0	1.2	3.8

whether the direction of the distance is perpendicular to the line of sight (a horizontal interobject distance), or is parallel to the direction of gaze (a radial interobject distance). I have already commented on why it might be interesting to examine this difference. In addition, many theorists, especially in the Helmholtzian tradition, believe that distances radiating out from the observer to objects are perceived by different (and presumably less direct) methods than are distances between objects more perpendicular to the line of sight. If this is true, then the observer's position, which defines the orientations of the interobject distances, becomes a determinant of the perception of the scene.

To test the relative accuracy of radial versus horizontal distance estimates, we separately examined the magnitudes of those interobject distances that are roughly perpendicular to the line of sight of the observer when sitting at one location and also roughly parallel to the line of sight from the other position. These define a class of interobject distances that are radial when viewed from one position but horizontal from the other, and a second class that are just the reverse (see Fig. 10). If any overall systematic distortion occurs in the perception of one direction of distance relative to the other, then contrasting the estimates of the same distance when viewed from two different postions should reveal a difference.

We tested the differences in the distance estimated for each of these classes of interobject distances as a function of where the subject sat. We found a consistent significant difference for each of the three response measures, in which an interobject distance viewed as radial was estimated to be shorter than when the same interobject distance was viewed as horizontal. We analysed this further with just the four subjects who shifted position, allowing a within-subject comparison, with the same result. The average magnitude of the radial–horizontal difference was about seven feet for the absolute distance estimates, or nearly a half standard deviation of the distribution of all of the interobject distances. Because the underestimation of the radial, compared to the horizontal interobject distances was found in all three measures, the effect cannot be due to properties of distance estimation themselves, but must be an effect that is occurring in the observers' perception of the scene itself. With radial distance foreshortened relative to horizontal distance, a physically round scene is perceived with an ellipical layout, with the short axis parallel to the line of sight. Whether this is a general property of perceived layout requires testing of a variety of scenes. However, the foreshortening of the radial distances is consistent

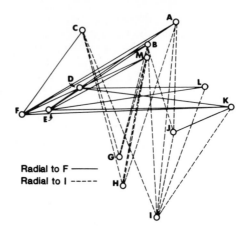

FIG. 10. A subset of the interobject distances from the stake scene. The solid lines represent interobject distances that are radial to an observer when sitting at *F* and horizontal when sitting at *I*. The dashed lined are radial to an observer sitting at *I* and horizontal when sitting at *F*.

with less than unity exponents found in Stevens functions for radial distances in the literature.

5. HOW GOOD ARE THESE MEASURES OF PERCEIVED LAYOUT OF SPACE

I have presented evidence concerning four psychophysical aspects of the constructions I have called measures of perceived layout of a scene. These show, first, that subjects can make absolute, relative, and drawn distance estimates that possess most of the properties of real distances. Second, these distance responses can be used to produce scaled constructions of the arrangements of the objects in the scene that are internally highly consistent using only two dimensions to account for all of the judgments, and that are stable across a replication. Third, when the scaled constructions are fit to the physical layout of the scene, the average discrepancy in locating the objects is only about a quarter standard deviation of all of the interobject distances in the scene—in this experiment about 4 ft in a scene 70 ft across. Thus, the scalings recover much of the location information from the physical layout of the scene. Finally, the constructions of the scene made from responses taken at one viewpoint differ systematically from one made from a different viewpoint, suggesting that the perceived layout is dependent on viewing position. The systematic distortion arises from differences in the estimates of horizontal vs radial interobject distances.

The above conclusions are supported by data taken from each of the three response measures. Two-dimensional constructions of the scene, whether made by the subject directly as a drawn map, or scaled as a multi-dimensional solution from the absolute or relative interobject distance responses, all yield the same information. Therefore, all three of the constructions can be used as measures of an observer's perceived layout of space, as they all meet the minimum psychophysical properties tested here.

However, these have been primarily tests internal to the data. We can also ask whether these measures of perceived layout provide the best index of perceived layout possible. This question has two sides: do the measures reflect all of the information about layout that the observer perceives; and are the measures completely sensitive to the properties of the scenes being observed. Some of the analyses already presented are relevant to these questions. For example, overall accuracy seems pretty good—an average error of only one-quarter standard deviation of the interobject distances contained in the scene. On the other hand, mislocating an object by three feet is not exactly a trival error. So it would be nice to know what the upper limits on such accuracy can be. Sensitivity to properties of the scene was more difficult to test in this experiment because the scene was quite constrained. While the perceived layout contained two dimensions, exactly matching the number of the dimensions in the scene, it would be nice to know if the scaled construction contains three dimensions for 3-dimensional scenes. To answer these questions about how well the measures reflect the perceiver's accuracy and the scene's properties, further experiments are needed. The following two are examples.

I have already raised the question of the effects of familiarity and practice on the response measures themselves. Since most people have never had to draw a map, or at least one that had to be consistently scaled, perhaps the drawn maps suffered as measures of perceived layout of space simply from lack of practice. Similarly, while most people do make absolute and relative distance judgments, they rarely receive accurate and consistent feedback about their judgments. Ferris [27] showed that subjects did improve in their distance estimates with feedback, but he only tested his subjects over and over on the same scene, so we do not know about the generality of the training. I have been unable to find any literature on procedures to train subjects to draw maps, or to make distance estimates, nor any evidence that such training is effective. Consequently, I have begun studies in which subjects undergo training on one of the response measures. The training is on a different scene from the one being used to assess perceived layout of space, so the training has to improve a general skill of map drawing or distance estimation, and not just improve the subject's memory for the layout of a particular scene.

The design of these studies asks subjects to view a scene and respond using both the absolute distance and the drawn map measures. Half of the subjects then undergo training on one of those measures, while looking at a variety of different and unrelated scenes. Finally, all subjects are retested on the original scene, again using both the trained and untrained measures. I expect that I can demonstrate an improvement as a function of practice, so that the degree of overlap between the perceived and the actual scene is increased.

To demonstrate that the measures reflect known properties of scenes, we need to introduce greater variation in the scenes being tested. For example, the experiment just described had a relatively even and flat ground surface. We are now testing a scene with a ground that contains a sharply rising hill. The objects are small balloons resting on the grass, each showing a large letter facing the subject. The scene is about 50 by 50 ft across, with the largest vertical difference in elevation about 10 ft. The objects are all visible, but otherwise distributed over the scene on the level parts, the slopes, the valley bottom and the hill top. The subject is asked to estimate all of the direct line interobject distances in feet. If the constructions made by the subject' responses reflect the layout of the scene, including the ground variation, then three dimensions will be needed to satisfy all of the estimated interobject distances. We can determine then whether the third dimension is reflected in the data analyses to the same extent as are the two dimensions already reported.

There are, of course, other variations to be tried. For example, instead of (or in addition to) rolling terrain, we could test a scene that had objects located at different heights above the terrain. Such a scene might be a playground, with a tree house 20 ft above the ground, a slide with its top 15 ft high and a middle dip 10 ft up, a peak bar of a jungle gym 5 ft high, and so forth. The question then is whether the interobject distance estimates between these objects reflect this vertical distribution of distances as well as it reflects where the objects each intersect the ground plane. Since the scene has significant variation in the vertical elevations of the objects, the measures of perceived layout should also reflect that variation.

These two projects, with pretraining on the responses and with 3-dimensional scenes, illustrate procedures to provide further evidence on the validity of these measures of perceived layout of space.

6. PROPERTIES OF THE PERCEIVED LAYOUT OF SPACE

Most of my discussion up to this point has been focused on methodological issues, concerning the usefulness of the measures of perceived layout of space. Now I want to reverse the emphasis. Let us simply accept the usefulness of these measures, and focus on what they tell us about the way space appears. Since so little data is available, I shall discuss just two questions about perceived layout: how accurate the perceived layout is, and how many dimensions it has. Some aspects of these properties are simple empirically interesting, but others have profound implications for the nature of visual perception, or the adequacy of one or more of the present theories of visual perception. My interest in this paper is on both the properties and the theoretical issues (see also [119, 120, 57] for more theoretical discussion).

The Accuracy of Perceived Layout

Several kinds of accuracy can be assessed as properties of perceived layout, including the amount of overall overlap between the perceived and the actual layout, the resemblance in shape between the two, and the specific patterns of distortions in accuracy.

The most general accuracy property of a perceived layout of space is the degree to which it matches the physical layout of the scene being observed. This kind of accuracy is captured by the D measure as an index of overlap of the perceived and physical scene, and can be used for flat scenes (such as Toye studied). It can also be used for scenes requiring three dimensions to specify the location of the objects, by adding the corresponding terms to the equation.

When the accuracy averaged over all objects and dimensions is less than perfect, then a measure of overall accuracy is not sufficient. We want to know the kinds of inaccuracies or errors made by the observer: in what ways did the perceived and actual layouts fail to match? Toye found one way: since a distance viewed perpendicular to the line of sight was perceived as longer than when viewed parallel to the line of sight, the entire scene must have been perceived to be slightly more elliptical than it really was. So at least for the kind of scene used by Toye, we can describe accuracy in terms of a match in the overall shape of the perceived and actual scene.

Another mismatch could be in terms of preceived scale. Observers could perceive a scene to be its true shape, but not its proper size. Toye could not make that comparison directly, given the nature of the multi-dimension scaling programs and Procrustean rotations that he used. However, from the analysis of the scaling properties of the absolute distance estimates, especially the convergence of exponents and the slopes of the Stevens functions around unity, the preceived size of the layouts of his observers must have been quite close to the size of the actual layout.

With respect to the accuracy of the locating individual objects, Toye was unable to provide an analysis of the errors made in perceiving the location of each object separately, also because of the nature of the rotations of the multi-dimensional scalings. I have suggested several ways in which modifications in data collection would permit future analyses of this kind to be carried out, so that each object's perceived location can be determined absolutely, and independently of all other locations.

Besides using the individual object location errors to support the overall shape analysis, the accuracy of locating the individual objects contribute to other properties of perceived layout. As I will discuss in some detail below, certain patterns of the physical locations of objects can cause errors in their perceived locations. It is possible that there is a "good" perceived layout, showing the effects of systematic organizational tendencies, in much the same way that some forms or patterns are systematically misperceived as being more regular than they really are (see [124] for many examples of this in map perception). To test for such goodness of perceived layout, and other Gestalt-like tendencies, we have to be able to measure the errors in perceiving the location of each individual in the scene.

The several kinds of accuracy description just discussed (overall overlap, shape resemblence, and specific patterns of distortions of inaccuracy) provide a beginning of an analysis of the properties of perceived layout that are concerned with accuracy. I could provide further examples, but given the severe limitations of data, I have already speculated too much. After we have some experimental demonstrations, of the kind proposed in the next section, then we can go back to the theory underlying accuracy.

The Dimensions of Perceived Layout

A quite different property of perceived layout concerns the number of dimensions it contains. Toye has shown convincingly, at least for one example of a 2-dimensional scene, that observers perceive the scene in two dimensions. Such perceived layouts of scenes have similar properties to survey maps, in which the locations of objects are represented as points on a 2-dimensional coordinate display, as if the observer was looking directly down on the scene, rather than viewing it from its edge. The translation from a perspective view to a birds-eye view seems so natural that no subject ever asked us which way we wanted their map to be drawn. But does this mean that only birds-eye perceived layouts exist? What would happen to the accuracy of perceived layout if the scene is viewed from an elevated position, or even from directly above its center? While elevated viewing reduces the differences between perspective and birds-eye representations, if the construction of a birds-eye perceived layout requires a perspective viewpoint of a scene from its edge, then elevated viewing may introduce more systematic distortions in perceived layout. These questions are not just methodological concerns with the measurement of perceived layout, but focus on basic questions of the nature of perceptual representations.

Survey maps have a number of other properties that may not be possessed by perceived layouts: the scale of the survey map is independent of the scale of the scene, and is only arbitrarily related to it by an indication noted on the legend on the map; survey maps are truly independent of the location of the observer, whereas perceived layouts seem to depend on where the observer stands; the effects of turning a survey map around may be quite different from the effects of viewing the scene from the other side; and the different kinds of markings on a survey map are interpretable by conventions which have to be learned (or read from a legend), whereas we know nothing about the specification of details on perceived layouts, or how they are interpretated. I can make this list of possible differences between survey maps and perceived layouts longer, but again, we need some data to shape the speculation.

It seems reasonable that scenes with significant vertical contents would be perceived in three dimensions: the first experiment to test this is in progress. If this expectation is correct, then the analogy between perceived layout and survey maps may be no longer useful, since survey maps use geometical coordinates to specify only two dimensions, relying on marking conventions (e.g., shading, color, or contour lines) to represent elevation. Further, since for most scenes, the scale needed to represent the X and Y dimensions is many times larger than that for the vertical Z dimension, the absolute scale values among the three dimensions are not the same on survey maps. Whether this is true for the three coordinate scales of perceived layout is not known yet.

I have only described two classes of properties—accuracy and dimensionality. Some other potential properties are more easily discussed in the context of experiments that manipulate perceived layout.

7. VARIABLES THAT AFFECT THE PERCEIVED LAYOUT OF SPACE

I have separated four main classes of independent variables that might have some effect of the properties of perceived layout: the conditions of viewing, the position of the observer during viewing, properties of the scene itself, and properties of the observer (see Table 2). Many of the variables have been studied extensively in other contexts, primarily ones concerning radial distance. Some of these have not been investigated at all, usually because they do not apply to radial distance or to other aspects of distance perception. Consequently, little is known about most of these, especially in the context of perceived layout, so we need experiments to provide the necessary information. I have not attempted to provide references to previous work on all of these variables, since most of those would be irrelevant to the study of perceived layout.

Conditions of Viewing

The important variables that fall under the category of viewing conditions are the movement of the observer, and the conditions of illumination. Secondary variables that are occasionally important concern whether viewing is binocular or monocular, restriction of the size of the natural field of view, and the use of any optical distortions or enhancements, such as viewing through a telescope.

TABLE 2

A List of the Variables That Might Affect the Properties
of the Perceived Layout of Space.

Conditions of viewing
1. Observer motion
2. Illumination
3. Visual field size and optical enhancements
4. Monocular viewing
5. Demand characteristics

Position of viewing
1. Edge, center or distance position
2. Level or elevated viewing
3. Momentary occlusions

Properties of scenes
1. Gestalt laws of scene arrangements
2. Size
3. Richness
4. Number of objects

Observer variables
1. Experience
2. Spatial abilities
3. Age and developmental history
4. Visual apparatus tolerances
5. Meaning of scene

Note. See text for further details.

1. *Observer motion.* Both motion parallax produced by head movements, and motion perspective produced by body motion through the scene, are thought to improve the accuracy of the perception of radial distance. There are hundreds of references to experiments on the role of motion in perceiving the distance of objects from the observer, both for the observer's head moving sideways, and for the observer moving toward objects. However, many of these failed to find an effect of observer motion, and at least some researchers (e.g., [131]) question whether observer motion should ever be expected to be useful. I know of no data on the role of observer motion on the accuracy of perceived layout. It seems reasonable to me that, other things being equal, a moving observer has a more accurate perceived layout of a scene than does a stationary one. However, it may be that this prediction fails for natural and informative scenes (see below), since perceived layout may already be as accurate as it can be, so that adding observer motion has no further effect.

2. *Effects of amount and uniformness of illumination.* To the extent that reduced illumination removes some sources of information, then twilight and evening viewing should produce a less accurate perceived layout. The nature of the inaccuracies are hard to predict in the absence of any data: all objects may simply be less precisely located; far objects may be less precisely located; or perhaps far objects may be seen as closer then they really are.

Similarly, the effects of shadows on the perceived locations of objects has not been investigated. A long shadow cast by an object could displace the perceived location of the base of the object toward its shadow, so that as the sun moved across a scene of objects the perceived locations of the objects would systematically shift back and forth. It is also possible that the reduced visibility of the terrain texture covered by the shadowed light would produce distortions or simply error in the perceived layout.

3. *Reduced field of view and optical enhancements.* I have lumped these together because they tend to be confounded in practice. Telescopes and binoculars, which magnify parts of the scene, also drastically reduce the field of view. Dolezal [21] has shown that many of the effects of optical distortions, such as viewing scenes through prisms and mirrors, can be accounted for in terms of the reduced field of view alone, without any contribution from the optical distortion. What happens to the perceived layout of the objects in a scene when it is viewed through a reduction tube that restricts the field of view to only ten or twenty degrees? This could be contrasted with magnified telescopic viewing, both monocular and binocular. The expected effect of the pulling in of far space should be found with magnification (Lumsden, 1983), but is also likely to be present with a purely reduced field of view as well. In addition, since a reduced field of view prevents many of the objects in a scene from being seen in each glance, whatever problems are created by the difficulties of integrating across glances (see below) should be manifest here too.

4. *Monocular viewing.* Observers rarely look at scenes with only one eye if they have two available, but some aspects of perceptual theories can be tested by contrasting 1- and 2-eyed viewing (see [30, 75].) Further, some observers only have one eye, or if two, do not have a functioning stereoscopic system. Consequently, we can ask questions about changes that might be found in perceived layout under monocular viewing, or under non-stereoscopic binocular viewing.

5. *Demand characteristics of the testing.* Presumably observers would attend to the layout of a scene more carefully when they expected to be questioned about layout. In such cases, perceived layout might be more accurate, though again, there is little data on demand characteristics for most perceptual tasks. There is some recent work on the effects of instructions on radial distance estimates (e.g., [16, 68]) showing in general that estimates are impervious to changes in instructions.

Position of Viewing

Three different kinds of position variations might produce substantial differences in perceived layout: is viewing from the edge of the scene, from its center, or from a distance; is the observer standing on the same ground surface that supports the objects, contrasted to viewing from an elevated position without a common ground surface; and there substantial occlusions of some of the objects by terrain elevations or large nearby objects.

1. *Edge, center, or distance viewing.* When observers stand at the edge of a scene, so that all of the objects are in front of them, then most of the location relationships among the objects can be seen in each momentary glance. This "simultaneity" is enhanced as the distance between observer and scene is increased. When the observer is close to the scene, then it is necessary to make eye (or head)

movements in order to look at each of the objects. The question of integration of successive views across saccades is being actively pursued in the literature now (e.g., [71, 101, 65]), but has not been studied in the context of perceived layout. Hochberg and Fallon [66] and Hochberg and Gellman [67] have examined the role of landmarks present in each single glance of a picture in the integration process, but only with flat displays. At the extreme, if the observer stands in the middle of the scene, then massive head and body movements are needed to see all of the objects, and only a few of the interobject arrangements can be seen simultaneously. If the observers in Toye's experiment had stood in the middle of the stake scene, most of the interobject distance judgments would have required them to look first at one object, then turn to look at the other object, and estimate the distance between them without being able to see both objects simultaneously. This is similar to a successive judgment task, in which a significant memory component is added, possibly altering the perceived layout of the scene substantially. A scene can also be viewed from a distance, in which the average interobject distance is much less than the distance between the observer and even the nearest object. It may be much more difficult for observers to perceive the arrangements among the objects accurately when they themselves are more distant from the scene, especially the more radial interobject distances. There is a large literature on the effects of absolute distance on perceived radial distance, most of which suggests that as the distances increase, the perceived distance of far objects are underestimated (see [40] for a review). I know of no evidence regarding distortions in interobject distances between very distant objects that are both the same distance from the observer.

2. *Level vs elevated viewing.* Observers typically view a scene while standing on the same ground that supports the objects, with that ground extending away into the scene. The ground surface provides substantial information about the distances and placements of the objects. Gibson [33] referred to this as recession viewing, contrasting it to air viewing, in which empty space intervenes between the viewer and the objects. Gibson objected to much of laboratory research on distance, in which a continuous ground surface was missing (see [123]), but air viewing often occurs naturally. When looking down on a scene of objects, say from a balcony, or from an aircraft, each radial distance from observer to object lacks the continuous ground that provides a receding textured surface specifying information as to the recession. Of course, the interobject distances among the objects attached to the ground still have the ground texture available, but the observer is not attached to that same ground, so that the perception of the scale of recession is not as obviously direct as Gibson claimed.

3. *Momentary occlusions.* Toye verified for the stakes scene that no stake occluded any other one at either of the two viewing postions he used. But this is an unlikely restriction for most scenes, so that some objects are inevitably behind others, wherever the observer stands. Further, even if all of the objects are visible, the ground surface extending between some of the objects may be blocked by a nearby objects. Consequently, the presence of significant occlusion of some of the objects or of the ground may distort the perceived arrangement of parts of the scene. This may vary as a function of the prominence of the occluding objects. In contrast, Gibson [35] focuses much of his analysis of space perception on the information available from occluding edges, especially occlusions that change during observer

motion. To the extent that the observers use this information, arranging a scene to reduce occlusion may reduce information that is naturally present.

Properties of Scenes

The variables involved in descriptions of the properties of scenes are not well worked out yet, since the literature has only recently begun to provide information about a taxonomy of scenes (e.g., [125]), ways of scaling scenes (e.g., [6]), or even ways of comparing one scene to another along different dimensions (e.g., [129]). A theoretical analysis of scenes will be difficult to develop until we have access to more data than exist at present. The following categories of properties would seem to lend themselves to experimentation.

1. *Gestalt laws of scene arrangements.* I expect that the appearance of the arrangements of objects in a scene is affected by the presence of borders or fences, by paths or dividers bisecting parts of the scene, by significant occlusion of some objects by others, by very prominent objects, by significant vertical elevations or vertical variation of the ground plane, by very tall objects whose upper reaches are important parts of the scene, by the presence of movement of some of the objects, and by certain physical layout arrangements of objects, such as trees all in a row, or objects arranged in a square pattern. I have already described an example of the effects of barriers shown by Kosslyn *et al.* [78]. I refer to these factors as Gestalts, by analogy to the Gestalt principles offered to describe the way 2-dimensional patterns and forms are perceived. I am extending them to three dimensional scenes, but as the above list suggests, there is little overlap between the "laws" for 2-dimensional patterns (of the kind described by Tversky [124], when perceiving maps) and 3-dimensional scenes. However, overlap in lists of laws is an empirical matter—we have to run experiments in which scenes are varied in the different ways suggested above, and see what happens to perceived layout.

2. *Size of scene.* Natural scenes come in all sizes, from the objects stuffed into a closet or arranged on a shelf, to room sizes, to the views beyond the windshield of a car on the highway. There is no reason to believe that the properties of perceived layout are invariant over this wide range of sizes.

3. *Richness of scene.* In the absence of a theoretically based ranking of scenes from rich to impoverished, a reasonable procedure to study richness is to vary the properties of visual information already identified by theory or research as important for the perception of distance: texture of a ground surface, texture of object surfaces, familiar sized objects, visible horizon, some object motion, sufficient number of objects, or variation in surface features to produce relative motion effects as a result of observer motion, etc. It seems likely that removing important information about a scene would reduce the accuracy of the perceived layout of space.

4. *Number of objects in a scene.* A natural scene contains at least some objects (probably by definition), but that number can vary over a wide range, as can the familiarity of the objects, their density, their similarity to one another, and their arrangement within the scene. Some of these variations may affect perceived layout of the scene.

Observer Variables

Current perceptual theories have given little emphasis to individual differences in visual perception (see [17] for a review of exceptions), even though substantial differences in performance exists (e.g., [20]). Several classes of variables are relevant to the study of perceived layout: prior experience, training and practice on layout tasks; age and developmental history; general spatial ability; and the accuracy of acuity, contrast sensitivity, stereopsis, and the like.

1. *Experience*. Surveyers, architects, and some kinds of athletes have had so much practice and experience perceiving layout with immediate feedback as to accuracy, that their performance on layout tasks should be superior to those observers without comparable practice. As one example, Lee, Lishman, and Thomson [86] studied long jumping in skilled athletes, and found supurb accuracy of radial distance performance.

2. *Spatial abilities*. Research on spatial cognition has already identified several varieties of general spatial abilities as predispositional measures of individual differences (see [100] for reviews). Since that research invariably confounds memory with perception, the correlation between general spatial ability assessment and remembered layout variables may have nothing to do with perceived layout, so it needs to be tested directly on perceived layout.

3. *Age and developmental history*. Much of the spatial cognition literature is concerned with developmental changes (e.g., [99]). Again, they cannot separate out changes that occur in perception from those in memory, so developmental manipulations need to be made on the measurement of perceived layout directly.

4. *Visual apparatus tolerances*. Reduction in the accuracy of perceived layout might be expected to occur in subject groups who have impairments in visual acuity for high spatial frequencies, reduced contrast sensitivity, including sensitivity to low spatial frequencies, defective stereo-mechanisms, or other impairments to normal visual functioning.

5. *Familiarity and meaning of the scene to the observer*. Do observers regard scenes differently, depending on the meaning that the scene has for them, the purpose the scene serves in their lives, or the amount of familiarity they have with it? While these variables have been studied in other contexts, and have a mixed pattern of results, it is not obvious how perceived layout might be affected by familiarity or meaningfulness. No one has asked the question before.

This list of variables is indicative of those that might affect properties of the perceived layout of space. It is not intended to be exhaustive, or even properly organized, but it should impress us with how little we know about perceived layout.

8. THE THEORETICAL IMPORTANCE OF THE STUDY OF PERCEIVED LAYOUT

In this paper I have attempted to make a case for the theoretical importance of perceived layout as one aspect of what observers see when looking at a scene. Since this case has not been made before, I have also reported a psychophysical study on the measurement of perceived layout to demonstrate that perceived layout can be measured, and that its properties reflect our intuitions about both perceivers and scenes. Finally, I have outlined a substantial research program needed to provide an understanding of the properties of perceived layout, and the variables that might affect it. In this final section, the impace of the study of perceived layout is examined.

Perceived Layout and the Visual Control of Locomotion

Recent work by Lee (e.g., [86]), Turvey (e.g., [28]), Warren [130], Todd [118], and others (see also Strelow, [113] for a review) has focused on a number of aspects of the visual environment that provide both stimulation and confirmation for motor responses underlying movement through the natural world. What is still needed is a model of perceived layout, such as I have begun to sketch here, to provide a general description of what moving observers perceive about arrangements of objects in a scene, the locations of paths, barriers and barriers, and boundaries, and variation in the evenness of the ground surface.

If perceived layout is virtually identical to physical layout, then a theory of visually controlled locomotion can rely on the properties of the physical layout as its source of information. But even the initial results of Toye's experiment suggest that such an equation is less than perfect, and varies at least according to viewing position, if not a host of other variables. If this preliminary conclusion is supported by further research, then models of visual control of locomotion must be combined with models of perceived layout in order to provide a proper description of the information used to control motor responses.

Perceived Layout and Remembered Layout

Theorists in the Gibsonian tradition can assume that perceived layout is available to observers from the direct pickup of information contained in the light reflected from the ground and the objects of a scene, without any need to posit a continuing representation of that layout. When I refer to the scaled constructions produced from the multi-dimensional scaling program as a perceived layout of space, I make no assumption about it as a continuing representation: all I suggest is that the properties of that construction are consistent with the way the scene appears when the observer looks at it. This seems a safe enough statement, as long as the mover remains in direct visual contact with the parts of the scene being observed and moved through. But we do not maintain visual contact with all parts of a scene as we move through it, even those parts that are in or near our path of travel. Presumably, object position information is maintained even in the absence of continuous orientation of the eyes to each part of the scene.

The outcome of the theoretical status of Gibson's direct perception model notwithstanding, there is little alternative but to posit a representation of a scene previously seen but no longer on view. Some property of a memory structure allows us to retain spatial knowledge about a scene not presently before the eyes. My argument, a simple one, is that the properties of the memory representation of the layout are based at least in part on the properties of the perceived layout. We must know what was perceived of the scene in order to understand the form and structure of what is remembered about the scene. This should be true even for scenes that have no antecedent perceptual input, such as those from verbal instructions. Based on a lifetime of perceiving scenes, and remembering scenes previously perceived, it seems quite reasonable that the memory for scenes only partly perceived, or never perceived, utilize the same memory processes, and the same structures, whatever those may be. By this assumption, we must know the character of perceived layout to understand spatial memory, even spatial memory that is not based on any previous perceived layout.

Perceived Layout and Models of Intrinsic Perception

The study of perceived layout addresses questions currently being considered by researchers working on computational models of visual perception. One relevant concern is the stress on the extraction of an intrinsic representation of a scene by a computational approach (e.g., Barrow and Tannenbaum [3]). However, if changing the position of the observer changes the perceived layout of a scene, implying that perceived layout may not be independent of viewing position, then the comparison between the physical layout of a scene and its perceived layout always must take the position of the viewer into account. If so, then attempts to develop computer vision models of scene perception that are based on the intrinsic properties of the scene are doomed to failure. There may be no intrinsic layout, only a varying perceived layout depending on where the viewer stands while observing the scene.

Horizontal vs Radial Distortions in Perceived Layout

Another issue of some importance concerns the implications of the radial–horizontal differences in distance estimates. As I suggested earlier, theories in the Helmholtzian tradition, stressing the inferential basis for distance perception, might be expected to predict that radial distance is processed differently from horizontal distance. Further, a number of studies have already reported a foreshortening of far space compared to near space—an underestimation in radial distance. Since that literature did not measure the accuracy of perceiving interobject distances perpendicular to the line of sight, there is little evidence on the relative estimation errors for the two kinds of distances. Before further model building is done on this question, we need to have the data from some of the experiments described in the previous section, especially to see if the radial–horizontal differences increase or decrease when the scene is viewed from a distance, from above, or from inside, or when the scene is surrounded by a fence, and so forth.

The Role of Experience in the Development of Perceived Layout

In the previous section, I provided a list of variables that could theoretically affect the accuracy or other aspects of perceived layout. The results reported from Toye's experiment provide only a few glimpses about the potential outcome of all of the experiments that have yet to be run. At one extreme of prediction, it is possible that the perceived layout of space is relatively impervious to these variables, being an accurate representation of the physical layout of a scene under all conditions (at least until the conditions are so impoverished that all perceptual processes are impaired). If we see the arrangements of a scene correctly irrespective of how we look at it, where we stand, or what the scene contains, then this suggests that the perceptual processes underlying preceived layout are likely to be entirely prewired, and handled fairly peripherally in the visual system. Further, the relation between perceived layout and locomotion control is also likely to be prewired, peripheral, and relatively independent of development, learning, practice, attention, or intention.

In contrast, we might find that when the appropriate experiments are run, nearly all of these variables produce changes in the perceived layout of space. In this case, the arrangements of the objects among themselves, and to the ground surface would be continually varying, depending on viewing conditions, position, scene qualities, and observer characteristics. This would suggest processing mechanisms far more sensitive to practice and development, and to attention and intention: making these more likely to be learned connections located more centrally in the visual nervous system. Such mechanisms would also be expected to display large individual differences.

ACKNOWLEDGMENTS

Part of this paper is theoretical and part empirical. Most of the research reported here was carried out by Rick Toye, as part of his Ph.D. dissertation [119, 120]. Rick has also helped me with subsequent analyses reported here for the first time. I have also been assisted by Bernadette Berardi and Janusz Przeorek, both graduate students at the University of Illinois at Chicago. Partial support for the research reported here was provided by the Office of Social Science Research, and by the University Research Board, both of the University of Illinois at Chicago.

REFERENCES

1. P. Arbie and S. A. Boorman, Multidimensional scaling of measures of distance between partitions, *J. Math. Psychol.* **10**, 1973, 148–203.
2. F. Attneave, Dimensions of similarity, *Amer. J. Psychol.* **63**, 1950, 516–556.
3. H. G. Barrow and J. M. Tannenbaum, Recovering intrinsic scene characteristics from imagex, in *Computer Vision Systems*. Academic Press, New York, 1978.
4. D. R. Baum and J. Jonides, Cognitive maps: Analysis of comparative judgments of distance, *Mem. and Cognit.* **7**, 1979, 462–468.
5. J. K. Bengston, J. C. Stergios, J. L. Ward, and R. E. Jester, Optic array determinants of apparent distance and size in pictures, *J. Exp. Psychol., Human Percept. and Perform.* **6**, 1980, 751–759.
6. I. Biederman, On the semantics of a glance at a scene, in *Perceptual Organization* (M. Kubovy and J. R. Pomerantz, Eds.), pp. 213–254, Erlbaum, Hillsdale, N. J. 1981.
7. I. Biederman, Do background depth gradients facilitate object identification? *Perception* **10**, 1981, 573–578.
8. J. A. Brabyn and E. R. Strelow, Computer-analysed measures of characteristics of human locomotion and mobility, *Behav. Res. Methods and Instrum.* **9**, 1977, 456–462.
9. D. R. Bradley and D. Vido, Psychophysical functions for perceived and remembered distance, *Perception* **13**, 1984, 315–320.
10. M. Brady, *Computer Vision*, MIT Press, Cambridge, Mass, 1982; Reprinted from *Artif. Intell.* **18**, 1982.
11. M. L. Braunstein and G. J. Andersen, Velocity gradients and relative depth perception, *Percept. & Psychophys.* **29**, 1981, 145–155.
12. J. F. Brown and A. C. Voth, The path of seen movement as a function of the vector-field, *American J. Psychol.* **44**, 1937, 543–563.
13. R. W. Byrne and E. Salter, Distances and directions in the cognitive map of the blind, *Can. J. Psychol.* **37**, 1983, 293–299.
14. F. W. Campbell and L. Maffei, The tilt after-effect: A fresh look, *Vision Res.* **11**, 1971, 833–840.
15. J. D. Carrol and J. J. Chang, Analysis of individual differences in multi-dimensional scaling via an *n*-way generalization of "Eckart–Young" decomposition, *Psychometrika* **35**, 238–319.
16. J. A. Da Silva and A. Dos Santos, The effects of instructions on scales for perceived egocentric distance in a large open field, *Bull. Psychon. Soc.* **22**, 189–192.
17. J. B. Davidson, *Differences in Visual Perception: The Individual Eye*, Academic Press, New York, 1975.
18. D. Degelman and R. R. Rosinski, Motion parallax and children's distance perception, *Dev. Psychol.* **15**, 1979, 147–152.

19. E. De Renzi, *Disorders of Space Exploration and Cognition*, Wiley, New York, 1982.
20. R. F. Dillon and R. R. Schmeck, *Individual Differences in Cognition*, Academic Press, New York, 1983.
21. H. Dolezal, *Living in a World Transformed: Perceptual and Performatory Adaptation to Visual Distortion*, Academic Press, New York, 1982.
22. W. Epstein, *The Stability of Visual Perception*, Wiley, New York, 1977.
23. W. Epstein and J. Park, Examination of Gibson's psychophysical hypothesis, *Psychol. Bull.* **62**, 1964, 180–196.
24. E. S. Eriksson, Movement parallax during locomotion, *Percept. and Psychophys.* **16**, 1974, 197–200.
25. J. M. Farber and A. B. McConkie, Optical motions as information for unsigned depth, *J. Exper. Psychol., Human Percept. and Perform.* **5**, 1979, 494–500.
26. J. A. Feldman, Four frames suffice: A provisional model of vision and space, *Behav. and Brain Sci.* **8**, 1985.
27. S. H. Ferris, Motion parallax and absolute distance, *J. Exp. Psychol.* **95**, 1972, 258–263.
28. H. Fitch and M. T. Turvey, On the control of activity: Some remarks from an ecological point of view, in *Psychology of Motor Behavior and Sports* (D. Landers and R. Christina, Eds.), Human Kinetics, Urbana, 1978.
29. J. E. Foley and A. J. Cohen, Mental mapping of a megastructure, *Can. J. Psychol.* **38**, 1984, 440–453.
30. J. M. Foley, Binocular distance perception, *Psychol. Rev.* **87**, 1980, 411–434.
31. J. M. Foley and R. Held visually directed pointing as a function of target distance, direction and available cues, *Percept. and Psychophys.* **12**, 1972, 263–267.
32. E. J. Gibson, J. J. Gibson, O. W. Smith, and H. Flock, Motion parallax as a determinant of perceived depth, *J. Exp. Psychol.* **58**, 1954, 40–51.
33. J. J. Gibson, *The Perception of the Visual World*, Houghton Mifflin, Boston, 1950.
34. J. J. Gibson, On the analysis of change in the optic array, *Scand. J. Psychol.* **18**, 1977, 161–163.
35. J. J. Gibson, *The Ecological Approach to Visual Perception*, Houghton Mifflin, Boston, 1979.
36. J. J. Gibson and W. Carel, Does motion perspective independently produce the impressing of a receding surface?, *J. Exp. Psychol.* **44**, 1952, 16–18.
37. J. J. Gibson, J. Prudy, and L. Lawrence, A method for controlling stimulation for the study of space perception: The optical tunnel, *J. Exp. Psych.* **50**, 1955, 1–14.
38. A. S. Gilinsky, Perceived size and distance in visual space, *Psychol. Rev.* **58**, 1951, 460–487.
39. W. C. Gogel, *The Visual Perception of Spatial Extent*, FAA-CARI document No. 63-20, Oklahoma City, Sept. 1963.
40. W. C. Gogel, cognitive factors in spatial responses, *Psychologica* **17**, 1974, 213–225.
41. W. C. Gogel, An indirect method of measuring perceived distance from familiar size, *Percept. and Psychophys.* **20**, 1976, 419–429.
42. W. C. Gogel and P. J. McCracken, Depth adjacency and induced motion, *Percept. and Motor Skills* **48**, 1979, 343–350.
43. W. C. Gogel and H. W. Mertens, Perceived depth between familiar objects, *J. Exp. Psychol.* **77**, 1968, 206–211.
44. W. C. Gogel and J. D. Tietz, Absolute motion parallax and the specific distance tendency, *Percept. & Psychophy.* **13**, 1973, 284–292.
45. W. C. Gogel and J. D. Tietz, A comparison of oculomotor and motion parallax cues of egocentric distance, *Vision Res.* **19**, 1979, 1161–1170.
46. F. E. Goodson, T. Q. Snider, and J. E. Swearingen, Motion parallax in the perception of movement by a moving subject, *Bull. Psychon. Soc.* **6**, 1980, 87–88.
47. C. H. Graham, K. G. Baker, M. Hecht and V. V. Lloyd, Factors influencing thresholds for monocular movement parallax, *J. Exp. Psychol.* **38**, 1948, 205–222.
48. W. L. Gulick and R. B. Lawson, *Human Stereopsis*, Oxford, New York, 1976.
49. J. Gyr, R. Willey, and A. Henry, Motor-sensory feedback and geometry of visual space: An attempted replication, *Behav. and Brain Sci.* **2**, 1979, 59–94.
50. R. N. Haber, Visual perception *Annu. Rev. Psychol.* **29**, 1978, 31–59.
51. R. N. Haber, Perceiving the layout of space in pictures: A perspective theory based on Leonardo da Vinci, in *Perception and Pictorial Representation* (C. F. Nodine and D. F. Fisher, Eds.), pp. 84–99, Praeger, New York, 1979.
52. R. N. Haber, When is sensory-motion information necessary, when only useful, and when superfluous? *Behav. and Brain Sci.* **2**, 1979, 68–70.

53. R. N. Haber, How we perceive depth from flat pictures, *Amer. Sci.* **68**, 1980, 370–380.

54. R. N. Haber, Perceiving space from pictures: A Theoretical analysis, in *The Perception of Pictures: Volume I, Alberti's Window* (M. A. Hagen, Ed.), pp. 3–31, Academic Press, New York, 1980.

55. R. N. Haber, The power of visual perceiving, *J. Ment. Imagery* **5**, 1981, 1–40.

56. R. N. Haber, Stimulus information and processing mechanisms in visual space perception, in *Machine and Human Visual Perception* (J. Beck, B. Hope, and A. Rosenfeld, Eds.), pp. 157–236, Academic Press, New York, 1983.

57. R. H. Haber, The control of mobility by perceived spatial layout: Application from sighted to blind travelers, in *Visual Prothetic Devices for the Blind* (E. R. Strewlow and D. Warren, Eds.), Nijhoff, Amsterdam, 1985.

58. M. A. Hagen and M. Teghtsoonian, The effects of binocular and motion-generated infromation on the perception of depth and height, *Percept. and Psychophys.* **30**, 1981, 257–265.

59. A. Hein and M. Jeannerod, *Spatially Oriented Behavior*, Springer-Verlag, New York, 1983.

60. W. Hell, Movement parallax: An asymptotic function of amplitude and velocity of head movement, *Vision Res.* **18**, 1978, 629–635.

61. W. Hell and R. B. Freeman, Detectability of motion as a factor in depth preception by monocular movement parallax, *Percept. and Psychophys.* **22**, 1977, 526–530.

62. R. Held, H. W. Leibowitz, and H.-L. Teuber (Eds.), *Handbook of Sensory Physiology: Vol. VIII, Perception*, Springer-Verlag, Heidelberg, 1978.

63. J. Hochberg, *Perception*, 2nd ed. Prentice–Hall, Englewood Cliffs, N. J., 1978.

64. J. Hochberg, Pictorial limitations on perception, in *Perception and Pictorial Representation* (C. F. Nodine and D. F. Fisher, Eds.), pp. 313–350, Praeger, New York, 1979.

65. J. Hochberg and V. Brooks, The perception of motion pictures, in *Handbook of Perception: Vol. X, Perceptual Ecology* (E. C. Carterette and M. P. Friedman, Eds.), pp. 259–306, Academic Press, New York, 1978.

66. J. Hochberg and P. Fallon, Perceptual analysis of moving patterns, *Science (Washington, D. C.)* **194**, 1976, 1081–1083.

67. J. Hochberg and L. Gellman, Feature saliency, "mental rotation" times and the integration of successive views, *Mem. and Cognit.* **5**, 1977, 23–26.

68. H. W. Hock and M. Sullivan, Alternative spatial reference systems: Intentional vs. incidental learning, *Percept. and Psychophys.* **29**, 1981, 467–474.

69. I. P. Howard, *Human Visual Orientation*, Wiley, New York, 1982.

70. T. Indow, Application of multidimensional scaling in perception, in *Handbook of Perception: Vol. II, Psychological Judgment and Measurement* (E. C. Carterette and M. P. Friedman, Eds.), Academic Press, New York, 1974.

71. D. E. Irwin, S. Yantis, and J. Jonides, Evidence against visual integration across saccadic eye movements, *Percept. and Psychophys.* **34**, 1983, 49–57.

72. W. H. Ittelson, Environmental perception and comtemporary perceptual theory, in *Environment and Cognition* (W. H. Ittelson, Ed.), Seminar, New York, 1973.

73. W. H. Ittelson, Environmental perception and urban experience, *Environ. and Behav.* **10**, 1978, 193–213.

74. G. Johansson, Studies on the visual perception of locomotion, *Perception* **6**, 1977, 365–376.

75. R. K. Jones and D. N. Lee, Why two eyes are better than one: The two views of binocular vision, *J. Exp. Psychol., Human Percept. and Perform.* **7**, 1981, 30–40.

76. R. Klein, Stereopsis and the representation of space, *Perception* **6**, 1977, 327–332.

77. J. J. Koenderlink and A. J. Van Doorn, Local structure of motion parallax of a plane, *J. Opt. Soc. Amer.* **66**, 1976, 717–723.

78. S. M. Kosslyn, H. L. Pick, and G. R. Fariello, Cognitive maps in children and men, *Child Dev.* **45**, 1974, 707–716.

79. S. M. Krest and J. H. Howard, Memory psychophysics for visual area and length, *Mem. and Cognit.* **6**, 1978, 327–335.

80. J. B. Kruskal, Multidimensional scaling by optimizing goodness of fit to a nonmetric hypothesis, *Psychometrika* **29**, 1964, 1–27.

81. J. B. Kruskal, Nonmetric multidimensional scaling: a numerical method *Psychometrika* **29**, 1964, 115–129.

82. J. B. Kruskal, F. W. Young, and J. B. Seery, *KYST*, Bell Telephone Laboratories, Murray Hill, N. J. 1973.

83. R. W. Kulhavy, N. H. Schwartz, and S. H. Shaha, Spatial representation of maps, *Amer. J. Psychol.* **96**, 1983, 337–351.
84. J. M. Kunnapas, Scales for subjective distance, *Scand. J. Psychol.* **1**, 1960, 187–192.
85. D. N. Lee and R. Lishman, Visual control of locomotion, *Scand. J. Psychol.* **18**, 1977, 224–230.
86. D. N. Lee, J. R. Lishman, and J. A. Thomson, Regulation of gait in long jumping, *J. Exp. Psychol., Human Percept. and Perform.* **8**, 1982, 448–459.
87. M. Levine, L. N. Jankovic, and M. Palij, Principles of spatial problem solving, *J. Exp. Psychol., General* **111**, 1982, 157–175.
88. M. S. Lewis, Determinants of visual attention in real-world scenes, *Percept. Motor Skills* **41**, 1975, 411–416.
89. L. S. Liben, A. H. Patterson, and N. Newcombe, *Spatial Representation and Behavior Across the Life Space: Theory and Application* Academic Press, New York, 1981.
90. E. A. Lumsden, Perception of radial distance as a function of magnification and truncation of depicted spatial layout, *Percept. and Psychophys.* **33**, 1983, 177–182.
91. L. Marks, *Sensory Processes: The New Psychophysics*, Academic Press, New York, 1974.
92. D. C. Marr, *Vision*, Freeman, San Franscisco, 1982.
93. L. Matin, Saccades and extra-retinal signals for visual direction, in *Eye Movements and Psychological Processes* (R. A. Monty and J. W. Senders, Eds.), pp. 205–220, Erlbaum, Hillsdale, N. J., 1976.
94. C. F. Michaels and C. Carello, *Direct Perception*, Prentice–Hall, Englewood Cliffs, N. J. 1981.
95. R. S. Moyer, P. Sklarew, and J. Whiting, Memory psychophsics, in *Psychophysical Judgment and the Process of Perception* (H. G. Geissler and P. Petzold, Eds.) pp. 35–46, VEB, Berlin, 1982.
96. K. Nakayama and J. M. Loomis, Optical patterns, velocity-sensitive neurons, and space perception: A hypothesis, *Perception* **3**, 1974, 63–80.
97. U. Neisser, *Perceptual Reality*, Freeman, San Francisco, 1976.
98. D. R. Olsen and E. Bialystok, *Spatial Cognition: The Structure and Development of Mental Representations of Spatial Relations*, Erlbaum, Hillsdale, N. J., 1983.
98a. M. Palij, M. Levine, and T. Kahan, The orientation of cognitive maps, *Bull. Psychon. Soc.* **22**, 1984, 105–108.
99. H. L. Pick, Jr. and L. P. Acredolo, *Spatial Orientation: Theory, Research and Application*, Plenum, New York, 1983.
100. M. Potegal (Ed.), *Spatial Abilities: Development and Physiological Foundation*, Academic Press, New York, 1982.
101. K. Rayner and A. Pollatsek, Is visual information integrated across saccades?, *Percept. and Psychophys.* **34**, 1983, 39–48.
102. I. Rock, On unconscious inference, in *The Stability of Visual Perception* (W. Epstein, Ed.), pp. 313–330, Wiley, New York, 1977.
103. S. Runeson, On the possibility of "smart" perceptual mechanisms, *Scand. J. Psychol.* **18**, 1977, 172–179.
104. W. L. Shebilske, C. M. Karmiohl, and D. R. Proffitt, Induced esophoric shifts in eye convergence and illusory distance in reduced and structured viewing conditions, *J. Exp. Psychol., Human Percept. and Perform.* **9**, 1983, 270–277.
105. W. L. Shebilske and D. R. Proffitt, The priority of perceived distance for perceiving motion has not been demonstrated: Critical comments on Gogel's "The sensing of retinal motion." *Percept. and Psychophys.* **29**, 1981, 170–172.
106. W. L. Shebilske, D. R. Proffitt, and S. K. Fisher, Efferent factors in natural events can be rationalized and verified: A reply to Turvey and Solomon, *J. Exp. Psychol., Human Percept. and Perform.* **10**, 1984, 455–460.
107. R. N. Shepard, The analysis of proximities: Multidimensional scaling with an unknown distance function, I, *Psychometrika* **27**, 1962, 125–140; II, *Psychometrika* **27**, 1962, 219–246.
108. R. N. Shepard, Attention and the metric structure of the stimulus space, *J. Math. Psychol.* **1**, 1964, 54–87.
109. F. A. Singer, Z. E. Tyer, and R. Tasnak, Assumed distance as a determinant of apparent size, *Bull. Psychon. Soc.* **19**, 1982, 267–268.
110. K. A. Stevens, Surface tilt (the direction of slant): A neglected psychophysical variable, *Percept. and Psychophys.* **33**, 1983, 241–250.
111. S. S. Stevens, *Handbook of Experimental Psychology*, Wiley, New York, 1951.
112. S. S. Stevens, Perceptual magnitude and its measurement, in *Handbook of Perception: Vol. II.*

Psychophysical Judgment and Measurement (E. C. Carterette and M. P. Friedman, Eds.), pp. 361–390, Academic Press, New York, 1974.

113. E. R. Strelow, What is needed for a theory of mobility: Direct perception and cognitive maps; some lessons from the blind, *Psychol. Bull.* **97**, 1985.

114. E. R. Strelow and J. A. Brabyn, Use of foreground and background information in visually guided locomotion, *Perception* **10**, 1982, 191–198.

115. R. Teghtsoonian and M. Teghtsoonian, Range and regression effects in magnitude scaling, *Percept. and Psychophys.* **24**, 1978, 305–314.

116. P. W. Thorndyke, Distance estimation from cognitive maps, *Cognit. Psychol.* **13**, 1981, 526–550.

117. P. W. Thorndyke and B. Hayes-Roth, Differences in spatial knowledge acquired from maps and navigation, *Cognit. Psychol.* **14**, 1982, 560–589.

118. J. T. Todd, Visual information about moving objects, *J. Exp. Psychol., Human Percept. and Perform.* **7**, 1981, 795–810.

119. R. Toye, Judging the locations of objects in space: Do we really know where things are, unpublished Ph.D. dissertation, University of Illinois at Chicago, 1984.

120. R. Toye, The effects of viewing position on the perceived layout of space, submitted for publication.

121. M. T. Turvey, Contrasting orientations to a theory of visual information processing, *Psychol. Rev.* **84**, 1977, 67–88.

122. M. T. Turvey, The thesis of the efference-mediation of vision cannot be rationalized, *Behav. and Brain Sci.* **2**, 1979, 81.

123. M. T. Turvey and J. Solomon, Visually perceiving distance: A comment on Shebilske, Karmiohl, and Proffitt (1983), *J. Exp. Psychol., Human Percept. and Perform.* **10**, 1984, 449–454.

124. B. Tversky, Distortions in memory for maps, *Cognit. Psychol.* **13**, 1981, 407–433.

125. B. Tversky and K. Hemenway, Catagories of environmental scenes, *Cognit. Psychol.* **15**, 1983, 121–149.

126. Z. E. Tyer, J. A. Allen, and R. Pasnak, Instruction effects on size and distance judgments, *Percept. and Psychophys.* **34**, 1983, 135–139.

127. H. C. van der Meer, Interrelation of the effects of binocular disparity and perspective dues on judgments of depth and height, *Percept. and Psychophys.* **26**, 1979, 481–488.

128. R. T. Verrillo, Stability of line-length estimates using the method of absolute magnitude estimation, *Percept. and Psychophys.* **33**, 1983, 261–265.

129. L. M. Ward and J. A. Russell, The psychological representation of molar physical environments, *J. Exp. Psychol., General* **110**, 1981, 121–152.

130. W. H. Warren, Perceiving affordances: visual guidance of stair climbing, *J. Exp. Psychol., Human Percept. and Perform.* **10**, 1984, 683–713.

131. D. G. Wheeler and I. Rock, What is the role of motion parallax in perception?, presented at the Psychonomics Society Convention, November 1982.

Generative Systems of Analyzers

Michael Leyton

*Department of Psychology and Social Relations, Harvard University,
Cambridge, Massachusetts 02138*

Received March 7, 1985

It is argued that human visual analyzers are organized into generative systems and that these systems are decomposed into nested structures of control. Any such system is structured as a transformation group G and the nested analyzer hierarchy can be expressed by an algebraic decomposition $G_1.G_2.\ \ldots\ .G_n$ of that group. The paper shows how several important aspects of this analyzer architecture determine several important aspects of any perceptual organization. For example, there is a division of the analyzer hierarchy into two sub-hierarchies, one encoding the stimulus set as generated via a sequence of successively modified prototypes, and the other encoding the stimulus set as generated internally from a subset. The structure of the latter analyzer sub-hierarchy is responsible for the encoding of grouping in the stimulus set. Principles are proposed that determine the way these two analyzer sub-hierarchies are wired together: symmetry axis analyzers of the grouping sub-hierarchy are wired as encoding lines of flexibility in the sub-hierarchy describing the percept as deformed via a sequence of prototypes. In addition, it is found that one particular example of such a combined structure is significantly salient across many perceptual organizational situations. Several aspects of its architecture are examined, and it is found to provide us with a detailed theory of the perceptual encoding of highly complex shape. © 1985 Academic Press, Inc.

1. INTRODUCTION

In this paper, an attempt is made to infer structural aspects of human visual analyzer-systems from perceptual organizational data. The two main proposals of the paper are:

(1) *Perceptual analyzers are structured into* **generative systems**.

(2) *These generative systems are decomposed into* **nested structures of control**.

The method of argumentation will be to consider a number of perceptual-organizational phenomena that are currently of great concern—Gestalt grouping, the orientation and form phenomenon, relative motion perception, the organization of complex shape—and show that a single highly constrained form of analyzer structure will explain these wide-ranging examples.

2. AN EXAMPLE

One of the goals of this paper will be to describe an analyzer architecture that can deal with complex natural and abstract shapes such as those shown in Fig. 1. Before we can do that, a number of theoretical principles will need to be developed. Thus we shall, for some time, be handling simple shapes. However, the reader should bear in mind that, when we later put the theoretical principles together, we will have a system that will provide an analysis of the complex shapes shown.

Let us begin by working through a simple example. In a convergent series of experiments reported in Leyton ([14], see also [15, 17]), I found that, when subjects are presented with a rotated parallelogram, illustrated in Fig. 2a, they reference it to

149

FIG. 1.   The complex natural and abstract shapes used in Experiment 13 [14].

a non-rotated one (Fig. 2b), which they reference to a rectangle (Fig. 2c), which they reference to a square (Fig. 2d).

To explain this successive reference phenomenon, I argued [15] first the following: The cognitive system has a reference frame of shapes which is structured by a particular transformation group called $SL_2 R$. In mathematics, a transformation group is a system of transformations which obey the following conditions that hold also for numbers; and will thus be illustrated here using numbers:

(1) *Closure.* Given any pair of numbers n and m, there is always another number q that is the multiple of n and m.

(2) *Associativity.* The bracketing of multiplication can be in either of two ways:

$$(2 \times 3) \times 5 = 30 = 2 \times (3 \times 5).$$

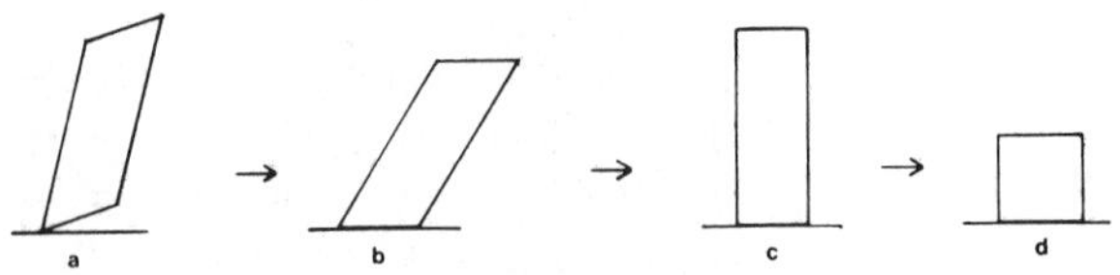

FIG. 2.   The successive shape sequence found in [14].

(3) *Identity element*. There exists an element with no multiplicative effect. For numbers, it is 1; for example,

$$5 \times 1 = 5 = 1 \times 5.$$

(4) *Inverse*. There is always a multiplicative inverse; for example,

$$5 \times \tfrac{1}{5} = 1 = \tfrac{1}{5} \times 1.$$

In a transformation group, one replaces (a) numbers by transformations and (b) multiplication of numbers by combination of transformations. Corresponding to the above four conditions one has the following: (1) The combination of any pair of transformations leads to another transformation, also in the system; (2) the transformations can be bracketed as shown above; (3) there is a transformation e called the identity element that has no effect; (4) for each transformation T there is an inverse transformation—one that reverses the effect of T. (A highly readable introduction to group theory is [10].)

Let us now consider the group SL_2R. This is a group of transformations with the following properties: (1) The transformations act on the plane; (2) they are linear; that is, straight subspaces of the plane (e.g., lines) are sent to straight subspaces; and (3) the transformations preserve area.

Another important property is that SL_2R splits into three subgroups. (Subgroups are subsystems that are also transformation groups.) The three subgroups are shown in Fig. 3, where they are illustrated by their effects on the square placed at the top of the figure. The three subgroups are described as follows:

(1) A, the group of *pure deformations*. These stretch and contract objects along the x and y axes (Fig. 3a).

(2) N, the group of *shears*. These tilt a pair of opposite sides of a square (Fig. 3b).

(3) SO_2, the group of *rotations* of the plane (Fig. 3c).

Any member of the entire group can be written as the product of a pure deformation a, a shear n, and a rotation r. That is, the group decomposes in this

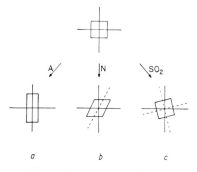

FIG. 3.   Three subgroups of $SL_2 R$.

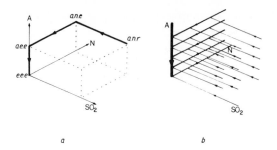

FIG. 4.   Successive reference in $SL_2 R$: (a) a single trajectory; (b) the set of trajectories.

way:

$$SL_2 R = A.N.SO_2$$

and any member g of $SL_2 R$ can be written

$$g = a.n.r.$$

The three subgroups can each be given by a single parameter as follows: (1) For A it is ratio of horizontal to vertical stretches; (2) for N it is angle of shear; and (3) for SO_2 it is angle of rotation.[1] This definition, in terms of three parameters, allows $SL_2 R$ to be represented by a 3-dimensional space as shown in Fig. 4a.

Now let us return to the experimental results summarized in Fig 2. The first stimulus (Fig. 2a) has rotation, shear, and pure deformation; so one can represent it by some point $a.n.r$ shown in the 3-dimensional space in Fig. 4a. Note that, for this first stimulus, neither a, n, nor r is an identity element e of its own subgroup. The reference from the first stimulus (Fig. 2a) to the second (Fig. 2b) removes rotation. This can be represented in Fig. 4a by moving down the bold trajectory from $a.n.r$ to the point $a.n.e$ which represents the second stimulus. That is, the second point is at the identity element e of SO_2 (rotation). One has removed the dimension labeled by SO_2; that is, the point $a.n.e$ has zero value on the SO_2 axis. The reader can easily check that the remainder of the bold trajectory in Fig. 4a represents the remainder of the successive shape reference in Fig. 2; i.e., one then removes the N (shear) dimension obtaining the rectangle at point $a.e.e$ in the space; and finally one removes the A (stretch) dimension obtaining the square the origin $e.e.e$.

Observe that, in terms of the product,

$$SL_2 R = A.N.SO_2$$

one is algebraically factorizing the SO_2-subgroup (rotation), then the N-subgroup (shear), and then the A-subgroup (stretch).

Two questions concern us now: (1) Why did the subjects choose a decomposition? For example, why did they not move directly from $a.n.r$ to the origin $e.e.e$? (2)

---

[1] In fact, I will take $SL_2 R$ to stand for any 3-parameter group, where the parameters are those just defined. The restriction of area preservation need not be complied with, although some pilot results indicate that it might have been the intention of subjects to preserve area.

Why did they choose a particular ordering on the decomposition? The answers to these questions are given by further experiments in Leyton [14; see also 17]: It was found that the subjects were successively *stabilizing* the initial percept by removing the properties of the percept in order of increasing stability; the orientation value being the most unstable, the shear value being the next most unstable, and the pure deformation value being the most stable. (Stability was taken to be observer defined persistence.)

Thus it is argued in Leyton [14, 15, 17, 18] that the reference process itself is that of going to successively more stable percepts. Another way of saying this is, that subjects stratify the properties defined by SL_2R into levels of stability and reference by removing those levels in order of increasing stability.

Up to now our considerations have been purely perceptual. However, let us now turn our attention to analyzer structure. In fact, let us see how the above successive reference sequence can be encoded by an analyzer system. What we will do is to pull the SL_2R space apart in a specific way that accords with the trajectories—and assign the parts to different analyzer systems. To see how to do this, let us return to Fig. 4a. The set of all possible trajectories of the form $a.n.r \rightarrow a.n.e \rightarrow a.e.e \rightarrow e.e.e$, shown in Fig. 4a, are represented in Fig. 4b. That is, one first travels down one of the faint lines parallel to the SO_2 axis, until one hits the $A.N$ plane; one then travels down one of the slightly bolder lines parallel to N until one hits A and one finally travels down A.

This causes the entire space to be partitioned in a certain way: For each *point* on A there is a *trajectory* through it parallel to N. If one now looks at only a *point* on the latter trajectory, one sees that the point determines a whole *trajectory* parallel to SO_2. The reverse is not the case.

As we shall see this means that, under the described reference, SL_2R can be partitioned into lines such that each line is represented by an analyzer array in the hierarchy shown in Fig. 5. Observe that the considerations of the previous paragraph translate into the following: A *single analyzer* on level A corresponds to an *entire array N* on the level below. Again, a *single analyzer* in one of the arrays N corresponds to an *entire array SO_2* on the level below. We shall say that each analyzer *covers* the array below it.

Now observe that each of the analyzers on the lowest level represents a single point in SL_2R, by a process I will call *collecting coordinates*: Consider the analyzer marked r in the *right-most SO_2*-system (lowest level). Its SO_2 coordinate is r. However, it is covered by analyzer n on the level above it, and by analyzer a on the level above that. Thus it has coordinates $a.n.r$ in SL_2R. This means that it corresponds to the stimulus, a rotated parallelogram, shown below that r-analyzer. We shall say that the three analyzers *encode* that stimulus.

Now observe that the non-rotated parallelogram is the last but one stimulus in the bottom row of stimuli in Fig. 5. It is encoded by analyzer e (no rotation) in the lowest system; by analyzer n (non-trivial shear) in the next higher system; and finally by analyzer a (non-trivial stretch) in the system at the top. This is in accord with Fig. 4a. The reader can check the corresponding facts to hold in Fig. 5 for the rectangle (fifth stimulus along from the left in Fig. 5), and for the square (first stimulus on the left).

Observe now that the reference sequence corresponds to an apparently irregular sequence of shapes on the lowest level of this diagram. The sequence is: stimulus

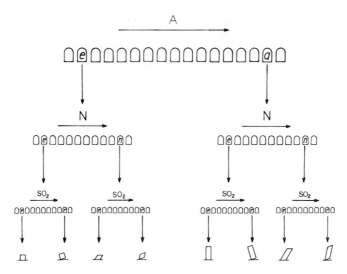

FIG. 5.   The analyzer partition of SL_2R in accord with the trajectories in Fig. 4b.

$8 \rightarrow 7 \rightarrow 5 \rightarrow 1$. The regularity, in fact, lies elsewhere. Figure 6 shows what the successive reference means in terms of the analyzer structure. Given any array, one moves leftward to the identity element, then upward to the covering analyzer, then leftward to the identity element, then upward, etc.; repeating these two operations in turn until one reaches the top level.

It is important to observe two crucial features of the system diagramed in Fig. 5: The hierarchy corresponds to the stability stratification prescribed by the subjects; that is, higher levels are more stable than lower levels. Second, the higher levels act as control levels with respect to lower levels. The term *control*, used about a level, is

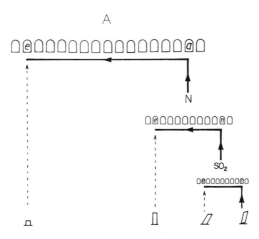

FIG. 6.   Successive reference in the SL_2R analyzer system.

employed here not only in the sense that an analyzer on that level *selects* one of the systems on the next lower level, but in the sense that the control level maps lower level systems onto each other; thus encoding *generativity* between levels. For example, on the top level of Fig. 5, by moving from analyzer e to a, one establishes a correspondence between analyzers in the left-hand N-system and analyzers in the right-hand N-system. For example, analyzers marked e and n in the left-hand system correspond to those marked e and n in the right-hand system. More precisely, by collecting coordinates for these analyzers, the correspondence sends $e.e$ and $e.n$ to $a.e$ and $a.n$.

Thus there is a crucial relationship embodied in the analyzer system: *the stability hierarchy corresponds to the control hierarchy*. The associated stratification of the group G will be denoted

$$G = G_1.G_2. \ldots .G_n,$$

where a G_i nearer the beginning of the sequence represents a perceptual property of a higher stability ranking, or an analyzer system of a higher control level. An example of a sequence $G = G_1.G_2. \ldots .G_n$, is the sequence $SL_2R = A.N.SO_2$. The correspondence of stability stratification and control stratification is discussed at greater length in Leyton [14, 15, 17], where I propose a Principle of Nested Control: Given an asymmetric sequential reference structure $G_1.G_2. \ldots .G_n$, determined by a stability stratification, higher stability levels are cognized as controlling lower levels.

Again, observe that a stability ranking is defined also along the analyzer arrays: stability increases as one moves along the array toward the identity analyzer. Thus combining the between-level and within-level stability ranking, one finds that the analyzer path shown in Fig. 6 decreases instability along each limb of the path. This correspondence of stability and control can be partially understood in this way. Given a stimulus set S, we shall let the map

$$D: G \rightarrow S$$

denote the encoding of S by an analyzer system structured by the group G. The encoding D is a map in the strict mathematical sense of being an assignment to each member of G a member of S. What we shall argue is that the algebraic structure $G_1.G_2. \ldots .G_n$ of G transfers, via D, into a perceptual organization of S. This will be because the algebraic structure determines the structure of the encoding system.

One further point should be made here: It will be assumed that each analyzer system forms a complete group G. Thus it might be the case that some of the analyzers in G are not instantiated in S. The consequence is that the stimuli will be perceived as incomplete; as when a side is missing from an octagon. Thus, more strictly, we will say that the encoding is of the form

$$D: G \rightarrow S \cup \{\text{OFF}\}$$

where some of G can be assigned to the OFF state. Note that this is just a simple example of the way in which the algebraic structure of the analyzer system results in a perceptual phenomenon; i.e., Gestalt closure (see Leyton [13, 16] for further discussion on closure).

3.1. Generation and Reference

The analyzer system shown in Fig. 5 provides an organization of referential relations between the shapes shown along the bottom of the figure. Reference in *any* part of the analyzer system takes the form which was illustrated in Fig. 6 for the particular case of the right-most stimulus. Thus the encoding of that set of shapes by the analyzer system can be regarded as the imposition of a *reference frame* on those shapes. In this paper, I will attempt to argue that quite a variety of perceptual reference-frame phenomena result from an encoding by an analyzer system of this form.

Observe now that, in a system such as that shown in Fig. 6, the term *reference* takes on a highly specific meaning: it is the reversal of an operation that was applied to some starting state *e*. For example, in the described system, a rectangle is *referred* to a square because a rectangle is encoded as generated by applying a stretch operation to a square. Thus a reference sequence is understood here as the reversal of a sequence of generating operations. Therefore, reversing the reference directions, upward and leftward to identity elements, creates a structure of generation downward and to the right. It is for this reason that I will call the analyzer structure to be discussed, a *generative system of analyzers*. In fact, the concept of control considered earlier belongs to the generative direction rather than the reference direction. Thus we shall speak of the analyzer structure as forming a generative system organized into a nested structure of control. Any such structure will be represented algebraically as a product $G_1.G_2. \ldots .G_n$, where it will be understood that going from left to right in this sequence corresponds to descending through the analyzer hierarchy. A central claim to be made is that particular properties of the algebraic structure correspond to perceptually significant aspects of the analyzer structure.

3.2. External and Internal Generation

Let us now consider the concept of generation in greater detail. The first theoretical notion we require is to distinguish between two forms of generation:

DEFINITION 1.   The **external generation** of a set S is the application of a sequence of operations $g_1, g_2, \ldots, g_n$ to some set S_0 such that the outcome of the final operation is S; that is,

$$S = g_n.g_{n-1}. \ldots .g_1(S_0).$$

For example, the above discussion implies that, cognitively, a rotated parallelogram is generated by applying a sequence $a.n.r$ to a square.

However, a different type of generation process is that of generating a square from one side S_0. This time the starting set S_0 (a side) is a *proper subset* of the final set S (a square). Let us see if Definition 1 works for this type of generation. Let r_{90}, r_{180}, r_{270} be a sequence of 90° rotations applied to the initial side. However, a rotated side is only some other side and so the final operation yields only a side.

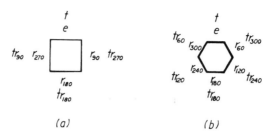

FIG. 7. The internal analyzer encoding of (a) a square, (b) a hexagon.

That is, $g_n \cdot g_{n-1} \cdot \ldots \cdot g_1(S_0)$ is only a side. So Definition 1 does not apply. To obtain the entire square, one has to collect, into one set, all the sides yielded by all the preceding generation strings in the sequence. These preceding sequences will be called *initial subsequences*, or simply *i-subsequences*. Thus we have

DEFINITION 2. The **internal generation** of a set S, by the operations $g_1, g_2, \ldots, g_n$, is the union of the application of all *i*-subsequences to some set S_0; that is,

$$S = \bigcup_{j=1}^{j=n} \left\{ g_j \cdot g_{j-1} \cdot \ldots \cdot g_1(S_0) \right\}.$$

We have considered $SL_2R = A.N.SO_2$ as the external generative structure of a sequence. Now let us consider the square's internal generative structure. First, observe that the square can be internally generated from a side using the following group of eight transformations:

$$D_4 = \left\{ e, r_{90}, r_{180}, r_{270}, t, tr_{90}, tr_{180}, tr_{270} \right\}.$$

The operations are: e the identity element; r_θ rotation by $\theta°$; t reflection about the vertical axis bisecting the top and bottom sides; and tr_θ which is reflection about one of the non-vertical axes. If one were to take the starting side to be the top side, then an analyzer system structured by D_4 would encode the square as shown in Fig. 7a. That is, Fig. 7a shows how the individual analyzers e, r_{90}, r_{180}, r_{270}, t, tr_{90}, tr_{180}, and tr_{270} are assigned to the individual sides. A corresponding diagram, Fig. 7b, holds for a hexagon. Note that these examples, simple as they are, will be generalized later to handle highly complex shapes.

However, another organization aspect has not yet been accounted for. This is the internal organization of a single side. In Leyton [14, Experiment 6] subjects were given pairs of polygons as shown in Fig. 8a with two dots, one each on a common side. They were asked which of these two marked positions was the referent with respect to which the other position was judged. The statistically significant answer was the center. Thus, taking reference as the reversal of a transformation, the implication is that there is a generative description of a side in which each point is

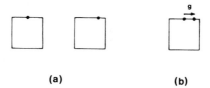

(a)   **(b)**

FIG. 8. (a) An example of the comparison pairs used in [14, Experiment 6]. (b) The implied reference on a side.

obtained by some translation g from the central point as illustrated in Fig. 8b.[2] Under the view we are developing, this implies that each side is encoded by a generative analyzer system that has the structure of R, the group of translations along a line. The central point on the side receives the analyzer e and each other point receives some translation analyzer g. The generative encoding is thus of the form $R \to S \cup \{\text{OFF}\}$, which reads: analyzers in R encode the points on the side S. Hence the points are encoded as translations. Note that the encoding will send all analyzers that are beyond the end of the side to the state OFF.

To summarize: we have two generative encodings, one by a D_4-analyzer system, generating the four sides from one side, and the other by a R-analyzer system generating a side from a point.

The important thing now to observe is that the two systems form a control hierarchy. This is due to the simple fact that, as was demonstrated in Leyton [14, Experiment 7; see also 17] the members of D_4 take the generative structure of one side and map it onto the generative structure of each other side: subjects were asked to correspond points on adjacent sides of regular polygons; the correspondence in each case turned out to be a rotation or reflection.

Figure 9 shows what is going on here in terms of the analyzer systems. The lower analyzer level in the diagram has two R-systems: One encodes the stimuli on one side (called side 1, below the left-hand R-system in Fig. 9), and the other encodes the stimuli on another side (called side 2, below the right-hand R-system). In the left-hand R-system, two analyzers have been distinguished, e_2 and g, which encode two stimuli x_1 and x_2, below on side 1. On the highest level, the D_4-system takes these two analyzers and corresponds them to the analyzers e_2 and g in the right-hand R-system. The latter two analyzers encode the two points x_3 and x_4, respectively. Now, by our method of collecting coordinates (Sect. 2), we take any stimulus on any side, and follow the arrows upward, picking up coordinates as we go. These coordinates give the generative description of that stimulus. Thus, for example, the point x_2 on side 1, has coordinates g on the R-level, and e_1 on the D_4-level. Note that because the control hierarchy is given by the ordered sequence $D_4 . R$ (because D_4 is on the higher control level), the coordinates will be written in the order (e_1, g). Similarly, by checking the diagram, we see that the point x_4 in side 2 (bottom right of Fig. 9) has coordinates g on the R-level, and r on the D_4-level, thus yielding the coordinate pair (r, g).

---

[2] Leyton [17] argues that there can be two other generative descriptions of a side, each taking a side end-point as a referent. The set of such descriptions forms a generative class on the same group R. Above we are considering only one member of the class.

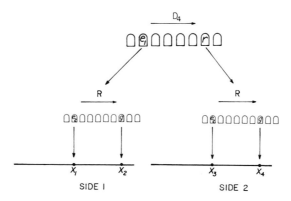

FIG. 9. The analyzer hierarchy $D_4 . R$.

Figure 10 shows the *perceptual-organizational* consequence of the encoding by the above system of analyzers. The four points we have discussed are the four points shown on the square in Fig. 10. The reader can easily check that the coordinates given in Fig. 10 correspond to the coordinates in the analyzer system depicted in Fig. 9. Observe that the large arrow r, in Fig. 10, is the D_4-rotation that takes a translation g on one side and maps it onto the translation g on the other. This map is the analyzer r on the upper level in Fig. 9; it takes the lower level analyzer systems and maps them to each other. Thus, we see that the perceptual organization of the square is literally the organization of the analyzer system. The reader familiar with group theory will also realize that the structure of both the analyzer system and the perceptual organization is the Cayley graph of D_4.

3.3. The Structure Postulate

In order to account for perceptual data, the previous section proposed two analyzer systems for the perceptual organization of a square (1) a system $SL_2 R = A.N.SO_2$ which encodes the square as part of an external space of generation, and (2) a system $D_4.R$ which encodes the square as internally generated from a single point.

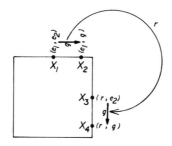

FIG. 10. The structuring effect of the hierarchy illustrated in Fig. 9.

The reader might as first think that these two types of systems can be defined only for simple shapes like a square. However, it is the central aim of this paper to show that analyzer structures of exactly the above algebraic type provide a rich perceptual analysis of complex natural and abstract shapes such as these shown in Fig. 1. To be precise, the following will be the main proposal of the paper:

STRUCTURE POSTULATE.

(1) *A perceptual organization is given by an encoding of a stimulus set S by two generative analyzer systems*:
  (i) *one structured by a group G_E which has an algebraic decomposition $G_{E_1}.G_{E_2}. \ldots .G_{E_n}$ encoding S within an external generative sequence,*
  (ii) *the other structured by a group G_1 which has an algebraic decomposition $G_{I_1}.G_{I_2}. \ldots .G_{I_m}$ encoding S within an internal generative sequence.*

(2) *In both cases, the algebraic decomposition has two correlates*:
  The Analyzer Correlate. *The algebraic decomposition corresponds to the structuring of the analyzer system into a control hierarchy.*
  The Perceptual Correlate. *The algebraic decomposition corresponds to the perceptual stratification of S into stability levels.*

(3) *G_E and G_I are wired together in accord with two interconnection principles.*

Part (3) of the postulate proposes an *interconnection* between the external and internal analyzer systems. The two principles determining this interconnection will be deduced later. It will be these principles that will allow us to provide an analysis of complex shape.

4. THE STRUCTURE OF GROUPING

The Gestalt psychologists (e.g., Wertheimer [24]) made the following profound discovery: At the lowest levels of processing, the organism receives a collection of stimuli which can be grouped in an almost infinite number of ways. Different groupings will lead to different percepts. Thus perception depends crucially on grouping.

Although the Gestalt school discovered several important criteria which the perceptual system uses in its choice of grouping, a fundamental problem has remained unsolved: No one has proposed *substantively* what a grouping is. In this section, two substantive proposals will be offered and shown to be equivalent. The first is very simple to understand but does not reveal much about the structure of grouping. The second is more complicated but reveals a profound relationship between the phenomenon of grouping and control. The first is this:

PROPOSAL 3.   *Any stimulus set encoded by a single analyzer becomes psychologically a grouping.*

To illustrate this proposal consider first a square. Psychologically, the groupings or parts (i.e., subgroupings) of a square are its points, its sides, and the whole. Let us look again at Fig. 9. Proposal 3 says that if one selects an analyzer one will obtain a grouping. If the selection is from any one of the *R*-systems (e.g., the analyzer *g* in the left-hand *R*-system) one finds that it encodes a point. Now if one selects any analyzer on the D_4-level one finds that it covers an entire *R*-system which, of course,

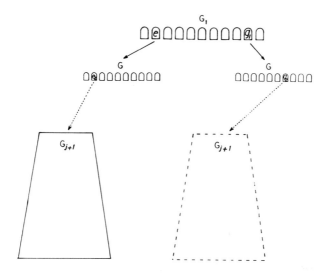

FIG. 11.   The trapezoidal blocks circumscribing cosets of *i*-subsequences.

encodes a side. So single analyzers correspond to psychological groupings in this case.

While the prediction that any analyzer yields a psychological grouping might be interesting in itself, there is much more to be revealed about the relation of these analyzer systems to grouping than the correspondence directly exhibits. Let us therefore develop an alternative but equivalent definition that opens up more of what is happening here.

In the previous section we saw that, in the perceptual analysis of a square, the D_4-system—which is the level of control in the analyzer encoding sequence $D_4.R$—sends copies of the R-systems onto each other. However, the R-systems correspond to the sides of the square and the sides are perceptual *parts* or *subgroupings* within the square. This phenomenon hints at a possible relationship between the phenomenon of grouping and the phenomenon of analyzer control. First of all let us introduce a couple of concepts:

DEFINITION 4.   Let $G = G_1.G_2.\ \ldots\ .G_n$ be a control hierarchy. Given any level G_j in the hierarchy, the subsequence $G_{j+1}.G_{j+2}.\ \ldots\ .G_n$, algebraically to the right of G_j, is called the **i-subsequence** of G_j.

The term *i-subsequence* is chosen because the entire sequence, $G = G_1.G_2.\ \ldots\ .G_n$, is a sequence of *nested* control, and any right subsequence is therefore a sequence of *inner* levels in the nesting structure. Thus, in any analyzer control diagram (such as Fig. 5), an *i*-subsequence is a G_{j+1} analyzer system, together with all the analyzer systems which it *covers* (i.e., all the systems below it and dominated by it). For example, the large trapezoidal block on the left in Fig. 11 is an *i*-subsequence.

Consider now the coordinates of this particular block in the entire hierarchy. We see that each analyzer that covers it (i.e., each analyzer that is above and dominates it) is an identity element e_i. Thus by our method of collecting coordinates, we see that the i-subsequence $G_{j+1}.G_{j+2}. \ldots .G_n$ can also be described as

$$e_1. \ldots .e_j.G_{j+1}. \ldots .G_n.$$

Of course, because the e_i are simply identity elements, one can multiply these elements out, and obtain simply the sequence $G_{j+1}.G_{j+2}. \ldots .G_n$.

However, consider now the block defined by the broken line in Fig. 11. It is covered (i.e., from above) by a string of analyzers of the form g_i. Thus its description is

$$g_1. \ldots .g_j.G_{j+1}. \ldots .G_n.$$

This cannot be reduced down to $G_{j+1}.G_{j+2}. \ldots .G_n$ because some of the elements g_i are not identity elements. Thus, strictly speaking, this second block is not an i-subsequence. It is an i-subsequence, *multiplied* by $g_1. \ldots .g_j$.

To describe this situation more clearly, let us use the notion of *coset* from group theory. A coset is a subgroup H multiplied by an element g from the group. That is, a coset is a set of the form gH. Thus the notion of coset involves the four following constructs:

group	G
subgroup	H
coset	gH
coset leader	g.

An important result from elementary group theory is that the entire set of cosets $g_1 H, g_2 H, g_3 H, \ldots,$ of a subgroup H, partitions the group G. The terms in the above list apply to our analyzer considerations in the following way:

group	$G_1.G_2. \ldots .G_n$
subgroup	$G_{j+1}.G_{j+2}. \ldots .G_n$
coset	$g_1. \ldots .g_j.G_{j+1}. \ldots .G_n$
coset leader	$g_1. \ldots .g_j$.

In other words, the block on the left of Fig. 11, that is, the i-subsequence $G_{j+1}.G_{j+2}. \ldots .G_n$ is a subgroup H; and the block, $g_1. \ldots .g_j.G_{j+1}. \ldots .G_n$, shown on the right of Fig. 11, is a *coset of an i-subsequence*.

It is now possible to state the main proposal of our theory of grouping:

PROPOSAL 5.   *Any stimulus set that is encoded by a coset of an analyzer-system i-subsequence becomes psychologically a grouping.*

To illustrate the above proposal, let us go first to our simple example, the square. Complex examples will be given later. Recall that the square has the encoding hierarchy $D_4.R$. In fact, any encoding hierarchy can be preceded by a trivial set $\{e\}$, encoding the point. This gives the total hierarchy of a square to be $D_4.R.\{e\}$. This analyzer sequence is illustrated in Fig. 9, where the dots at the bottom should now be regarded as the analyzers $\{e\}$. Proposal 5 says that, to obtain those stimulus subsets that are perceived as groupings, one should elaborate the cosets of i-subsequences in the analyzer structure. The i-subsequences are as follows:

i-subsequences of $D_4.R.\{e\}$

$$\{e\}$$
$$R.\{e\}$$
$$D_4.R.\{e\}.$$

The first i-subsequence is $\{e\}$. By algebraic inspection of the full sequence, $D_4.R.\{e\}$, one can see that all the cosets of $\{e\}$ are of the form $g_i.g_j.\{e\}$. Note that the coset leader is $g_i.g_j$ because $\{e\}$ is the subgroup. One interprets the sequence $g_i.g_j.\{e\}$ as follows: Consider the analyzer wiring diagram Fig. 9. The symbol g_j in the sequence $g_i.g_j.\{e\}$ is an analyzer from one of the R-systems in the middle level. For example, it could be e_2 or g (in Fig. 9). But the question is: In which R-system is it located? The answer is provided by the g_i in the sequence $g_i.g_j.\{e\}$. The g_i is an analyzer on the top level, that is, the D_4-system. As illustrated in Fig. 9, the top level analyzer selects the R-system in which the g_j-analyzer will be situated.

Now recall, from Fig. 10, that $g_i.g_j$ are the coordinates of any point. Thus the partition of $D_4.R.\{e\}$ into cosets of $\{e\}$ is the partition of the shape into its points.

Now consider the next i-subsequence in the above list; that is, consider $R.\{e\}$. By algebraic inspection of the entire sequence $D_4.R.\{e\}$, we see that cosets of $R.\{e\}$ have the form $g_i.R.\{e\}$. One interprets this sequence as follows. The i-subsequence $R.\{e\}$ is a side; i.e., it is determined by a middle level analyzer system in Fig. 9. In fact, consider first, just the two R-systems shown in Fig. 9. Let us collect coordinates for the left-hand R-system. The latter is covered by analyzer e_1 on the D_4-level. This means that it is specified as $e_1.R.\{e\}$. Similarly, the right-hand R-system is covered by r on the D_4-level, and is thus specified as $r.R.\{e\}$. In fact, there are eight R-systems on the middle level, one for each coordinate in D_4. By collecting coordinates, we see that they are all of the form $g_i.R.\{e\}$. That is, they are the cosets that we obtained by algebraic inspection at the beginning of this paragraph. This means that the algebraic partition of $D_4.R.\{e\}$ into cosets $g_i.R.\{e\}$ corresponds to the analyzer encoding of salient groupings, i.e., the sides.

Finally, by looking at the list of i-subsequences given earlier for $D_4.R.\{e\}$, we have the last i-subsequence which is $D_4.R.\{e\}$ itself. This equals its own cosets and visually corresponds to the entire square as a grouping. In terms of the analyzer control diagram in Fig. 9, it is the "trapezoid" that encompasses the entire diagram.

The above discussion has shown that if one algebraically enumerates the cosets of i-subsequences, and identifies those analyzer systems to which they correspond, one finds that the analyzer systems are those which encode the perceptually defined parts (subgroupings) of a percept. In the case of the square these are the points, the sides, and the whole. Brief consideration reveals that Proposal 3 and Proposal 5 are equivalent. The single analyzer in Proposal 3 is the analyzer g_j in the i-subsequence coset $g_1. \ldots . g_j.G_{j+1}. \ldots .G_n$ of Proposal 5. Let us, however, stay with the analysis following from the latter proposal.

The example we have just considered in fact demonstrates the intimate relationship between the phenomenon of control and that of grouping. To make this more obvious, let us simply reverse the generative encoding factors D_4 and R, thus obtaining the sequence $R.D_4.\{e\}$. We shall see that this does not lead to a set of perceptual parts (subgroupings) for a square.

Observe first that the $i$subsequences are as follows:

i-subsequences of $R.D_4.\{e\}$

$\{e\}$

$D_4.\{e\}$

$R.D_4.\{e\}.$

In fact, the first i-subsequence $\{e\}$ causes no problem. But consider the middle level i-subsequence $D_4.\{e\}$. Because the set $\{e\}$ is a point (e.g., the central point), the set $D_4.\{e\}$ is the point with the operations of D_4 applied. An example of such a subset is the cross-like subset shown on the square at the bottom left of Fig. 12.

However, observe that by algebraic inspection of the sequence $R.D_4.\{e\}$, any of the cosets of $D_4.\{e\}$ is a set of the form $g_i.D_4.\{e\}$. This is the cross-like set with a translation g_i from R applied to each point, as shown on the square at the bottom-right of Fig. 12. This subset is not usually perceived as a subgrouping of a square. The psychologically salient parts are points, sides and the whole. These are the i-subsequence cosets of the other ordering $D_4.R.\{e\}$. Thus, the example shows that the generative ordering is crucial. The sequence $D_4.R.\{e\}$ leads to a psychologically salient set of parts, whereas the sequence $R.D_4.\{e\}$ does not.

We have obtained the coset $g_i.D_4.\{e\}$ by examining the full sequence $R.D_4.\{e\}$ algebraically. But we can learn something from obtaining it by the procedure of collecting coordinates in the associated control wiring diagram; i.e., Fig. 12. Observe

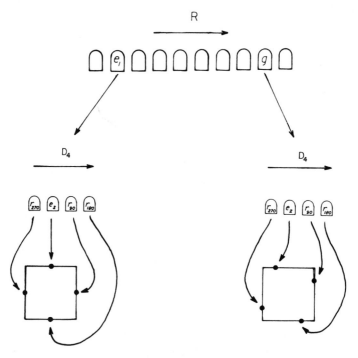

FIG. 12.   The structuring effect of the analyzer hierarchy $R.D_4.\{e\}$.

FIG. 13.   Grouping by rows or columns.

that in the diagram, the R-analyzer system is now at the top level and a collection of D_4-systems are now on the middle level. Consider the left-hand D_4-system. It is encoded by a single analyzer e from the higher R-level. Therefore, collecting coordinates, it is given by $e.D_4$. Again, because the right-hand D_4-system is covered by g on the R-level, it is specified by $g.D_4$

The important thing to observe now is that the analyzers r_{270}, e, r_{90}, and r_{180} in the left-hand D_4-system encode the points on the square shown below that system, but the *same* analyzers in the right-hand D_4-system map to four different points on the square below that system. This difference is given by the analyzer g on the R-level, which is responsible for the map from the D_4-analyzers, r_{270}, e, r_{90}, r_{180}, on the left-hand side to the same ones on the right.

This mapping action is exactly what I have meant by a *generative control parameter*. The fact that we do not usually see the resulting sets of points as groupings therefore is embodied in a single fact: It is harder to see the translation group as a control parameter mapping D_4-sets to D_4-sets (i.e., cross-like sets to skewed cross-like sets) than it is to see D_4 as a control parameter mapping R-sets to R-sets (i.e., sides to sides).

The crucial point, that the grouping structure depends on the structure of *wiring* of the analyzer systems, can be illustrated in the following famous example from the Gestalt school. Figs. 13a and b each show a rectangular grid of dots. However, in Fig. 13a, the collection is visually grouped into rows, whereas in Fig. 13b, the collection is visually grouped into columns.

In order to explain this phenomenon, let us consider three analyzer systems structured respectively by

$\{e\}$ the trivial group
Z_H the group of integer translations in the horizontal direction
Z_V a vertical version of Z_H.

Supposing now one connected these three systems into the hierarchy $Z_V.Z_H.\{e\}$; that is, where Z_V controls Z_H, which in turn controls $\{e\}$. Then there would be three i-subsequences:

$$\{e\}$$
$$Z_H.\{e\}$$
$$Z_V.Z_H.\{e\}.$$

By algebraic inspection, the cosets of the first i-subsequence are all of the form $g_i.g_j.\{e\}$; where $g_i.g_j$ is a coset leader. The coordinate g_j is an analyzer on the

Z_H-level and the coordinate g_i is an analyzer on the Z_V-level. Therefore, $g_i.g_j$ gives the point its vertical and horizontal coordinate. Thus the algebraic partition of the analyzer hierarchy $Z_V.Z_H.\{e\}$ into cosets of $\{e\}$, corresponds to the partition of the percept into points.

The next i-subsequence is $Z_H.\{e\}$ which has cosets of the form $g_i.Z_H.\{e\}$. Going backwards through this sequence, i.e., upward through the hierarchy, one obtains first $\{e\}$ a point, Z_H the translation of the point horizontally (i.e., a row), and finally the coset leader g_i. Observe that g_i is an analyzer on the Z_V-level, and therefore assigns a vertical coordinate to the row.

From this discussion we can see that if the analyzer hierarchy were set up as $Z_V.Z_H.\{e\}$, then the visual effect would be to partition the percept into rows. A corresponding argument shows that if the analyzer hierarchy were set up as $Z_H.Z_V.\{e\}$ then the visual effect would be to partition the percept into columns. Thus we can see that the two groupings, Figs. 13a and b, correspond to the wiring of analyzer systems into two alternative control hierarchies. In Leyton [16] several more of the standard Gestalt examples are considered and shown to be explained by this type of analysis.

Although we will be considering complex shape mainly in Section 8, let us take a preliminary look at the encoding of a part of such a shape; e.g., the encoding of the ear of the mouse in the top left of Fig. 1, as a part. Hoffman and Richards [11] and Richards and Hoffman [22] argue that a part of such a contour is obtained by segmenting the boundary at concave cusps. Observe, however, that their justification for such a rule is that, in the 3-dimensional world, the joining of two simpler parts typically creates concavities at the joint (see Fig. 2, Richards and Hoffman [22]). Thus the parts are, initially, wholes. In Section 8, I argue that each such part is given by an encoding hierarchy of the form $R.D\hat{i}(Z_2(\times_{sd})SO_2).\{e\}$. Furthermore, because each is initially a whole (thus giving the concavity condition) each is a coset of an i-subsequence (in fact, a coset of itself), thus corroborating Proposal 5. Therefore, the concavity rule can be seen as leading to the description of the boundary in terms of two independent i-subsequence cosets.

5. WIRING TOGETHER THE EXTERNAL AND INTERNAL ANALYZER SYSTEMS

We now come to two crucial proposals that will allow us in later sections to deal with the perceptual analysis of highly complex shapes such as those shown in Fig. 1.

Recall that part (1) of the Structure Postulate claims that a perceptual organization is the result of an encoding by the interconnection of two generative analyzer systems: an external one and an internal one. So far we have been examining these two systems independently. However, part (3) of the Structure Postulate claims that the two systems are wired together into one system, and the wiring always conforms to two principles. The present section will deduce these principles. In preparation for some of the main concepts to be used, let us go back to the SL_2R example, illustrated in Fig. 2.

5.1. A Stability Criterion

What we will first do is to develop a principled explanation of why subjects defined the stability stratification on SL_2R to be $A.N.SO_2$—that is, rotations SO_2 followed by shears N followed by pure deformations A. Why did subjects not choose an alternative decomposition and ordering for the stability stratification? The explanation I will propose is based on the concept of *eigenspace*, taken from linear algebra:

An **eigenspace** is a straight subspace (e.g., a line) which goes through the origin and remains over itself under a transformation of the overall space.

To illustrate this concept consider again Figs. 3a, b, and c, which show the groups A, N, and SO_2, respectively. In the case of the group A, the transformation of the square (at the top) to the rectangle (on the left) leaves the x and y axes over themselves, while moving every other line off itself. This means that the x and y axes are eigenspaces. Now look at the shear illustrated in Fig. 3b. Here, in the transformation of the square (at the top) to the rhombus, all the straight lines shift except the x axis. This means that the x axis is the only eigenspace. Finally, examination of the rotation in Fig. 3c shows that, under a rotation, *all* lines move, without exception. This means that a rotation does not have a (real) eigenspace.

The notion of eigenspace is relevant to our discussion because it is a *stability* concept: The *size* of the eigenspace of a transformation is the amount of subspace that is invariant and this is clearly a measure of the amount of *linear stability* associated with the transformation.

What is remarkable is that the stability stratification $SL_2 R = A.N.SO_2$, which had been chosen by the subjects in Leyton [14], exactly obeys this criterion. By examining Fig. 3, we see that there are two eigenspace lines for the group A, one for the group N, and none for the group SO_2. Thus, the stability ordering chosen by the subjects is the ordering of the eigenspace size.

5.2. The Interconnection Principles

The concept of eigenspace is crucial to the theory being developed. For example, it will be central to the analysis later of complex shapes.

The Structure Postulate states that a perceptual organization is given by the interconnection between two generative analyzer encodings: one by an internal and one by an external system. The interconnection to be proposed can now be illustrated using the $SL_2 R$ example. Consider again Fig. 3a. The two axes are eigenspaces of the pure deformation group. However, these two lines have another important property. Observe that the pure deformation group is acting here on the square. Simple inspection reveals that the two axes in Fig. 3a were symmetry axes of the square upon which the pure deformation shown is applied. Thus the two axes have two functions: (1) With respect to the *internal* geometry of the square they are symmetry axes. (2) With respect to the *external* actions on the square they are eigenspaces.

The experiments to be reviewed later will show that this phenomenon is extremely wide ranging, and will allow us to provide an analysis of complex shape and motion phenomena.

Now let us return to analyzer systems. The above perceptual phenomena imply the following principle concerning the wiring of internal analyzer systems to external ones.

FIRST INTERCONNECTION PRINCIPLE. *Analyzers that comprise symmetry axes in the internal system are wired as eigenspaces in the external system.*

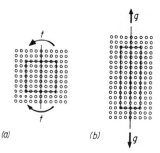

FIG. 14.   An illustration of the interconnection principles: The symmetry axis of t is wired as the eigenspace of g.

To illustrate this proposal, consider Fig. 14a. It shows a 2-dimensional array of analyzers that covers a square. If the vertical symmetry of the square is perceived, there is an analyzer t mapping the left half of the system to the right half. However, observe that each analyzer on the central axis maps to itself. That is, these analyzers are *transformationally static*. However, now consider the pure deformation g, shown in Fig. 14b. Under this transformation, the axis stimuli lie along the direction of transformation. Thus, although the analyzers represent transformationally static points on the internal level, they represent *transformationally mobile* points on the external level.

Another crucial factor will now be examined. First of all let us consider why the wiring of symmetry axes to eigenspaces would be perceptually useful. Consider again Figs. 14a and b. In going from Fig. 14a to Fig. 14b, we can see illustrated this important notion: when the symmetry axis is an eigenspace, the *symmetry is not destroyed in the external transformation*. For example, the rectangle (Fig. 14b) has the same symmetry t as the square (Fig. 14a). In other words, the internal reflection analyzer t, active on the left, is still active on the right. Thus an external transformation g which accords with the First Interconnection Principle preserves the activity of the internal analyzer system. Perceptually, this means that the external analyzer is *structure-preserving*.

What should now be noted is that a transformation which is structure-preserving can be regarded as more stable. However, I have argued that the more stable a transformation is, the higher its level of control; i.e., by the Structure Postulate part (2).

Now observe that the discussion of the previous two paragraphs must be extended to involve the phenomenon of axis-salience. If an axis were not salient, then an external analyzer that encoded the axis as an eigenspace (line of flexibility) would not be particularly structure-preserving and thus would not be particularly stable. However, for a highly salient axis, an external analyzer which encoded the symmetry axis as an eigenspace would be significantly structure-preserving, and thus perceptually stable. This is illustrated again in the $SL_2 R$ example of Fig. 3. A square has perceptually salient axes bisecting the sides. Therefore these axes become eigenspaces of the pure deformation group which subjects rate as *the most stable* of the three groups. However, the square also has symmetry axes along the diagonals. But these are *not* salient. If they were, the figure would be seen as a diamond. (Leyton [14, Experiment 11] has shown that regular four-sided figures, where the salient axes are diagonal, are seen as diamonds.) Thus, there is no attempt to preserve the diagonals of a square in the most stable external analyzers. If there were such an attempt the figure would be seen as a diamond. (Leyton, [14, Experiment 12] has shown that elongations of a regular four-sided figure along the *diagonals* are seen as elongations of a diamond.) In general then the following principle is proposed:

SECOND INTERCONNECTION PRINCIPLE.   *The more salient an analyzer array is as a symmetry axis, the higher the control level of the external analyzer to which it is wired as an eigenspace.*

The fact that the internal system G_I is wired to the external system G_E in accord with the Interconnection Principles will be denoted by replacing the writing of the overall analyzer sequence $G_E.G_I$ by $G_E \hat{\imath} G_I$; that is, $\hat{\imath}$ denotes a product that accords with the Interconnections Principles.

Perceptual evidence. We now summarize perceptual evidence in support of the Interconnection Principles. The evidence, from Experiments 9–13 in [14], involves large classes of shapes, regular and irregular. Experiments 9 and 10 tested the above proposals for nine types of regular n-sided polygons (e.g., from $n = 3$ to $n = 8$ including squares as well as diamonds; adding also circles). Experiment 13 tested the proposals for the 22 complex, highly irregular, shapes shown in Fig. 1; i.e., animals, birds, plants, and abstract forms. For the regular shapes, two alternative methods were used for creating axis-salience: gravitational alignment or division of the figure along the axis. Subjects had to compare each regular polygon, which had a salient axis, with a variety of elongations of that polygon. With statistical significance, subjects chose the elongation along the salient axis as preserving similarity to the regular polygon (Gravitational condition: $n = 6$, 15 comparisons per subject; expected mean = 7.5 sets in which gravitational alignment is chosen; actual mean = 12.5, $t(5) = 9.444$, $p < 0.0005$, one tailed. Division condition: $n = 6$, 15 comparisons per subject; expected mean = 7.5 sets in which every matching is a salient axis/eigenspace pairing; worst score = 12 yielding $t(5) = 14.118$, $p < 0.0005$, one tailed.). In the case of the complex shapes, subjects were asked to assign directions of flexibility to each figure at four designated points in the figure. With considerable statistical significance, they chose the salient local symmetry axis through each designated point ($n = 12$; 88 choices per subject; expected mean = 44; actual mean = 77.58; $t(11) = 27.228$, $p < 0.0005$, one tailed).

6. ANALYZER SYSTEMS ENCODING THE CARTESIAN REFERENCE FRAMES

6.1. Introduction

A theory of the encoding of cartesian frames will be crucial to us when we later give a theory of complex shape perception. Cartesian reference frames seem to be generally involved in perception. For example, Binford [3] and Marr and Nishihara [20] argue that an important stage in the analysis of a complex shape such as one of those shown in Fig. 1, is that a cartesian reference frame is assigned locally to each limb. One axis is coincident with the 2-dimensional symmetry axis of the limb (as a 2-dimensional outline), and this axis is then interpreted as the 3-dimensional *rotation* axis of a postulated cylinder comprising the limb. Another important perceptual area is the orientation and form problem which is this: Imposing a cartesian reference frame on a figure in two different orientations can lead to two phenome-

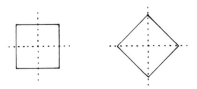

FIG. 15.   The square–diamond effect.

nally different percepts. The most famous example is the square–diamond effect shown in Fig. 15. A more compelling example, however, is shown in Fig. 20. Fig. 20a can be seen either as a sheared square, Fig. 20b, or as a stretched diamond, Fig. 20c. The orientation and form problem has remained unsolved in its entire 100 year history.

In order to solve the orientation and form problem, and show a common analyzer structure to several perceptual areas involving cartesian reference frames, we need a very different understanding of what a cartesian reference frame is than the conventional understanding. What we will do is to describe such a frame as a *generative* structure and claim that there is substantial evidence to show that the latter constitutes the structure of a strongly salient analyzer system. We begin by considering external generative aspects and will then move onto internal aspects.

6.2.   The External Generative Structure

Although the perceptual evidence will be considered later, some simple referential phenomena will motivate the proposal that the cartesian system has an external referential structure. The phenomena are simply this: People see any cartesian frame in which vertical units are larger than horizontal units (or vice versa) as a stretched version of a frame in which vertical and horizontal units have the same length. The latter frame will be said to be equal-sided. Again, people see any cartesian frame in which vertical and horizontal axes are not at a 90° angle to each other as a sheared version of a rectangular frame. Finally, people see any frame in which the axes are not gravitationally aligned as a rotated version of a frame in which the axes have been so aligned.

These considerations imply that the standard cartesian reference frame (one which is equal-sided, rectangular, and gravitationally aligned) is the reference point in a space of frames where reference is provided respectively by the pure deformation group A, the shear group N, and the rotation group SO_2. Thus we shall say that the external generative structure of the cartesian frame is $SL_2R = A.N.SO_2$.

In fact, it will be claimed that the successive reference example shown in Fig. 2, was the result of an encoding of the stimulus set by a system of analyzers $SL_2R = A.N.SO_2$ which will be called the *external cartesian frame-system*. Thus, as shown in Fig. 16a, a plane of analyzers is imposed on the first figure, and this subsystem is rotated, straightened, and unstretched as one moves through successively higher control levels in the external structure of this plane.

6.3.   The Internal Generative Structure

We have just examined the external referential or external generative structure of the cartesian frame. Now let us look at the internal generative structure. It is clear

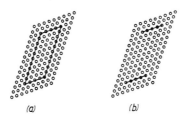

(a)   (b)

FIG. 16. (a) The encoding of the rotated parallelogram as a subset of a cartesian plane which itself has external coordinates $a.n.r.$ (b) Four points in the plane that are symmetrically arranged on the square.

that the cartesian frame can be internally generated in two very different ways:

(1) The entire set of points of the plane can be generated by taking only a single point and applying (to the point) the group of 2-dimensional translations R^2.

(2) One can generate the plane by taking the left half and applying (to it) the reflection t_V about the central vertical axis. The operation t_V generates the group $Z_2 = \{e, t_V\}$ because two applications of t_V are equivalent to no action, e. Similarly, one can generate the plane by taking the bottom half and applying the reflection t_H about the horizontal axis. The operation t_H generates the group $Z_2 = \{e, t_H\}$. Finally, the operations t_V and t_H together generate the group:

$$Z_2 \times Z_2 = \{e, t_V, t_H, t_V \cdot t_H\}.$$

The two generative systems just described—the double reflection system $Z_2 \times Z_2$ and the translation system R^2—can be combined into one generative system:

$$(Z_2 \times Z_2) . R^2.$$

However, in this case, the product "." has a special property:

Observe that the two systems $Z_2 \times Z_2$ and R^2 have, in fact, a close inter-relationship. Quite simply: if one applies any reflection from $Z_2 \times Z_2$ to the translation system R^2, one obtains another translation system R^2. For example, if one applies the vertical reflection t_V to R^2, one obtains a copy of R^2 where the translations in the horizontal direction are reversed. The fact that the generative system $Z_2 \times Z_2$ makes copies of the generative system R^2 is summarized by saying that the product of the two generative systems is a *semi-direct product*. In accord with this, the product system "." above will be replaced by the symbol ($\times_{sd}$). Thus the combined generative system is:

$$Z_2 \times Z_2 (\times_{sd}) R^2.$$

In the following sections, a variety of perceptual experiments will be reviewed in support of our proposal that there is a particularly salient analyzer system of the form $Z_2 \times Z_2 (\times_{sd}) R^2$. To show the form that such a system must take, consider Fig. 17. Here, the R^2-systems have been arranged one above the other, for example, as they might be in some ascending column of the visual system. This arrangement is proposed here because, under $Z_2 \times Z_2$, the R^2-systems encode the same region in retinal space. The vertical fibers on the left descend from the analyzer system $Z_2 \times Z_2$. Each of the four fibers corresponds to one of the analyzers $e, t_V, t_V \cdot t_H \cdot t_H$ of the $Z_2 \times Z_2$-system.

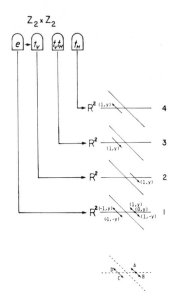

FIG. 17.   The analyzer system encoding the internal cartesian frame.

To gain an understanding of the system, let us consider the encoding of some stimulus input by this analyzer space. The input is shown at the bottom of Fig. 17. It consists of two sides of a square. First note that each R^2-system above is a space of translation analyzers. One can in fact regard them as movement analyzers except that the time parameter is substituted by a distance parameter.

In the lowest R^2-system (system 1), in the figure, we see a set of analyzers encoding points on two sides in the stimulus set represented below. Locate analyzer $(0, y)$ in this first system. Let us assume, without loss of generality, that it is responding to the central point on one side. Now consider the analyzer $(1, y)$ in system 1. It encodes point A below in the stimulus input. Thus it encodes the point as a *translation* from the central point by a distance of y units. This explains the perceptual phenomenon that a non-central point on a side is perceptually referenced to the central point on the side (Experiment 6 [14]).

Now consider stimulus point B. It is encoded by the analyzer $(1, -y)$ in the first R^2-system (system 1). However, notice something important. It is also encoded by the analyzer $(1, y)$ in the R^2-system just above that (system 2). In other words, although it is encoded by analyzer $(1, -y)$ in system 1, it has the same value $(1, y)$, in system 2, as point A has in system 1. That is, there are two R^2-analyzers having the value $(1, y)$; one in system 1, and the other in system 2, but the two analyzers do not encode the same stimulus. What accounts for the assignment of the same value to two different stimulus positions? The answer is found by considering the $Z_2 \times Z_2$-system above. Recall that a higher system acts as a control variable. This means that the arrow shown between the e- and t_V-analyzer in the $Z_2 \times Z_2$-system, maps analyzers in the first R^2-system to analyzers in the second R^2-system. Via this map, the same R^2-value $(1, y)$ is assigned to an analyzer in the first R^2-system and an analyzer in the second R^2-system, despite the fact that they encode different stimulus positions. Of course, even though the two positions have the same R^2-value, they do not have the same value in the entire analyzer system. By the method of counting coordinates, they have values respectively e and t_V on the $Z_2 \times Z_2$-level. That is, the positions A and B have analyzer coordinates $(e, 1, y)$ and $(t_V, 1, y)$, respectively.

Now consider the analyzer $(-1, -y)$ on the first R_2-plane. It encodes stimulus point C. Observe that, within the first R_2-system, we can find no relationship between the analyzer that encodes C, and the analyzer $(1, y)$ that encodes A. However, follow the vertical fiber from the first R_2-system up to the $Z_2 \times Z_2$-level, then follow the control parameter from the e-analyzer to the $t_V . t_H$-analyzer, and then follow the vertical fiber down from the $t_V . t_H$-analyzer to the third R^2-system. Here we find that the stimulus point C has coordinates $(1, y)$; that is, the same coordinates as A has in the first R^2-system. This is explained by the control action of the $t_V . t_H$-analyzer on the $Z_2 \times Z_2$-level. Finally, as the reader can easily check, equivalent considerations connect analyzer $(1, y)$, in R^2-system number 4, to analyzer $(1, y)$ in R^2-system number 1, even though they encode quite different stimulus points.

6.4. The Full Generative Structure

The above discussion developed two analyzer systems that describe the cartesian reference frame as two generative structures, respectively: (1) an external system $SL_2 R = A.N.SO_2$, which allows a frame of any stretch, shear, and orientation to be referenced to the conventional equi-sided, perpendicular, gravitational frame; and (2) an internal system $Z_2 \times Z_2 (\times_{sd}) R^2$ which is structured by the double-reflection group combined with the 2-dimensional translation group.

Because $A.N.SO_2$ is an external system and $Z_2 \times Z_2 (\times_{sd}) R^2$ is an internal system, the former acts on the latter. That is, the former is a control group with respect to the latter. Thus the entire wiring diagram is Fig. 5, the diagram of $SL_2 R$, with a copy of Fig. 17, the diagram of $Z_2 \times Z_2 (\times_{sd}) R^2$, wired to each of the terminal nodes of the former. The result is Fig 18. Note that Fig. 17 corresponds to the left-most column in the lower half of Fig. 18; and the successive columns, from left to right in Fig. 18 are successive images of Fig. 17 undergoing the control operations defined above. Thus, for example, the encoding shown in Fig. 16a is performed by the column on the far right of Fig. 18. In particular, the point $(1, y)$ which was represented in four different positions in Fig. 17, is now in four different positions on the rotated parallelogram. These particular points are shown in Fig. 16b as the two black dots on the top side and the two on the bottom side. Each of these four points is given by an analyzer $(1, y)$ on one of the four levels of the right-hand column in Fig. 17.

Observe now that the Interconnection Principles of Section 5.2 prescribe important aspects of the wiring in this entire system: the symmetry axes of the $Z_2 \times Z_2 (\times_{sd}) R^2$-system are wired as eigenspaces with respect to the system A on the top level. This means that the axes shown down the left-most column are innervated by fibers which connect to system A above in the way described by the Interconnection Principles. Thus, descending through the control levels of the

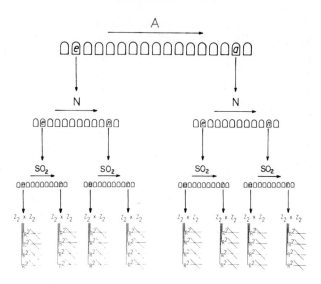

FIG. 18.   The cartesian frame-system.

diagram, we see that the entire system is given by the product

$$(A . N . SO_2) \hat{\imath} \big((Z_2 \times Z_2)(\times_{sd}) R^2 \big).$$

To understand this rather lengthy string of symbols, let us go through the sequence from left to right, explaining the symbols one by one:

A	the pure deformation system
N	the shear system
SO_2	the rotation system
$\hat{\imath}$	the wiring of symmetry axes as eigenspaces
$Z_2 \times Z_2$	the double reflection group
$(\times_{sd})$	the semidirect wiring operation
R^2	the 2-dimensional translation system.

Note that the full string can be regarded either as an algebraic structure or as the sequential listing of the descending analyzer levels; i.e., as stated in part (2) of the Structure Postulate. It is a central feature of this theory that the algebraic interpretation corresponds to the analyzer interpretation. As stated above, the entire system will be named as follows:

DEFINITION 6.   The **full cartesian frame-system** is the hierarchical analyzer system

$$(A . N . SO_2) \hat{\imath} \big((Z_2 \times Z_2)(\times_{sd}) R^2 \big).$$

The present paper will attempt to adduce *perceptual* evidence showing that the above system is a highly salient analyzer system in human vision.

It is now possible to develop a new view of what it might mean to impose a cartesian reference frame on a figure. Recall that the Structure Postulate claims that the perceptual organization of a stimulus set is an encoding by an interconnection between two generative analyzer systems: an external system G_E and an internal system G_I. Both have a hierarchical decomposition and thus the full analyzer system is $G_{E_1}.G_{E_2}.\ \ldots\ .G_{E_n}.G_{I_1}.G_{I_2}.\ \ldots\ .G_{I_m}$, where the first n factors comprise G_E and the second m factors comprise G_I.

On the other hand, the full analyzer system of the cartesian frame is the hierarchical product $(A.N.SO_2)\hat{\imath}((Z_2 \times Z_2)(\times_{sd})R^2)$. The claim to be made now is

PROPOSAL 7.   *The basis for the impression that a cartesian reference frame has been imposed on a perceptual organization is this*: *The analyzer system*

$$(A.N.SO_2)\hat{\imath}\big((Z_2 \times Z_2)(\times_{sd})R^2\big)$$

encoding the frame, occurs as a subsystem of the analyzer system

$$G_{E_1}.G_{E_2}.\ \ldots\ .G_{E_n}.G_{I_1}.G_{I_2}.\ \ldots\ .G_{I_n}$$

encoding the organization.

As an example, consider the imposition of a cartesian frame on a hexagon. As shown in Fig. 7b the analyzer system encoding a hexagon is structured by

$$D_6 = \big\{\, e, r_{60}, r_{120}, r_{180}, r_{240}, r_{300}, t, tr_{60}, tr_{120}, tr_{180}, tr_{240}, tr_{300} \,\big\}.$$

Furthermore, the analyzer system defining the cartesian frame includes

$$Z_2 \times Z_2 = \big\{\, e, t_V, t_H, t_V.t_H \,\big\}.$$

It turns out that the latter set of analyzers is a subsystem of the former: The analyzers e, t_V, t_H, $t_V.t_H$ in $Z_2 \times Z_2$ are respectively the analyzers e, t, r_{180}, tr_{180} in D_6. This corroborates Proposal 7.

Finally, let us note something else about the cartesian frame-system. By referring back to Fig. 3, we can trace the fate of symmetry axes and eigenspaces through the analyzer hierarchy defining the frame. In Fig. 3, the two eigenspace lines of the first group A were the symmetry axes of the $Z_2 \times Z_2$-subsystem of D_4. Again, we see that, in Fig. 3b, one of the eigenspace lines remains and the other is sheared. Finally, the rotation group moves the lines off themselves. Thus the fate of the initial symmetry axes are as follows:

$$Z_2 \times Z_2(2 \text{ sym. axes}) \rightarrow A \ (2 \text{ eigs})$$

$$\rightarrow N(1 \text{ eig})$$

$$\rightarrow SO_2 \ (0 \text{ eig}).$$

Finally, returning to Fig. 18, we see that this sequence shows the fate of the symmetry axes from column 1, to column 5, to column 7, to column 8.

FIG. 19.   Two fields of ambiguous shapes that are always simultaneously disambiguated.

6.5. The Cartesian Bundle System

The geometries of figures, presented simultaneously in visual space, influence each other. For example, Attneave [2] has observed that multistable figures can disambiguate each other. The four tetragons on the left of Fig. 19a are perceived as squares, whereas those on the right of Fig. 19a are perceived as diamonds. Again, Attneave noted that certain fields of ambiguous (equal-sided) triangles, as in Fig. 19b, always point in the same direction simultaneously.

The above phenomena imply an important property of the human nervous system: A collection of separate stimulus sets, each at a different location in visual space can be structured in parallel such that correspondences between those structures are established. Observe that locally one does not simply have a *feature* but an *entire structure*. Thus the situation is not amenable to a simple flow-field analysis; i.e., a global analysis which picks out line elements at each point. For, in such an analysis, the above examples would produce, perceptually, a field of corresponding sides rather than a distribution of structures. Observe that in the case of triangles, any line-field would lie in a different direction from the perceived pointing. The pointing is directed along the symmetry axis in each case, and the axis is not explicitly in the stimulus set: The axis emerges from the imposition of a structure locally. Observe that if a line-field does perceptually emerge here, it is in fact the field of bottom sides; i.e., the perpendicular axis to the triangle's symmetry axis.

The above argues for a nested structure of analyzer systems, of the type we have been considering. That is, (1) an organization is locally given by an analyzer system structured generatively as a group; and (2) on the next level, these analyzer systems are mapped to each other by a control analyzer system which is also structured as a group. In particular, the lower and higher systems seem to be structured as follows: One can assume that, at the local level, salient aspects of the perceptual organization are given as a result of an encoding by the cartesian frame-system; e.g., this causes the triangles, squares, and diamonds to be seen as bilaterally symmetric. On the higher level, the control analyzer system is structured simply by the translation group R^2. Thus it appears that the nested analyzer structure is

$$R^2.(A.N.SO_2)\hat{\imath}\big((Z_2 \times Z_2)(\times_{sd})R^2\big).$$

Observe that the wiring of the R^2-system to the rest of the analyzer structure accords with the Interconnection Principles: The symmetry axes of the lower systems are wired as eigenspaces (invariant lines) of the R^2-system. The full system elaborated above will be defined as follows:

DEFINITION 8.   The **cartesian bundle-system** is the hierarchical analyzer system

$$R^n.(A.N.SO_2)\hat{\imath}\big((Z_2 \times Z_2)(\times_{sd})R^2\big).$$

The dimension of R^n can vary; e.g., in the case of a contour, $n = 1$; in the case of a surface, $n = 2$, etc. Definition 8 is an example of what is called, in differential geometry, a *principle bundle* (i.e., a manifold, in this case R^n, with a group defined at each point on the manifold. The group in this case is the i-subseqence $(A.N.SO_2)\hat{i}((Z_2 \times Z_2)(\times_{sd})R^2)$ of R^n in Definition 8). In fact, the above is a nested system of principle bundles. This system will be of considerable importance later when we analyze motion and complex-shape phenomena.

6.6. Solving the Orientation and Form Problem

The orientation and form phenomenon is this: Different orientations of the same stimulus set, or differently orientated placements of the cartesian reference frame over the same stimulus set, can yield different percepts. That is, different orientations can yield different *forms*; i.e., the stimuli are organized differently. Historically, the first example adduced was that of the square–diamond effect (Mach [19]; see also Goldmeier [9] and Rock [23]). The importance of this phenomenon cannot be overestimated: it shows that perception is not a process of passive reception of environmental structures but a type of *description* that defines structure. The phenomenon of description is, I claim, captured in the notion of *analyzer covering*. This notion will be used to solve the orientation and form problem.

First of all observe that, according to Proposal 7, a cartesian reference frame must have three coordinates (a, n, r) in the analyzer system $A.N.SO_2$, describing the frame's stretch shear, and orientation value. Now suppose that a stimulus set has a cartesian frame imposed on it in two different ways. That is, the encoding analyzers are (a_1, n_1, r_1) in one case and (a_2, n_2, r_2) in the other case. This will mean that the eigenspace lines of these external analyzers will encode the stimulus set differently in the two cases. However, the Interconnection Principles state that the analyzers lying along the eigenspace lines must be wired such that they are also analyzers along symmetry axes. Thus, if the eigenspace lines encode the stimulus set differently in the two cases, then the symmetry-axis analyzers must encode the stimulus set differently in the two cases. Therefore, these analyzers define the symmetry structure in the stimulus set to be different in the two cases. Thus the set is given two different perceptual organizations, i.e., forms. This solves the orientation and form problem.

Let us now restate the argument, filling in more details: If a stimulus set has a cartesian frame imposed on it, then, by Proposal 7, it has an internal organizing structure given by a $Z_2 \times Z_2(\times_{sd})R^2$-system, and a set of external coordinates (a, n, r). Thus collecting coordinates upward through the analyzer hierarchy, the encoding analyzer system is

$$(a.n.r)\hat{i}((Z_2 \times Z_2)(\times_{sd})R^2)$$

which turns out to be one of the columns in Fig. 18. However, the coordinates $a.n.r$ define an eigenspace structure, and, by the Interconnection Principles, this must be coincident with the axis structure in the organizing $Z_2 \times Z_2$-system. Thus, different external coordinates $a.n.r$ prescribe different placements of the $Z_2 \times Z_2$-system over the stimulus set. Hence one obtains a different perceptual structure. Thus the above argument can be summarized as:

Different external encodings can determine different internal encodings.

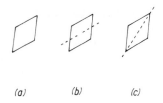

FIG. 20.   (a) A perceptually ambiguous shape that can be interpreted as (b) a sheared square or (c) a stretched diamond.

Translated into perceptual terms, one has simply: Different external coordinates can determine different internal organizations. Note that this generalizes the orientation and form phenomenon. The statement of the phenomenon is that different *orientations* can determine different forms. The above has said that a difference in *any* external coordinate (not just orientation) can determine a different form.

In order to understand more fully the above concepts, consider the perceptually ambiguous shape in Fig. 20a. It can either be seen as a sheared square, Fig. 20b, or a stretched diamond, Fig. 20c. In either case, the figure has a particular imposition of the cartesian reference frame. By Proposal 7, this means that the encoding analyzer system contains $(A.N.SO_2)\hat{\imath}((Z_2 \times Z_2)(\times_{sd})R^2)$ as a subsystem. Let us look at the external coordinates of Fig. 20b, in $A.N.SO_2$. They are respectively

$$e_A \qquad \text{no stretch}$$
$$n \qquad \text{non-trivial shear}$$
$$r_1 \qquad \text{a particular rotation value.}$$

This means that the figure is given by an analyzer system:

$$(e_A.n.r_1)\hat{\imath}((Z_2 \times Z_2)(\times_{sd})R^2).$$

Now observe that the system just defined is the fourth column (from the left) in Fig. 18; for, observe that this column is the only one covered by the identity analyzer from the A-system, and a non-identity analyzer each from the N- and SO_2-systems.

Now consider Fig. 20c. It has external values

$$a \qquad \text{non-trivial stretch}$$
$$e_N \qquad \text{no shear}$$
$$r_2 \qquad \text{a particular rotation value.}$$

Thus by Proposal 7, the figure is encoded by an analyzer system of the form

$$(a.e_N.r_2)\hat{\imath}((Z_2 \times Z_2)(\times_{sd})R^2).$$

This system, in fact, turns out to be the sixth column in Fig. 18; as can be seen by the fact that only this column is covered by a non identity A- and SO_2-analyzer, and also by the identity analyzer of the N-system.

Thus we can see that the same stimulus set Fig. 20a, can be encoded by two different analyzer systems. Encoding by column 4 yields the percept shown in Fig. 20b, and encoding by column 6 yields the percept shown in Fig. 20c.

However, the analyzer difference is greater even than this. Not only do the two columns differ in their encodings, but it turns out that the entire surrounding system encodes differently in each case, as we shall now see.

Consider first Fig. 20b. As was said above, it is encoded by analyzers $e_A.n.r_1$. Figure 6, showed how a percept is referred via the analyzer system to the left-most column. It will turn out that a useful question to ask is this: What figure is encoded by this first column? Let us go back through the reference sequence $e_A.n.r_1$, till we reach the left-most column. What we will do is to perform this reference while going backward through the sequence given at the end of Section 6.4, to trace the fate of the eigenspaces. By removing the rotation coordinate r_1, we obtain the single eigenspace of the shear coordinate n (as claimed in the sequence at the end of Section 6.4). Observe, in Figure 20b, that this eigenspace is a side bisector. Now according to the sequence at the end of Section 6.4, when one removes n, the second eigenspace emerges, and this also was a side-bisector (because it was parallel to the angle of shear). Since we now have only external identity elements, we must be at the first column. At this point, we use the Interconnection Principles. They state that the eigenspaces just identified must be symmetry axes. This means that the symmetry axes are side-bisectors in this column. Therefore, the figure that is encoded by this column is a square (because the salient symmetry axes of a square are its side-bisectors).

In contrast, consider Fig. 20c, which is encoded by column 6, and external analyzers $a.e_N.r_2$. Let us go back through the latter sequence till we reach the first column. By removing r_2, we are left at the identity element e_N of the shear group. But because there is no shear, the two eigenspaces from the pure deformation stage a are still present. However, these eigenspaces are angle-bisectors; i.e., Fig. 20c is visually interpreted as stretched along the angle-bisectors. Then, by removing the first stage a and obtaining the first column, we still have angle-bisectors as eigenspaces. Now use the Interconnection Principles. These state that the eigenspaces are the symmetry axes in the column. Therefore, the symmetry axes are the angle-bisectors. This means that the figure, encoded by this column, must have been a diamond. (Leyton [14, Experiment 11], shows that a square is distinguished from a diamond in that the former has salient symmetry axes along the side-bisectors and the latter has salient symmetry axes along the angle-bisectors.)

The argument thus shows that if analyzer column 4 encodes Fig. 20a, then the figure encoded by the first column is a square, and if analyzer column 6 encodes Fig. 20a, then the figure encoded by the first column is a diamond. However, if a different figure is encoded in the first column, then, as one progresses through all the columns from left to right, one obtains an entirely different system of figures. This means that the encoding of Fig. 20a, by column 4, forces the entire system to encode a different space of figures from that encoded when column 6 is chosen for Fig. 20a. Thus, recalling the statement made earlier that different external encodings can lead to different internal encodings, what we can now see is that the internal encoding is different not just with respect to the presented figure but with respect to the entire set of figures which the full analyzer system encodes.

7. THE JOHANSSON MOTION PHENOMENON

Johansson [12] has given an elegant analysis of relative motion phenomena, of which Fig. 21a is typical. The two dots in Fig. 21a are moving perpendicularly from

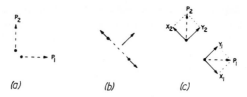

FIG. 21.   The Johansson motion phenomenon: (a) the physical system of movement; (b) the visual interpretation; (c) Johansson's analysis.

each other, in phase and in harmonic motion. If each dot is shown separately, it is seen as a dot moving along its line of motion. However, if the dots are presented at the same time, they are not seen as the superposition of their separate movements. Instead, they are seen as moving to and from each other along a diagonal line, the dashed line in Fig. 21b. The impression is often that the dots are the ends of an invisible rod that is stretching and contracting. Furthermore, the rod is seen as moving in the opposite diagonal direction. The perceived motion is represented in Fig. 21b.

Johansson's analysis is as follows: Each of the motion vectors P_1 and P_2 shown in Fig. 21a, are split into two vectors: (1) One vector describes the *relative* motion of the two dots, i.e., to and from each other. This is shown in Fig. 21c as a vector in the X direction. (2) The other vector is the motion *common* to both dots. This is shown in Fig. 21c as the Y vector. Johansson demonstrated that this analysis holds for a wide variety of examples.

Let us now analyze Johansson's results in terms of the theory being offered in the present paper. Observe first that mathematically the entire set of available vectors in a plane forms a group under addition. (Two vectors can be added by the "parallelogram of forces" construction.) In the case here, the vectors are motion vectors, and it would not seem controversial to suppose that each motion vector is given by a motion detector or analyzer. Let G therefore be the entire system of motion analyzers. It is structured as a group because a vector space forms a group. The Johansson experiments imply that, in the described circumstances, this detector system factorizes as follows:

$$G = G_1.G_2$$
$$= \text{common motion system} \times \text{relative motion system}.$$

Thus the total motion P_i in Fig. 21a, is given by an analyzer Y in system G_1 and an analyzer X_i in system G_2. Observe that system G_1 *controls* system G_2. That is, the perceptual organization imposed on the entire motion is that of a stretching and contracting rod—i.e., with relative velocity given by G_2—being pulled through space by G_1. Thus the G_1-analyzer system covers a collection of G_2-systems.

However, let us look more carefully at how these analyzer systems must be wired together. To do this we start at the lowest level possible and work upwards. At the lowest level, because each of the two points is perceived as a point, each must be encoded by what is effectively a point-analyzer $\{e\}$. However, observe that the two points are perceived as reflectionally symmetric about the Y axis. This implies that the two point-analyzers are together covered by an analyzer system with the structure Z_2 (the reflection group), mapping each point-analyzer to the other. Again, observe that the two points are perceived as reflectionally symmetric about the X line. Therefore, one has another analyzer system also with the structure Z_2 covering the two point-analyzers, but this time mapping each to itself. The above considerations therefore imply that the rod is covered by an internal analyzer system of the form $(Z_2 \times Z_2).\{e\}$.

The perceptual results indicate that this system is acted on (controlled) by the analyzer system $G_1.G_2$, given above. First the relative motion system G_2, which detects stretches and contractions of the rod and hence of the $(Z_2 \times Z_2).\{e\}$-system, can be regarded as the pure deformation system A. This maps $(Z_2 \times Z_2).\{e\}$-systems onto themselves along the X line. Second, the common motion system G_1 which detects the motion along the Y direction can be regarded as the translation system R. This maps $(Z_2 \times Z_2).\{e\}$-systems to each other along the Y line. Thus the complete analyzer system we have been elaborating has the hierarchical structure

$$R.A\hat{\imath}(Z_2 \times Z_2).\{e\}.$$

It is important to observe that the full analyzer system just defined obeys the Interconnection Principles: symmetry-axis analyzers of the internal system $Z_2 \times Z_2$ are wired as eigenspaces of the external analyzer system $R.A$. This can be seen by consulting Fig. 21c. Perceptually, the symmetry axis X of one of the Z_2-systems is simultaneously the line of relative motion. Therefore it must be wired as an eigenspace of the analyzer system A. Again, as shown in Fig. 21c, the symmetry axis Y of the other Z_2-system is simultaneously the line of common motion. Therefore, it must be wired as an eigenspace of the analyzer system R.

Inspecting the sequence given above, one sees a number of the analyzer systems from the cartesian bundle-system (Definition 8). This attests to the considerable salience and frequent perceptual use of this system. It would be a simple matter to show that the entire cartesian bundle-system is involved. For example, the shear system N determines the angle betwen the X and Y vectors; the SO_2-system determines the orientation of the combined X and Y vectors, etc. Thus the entire analyzer system responsible for this motion phenomenon is none other than the one which we have diagramed in Fig. 18, and which has been of central concern in the rest of our discussion. Much more will be said about this in our final section on complex shape perception.

8. THE ANALYSIS OF COMPLEX SHAPE

It will now be argued that the generative analyzer structures of the highly restrictive type we have been discussing are the basis for the analysis of complex shapes such as those shown in Fig. 1.

Let us contrast the view we are to develop with that which has been provided by Marr and Nishihara [20]. The latter proposes that a complex shape is given by a hierarchy of successively greater detailing; i.e., a multi-resolution hierarchy. At each stage of resolution the figure is represented by a concatenation of cylinders as argued by Binford [3]. At the coarsest level, a man is simply a cylinder. At the next level of fineness, the cylinders describing the limbs are discerned, etc. An example is shown in Fig. 22a.

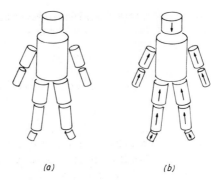

(a)   (b)

FIG. 22. (a) An example of the Binford analysis of a man. (b) The interpretation as a deformation hierarchy in accord with the interconnection principles.

However, in accord with the theory developed in the present paper, a different view will be proposed and explored in this section. It will be argued that the human visual system constructs a deformation hierarchy. This proposal does not exclude the possibility of a resolution hierarchy; it only asserts that a deformation hierarchy is crucial in the analysis of complex shape.

Before considering a full figure, let us begin by examining what Marr and Nishihara [20] regard as the basic module, the cylinder. This unit of analysis was proposed by Binford [3] and called the generalized cone. As shown, in Fig. 23c, it consists of a cross section which is moved along some axis, generally called the *spine*, while undergoing a deformation action called a *sweeping rule*.

What we shall now see is that Binford's proposal is exactly the kind of structure one would obtain from the type of analyzer control hierarchy being proposed in this paper. Consider first the cross section. Since the experiments cited earlier indicate that a regular polygon is perceived as generated from a side by D_n, one can simply generalize this by letting $n \to \infty$ and propose that a circle is visually generated from a point by the rotation group SO_2, as shown in Fig. 23a. This implies an analyzer system with structure SO_2 mapping points in space rotationally onto each other. Furthermore, observe that, visually, the cross section is reflectionally symmetric, as shown in Fig. 23b. Therefore, it appears that an analyzer system structured by the reflection group Z_2 maps the cross section to itself reflectionally. That is, the Z_2-system makes reflected copies of SO_2. Mathematically, one describes this by saying that the two groups are combined as a semi-direct product $Z_2(\times_{sd})SO_2$

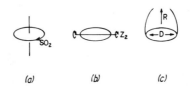

(a)   (b)   (c)

FIG. 23. (a) The cross section of a generalized cone as generated by the rotation group. (b) A reflection of the cross section. (c) The creation of the generalized cone.

(reflection times rotations where reflections are automorphisms of rotations). Thus to summarize so far, the perceptual structure of the cross section implies that it is generated by an analyzer system with the structure $(Z_2(\times_{sd})SO_2).\{e\}$.

Now, if one perceives the cylinder itself as generated in the way proposed by Binford, then two external analyzer systems must act on the system just described: The first encodes deformations of the cross section, i.e., it is an analyzer system structured by the deformation group D. The second encodes movement of the cross section along the spine of the cylinder, and is thus a system structured by R the translation group. This means that the entire analyzer control hierarchy we have been discussing has the structure

$$R.D\hat{\imath}(Z_2(\times_{sd})SO_2).\{e\} \qquad \text{(Binford/Marr situation)}.$$

However, something remarkable can now be seen: Recall the analyzer structure we deduced for the Johansson motion phenomenon:

$$R.A\hat{\imath}(Z_2 \times Z_2).\{e\} \qquad \text{(Johansson situation)}.$$

What is remarkable is that this structure is essentially identical to what we deduced for the Binford/Marr situation. Let us compare the two structures, level by level, starting at the lowest level of the hierarchy. At this level, one has the point analyzer $\{e\}$. Next one has the analyzer system $Z_2(\times_{sd})SO_2$ in the Binford/Marr example, and the system $Z_2 \times Z_2$ in the motion case. These two systems are the same except that the latter is simply a 2-dimensional version of the former. On the next higher level, both hierarchies have a deformation component. Although, in the motion case, this component was regarded as A (the system with unequal stretches on the two perpendicular axes), it could also have been a 1-dimensional version of D (the dilation system with equal stretches in all directions). On the top level, both hierarchies have the R-translation system.

Thus the argument seems to show that the same analyzer structure underlies the perception of two phenomena which we would not have suspected to possess commonality at all. To show even more clearly how the two phenomena are related to each other, consider the following. As can be seen in Fig. 23c, the action of the D-system is that of defining the changing cross section in Binford's generalized cone. The rule defining this change is generally called the *sweeping rule*. In the Johansson motion case, the pure deformation action is in the direction of the X vectors; i.e., it is the relative motion component in Fig. 21c. Now consider the action of R in the Binford case shown in Fig. 23c. It translates the cross section of the cylinder through space, and thus defines the *spine* of the cylinder. In the Johansson motion example, the action of R is movement in the Y direction (see Fig. 21c). This is the common motion vector. Thus, what the above considerations have done is to show that the sweeping rule in the generalized cone becomes the relative motion vector in the Johansson phenomenon, and the spine of the generalized cone becomes the common motion vector of the Johansson case.

Let us now consider some other aspects of the Binford/Marr situation. Observe that the analyzer system deduced for this situation must be wired in accord with the Interconnection Principles (Sect. 5.2) as follows: The cross-section system $Z_2(\times_{sd})SO_2$ constitutes an internal system under the external action of the R and D

systems. The Interconnection Principles state that the symmetry axes of the internal system are wired as eigenspaces of the external system. Consider first the SO_2-system. As shown in Fig. 23a, it analyzes the cross section such that the symmetry axis is the rotation axis vertically through the plane of the cross section. However, observe that this is the direction of the R-component shown in Fig. 23c, that is, the eigenspace (invariant line) of the R-analysis—in accord with the Interconnection Principles. Now consider the Z_2-system. As shown in Fig. 23b, it analyzes the cross section as having symmetry axes in the plane of the cross section. However, by looking at Fig. 23c, we see that the D-system analyzes these axes as eigenspaces—thus corroborating the Interconnection Principles.

Having checked the wiring principles, it is now possible to progress from the analysis of the single cylinder to that of the entire figure. For observe that the R-eigenspace is the direction of shortening and lengthening a limb of the figure. Therefore, the symmetry axis of the internal SO_2-system is wired as an eigenspace of a deformation system that analyzes the figure as stretched in that direction. To corroborate this perceptually, I conducted the following experiment [14, Experiment 13]. Subjects were presented with the 22 outlines of animals, birds, plants, and abstract shapes shown in Fig. 1. They were asked to assign the perceived direction of maximal flexibility at four regions of each figure (by selecting a spoke of an 8-spoke star placed in that region). With considerable statistical significance, they chose what corresponds to either the Z_2 axis or the SO_2 axis in the above system ($n = 12$; 88 choices per subject; expected mean = 44; actual mean 77.58; $t(11) = 27.228$, $p < 0.0005$, one tailed). Thus the subjects were converting symmetry axes into eigenspaces.

This experiment therefore corroborates the proposal that the shape hierarchy is one of deformation, not just of resolution as Marr and Nishihara [20] propose. The deformation hierarchy can be represented by a diagram such as that shown in Fig. 22b, where the arrows reverse the generating deformations. Note that the arrows act simultaneously as symmetry axes and as eigenspaces.

What we will do now is take the concepts developed so far in this section and elaborate a more detailed, more complete, view of the analyzer organization encoding complex shape. In the following discussion, the full referential structure will be divided into five successive referential levels corresponding to five ascending levels in the analyzer hierarchy. Note that one could regard the levels as successive phases of an algorithm. However, we are choosing here to regard them as constituting successive sections of the referential path upward and leftward through the analyzer structure, as illustrated by the path in Fig. 6. Note finally that the analysis will be applied to a contour in the 2-dimensional plane. Thus we will be able to consider part of that analyzer structure to be the sequence $R.A\hat{\imath}(Z_2 \times Z_2).\{e\}$ deduced for the Johansson phenomenon. However, more will now be added to this structure. The five referential stages are:

LEVEL 1. The first level of the encoding can be simply summarized as follows: $Z_2 \times Z_2$ analyzer systems encode reflectional symmetry where possible in the image. In the literature, there are a number of different views as to what a full reflection-symmetry encoding looks like. The one which we shall adopt here is that developed by Brady [5–8] which he calls *smoothed local symmetry* (SLS). It is important to understand Brady's structure theory at this point, in order to understand the four subsequence levels I develop later.

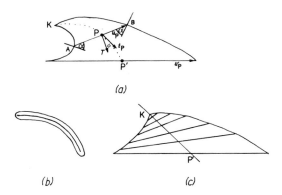

(a)

(b)   (c)

FIG. 24.   (a) Brady's SLS analysis of a contour. (b) A flexed symmetry. (c) An SLS with only local shear and local pure deformation, but no rotation.

Figure 24a summarizes the SLS analysis. Points A and B are located on the contour such that the line AB subtends the *same* angle α with the normal at A and the normal at B. The symmetry point is P, the point bisecting AB. Thus Brady's system produces a smooth locus of symmetry points as shown (the line of dots from K to P'). The locus is the SLS. I will make the assumption that Brady's system describes the analysis performed by human perception.

Considering Fig. 24a again, three vectors will be of particular importance to us: (1) the vector u_P, based at P and pointing to B; (2) the vector T perpendicular to u_P and equal to the difference between the tangent vector at A and that at B; (3) t_P the tangent to the SLS.

What is crucial for us to observe is that t_P is not necessarily coincident with T; that is, there is a non-zero angle ϕ between t_P and T. As Brady and Asada [8] argue, the case of $\phi = 0$ corresponds to what Blum and Nagel [4] call a *flexed symmetry*, an example of which is the "worm" shown in Fig. 24b. It is in this particular case that the SLS-analysis is the same as the generalized-cone analysis [8, p. 44].

LEVEL 2. The importance of Brady's description to us is that it allows us to bring into consideration the SL_2R-analysis that was developed in the present paper. The clue is the fact that ϕ is not necessarily zero. In accord with the type of analysis provided in this paper, this must imply that the frame (u_P, t_P), generated by the basis vectors u_P and t_P, is a *sheared* frame. Thus as one travels along the SLS, one has four groups acting:

(1) the rotation group SO_2 which successively rotates the local frame (u_P, t_P) along the SLS (e.g., in Fig. 24a, the vector u'_P, at the base, rotates on its way to becoming u_P);

(2) the shear group N which successively shears the local frame (u_P, t_P);

(3) the pure deformation group A which induces stretch and contraction in the local frame (u_P, t_P) (e.g., in Fig. 24a, the vector u'_P contracts on its way to becoming u_P);

(4) the translation group R which moves the frame (u_P, t_P) along the SLS.

This means that, at each point on the SLS, there is an analyzer system structured by $SL_2R = A.N.SO_2$. We will assume that the stability ordering on the SL_2R-system is the same as that obtained by the experimental results summarized in Fig. 2; and we will soon investigate the perceptual consequences of this on the contour structure.

It was observed above that each such SL_2R-system acts on a local $Z_2 \times Z_2$-system, the (u_p, t_p) frame; and furthermore that the SL_2R-system is itself acted on by a translation control-level structured by R. In consequence, we see that an SLS analysis implies the structuring of the contour by the cartesian bundle-system (Definition 8):

$$R.(A.N.SO_2) \hat{\imath} ((Z_2 \times Z_2)(\times_{sd})R^2).$$

Recall now that the first level of analysis was the encoding by $Z_2 \times Z_2$-systems in the way implied by Brady's SLS-theory. With the local external action of SL_2R, the implication is that at each point P there is an analyzer system with the structure depicted in Fig. 18. This means that each frame along the symmetry line, is a result of encoding by one of the columns in that analyzer system; e.g., the frame (u_p, t_p) in Fig. 24a would be the result of encoding by the final column in Fig. 18.

Now recall that the successive reference in Fig. 18 is given by the repeated leftward-upward path shown in Fig. 6. This implies that the second level of reference is that of removing the rotation coordinate. What does this mean visually?

Recall that if only this SL_2R-coordinate were present—i.e., there is no shear or pure deformation—one would have the worm shown in Fig. 24b. Thus if one factored rotation, one would be factoring the "worm" from the structure. This would yield the structure shown in Fig. 24c which I will call a "simple wave." The worm has only rotation, the simple wave has only shear and pure deformation. Note that, while the symmetry axis of the simple wave is straight, the successive frames along the axis are sheared.

LEVEL 3. The successive reference structure in Fig. 6 shows that the next level of reference is that of removing shear. The resulting figure can be easily computed. Putting together Eqs. (6) and (7) in Brady [7], one has, for any SLS, the following relation between the curvature κ_P of the SLS at P, the curvature κ_A of the contour at A, and the curvature κ_B of the contour at B:

$$\kappa_P = \phi' + \frac{\kappa_A \sin(\alpha + \phi)}{2 \sin 2\alpha} + \frac{\kappa_B \sin(\alpha - \phi)}{2 \sin 2\alpha}.$$

However, at level 2 one factors SO_2, which means that the SLS has no curvature; that is, $\kappa_P = 0$. Then, when one reaches Level 3, shear is removed and thus one also has $\phi = 0$ and $\phi' = 0$. A simple substitution of these values in the above equation reveals

$$\kappa_A = -\kappa_B.$$

Therefore at this third reference level one obtains a figure which is curvature symmetric; e.g., a simple hill or spike.

LEVEL 4. The next level of reference deals with the pure deformation system A and the translation system R. Note first, that the Interconnection Principles state that the $Z_2 \times Z_2$-axes are wired as eigenspaces of the A- and R-systems. Thus reference through the A-system will alter the local frame such that the axes u_p and t_p are the directions of flexibility. Again, reference in the R-system will translate the frame along the t_p axis. The question we must now answer is: which of the frames (u_p, t_p) are altered in the reference and how; are the axes stretched or contracted; are they translated away from the base u'_p, or towards it?

Let us answer this question in the particular but frequent case where the SLS terminates at a point K of maximal local curvature on the contour, as shown in Fig. 24a. By Attneave [2], K is a point of local maximal information. Resnikoff [21] gives a precise quantification of this notion; and I will elsewhere attempt to show that Resnikoff's informational measure corresponds to the instability measure in the present paper. Thus, if the direction of reference in our system is that of increasing stability, it will correspond in the Attneave–Resnikoff analysis to decreasing curvature; i.e., deforming the boundary so that the curvature at K diminishes. But how should this curvature reduction take place?

Observe that there is a contour region of a point K of maximal curvature, in which, as one moves down the SLS away from K, the u_p-vector increases in length. Now observe that, if this contour region is defined as a protrusion on some more main component, then each of the larger axes can be taken to represent a more stable continuation of the contour of the main component because a larger axis, being nearer the component, implies a continuation of lesser curvature. Therefore, referencing in the A and R analyzer-systems must respectively widen and translate the u_p-vectors till they become as large as, and coincident with, the base u'_p-vector. Therefore, this reference structure seems the logical one to diminish curvature. Observe that it contracts the protrusion till it disappears.

LEVEL 5. The final level of reference determines the order in which the several protrusions are contracted on a shape. I will call the entire analyzer system of the shape (e.g., including those subsystems encoding the several protrusions), the *complete* system. We shall put together its structure as follows. Recall that each protrusion is structured by the cartesian bundle-system $R.(A.N.SO_2)\hat{\imath}((Z_2 \times Z_2)(\times_{sd})R^2)$. Clearly, under the view developed in this paper, the reference path through the complete system (e.g., encompassing the protrusions) will contract each protrusion in turn (i.e., reference through each cartesian bundle-system) in order of their decreasing instability. The accurate evaluation of the instability of a protrusion sums the instabilities on all the analyzer levels of the cartesian bundle-system encoding the protrusion. A rough heuristic would simply be to take the stability of a protrusion to be its size, because this would often inversely correspond to its curvature. Thus, protrusions would be contracted in order of their size—the smaller being removed first. For example, consider the mouse in the top left of Fig. 1. The ear is smaller than the nose. Therefore, the ear would be removed first before the nose. Eventually, the mouse would be a smooth oval; and then, again by the Interconnection Principles (encoding symmetry axes as eigenspaces), the oval would be reduced to a circle. Thus, according to this analysis, the internal structure of a mouse is the rotation group SO_2. The encoding SO_2 analyzer system would correspond to the left-most and lowest-level system in the analyzer hierarchy. This would be covered by a string of identity elements upward through the hierarchy. Thus, translating the SO_2-system successively to the right, in its own hierarchy level, would induce the deformations that eventually create a mouse; i.e., the nose would be induced first, then the ear, etc.

This allows us to determine finally the precise structure of the complete system. We have said that the internal system is the generative structure of the most prototypical shape in the reference sequence (e.g., the circle). Notice that a contour is reflectionally symmetric locally at each point P' on the contour-line. In particular, on the most prototypical contour (e.g., a circle) one has, at each point P' on the contour, a local cartesian frame consisting of a tangent vector u'_p, and a normal t'_p. Each such local frame becomes a base frame, depicted as (u'_p, t'_p) in Fig. 24a, which is the starting frame of the cartesian bundle-system to be applied at that point. This means that the internal system of the most prototypical form (e.g., SO_2) is both an internal group and an external control group at the highest level in the hierarchy. As an *external* system each analyzer, in the system, covers a cartesian bundle system located at that point on the contour. In differential-geometric terms, the internal system, in its external capacity, becomes the base manifold of a principle bundle structure, where the bundle group is the cartesian bundle system. With respect to the contour, encoded as an *internal* system, each successive mapping of that system to its cosets on that level in the hierarchy, is the successive outward coordinatization through successive cartesian bundles. The set of coordinates within each such bundle is a coset leader. As we said, each of these coordinatizations generates a protrusion of successive local pure deformation, local shear and local rotation, in the way illustrated in Fig. 24. This completely encodes the complex shape as a generative structure.

REFERENCES

1. F. Attneave, Some informational aspects of visual perception, *Psychol. Rev.* **61**, 1954, 183–193.
2. F. Attneave, Triangles as ambiguous figures, *Amer. J. Psychol.* **18**, 1968, 447–453.
3. O. B. Binford, Visual perception by computer, in *IEEE Systems. Science, and Cybernetics Conf.*, Miami, Fla., 1971.
4. H. Blum and R. N. Nagel, Shape description using weighted symmetric axis features, *Pattern Recognit.* **10**, 1978, 167–180.
5. M. Brady, Parts description and acquisition using vision, in *Robot Vision* (A. Rosenfeld, Ed.), Soc. Photo-Opt. Instrum. Eng., pp. 20–28, Bellingham, Wash., 1982.
6. M. Brady, Smoothed local symmetries and local frame propagation, in *Proceedings of the 1982 Conference on Pattern Recognition and Image Processing*, pp. 629–633, IEEE Comput. Soc., New York, 1982.
7. M. Brady, Criteria for representations of shape, in *Human and Machine Vision* (A. Rosenfeld and J. Beck, Eds.), Erlbaum, Hillsdale, N.J., 1983.
8. M. Brady and H. Asada, Smoothed local symmetries and their implementation, *Int. J. Robotics Res.* **3**, 1984, 36–61.
9. E. Goldmeier, Uber Anlichkeit bei gehenen Figuren, *Psychol. Forschung* **21**, 1937, 146–209; English transl., Similarity in visually perceived forms, *Psychological Issues*, Monograph No. 29, **8**, No. 1, International Universities, New York, 1972.
10. I. Grossman and W. Magnus, *Groups and Their Graphs*, Math. Assn., Washington, D.C., 1964.
11. D. D. Hoffman and W. A. Richards, Parts of recognition, *Cognition* **18**, 1984, 65–96.
12. G. Johansson, *Configurations in Event Perception*, Almqvist and Wiksell, Stockholm, Sweden, 1950.
13. M. Leyton, (1982). A unified theory of cognitive reference frames, in *Proceedings of the Fourth Annual Conference of the Cognitive Science Society*, University of Michigan, Ann Arbor, Michigan, 1982, pp. 204–209.
14. M. Leyton, *A Theory of Information Structure*, Ph.D thesis, University of California, Berkeley, 1984.
15. M. Leyton, Perceptual organization as nested control, *Biol. Cybern.* **51**, 1984, 141–153.
16. M. Leyton, A theory of cognition. II. Perceptual organization, manuscript, Psychology Department, Harvard University, 1984.
17. M. Leyton, A theory of information structure. I. General Principles, submitted for publication, 1985.

18. M. Leyton, A theory of information structure. II. A theory of perceptual organization, submitted for publication, 1985.
19. E. Mach, *The Analysis of Sensations* (1897), English transl. Dover, New York, 1959.
20. D. Marr and H. K. Nishihara, Representation and recognition of the spatial organization of three-dimensional shapes, *Proc. R. Soc. London B* **200**, 1978, 169–294.
21. H. L. Resnikoff, *The Illusion of Reality: Topics in Information Science*, Springer-Verlag, New York, 1985.
22. W. A. Richards and D. D. Hoffman, Codon constraints on closed 2D shapes, *Comput. Vision, Graphics, Image Process.* **31**, No. 1, 1985.
23. I. Rock, *Orientation and Form*, Academic Press, New York, 1973.
24. M. Wertheimer, Laws of organization in perceptual forms (1923), in *A Source Book of Gestalt Psychology* (W. D. Ellis, Ed.), (English transl.) Harcourt Brace, New York, 1938.

Early Vision: From Computational Structure to Algorithms and Parallel Hardware

Tomaso Poggio

Artificial Intelligence Laboratory and Center for Biological Information Processing, Massachusetts Institute of Technology, 545 Technology Square, Cambridge, Massachusetts 02139

Received November 15, 1984

I review a new theoretical framework that from the computational nature of early vision leads to algorithms for solving them and suggests a specific class of appropriate hardware. The common computational structure of many early vision problems is that they are mathematically ill-posed in the sense of Hadamard. Standard regularization analysis can be used to solve them in terms of variational principles that enforce constraints derived from a physical analysis of the problem, see T. Poggio and V. Torre (Artificial Intelligence Lab. Memo No. 773, MIT, Cambridge, Mass., 1984). Studies of human perception may reveal whether some principles of a similar type are exploited by biological vision. It can also be shown that the corresponding variational principles are implemented in a natural way by analog networks, see T. Poggio and C. Koch (Artificial Intelligence Lab. Memo No. 783, MIT, Cambridge, Mass., 1984). Specific electrical and chemical networks for localizing edges and computing visual motion are derived. These results suggest that local circuits of neurons may exploit this unconventional model of computation. © 1985 Academic Press, Inc.

1. INTRODUCTION

One of the best definitions of early vision is that it is inverse optics—a set of computational problems that both machines and biological organisms have to solve. While in classical optics the problem is to determine the images of physical objects, vision is confronted with the inverse problem of recovering 3-dimensional shape from the light distribution in the image. Most processes of early vision such as stereomatching, computation of motion, and all the "structure from" processes can be regarded as solutions to inverse problems. This common characteristic of early vision can be formalized: *most early vision problems are "ill-posed problems" in the sense of Hadamard*. In this article we will first review a framework proposed by Poggio and Torre [54]. They suggested that the mathematical theory developed for regularizing ill-posed problems leads in a natural way to the solution of early vision problems in terms of variational principles of a certain class. They argued that this is a theoretical framework for some of the variational solutions already obtained in the analysis of early vision processes. They also showed how several other problems in early vision can be approached and solved. Thus the computational, ill-posed nature of early vision problems dictates a specific class of algorithms for solving them, based on variational principles of a certain class. It is natural to consider next which classes of parallel hardware may efficiently implement regularization algorithms. We are especially interested in implementations that are suggestive for biology. I will thus review a model of computation proposed by Poggio and Koch [53] that maps easily into biologically plausible mechanisms. They showed that a natural way of implementing variational principles of the regularization type is to use electrical, chemical, or neuronal networks. They also showed how to derive specific networks

190

for solving several low-level vision problems, such as the computation of visual motion and edge detection.

1.1. Variational Solutions to Vision Problems

In recent years, the computational approach to vision has begun to shed some light on several specific problems. One of the recurring themes of this theoretical analysis is the identification of physical constraints that make a given computational problem determined and solvable. Some of the early and most successful examples are the analyses of stereo matching (Marr and Poggio [43, 44]; Grimson [15, 16]; Mayhew and Frisby [45]; Kass [32]; for a review, see Nishihara and Poggio [50]) and structure from motion (Ullman [68]). In these studies constraints such as continuity of 3-D surfaces in the case of stereo matching and rigidity of objects in the case of structure from motion play a critical role for obtaining a solution.

More recently, variational principles have been used to introduce specific physical constraints. A variational principle defines the solution to a problem as the function that minimizes an appropriate cost function. Many problems can be formulated in this way, including laws that are normally expressed in terms of differential equations. In physics, for instance, most of the basic laws have a compact formulation in terms of variational principles, that require the minimization of a suitable functional, such as the Lagrangian for classical mechanics. In vision, the problem of interpolating visual surfaces through sparse depth data can be solved by minimizing functionals that embed a constraint of smoothness [16, 17, 60, 61]. Thus, the surface that best interpolates the data minimizes a certain cost functional which measures how much the surface deviates from smoothness. Computational of the motion field in the image can be successfully performed by finding the smoothest velocity field consistent with the data [26, 20, 21]: in other words, among all possible velocity fields that are consistent with the data a solution can be found by choosing the velocity field that varies the least. In a similar way, shape can be recovered from shading information in terms of a similar variational method [28].[1]

We wish to show that these variational principles follow in a natural and rigorous way from the ill-posed nature of early vision problems. We will then propose a general framework for "solving" many of the processes of early vision.

1.2. Ill-Posed Problems

Hadamard (1923) defined a mathematical problem to be *well posed* when its solution

   (a) exists

   (b) is unique

   (c) depends continuously on the initial data (this condition is essentially equivalent to saying that the solution is robust against noise, because it will change only a little for small perturbations of the input data).

---

[1] The computation of subjective contours [67, 4, 25], of lightness [24], and of shape from contours [1, 5] can also be formulated in terms of variational principles. Terzopoulos [60, 63] has recently reviewed the use of a certain class of variational principles in vision problems within a rigorous theoretical framework.

Most of the problems of classical physics are well posed, and Hadamard argued that physical problems have to be well posed. "Inverse" problems, however, are usually ill-posed. Inverse problems can usually be obtained from the direct problems by exchanging the role of solution and data. Consider, for instance,

$$y = Az \tag{1}$$

where A is a known operator. The direct problem is to determine y from z, the inverse problem is to obtain z when y ("the data") are given. Though the direct problem is usually well posed, the inverse problem is usually ill-posed, when z and y belong to a Hilbert space.

Typical ill-posed problems are analytic continuation, backsolving the heat equation, superresolution, computer tomography, image restoration, and the determination of the shape of a drum from its frequency of vibration, a problem which was made famous by Kac [30]. In early vision, most problems are ill-posed because the solution is not unique (but see later the case of edge detection), since the operator corresponding to A is usually not injective, as in the case of shape from shading, surface interpolation, and computation of motion (see Poggio and Torre [54]).

1.3. Regularization Methods

Rigorous regularization theories for "solving" ill-posed problems have been developed during the past years (see especially Tikhonov [64], Tikhonov and Arsenin [65], and Nashed [48, 49]. Most ill-posed problems are not sufficiently constrained. To regularize them and make them well posed, one has to introduce generic constraints on the problem. In this way, one attempts to force the solution to lie in a subspace of the solution space, where it is well defined. The basic idea of regularization techniques is to restrict the space of acceptable solutions by choosing the function that minimizes an appropriate functional. The regularization of the ill-posed problem of finding z from the data y such that $Az = y$ requires the choice of norms $\| \cdot \|$ (usually quadratic) and of a *stabilizing functional* $\|Pz\|$. The choice is dictated by mathematical considerations, and, most importantly, by a physical analysis of the generic constraints on the problem. Three methods that can be applied (see Bertero [3]) among the several standard regularization techniques are:

(I) Among z that satisfy $\|Pz\| \leq C$, where C is a constant, find z that minimizes

$$\|Az - y\|, \tag{2}$$

(II) Among z that satisfy $\|Az - y\| \leq C$, find z that minimizes

$$\|Pz\|, \tag{3}$$

(III) Find z that minimizes

$$\|Az - y\|^2 + \lambda \|Pz\|^2, \tag{4}$$

where λ is a regularization parameter.

The first method consists of finding the function z that satisfies the constraint $\|Pz\| \leq C$ and best approximates the data. The second method computes the function z that is sufficiently close to the data (C depends on the estimated errors and is zero if the data are noiseless) and is most "regular." In the third method, the regularization parameter λ controls the compromise between the degree of regularization of the solution and its closeness to the data. Standard regularization theory provides techniques to determine the best λ [65, 69]. It also provides a large body of results about the form of the *stabilizing functional P* that ensure uniqueness of the result and convergence. For instance, it is usually possible to ensure uniqueness in the case of Tikhonov's stabilizing functionals (also called *stabilizers of pth order*) defined by

$$\|Pz\|^2 = \int \sum_{r=0}^{p} c_r(\xi) \left(\frac{d^r z}{d\xi^r} \right)^2 d\xi, \tag{5}$$

where $c(\xi)$ are positive weighting factors. Equation (5) can be extended in the natural way to several dimensions. If one seeks regularized solutions of Eq. (1) with P given by Eq. (5) in the Sobolev space W_2^p of functions that have square-integrable derivatives up to pth order, the solution can be shown to be unique (up to the null space of P), if A is linear and continuous. This is because for every p the space W_2^p is a Hilbert space and $\|Pz\|^2$ is a quadratic functional (see Theorem 1, [65, p. 63]). They all correspond to either interpolating or approximating splines (for method II and method III, respectively). In the following, I will refer to regularization methods based on Tikhonov stabilizers as *standard regularization theory*. It turns out that most stabilizing functionals used so far in early vision are of the Tikhonov type (see also Terzopoulos, [60, 62]). I will discuss later the limitations of standard regularization theory and the need to develop nonstandard regularization methods (possibly, but not necessarily, of the type of Eqs. (2), (3), and (4)) for solving satisfactorily basic problems in vision.

1.4. Example I. Motion

Our first claim is that variational principles introduced recently in early vision for the problem of computation of motion and surface interpolation and approximation are exactly equivalent to standard regularization techniques. The associated uniqueness results are directly provided by regularization theory. We briefly discuss the case of motion computation in its recent formulation by Hildreth [20, 21].

Consider the problem of determining the 2-dimensional velocity field along a contour in the image. Local motion measurements along contours provide only the component of velocity in the direction perpendicular to the contour. The component of velocity tangential to the contour is invisible to a local detector that examines a restricted region of the contour. Figure 1 shows how the local velocity vector $\mathbf{V}(s)$ is decomposed into a perpendicular and a tangential component to the curve

$$\mathbf{V}(s) = v^\tau(s)\mathbf{T}(s) + v^\perp(s)\mathbf{N}(s). \tag{6}$$

The perpendicular component $v^\perp$ and direction vectors $\mathbf{T}(s)$ and $\mathbf{N}(s)$, are given directly by the initial measurements, the "data." The tangential component $v^\tau(s)$ is not and must be recovered to compute the full 2-dimensional velocity field $\mathbf{V}(s)$. Thus the "inverse" problem of recovering $\mathbf{V}(s)$ from the data is ill-posed because the

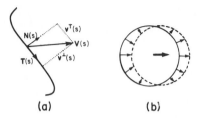

FIG. 1. Decomposition and ambiguity of the velocity field: (a) The local velocity vector $\mathbf{V}(s)$ in the image plane is decomposed according to Eq. (6) into components perpendicular and tangent to the curve. (b) Local measurements cannot measure the full velocity field; the circle undergoes pure translation; the arrows represent the perpendicular components of velocity that can be measured from the images [54].

solution is not unique. Mathematically, this arises because the operator K defined by

$$v^{\perp} = K\mathbf{V} \tag{7}$$

is not injective. Equation (7) describes the imaging process as applied to the physical velocity field $\mathbf{V}$ which consists of the x and y components of the velocity field on the image plane.

Intuitively, the set of measurements given by $v^{\perp}(s)$ over an extended contour should provide considerable constraint on the motion of the contour. An additional generic constraint, however, is needed to determine this motion uniquely. For instance, rigid motion on the plane is sufficient to determine $\mathbf{V}$ uniquely but is very restrictive, since it does not cover the case of motion of a rigid object in space. Hildreth suggested, following Horn and Schunck [26], that a more general constraint is to find the smoothest velocity field among the set of possible velocity fields consistent with the measurements. The choice of the specific form of this constraint was guided by physical considerations—the real world consists of solid objects with smooth surfaces whose projected velocity field is usually smooth—and by mathematical considerations—especially uniqueness of the solution. Hildreth proposed two algorithms: in the case of exact data the functional to be minimized is a measure of the smoothness of the velocity field

$$\|P\mathbf{V}\|^2 = \int \left(\frac{\partial \mathbf{V}}{\partial s}\right)^2 ds \tag{8}$$

subject to the measurements $v^{\perp}(s)$. Since in general there will be error in the measurements of $v^{\perp}$, the alternative method is to find $\mathbf{V}$ that minimizes

$$\|K\mathbf{V} - v^{\perp}\|^2 + \lambda \int \left(\frac{\partial \mathbf{V}}{\partial s}\right)^2 ds. \tag{9}$$

It is immediately seen that these schemes correspond to the second and third regularizing method, respectively. (The constraint of rigid translatory motion in the image plane corresponds to using the first regularizing method with the same P and $C = 0$.) Uniqueness of the solutions (proved by Hildreth for the case of Eq. (8)) is a direct consequence for both Eqs. (8) and (9) of standard theorems of regularization theories. In addition, other results can be used to characterize how the correct solution converges depending on the smoothing parameter λ (Geiger, in preparation).

1.5. Example II. Edge Detection

We have recently applied regularization techniques to another classical problem of early vision—edge detection. Edge detection, intended as the process that attempts to detect and localize changes of intensity in the image (this definition does not encompass all the meanings of edge detection) is a problem of numerical differentiation [66]. Notice that differentiation is a common operation in early vision and is not restricted to edge detection. The problem is ill-posed because the solution does not depend continuously on the data.

The intuitive reason for the ill-posed nature of the problem can be seen by considering a function $f(x)$ perturbed by a very small (in L_2 norm) "noise" term $\varepsilon \sin \Omega x$. $f(x)$ and $f(x) + \varepsilon \sin \Omega x$ can be arbitrarily close for very small ε, but their derivatives may be very different if Ω is large enough. This simply means that a derivative operation "amplifies" high-frequency noise.

In 1-D, numerical differentiation can be regularized in the following way. The "image" model is $y_i = f(x_i) + \varepsilon_i$, where y_i is the data and ε_i represent errors in the measurements. We want to estimate f'. We chose a regularizing functional $\|Pf\| = \int (f''(x))^2 \, dx$, where f'' is the second derivative of f. This choice corresponds to a constraint of smoothness on the intensity profile. Its physical justification is that the (noiseless) image is indeed very smooth because of the imaging process: the image is a bandlimited function and has therefore bounded derivatives. The second regularizing method (no noise in the data) is equivalent then to using interpolating cubic splines for differentiation. The third regularizing method, which is more natural since it takes into account errors in the measurements, leads to the variational problem of minimizing (see [57])

$$\sum \left(y_i - f(x_i) \right)^2 + \lambda \int \left(f''(x) \right)^2 dx. \tag{10}$$

Poggio et al. [55] have shown (a) that the solution f of this problem can be obtained by convolving the data y_i (assumed on a regular grid and satisfying appropriate boundary conditions) with a convolution filter R, and (b) that the filter R is a cubic spline with a shape very close to a Gaussian and a size controlled by the regularization parameter λ (see Fig. 2). Differentiation can then be accomplished by convolution of the data with the appropriate derivative of this filter. The optimal value of λ can be determined for instance by cross validation and other techniques. This corresponds to finding the optimal scale of the filter (see [54]).

These results can be directly extended to two dimensions to cover both edge detection and surface interpolation and approximation. The resulting filters are very similar to two of the edge detection filters derived and extensively used in recent years [42, 8, 66]. The Laplacian of the optimal filter found in this way seems, however, to have slightly better performance than the Laplacian of a Gaussian.

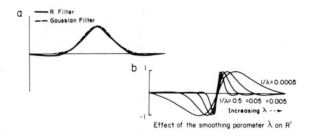

FIG. 2. The edge detection filter: (a) The convolution filter obtained (15) by regularizing the ill-posed problem of edge detection with method (III) (solid line). It is a cubic spline, very similar to a Gaussian (dotted line). (b) The first derivative of the filter for different values of the regularizing parameter λ, which effectively controls the *scale* of the filter. This 1-dimensional profile can be used for 2-dimensional edge detection by filtering the image with oriented filters with this transversal crossection and choosing the orientation with maximum response (see 16). The second derivative of the filter (not shown here) is quite similar to the second derivative of a Gaussian [66].

It is important to notice that the result about convolution holds true more in general: *if the data are given on a regular grid with appropriate boundary conditions, the solution of a standard regularization principle (Eq. 4, with Tikhonov stabilizers) is equivalent to convolving the data with a precomputed filter* [55].

Other problems in early vision such as shape from shading [28] and surface interpolation [16, 17, 60–62] in addition to the computation of velocity, have already been formulated and "solved" in similar ways using variational principles of the type suggested by regularization techniques (although this was not realized at the time—also, Ikeuchi and Horn's formulation is nonquadratic). It is also clear that other problems such as stereo and structure from motion can be approached in terms of, possibly nonstandard, regularization analysis (see [54]).

1.6. Physical Plausibility of the Solution

Uniqueness of the solution of the regularized problem—which is ensured by formulations such as Eqs. (2)–(4)—is not the only (or even the most relevant) concern of regularization analysis. Physical plausibility of the solution is the most important criterion. The decision regarding the choice of the appropriate stabilizing functional cannot be made judiciously from purely mathematical considerations. A physical analysis of the problem and of its generic constraints play the main role. Regularization theory provides a framework within which one has to seek constraints that are rooted in the physics of the visual world. This is, of course, the challenge of regularization analysis.

In our example of the computation of motion the constraint of smoothness is justified by the observation that the projection of 3-dimensional objects in motion onto the image plane tends, in a probabilistic sense, to yield smoother velocity fields (see [20, 21]). In the case of edge detection the constraint on the derivative of image intensity is justified by the bandlimiting properties of the optics. In the case of motion, however, as more dramatically in the case of surface reconstruction, the constraint of smoothness is not always correct. This suggests that more general stabilizing functionals are needed to deal with the general problem of discontinuities (see discussion).

A method for checking physical plausibility of a variational principle is, of course, computer simulation. A simple technique we suggest is to use the Euler–Lagrange equation associated with the variational problem. In the computation of motion, Yuille [70] has obtained the following *sufficient and necessary* condition for the solution of the variational principle equation (8), to be the correct physical solution

$$\mathbf{T} \cdot \frac{\partial^2 \mathbf{V}}{\partial s^2} = 0$$

where $\mathbf{T}$ is the tangent vector to the contour and $\mathbf{V}$ is the true velocity field. The equation is satisfied by uniform translation or expansion and by rotation only if the contour is polygonal. These results suggest that algorithms based on the smoothness principle will give correct results, and hence be useful for computer vision systems, when (a) motion can be approximated locally by pure translation, rotation, or expansion, or (b) objects have images consisting of connected straight lines.

In the case of edge detection (intended as numerical differentiation), the solution is correct *if and only if* the intensity profile is a polynomial spline of odd degree [55].

From a more biological point of view, a careful comparison of the various "regularization" solutions with human perception promises to be a very interesting area of research, as suggested by Hildreth's work on the computation of motion. For some classes of motions and contours, the solution of Eqs. (8) and (9) is not the physically correct velocity field. In these cases, however, the human visual system also appears to derive a similar, incorrect velocity field [20, 21].

2. ANALOG NETWORKS FOR SOLVING VARIATIONAL PROBLEMS

We consider now the question of which class of parallel hardware could efficiently solve variational principles of the regularization type. The specific architecture depends of course on the norm and the stabilizer P that are chosen. Standard regularization methods (with quadratic norms and Tikhonov's stabilizers) map into two main classes of algorithms: *convolution algorithms* (for data on a regular grid) and *multigrid algorithms*. These two classes of algorithms can be efficiently implemented by architectures of N simple processors with local interconnections (possibly with a multilevel structure) [60, 62]. Digital architecture of this type have only a limited interest for biology. Poggio and Koch [53] have suggested a more "exotic" type of hardware for implementing regularization solutions that suggests a new model for neural computations.

It is well known that analog networks—chemical, electrical, or mechanical—are a natural computational model for solving variational principles. The behavior of such systems can be described using variational principle. Electrical network representations have been constructed for practically all of the field equations of physics—many of them are equivalent to variational principles (for an electrical network implementation of Schrodinger's equation, see Kron [36]). A fundamental reason for the natural mapping between variational principles and electrical or chemical networks is Hamilton's least action principle (for more details see Koch and Poggio [35]).

The class of variational principles that can be computed by analog networks is dictated by Kirchhoff's current and voltage laws (KCL and KVL), which simply represent conservation and continuity restrictions satisfied by each network component (appropriate variables are usually voltage and current for electrical networks and affinity, i.e., chemical potential and chemical turnover rate for chemical systems). KCL and KVL provide the unifying structure of network theory. A large body of theoretical results is available about networks satisfying them, including classical thermodynamics [52]. In particular, KCL and KVL imply Tellegen's theorem. Tellegen's theorem captures the basic constraints provided by KCL and KVL. It is one of the most general and powerful results of network theory and is independent of any assumptions about constitutive relations or stationarity. (*Tellegen's theorem*: If $\mathbf{U}$ is the vector of branch potentials—with one component for each branch—and $\mathbf{J}$ is the vector of branch flows, then $\mathbf{U}^t \cdot \mathbf{J} = 0$. Thus the flow and the potential variables are orthogonal at any instant in time.)

For a network containing only sources and linear resistances, Tellegen's theorem implies Maxwell's minimum heat theorem: *the distribution of voltages and currents is such that it minimizes the total power dissipated as heat.* These results can be extended to nonlinear circuit components [39, 51, 53], but in the following we will restrict ourselves to linear networks (possibly with negative resistances). The power dissipated by each linear resistance in the circuit is a quadratic term of the form

$$I_k V_k \tag{11}$$

where I_k and V_k are the current and the voltage respectively, corresponding to the resistive process r_k. It follows that any network consisting of linear resistances and voltage sources E_k minimizes the following associated quadratic functional

$$\sum_k r_k I_k^2 - \sum_i E_i I_i, \tag{12a}$$

where the second sum includes all the batteries. For a network of resistances and current sources I_i, the functional is given by

$$\sum_k g_k V_k^2 - \sum_i I_i V_i, \tag{12b}$$

where the second sum includes all the current sources and $g_k = 1/r_k$.

It is then easy to show the equivalence of Eqs. (12) and the regularization principle Eqs. (4), (5). Thus, electrical networks of linear resistances and batteries (or current sources) can *solve* quadratic variational principles of the form of Eqs. (4), (5). The solution is unique when Eqs. (4), (5) yields a unique solution (which is usually the case, see [54]).

Electrical networks of resistances and batteries do not have any dynamics. In practice, however, small capacitances will be present and the *stability* of the network must then be considered. It turns out that networks implementing regularization principles of the form of Eqs. (4), (5) are indeed stable, under the same conditions that ensure a unique solution [53].

An equivalent way to see how electrical networks can implement variational principles of the form of Eqs. (4), (5) is to consider the associated Euler–Lagrange equations (the equivalence of variational principles with PDE also shows how to map them into parallel digital architecture). Since the functional to be minimized is quadratic, the Euler–Lagrange equations are linear, of the form $Qz = b$. They have a unique solution z, corresponding to the unique solution of the variational principle. In the discrete case, these equations correspond to n linear, coupled algebraic equations. These equations can be implemented in a network containing only linear resistances and sources. More precisely, the vector b, which depends on the data ($b = A^*y$), can always be represented in terms of current or voltage sources. The matrix Q corresponds to the symmetric, real matrix of the network resistances [53].

Although their procedure will always yield an electrical network with linear elements implementing $Q_z = b$, its physical realization might require negative resistances (if the corresponding term in Q is negative). An alternative implementation of variational principles, common on analog computers, involves operational amplifiers [29].

As pointed out by Terzopoulos in the context of vision (earlier, Horn [24] proposed an analog implementation of the lightness computation) a significant advantage of analog networks is their extreme parallelism and speed of convergence. Furthermore, resistive networks are robust against random errors in the values of the resistances [31]. A disadvantage is the limited precision of the analog signals.

2.1. An Example. Circuits for the Velocity Field Computation

We will consider next some specific networks for solving the optical flow computation. The simpler case is when the measurements of the perpendicular component of the velocity, $v_i^\perp$, at n points along the contours, are exact. In this case, the discretized Euler–Lagrange equations, corresponding to the regularization solution, Eq. (3), are [20]

$$\left(2 + \kappa_i^2\right)v_i^\mathsf{T} - v_{i+1}^\mathsf{T} - v_{i-1}^\mathsf{T} = d_i, \tag{13}$$

where κ is the curvature of the curve at location i, d_i is a function of the data $v_i^\perp$ and the curve and v_i^T is the unknown tangential component of the velocity v_i at location i to be computed. Figures 3a and 3b show two simple networks that solve Eq. (13), where one network is the dual of the other. The equation describing the ith node, in the case of Fig. 3b, is

$$\left(2g + g_i\right)V_i - gV_{i+1} - gV_{i-1} = I_i \tag{14}$$

where V_i is the voltage—corresponding to the unknown v_i^T—and I_i the injected current at node i—corresponding to the measurement $v_i^\perp$. It is surprising that this implementation does not require negative resistances. When the constraints are satisfied only approximately (Eq. (5)), the equations are

$$\left(2 + l_{xi}^2\right)V_{x_i} - V_{x_{i+1}} - V_{x_{i-1}} + c_i V_{y_i} = d_{x_i}$$
$$\left(2 + l_{y_i}^2\right)V_{y_i} - V_{y_{i+1}} - V_{y_{i-1}} + c_i V_{x_i} = d_{y_i} \tag{11}$$

where l_i depends on the contour and V_{x_i} and V_{y_i} denote the x and y component of

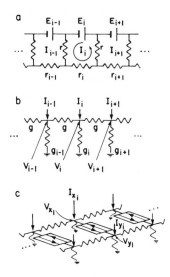

FIG. 3.   Resistive networks computing the smoothest velocity field. The first two networks correspond
to the situation where the constraints imposed by the data are to be satisfied exactly. The equation for the
current, which corresponds to the desired v^T in mesh i (for Fig. 1a), is given by $(2r + r_i)I_i - rI_{i+1} - rI_{i-1} = E_i$, where the value of the battery E_i depends on the velocity data $v_i^\perp$ at location i. The voltage
at node i, corresponding to v_i^T, for the network 1b, the dual of network 1a, is given by $(2g + g_i)V_i - gV_{i+1} - gV_{i-1} = I_i$, where the injected current I_i depends on the velocity data. Sampling the voltage
between nodes corresponds to linear interpolation between the node values. Network 1c, consisting of two
interconnected networks of the type shown in 1b, solves the velocity field problem when the data are not
exact. The equations for the ith nodes are $(2g_x + g_{x_i})V_{x_i} - g_xV_{x_{i+1}} - g_xV_{x_{i-1}} + c_iV_{y_i} = d_{x_i}$ and $(2g_y + g_{y_i})V_{y_i} - g_yV_{y_{i+1}} - g_yV_{y_{i-1}} + c_iV_{x_i} = d_{y_i}$. However, unlike the two purely passive networks shown above,
an active element may be required, since the cross-term c_i, relating the x and the y components of
velocity, can be negative. Such a negative resistance can be mimicked by operational amplifiers [53].

the unknown velocity v_i at location i. The corresponding network is shown in Fig.
3c. The resistances c_i can be either positive or negative, and may therefore require
active components such as operational amplifiers. More precisely, physically realizable linear resistances, whether in electrical or in chemical systems, must dissipate
energy, i.e., they are constrained to the upper right and the lower left quadrant in the
$I–V$ plane and can thus only be positive. There are at least three options for
implementing negative resistances using basic circuit components: (i) The positive
and negative resistances can be replaced in a purely resistive network by inductances
and capacitances, with impedance $i\omega L$ and $-i/(\omega C)$, respectively. The network
equations are then formulated in terms of the currents and voltages at the fixed
frequency ω. (ii) The negative resistance can be implemented by the use of operational amplifiers or similar active circuit elements. (iii) One may exploit the negative
impedance regions in such highly nonlinear systems as the tunnel diode.

In the limit, as the meshes of the circuit become infinitesimally small, the network
solves the continuous variational problem, and not simply its discrete approximation.

We have devised similar analog networks for solving other variational problems [53] arising from regularization analysis of several early vision problems such as edge detection [55] and surface interpolation [60, 62]. These networks are analog solutions to certain kinds of spline interpolation and approximation problems. For instance, in the case of surface interpolation the analog network solves the *biharmonic* equation which is the Euler–Lagrange equation corresponding to the variational problem associated with thin-plate splines [60]. The stabilizing functionals used in regularization analysis of vision problems typically lead to local and limited connections between the components of the network.

2.2. Solving Ill-posed Problems with Biological Hardware

Analog electrical networks are a natural hardware for computing the class of variational principles suggested by regularization analysis. Because of the well-known isomorphism between electrical and chemical networks (see, e.g., [7 or 10]) that derives from the common underlying mathematical structure, appropriate sets of chemical reactions can be devised, at least in principle, to "simulate" exactly the electrical circuits. Figure 4 shows chemical networks that are equivalent (in the steady state) to the electrical circuit of Figs. 3b and c.

Electrical and chemical systems of this type therefore offer a computational model for early vision that is quite difference from the digital computer. Equations are "solved" in an implicit way, exploiting the physical constraints provided by Kirchhoff's laws. It is not difficult to imagine how this model of computation could be extended to mixed electrochemical systems by the use of transducers, such as chemical synapses, that can decouple two parts of a system, similarly to operational amplifiers [53].

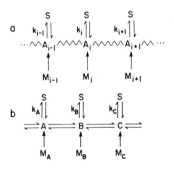

FIG. 4. Two examples of chemical networks solving the motion problem for exact measurements. They are equivalent, under steady-state conditions, to the electric circuit of Fig. 3b. Figure 4a illustrates a diffusion-reaction system. A substance A (the concentration of which corresponds to the desired v^τ) diffuses along a cable while reacting with an extracellular substance S (first-order kinetics). The corresponding on-rate k_i varies from location to location. This could be achieved by a differential concentration of an enzyme catalyzing the reaction or by varying the properties of the membrane where the reaction has to take place. The off-rates can either be constant or vary with location. The inputs are given by the influxes of substance A. Figure 2b shows a lumped chemical network, where n different, well-mixed substances, interact with each other and with the substrate S. Assuming first-order kinetics, these reactions can mimic a linear positive resistance under steady-state conditions. The input is given by the influx M_X and the output by the concentration of X [53].

Could neural hardware exploit this model of computation? Increasing evidence shows that electronic potentials play a primary role in many neurons [58] and that membrane properties such as resistance, capacitance, and equivalent inductance (arising through voltage and time-dependent conductances; see, e.g., [9, or 34] may be effectively modulated by various types of neurotransmitters, acting over very different time scales [41]. Dendrodendritic synapses and gap junctions serve to mediate graded, analog interactions between neurons and do not rely on all-or-none action potentials [14].

When implementing electrical networks in equivalent neuronal hardware, one can exploit a number of elementary circuit elements (for possible neuronal implementations; see Fig. 5). Patches of neuronal membrane or cytoplasm can be treated as resistance and capacitance. Voltage sources may be mimicked by synapses on dendritic spines [35] or on small dendrites, whereas synapses on large dendrites act as current sources. Chemical synapses could effectively serve to decouple different parts of a network (see [53]). Chemical processes such as the reactions associated with postsynaptic effects or with neuropeptides could also be thought as part of a complex electrochemical network. Obviously, the analogy cannot be taken too literally. It would be very surprising to find the exact neural analog of the circuit of Fig. 5 somewhere in the CNS. We are convinced, however, that the *style* of computation represented by analog circuits represents a very useful model for neural computations as well as a challenge for future VLSI circuit designs.

3. CONCLUSION

The concept of ill-posed problems and the associated regularization theories seem to provide a satisfactory theoretical framework for much of early vision. This perspective justifies the use of variational principles of a certain type for solving specific problems, and suggests how to approach other early vision problems. It provides a link between the computational (ill-posed) nature of the problems and the computational structure of the solution (as a variational principle). It also suggests computational "hardware" that is natural for solving variational problems of the type implied by regularization methods.

FIG. 5. This schematic figure illustrates a hypothetical neuronal implementation of the regularization solution of the motion problem. A dendrite, acting both as pre- and post-synaptic element has a membrane resistance that can vary with location. It can implement under steady-state conditions the circuit 3b. The inputs—corresponding to the measurements $v^\perp$ —are given by synaptic mediated currents, while the output voltages—corresponding to the desired v^τ —are sampled by dendro-dendritic synapses. The membrane resistance can be locally controlled by suitable synaptic inputs—corresponding to the curvature of the contour—from additional synapses that open channels with a reversal potential close to the resting potential of the dendrite. This scheme can be extended to the case where the measurements of the perpendicular velocities are not exact, by having a similar, second dendrite (see also Fig. 3c). The interaction between both dendrites takes place via two reciprocal chemical synapses. If the corresponding cross-term in Eq. (15) is negative, the chemical synapses must be inverting, presynaptic depolarization leading to a hyperpolarization [53].

Despite its attractions, this theoretical synthesis of early vision also shows the limitations that are intrinsic to the variational solutions proposed so far, and in any case to the *standard* (Tikhonov's) forms of the regularization approach. The basic problem is the degree of smoothness required for the unknown function z that has to be recovered. If z is very smooth, then it will be robust against noise in the data, but it may be too smooth to be physically plausible. For instance, in visual surface interpolation, the degree of smoothness obtained from a specific form of Eqs. (4), (5) —corresponding to so-called thin plate splines—smoothes depth discontinuities too much and often leads to unrealistic results (but see [60, 62]). An interesting approach to this problem is to parametrize with an additional parameter λ—a function of position—the order of the Tikhonov stabilizer. The question is then how to determine the optimal value of the parameter.

Different (e.g., nonquadratic) variational principles may be used to attack the general problem of discontinuities. Nonstandard variational principles may also arise in another one of the most fundamental problems in early vision, the problem of integrating different sources of information, such as stereo, motion, shape from shading, etc. This problem is ill-posed, not just because the solution is not unique (the standard case), but because the solution is usually overconstrained and may not exist (because of noise in the data). For instance, the problem of combining several different sources of surface information may easily lead to nonquadratic regularization expressions (though different "noninteracting" constraints can be combined in a convex way, see Terzopoulos, [60, 62]). These minimization problems will in general have multiple local minima.

Again, analog networks may be used to solve these minimization problems, with multiple local minima corresponding to the zeros of the *mixed potential* [6, 52]. Schemes similar to *annealing* [47, 33, 22] may be easily implemented by appropriate sources of Gaussian noise driving the analog network. The associated differential equation describing the dynamics of the system is then a stochastic differential equation. The stochastic differential equations ("Langevin" equations) describing an electrical or a chemical system with a source of Gaussian noise (e.g., voltage or the presence of a chemical reactive substance) can be formulated in terms of Ito or Stratonovitch calculus [13]. They can be solved with the Fokker–Planck or the Kolmogorov method. A "solution" of a stochastic differential equation is a characterization in terms of probability distributions of the "output" process. For linear networks, simpler correlation methods can also be used. If the noise is white and Gaussian, its spectral density is proportional to the "temperature" T. In a chemical network "noise" may be introduced in various, simple ways.

Needless to say, a number of biophysical mechanisms, such as somatic and dendritic action potentials, interactions between conductance changes, voltage, and time-dependent conductances, etc., are likely to be used by neurons and patches of membrane to perform a variety of nonlinear operations.

I conclude with a caution note, that hopefully will turn out to be too conservative. The range of applicability of variational principles is related to the deep question of the computational organization of a visual processor and its control structure. It is unlikely that variational principles alone could have enough flexibility to control and coordinate the different modules of early vision and their interaction with higher level knowledge. This also hints at the basic limitation of present regularization methods that makes them suitable only for the first stages of vision. They derive numerical representations—surfaces—from numerical representations—images. However, it is not difficult to see how the computation of the more symbolic type of representations that are essential for a powerful vision processor represent a form of regularization. The restriction of the solution space to a set of "symbols" regularizes an ill-posed problem. Standard regularization methods restrict the solution space to the set of generalized splines.

ACKNOWLEDGMENTS

This written version of my lecture is a porridge of two previous technical reports [54, 53]. The idea of vision problems as ill-posed problems originated from a conversation with Professor Mario Bertero of the University of Genoa. We are grateful to A. Yuille, E. Hildreth, D. Terzopoulos, J. Marroquin, T. Collett, and C. Koch for many discussions and comments. C. Bonomo made many less appreciated comments along the way as well. This paper reviews research done within the Artificial Intelligence Laboratory and the Center for Biological Information Processing (Whitaker College) at the Massachusetts Institute of Technology. Support for the A.I. Laboratory's research in artificial intelligence is provided in part by the Advanced Research Projects Agency of the Department of Defense under Office of Naval Research contract N00014-80-C-0505.

REFERENCES

1. H. G. Barrow and J. M. Tennenbaum, Interpreting line drawings as three dimensional surfaces, *Artif. Intell.* **17**, 1981, 75–117.
2. M. V. L. Benett, A comparison of electrically and chemically mediated transmission, in *Structure and Function of Synapses* (G. D. Pappas and D. P. Purpura, Eds.) Raven, New York, 1972.
3. M. Bertero, Problemi lineari non ben posti e metodi di regolarizzazione, in *Problem non ben posti ed inversi*, Istituto di Analisi Globale, Florence, Italy, 1982.
4. J. M. Brady, W. E. L. Grimson, and D. J. Langridge, Shape encoding and subjective contours, in *First Annual Natl. Conf. on Artificial Intelligence*, 1980, pp. 15–17.
5. J. M. Brady and A. Yuille, An extremum principle for shape from contour, *IEEE Trans. Pattern Anal. Mach. Intell.* **PAMI-288**, 1984, 301.
6. R. K. Brayton and J. K. Moser, A theory of nonlinear networks, I, *Quart. Appl. Math.* **22**, 1964, 1–33.
7. H. Busse and B. Hess, Information transmission in a diffusion-coupled oscillatory chemical system, *Nature (London)* **244**, 1973, 203–205.
8. J. F. Canny, Finding Edges and Lines in Images, MIT Artificial Intelligence Laboratory Technical Report TR-720, June 1983.
9. K. S. Cole, *Membranes Ions and Impulses*, Univ. of California Press, Berkeley, 1968.
10. M. Eigen, Molecules, information, and memory: From molecules to neural networks, in *The Neurosciences: Third Study Program* (F. O. Schmitt and F. G. Worden, Eds.), MIT Press, Cambridge, Mass. 1974.
11. S. A. Ellias and J. K. Stevens, The dendritic varicosity: A mechanism for electrically isolating the dendrites of cat retinal amacrine cells? *Brain Res.* **196**, 1972, 365–372.
12. S. Geman and D. Geman, Stochastic relaxation, Gibbs distributions, and the Bayesian restoration of images, IEEE *Trans. Pattern Anal. Mach. Intell.*, **6**, 1984, 721–741.
13. I. I. Gihman and A. V. Skorohod, *Stochastic Differential Equations*, Springer-Verlag, Berlin/New York, 1972.
14. K. Graubard and W. H. Calvin, Presynaptic dendrites: Implications of spikeless synaptic transmission and dendritic geometry, in *The Neurosciences: Fourth Study Program* (F. O. Schmitt and F. G. Worden, Eds.), MIT Press, Cambridge, Mass., 1979.
15. W. E. L. Grimson, A computer implementation of a theory of human stereo vision, *Philos. Trans. R. Soc. London B* **292**, 1981, 217–253.

16. W. E. L. Grimson, *From Images to Surfaces: A Computational Study of the Human Early Visual System*, MIT Press, Cambridge, Mass., 1981.
17. W. E. L. Grimson, A computational theory of visual surface interpolation, *Philos. Trans. R. Soc. London B* **298**, 1982, 395–427.
18. J. Hadamard, *Lectures on the Cauchy Problem in Linear Partial Differential Equations*, Yale Univ. Press, New Haven, Conn., 1923.
19. E. C. Hildreth, Implementation of a theory of edge detection, S.M. thesis, Department of Computer Science and Electrical Engineering, MIT, 1980; AI Lab. Technical Report 597, MIT, Cambridge, Mass. 1980.
20. E. C. Hildreth, *The Measurement of Visual Motion*, MIT Press, Cambridge, Mass. 1984.
21. E. C. Hildreth, Computation of the velocity field, *Proc. R. Soc. London B* **221**, 1984, 189–220.
22. G. E. Hinton and T. J. Sejnowski, Optimal perceptual inference, in *Proc. IEEE 1983 Conf. Computer Vision and Pattern Recognition*, Washington, D.C., 1983.
23. J. J. Hopfield, Neurons with graded response have collective computational properties like those of two-state neurons, in *Proc. Natl. Acad. Sci. USA*, 1984, in press.
24. B. K. P. Horn, Determining lightness from an image, *Comput. Graphics Image Process.* **3**, 1974, 111–299.
25. B. K. P. Horn, The Least Energy Curve, AI Memo 612, MIT AI Lab., Cambridge, Mass., 1981.
26. B. K. P. Horn and B. G. Schunck, Determining optical flow, *Artif. Intell.* **17**, 1981, 185–203.
27. R. Hummel and S. Zucker, On the Foundations of Relaxation Labeling Processes, Computer Vision and Graphics Laboratory TR 80-7, McGill University, 1980.
28. K. Ikeuchi and B. K. P. Horn, Numerical shape from shading and occluding boundaries, *Artif. Intell.* **17**, 1981, 141–184.
29. D. S. Jackson, *Analog Computation*, McGraw–Hill, New York, 1960.
30. M. Kac, Can one hear the shape of a drum? *Amer. Math. Monthly* **73**, No. 4, Part II, 1966, 1–23.
31. W. J. Karplus, *Analog Simulation: Solution of Field Problems*, McGraw–Hill, New York, 1958.
32. M. H. Kass, Computating Stereo Correspondence, M.S. thesis, MIT, 1984.
33. S. Kirkpatrick, C. D. Gelatt, Jr., and M. P. Vecchi, Optimization by simulated annealing, *Science* **220**, 1983, 671–680.
34. C. Koch, Cable theory in neurons with active, linearized membranes, *Biol. Cybern.* **50**, 1984, 15–33.
35. C. Koch and T. Poggio, A theoretical analysis of electrical properties of spines, *Proc. R. Soc. London B* **218**, 1983, 455–477.
36. G. Kron, Electric circuit models of the Schrodinger equation, *Phys. Rev.* **67**, 1945, 39–43.
37. B. C. Kuo, *Linear Networks and Systems*, McGraw–Hill, New York, 1967.
38. D. G. Luenberger, *Optimization by Vector Space Methods*, Wiley, New York, 1969.
39. A. G. J. MacFarlane, *Dynamical System Models*, Harrap, London, 1970.
40. R. H. MacNeal, The solution of elastic plate problems by electrical analogies, *J. Appl. Mech.* **18**, 1951, 59–67; in *The Bending and Stretching of Plates*, Macmillan, New York.
41. E. Marder, Mechanisms underlying neurotransmitter modulation of a neuronal circuit, *Trends Neurosci. (Pers. Ed.)* **7**, 1984, 48–53.
42. D. Marr and E. C. Hildreth, Theory of edge detection, *Proc. R. Soc. London B* **207**, 1980, 187–217.
43. D. Marr and T. Poggio, Cooperative computation of stereo disparity, *Science (Washington, D.C.)* **194**, 1976, 283–287.
44. D. Marr and T. Poggio, A theory of human stereo vision, *Proc. Roy. Soc. London B* **204** 1979, 301–328; earlier version, MIT AI Lab Memo 451, 1977.
45. J. E. W. Mayhew and J. P. Frisby, Psychophysical and computational studies towards a theory of human stereopsis, *Artif. Intell.* **17**, 1981, 349–385.
46. W. S. McCulloch and W. Pitts, A logical calculus of the ideas immanent in nervous activity, *Bull. Math. Biophys.* **5**, 1943, 115–133.
47. N. Metropolis, A. Rosenbluth, M. Rosenbluth, A. Teller, and E. Teller, Equation of state calculations by fast computing machines, *J. Chem. Phys.* **21**, No. 6, 1953, 1087–1092.
48. M. Z. Nashed, Approximate regularized solutions to improperly posed linear integral and operator equations, in *Constructive and Computational Methods for Differential and Integral Equations* (G. Auger, Ed.), pp. 289–296, Akademie Verlag, Berlin, 1974.
49. M. Z. Nashed, (Ed.), *Generalized Inverses and Applications*, Academic Press, New York, 1976.
50. H. K. Nishihara and T. Poggio, Stereo vision for robotics, in *Proceedings of the First International Symposium of Robotics Research*, in press.

51. G. F. Oster and C. A. Desoer, Tellegen's theorem and thermodynamic inequalities, *J. Theor. Biol.* **32**, 1971, 219–241.
52. G. F. Oster, A. Perelson, and A. Katchalsky, Network thermodynamics, *Nature* **234**, 1971, 393–399.
53. T. Poggio and C. Koch, Analog Networks: A New Approach to Neuronal Computation, Artificial Intelligence Lab. Memo No. 783, MIT, Cambridge, Mass., 1984.
54. T. Poggio and V. Torre, Ill-posed Problems and Regularization Analysis in Early Vision, Artificial Intelligence Lab. Memo No. 773, MIT, Cambridge, Mass., April 1984.
55. T. Poggio, H. Voorhees, and A. Yuille, Regularizing Edge Detection, Artificial Intelligence Lab. Memo No. 776, MIT, Cambridge, Mass., 1984.
56. I. Prigogine, *Thermodynamics of Irreversible Processes*, Wiley–Interscience, New York, 1967.
57. C. H. Reinsch, Smoothing by spline functions, *Numer. Math.* **10**, 1967, 177–183.
58. F. O. Schmitt, P. Dev, and B. H. Smith, Electrotonic processing of information in brain cells, *Science* (Washington, D.C.), **193**, 1976, 114–120.
59. B. G. Schunck and B. K. P. Horn, Constraints on optical flow computation, in *Proc. IEEE Conf. Pattern Recognition and Image Processing*, pp. 205–210, 1981.
60. D. Terzopoulos, Multiresolution Computation of Visible-Surface Representations, Ph.D. thesis, Dept. of Electrical Engineering and Computer Science, MIT, Cambridge, Mass., 1984.
61. D. Terzopoulos, Multilevel computational processes for visual surface reconstruction, *Comput. Vision Graphics, Image Process.* **24**, 1983, 52–96.
62. D. Terzopoulos, Multilevel Reconstruction of Visual Surfaces: Variational Principles and Finite Element Representations, Artificial Intelligence Lab. Memo 671, MIT; in *Multiresolution Image Processing and Analysis* (A. Rosenfeld, Ed.), pp. 237–310, Springer-Verlag, New York/Berlin, 1984.
63. D. Terzopoulos, Integrating visual information from multiple sources for the cooperative computation of surface shape, in *From Pixels to Predicates: Recent Advances in Computational and Robotic Vision*, (A. Pentland, Ed.), Ablex, Norwood, N.J., 1985.
64. A. N. Tikhonov, Solution of incorrectly formulated problems and the regularization method, *Soviet Math. Dokl.* **4**, 1963, 1035–1038.
65. A. N. Tikhonov and V. Y. Arsenin, *Solutions of Ill-Posed Problems*, Winston & Sons, Washington, D.C., 1977.
66. V. Torre and T. Poggio, On Edge Detection, Artificial Intelligence Lab. Memo No. 768, MIT, Cambridge, Mass., March 1984.
67. S. Ullman, Filling in the gaps: The shape of subjective contours and a model for their generation, *Biol. Cybern.* **25**, 1976, 1–6.
68. S. Ullman, The interpretation of structure from motion, *Proc. R. Soc. London B* **203**, 1979, 405–426.
69. G. Wahba, Ill-Posed Problems: Numerical and Statistical Methods for Mildly, Moderately, and Severely Ill-Posed Problems with Noisy Data, Tech. Report No. 595, Univ. of Wisconsin, Madison, 1980.
70. A. Yuille, The Smoothest Velocity Field and Token Matching Schemes, Artificial Intelligence Lab. Memo No. 724, MIT, Cambridge, Mass., August 1983.

Codon Constraints on Closed 2D Shapes

WHITMAN RICHARDS AND DONALD D. HOFFMAN*

*Natural Computation Group, Massachusetts Institute of Technology,
Cambridge, Massachusetts*

Received September 27, 1984

Codons are simple primitives for describing plane curves. They thus are primarily image-based descriptors. Yet they have the power to capture important information about the 3D world, such as making part boundaries explicit. The codon description is highly redundant (useful for error-correction). This redundancy can be viewed as a constraint on the number of possible codon strings. For smooth closed strings that represent the bounding contour (silhouette) of many smooth 3D objects, the constraints are so strong that sequences containing 6 elements yield only 33 generic shapes as compared with a possible number of 15,625 combinations. © 1985 Academic Press, Inc.

1. INTRODUCTION

An important task for object recognition is the description of the shape of a bounding contour, such as a silhouette that outlines an object. Although recognition need require only partial segments of such contours, the internal canonical description, against which the image contour is compared, is very likely a closed ring. Our concept of most "objects" should lead us to expect such a closed contour. The description of closed, 2D contours thus is an important ingredient of a system for object recognition. First we present such a scheme, described in more detail elsewhere [3, 4] and then show how the scheme leads to a hierarchical taxonomy of closed, 2D shapes.

2. THE REPRESENTATION

When we view shapes such as those in Fig. 1, we immediately see the ellipse and square as being "simpler" (in some psychological sense) than the lemniscate or epicycloid. Why? If we were to "measure" the simplicity of a shape contour by the degree of its polynomial equation, then the cardioid in the middle would have the simplest form, and the square the most complex, being the highest order polynomial. Clearly a polynomial representation seems quite inappropriate for our visual system, because it does not make explicit the meaningful properties of the shapes.

If we asked a child why the ellipse is "simpler" than the lemniscate, he would probably reply "because the latter has two parts, whereas the ellipse has only one." This simple observation is the basis for our representation for shapes: namely a shape should be described in terms of its natural "parts." Fortunately, the rule for finding "parts" is conceptually simple, for when 3D entities are joined to create complex objects, then concavities almost always are created at the join, as indicated by the small arrows in Fig. 2.

This regularity of natural objects follows a principle of transversality treated more fully elsewhere [5]. In the silhouette, these concavities appear as cusps, or as places

---

*D. D. Hoffman is now at the University of California, Irvine.

207

FIG. 1. An ellipse, square, cardioid, lemniscate, and epicycloid. The cardioid has the simplest (lowest order) equation; the square is the highest order polynomial equation.

FIG. 2. Joining parts generally provides concavities in the resulting silhouette.

of maximum negative curvature. Natural parts thus lie between concave cusps. In Fig. 1, the rule specifies that the ellipse and the square have no parts, whereas the lemniscate has two and the epicycloid has three. (The cardioid can not be broken simply into two parts, hence must be "simpler" than the two figures on its right.) Our first rule for representing (2D) shapes is thus as follows:

> *Segment a curve at concave cusps (or minima of negative curvature) in order to break the shape into its "parts."*

3. PART DESCRIPTORS: CODONS

Having now broken a curve into "parts" our next task is to describe the part. Again, we wish that our description capture some natural property of shapes, rather than an arbitrary mathematical formula, such as a polynomial equation. For example, at some stage in our representation, we would like to know whether it is round or polygonal. But even before such descriptors, is there a still simpler, more abstract, representation? Perhaps first we should represent the "sides" of the part, or its "top." As a step in this direction, we propose a very primitive representation based upon the singular points of curvature, namely the maxima, minima, and zeroes of curvature along the curve. An important property of these descriptors is that their ordinal relations remain invariant under translations, rotations, and dilations. Thus, regardless of the 3D orientation and size of a part to its whole, a

FIG. 3. Minima of curvature are indicated in slashes. Arrows indicate direction of traversal of curve. "Figure" is taken to be to the left of the direction of traversal.

relation between these descriptors is preserved in the 2D image. This property follows because the inflection of a 3D curve is preserved under projection, guaranteeing that at least the ordinal relations between minima, maxima, and zeroes of curvature will be preserved under projection. Our scheme thus provides a very primitive representation for a part, simply in terms of the ordinal relations of the extrema of curvature. This approach yields six different basic primitive shapes, or codons (see Fig. 4).

In order to define the codon types, it is first necessary to define maxima and minima of curvature. These definitions require that a convention be adopted for the sign of curvature. Consider Fig. 3. There are two directions along which the profile of the face may be traversed. In the upward direction (left) the minima of curvature (slashes) correspond to the points where the curve rotates at the greatest rate in the clockwise direction. If the same curve is traversed in the opposite direction, however, then the maxima and minima reverse. Our convention thus places "figure" to the left of the direction of traversal. When the figure is on the left, then the profile indeed looks like a face because the minima of curvature divide the curve into the natural parts—namely forehead, nose, mouth, and chin. (Note that the opposite view yields the "vase" of Rubin's famous figure–ground illusion observed as early as 1819 by Turton [14].) Thus, knowing which side is the figure determines the choice of orientation on a curve, or, conversely, choosing an orientation determines which side is the figure by convention. Minima are then typically associated with the concavities of the figure, whereas maxima are convexities.

To define our basic primitive codons, we first note that all curve segments lying between minima of curvature must have zero, one, or two points of zero curvature. If there are no zeroes (i.e., inflections), then the segment is designated as a type 0 codon (see Fig. 4). Those with two zeroes are called type 2 codons. If a segment has exactly one zero, then the zero may be encountered either before (type 1^-) or after (type 1^+) reaching the maximum point of the segment during traversal in the chosen orientation.

The type 0 codons may be further subdivided into 0^+, 0^- and (∞) to yield six basic codon types. Consider Fig. 3 once again. Note that as the ellipse is traversed in different directions, the minima of curvature change as expected. In the lower ellipse, which corresponds to a "hole" with figure outside, the minima have negative curvature, because the direction of rotation is clockwise. (Thus, the slashes suggest a part boundary by our rule, which will be repaired later when we discuss "holes.") In the upper ellipse, however, the minima have positive curvature (the rotation is always counterclockwise). Thus, the type 0 codon can be subdivided into 0^+ and 0^- with the superscript indicating the sign of curvature. Note that the 0^- codon can constitute a part boundary, whereas the type 0^+ codon must appear only as a shape

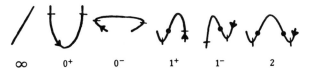

FIG. 4. The primitive codon types. Zeroes of curvature are indicated by dots, minima by slashes. The straight line (∞) is a degenerate case included for completeness, although it is not treated in the text.

descriptor. Finally, the type ∞ codon simply is the degenerate case of a straight line that has an ∞ of zeroes.

4. CONSTRAINTS ON SMOOTH CODON STRINGS

Not all sequences of codons are possible if the curve is smooth. Referring to Fig. 4 once again, note that a 1^- can not follow a 1^- codon unless a cusp is allowed. Similarly, a 1^+ can not follow a 1^+, because if such a join is attempted either a cusp will be created or, if the curve is indeed smooth, the 1^+ codon would have to be transformed into a type 2. To specify all legal smooth codon strings, we will first enumerate all pairs, and then show what pair substitutions are legal for one element in a sequence of pairs, thereby creating all possible triples.

Define the "tail" of a codon as the region about the first minima encountered when traversing the curve. The "head" of the codon is the subsequent minima. A smooth string of two codons is then allowable only if the head of the first codon has the same sign of curvature as the tail of the second codon in the string. Table 1a shows the sign of curvature for each codon type (excluding the degenerate type ∞). Table 1b is constructed simply by multiplying the sign of curvature of the "head" of the first codon (the left-most column) by the "tail" of the second (given in the second row). If the signs agree, then a (+) is entered, indicating a legal smooth join, otherwise the (−) product is an illegal smooth join. Thus, for these five codons, there are 13 legal joins out of a possible 25 combinations.

To enumerate the possible codon triples for a smooth contour, we now require that the curvature of both the head and tail of a middle codon match the tail of its successor or the head of its predecessor in the string. Table 2 provides the signs of the heads (and tails) of the legal pairs (left column) which must match the tail (or head) of the third codon in the string. For each column under the third codon, the legal triplets are indicated by a (+). If two pluses appear in brackets, then the third codon can either precede or follow the pair. Consider first the case where the third codon follows the pair (these are given in the columns headed "tail"). There are 34 legal smooth triplets of this type. Symmetry arguments yield a similar number of triplets when the third codon precedes the pairs (these are given in the columns headed "head"). Thus, there are only 34 legal codon triplets out of a possible $5^3 = 125$.

TABLE 1

Codon Signatures (a) and Legal Smooth Codon Pairs (b)

a CODON SIGNATURES			**b** LEGAL CODON PAIRS					
				2nd CODON (tail)				
CODON	TAIL	HEAD	1st CODON (head)	$0^-(-)$	$0^+(+)$	$1^-(-)$	$1^+(+)$	$2(-)$
0^-	−	−	$0^-(-)$	+	−	+	−	+
0^+	+	+	$0^+(+)$	−	+	−	+	−
1^-	−	+	$1^-(+)$	−	+	−	+	−
1^+	+	−	$1^+(-)$	+	−	+	−	+
2	−	−	$2(-)$	+	−	+	−	+

TABLE 2

Legal Smooth Codon Triplets

LEGAL CODON PAIRS			THIRD CODON									
			0^-		0^+		1^-		1^{+-}		2	
			−	−	+	+	−	+	+	−	−	−
	TAIL	HEAD	TAIL	HEAD	TAIL	HEAD	TAIL	HEAD	TAIL	HEAD	TAIL	HEAD
0^-0^-	−	−	[+	+]				+		+	[+	+]
0^-1^-	−	+		+	+				[+	+]		+
0^-2	−	−	[+	+]				+		+	[+	+]
0^+0^+	+	+			[+	+]		+	+			
0^+1^+	+	−	+			+	[+	+]			+	
1^-0^+	−	+		+	+				[+	+]		+
1^-1^+	−	−	[+	+]				+		+	[+	+]
1^+0^-	+	−	+			+	[+	+]			+	
1^+1^-	+	+			[+	+]		+	+			
1^+2	+	−	+			+	[+	+]			+	
$2\ 0^-$	−	−	[+	+]				+		+	[+	+]
$2\ 1^-$	−	+		+	+				[+	+]		+
$2\ 2$	−	−	[+	+]				+		+	[+	+]
NUMBER OF LEGAL PAIR SUBSTITUTIONS			5		2		3		3		5	
NUMBER OF PAIR SUBSTITUTIONS			9		4		6		6		9	

Note. The third codon can either follow or precede the pair. A (+) indicates a proper join. Because of symmetry, there are an equal number of total pluses in the head and tail columns.

Of the 34 possible triplets, there are 18 cases where the same codon can be attached to either end of the codon pair, indicated by [+ +]. This subset is particularly useful for establishing legal smooth codon strings of order higher than three. For example, consider a codon sequence C_{j-1}, C_j, C_{j+1}. We now desire to expand the sequence. This can be done simply by replacing C_j by $C_i C_k$, where $C_i C_k$ is one of the pairs that will accept C_j at either end. To extend the string, we thus have the following rewrite rule:

Any individual codon in a smooth string may be replaced by any pair yielding a [+ +] for the (third) codon in Table 2.

Thus, an 0^- codon may be replaced by any one of the following pairs: $0^-0^-, 0^-2, 1^-1^+, 2\,0^-, 22$, etc.

To calculate the number of possible quadruplets, we can determine from Table 2 how many times any given codon type appears in the middle portion of the string.

TABLE 3

A Comparison Showing How the Number of Possible Strings of Codon Elements is Reduced as First Smoothness (Open Strings) and Then Closure Are Imposed as Constraints on a Curve

NUMBER OF CODONS	NUMBER OF:		
IN STRING	COMBINATIONS	OPEN STRINGS	CLOSED STRINGS
1	5	5	(2)
2	25	13	3
3	125	34	5
4	625	89	9
5	3,125	233	17
6	15,625	610	33
7	78,125	1,597	65
8	390,625	4,181	129
9	1,953,125	10,946	257
10	9,765,625	28,657	513

Then we can multiply this number of occurrences by the number of possible pair substitutions. For example, the type 0^- codon appears as the middle codon in rows 1, 8, and 11. In each row, the only legal third codons whose tail curvature matches that of the head of 0^- are 0^-, 1^- and 2 (see Table 1). Thus the O^- codon appears as the middle codon in 9 of all the possible triplets. Similarly we find the following number of occurrences of the other codon types in the middle position of the string:

$$0^- = 9; 0^+ = 4; 1^- = 6; 1^+ = 6; 2 = 9. \Sigma = 34$$

Thus the total number of possible smooth codon quadruples will simply be the sum of each of these numbers times the number of possible pair substitutions for each type (next to last row of Table 2), less any duplicate strings. The total substitutions are 134, but the 0^- and 2's duplicate each other, reducing the total quadruples by 45. The answer is the difference of 89 out of a possible 625. Table 3 shows how the number of possible open strings increases with the number of codon elements. In general there will be less than $5 \cdot 7^{(N-1)/2}$ possible smooth strings of N codons compared with 5^N possible (see Appendix II).

5. CLOSED CODONS

Because most objects have closed bounding contours, matching to closed codon sequences is of greater interest for shape recognition than representing open strings. Clearly this constraint on the codon sequence will further reduce the number of allowable smooth shapes. Indeed, this constraint is so powerful that all closed shapes containing up to four codons will be enumerated shortly.

First, let us examine the generating rules. Closed codon pairs can be noted simply by inspecting Table 2. Here, the signs of the heads and tails of the pairs in the first column must agree. The only cases are 0^-0^-, 0^+0^+, 0^-2, 1^-1^+, and 22. These shapes are depicted in Fig. 5, with figure indicated by cross-hatching. Note that there are only three basic outlines, if figure and ground are ignored. Later, we will address

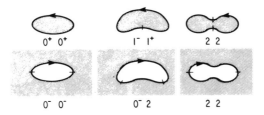

FIG. 5. Legal smooth, closed codon pairs. Figure is indicated by cross hatching. Part boundaries are noted by the slashes.

the problem of indexing identical codon descriptors that have different figure–ground relations (e.g., the 22 pair) and also the observation that the part boundaries (slashes) for the "holes" do not seem appropriate.

From these five legal codon pairs, we can now easily generate the legal closed triples. Simply consider the pair as a string of three elements and then replace each "middle" element by a pair according to Table 2. Thus, the closed pair 1^-1^+ may be rewritten as $1^-1^+1^-$ (or $1^+1^-1^+$) and the 1^+ (or 1^-) can then be replaced by 0^-1^-, 1^-0^+, 21^- (or $0^+1^+, 1^+0^-, 1^+2$). Such substitutions yield a total of 10 different codon triplets, or only 5 different outlines out of a possible 125 if figure and ground are ignored. These shapes are shown in Fig. 6 with their codon labels. Figure 7 shows the result of applying the same rewrite rules to the triples to enumerate all possible codon quadruples. Here there are only 9 outlines out of a total possible combination of 5^4 or 625 sequences. Appendix III shows that the upper bound on the number of closed smooth codons is $2^{N-1} + 1$, where N is the number of codons in the ring. The compression is thus about $2^{N-1}/5^N$, or over 10^4 for a 10-element ring. The reduction comes in part from a propagation of constraints through the closed string, very analogous to the constraint propagation used by Waltz [15] to solve for "blocks-world" shapes using constraints on legal trihedral joins.

6. MIRROR REVERSAL, HOLES, AND FIGURE–GROUND

In Fig. 5, three pairs of codon shapes are possible for a two element ring. For each pair, the outline is the same, but the figure–ground relation is reversed. The situation is similar to a lock–key arrangement, where the shapes in the upper row fit snugly into their "hole" complements in the lower row.

Two problems arise in representing these mirror shapes: First, a lock–key pair may have the same codon description, such as "22" on the right. This is easily rectified by adding an extra index. The second problem is perceptual. For each of

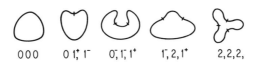

FIG. 6. Legal smooth, closed codon triplets.

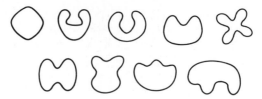

FIG. 7. Legal smooth, closed codon quadruples.

the shapes in the lower row, although "figure" is outside, we strongly prefer the "hole" as the figure. Why?

Some insight into why "holes" are preferred as figure can be obtained by noting that all the shapes in the lower row consist of two parts by our rule. (The slashes indicate the points of maximum negative curvature.) On the other hand, the "ellipse" and "peanut" in the upper row are single entities without parts. Certainly a single entity is "simpler" in some very basic sense than one with parts. Thus, it makes sense to describe the "hole" as the complementary figure if that complement has fewer parts. Note that for the 22 dumbbell shapes, the preference between the hole and its "key" is less strong. In fact, it is not too difficult to regard each "bump" in the hole as a part of the hole, whereas it is almost impossible to view the $0^- 0^-$ elliptical hole as having two parts. Our rule for representing "holes" is thus:

> Represent a "hole" by its figure–ground complement if that complement has fewer "parts."

Note that there are many linguistic examples where this rule has been applied. For example, "key-hole," "screw-hole," "oval window," etc., are all descriptions of a hole in terms of the figure–ground complement. (Appendix I shows how a figure–ground complement can be computed easily using a binary representation.)

7. INDEX DEVELOPMENT

The shapes of closed codon rings shown in Figs. 5–7 have all been drawn to preserve symmetry. Furthermore the axes of elongation tend to be straight, and the "parts" are neither too "thin" nor too "thick" for most peoples' taste. What are the rules that underly the canonical representation of these primitive shapes? What regularities of the world are captured here?

Clearly any time a rule is applied to put a codon ring in canonical form, then we have an implicit shape index which is being defaulted. An interesting extension of the abstract codon description is thus to develop indices that are meaningful. The fact that the codon hierarchy is small provides an opportunity for a rational development of such indices—at least for a start. (A more complete and useful set should relate each index to a desired real-world property.)

To give the flavor of this approach, consider the first three primitive codon shapes in Fig. 5: the "ellipse" (= 00), the "peanut" (= $1^- 1^+$), and the "dumbbell" (= 22). What useful properties can now be assigned to an ellipse outline? We have already mentioned the need to specify figure–ground. What about the orientation of the ellipse, or its eccentricity, or even perhaps its size? These four parameters will completely specify the elliptical shape relative to a reference frame. However, if we encounter an ovoidal shape having the same 00 codon description, then still another index may be required. For our single, most primitive closed shape we thus have already the following possible indices:

FIGURE–GROUND	0, 1
ORIENTATION (OF AXIS)	ϕ
ECCENTRICITY (ASPECT RATIO)	ρ
SIZE	Σ
SKEW	ν

As we proceed to the next more complex shape, the "peanut," the axis is now curved, and the left and right portions need not have identical size. Two more parameters thus must be added:

RELATION LEFT AXIS TO RIGHT AXIS	α
RELATIVE SIZE, LEFT TO RIGHT "PART"	σ_{lr}

These indices suffice for the dumbbell.

In a similar vein we may proceed up the closed codon hierarchy, adding additional indices. This procedure automatically provides an ordinal order to the indices (whether this order is perceptually appropriate is a separate issue!). Note that left–right "handedness" does not appear until we encounter four element codon rings. For codon rings greater than four or five, the complexity of the shape undoubtedly prohibits practical use. In sum, the codon hierarchy can thus be used to develop an ordered set of indices to the more metrical properties of shapes.[1]

8. MAPPING 3D ⇔ 2D

Codons are descriptors for 2D plane curves, and hence of necessity are an image-based representation. In Marr's [9, 10] terminology, they are part of the data structure of a primal sketch. An important aspect of the motivation for the codon description comes from the nature of the 3D world, however, namely the rule for locating part boundaries at maxima of negative curvature. This rule for partitioning a curve captures the concavity regularity created when two 3D parts are joined (see Fig. 2), as seen in the 2D image. Thus, the presence of a concavity in silhouette is used to infer a part boundary in the 3D world. (See [5] for a more rigorous treatment of this inference.) Can other inferences about the properties of 3D objects also be made from the codon descriptors?

To explore the kinds of inferences possible about 3D shape from 2D contours, we will consider some of the canonical, primitive shapes generated by codons shown in Figs. 5–7. Our aim is not to exhaust all possible inferences, but rather to indicate a profitable direction for future study.

There are two kinds of inferences to consider: (1) those that lead to the acceptance of a particular 3D shape and (2) those that reject a possible 3D shape [12, 11].

---

[1] It is expected that a mapping between our codon-based and axial-based (or "grassfire") representations for shapes can be made with a suitable list of indexed parameters. We see the advantage of the codon scheme being that crude part descriptions appear at the top level, allowing immediate access.

Consider the first three primitive outlines given in Fig 5: the ellipse, the peanut, and the dumbbell. An example of the rejection strategy is that the 2D peanut contour can not arise from a surface of revolution about a straight axis, for if it did, then the concavity in the outline would be eliminated. Similarly, the dumbbell can not be the projection of a 3D surface of revolution about a vertical axis, although it could be a 3D shape created by revolving the outline about the horizontal axis (i.e., a dumbbell in 3D).

An example of the accept strategy is the inference that the elliptical outline represents a 3D ellipsoid. But of course although it is true that a 3D ellipsoid will generate a 2D elliptical contour, so will any planar 2D ellipse or more awkwardly any shape whatsoever that has at least one elliptical cross section.

To infer the 3D shape from the 2D contour thus requires assumptions about (1) what the hidden 3D surface looks like, (2) whether the shape is 2D or 3D, and (3) whether the silhouette arises from a plane curve, etc. [13]. Clearly, then, the accept mode of inference is much more fragile than the rejection strategy. In one case the inference rests on assumptions, whereas in the other, possible assumptions are rejected.

What kinds of 3D properties then can be tested from 2D codons? We have already mentioned the surface of revolution constraint, which is a particularly popular basis for modelling shapes [2, 1, 8]. But still deeper insights into 3D shape can be obtained if the part boundaries are reinforced by spines and cusps which appear in the image [7]. For example, in Fig. 8 the silhouette of all three figures is the same. However, their interpretation is quite different. Assuming general position, outline (A) is seen as planar, (B) as three dimensional, whereas (C) suggests a 2D fin on a 3D ball, otherwise it would be an impossible object [6]. It is clear that as the codon representation is developed, the internal contours must play an important role. Their presence may force (or exclude) a particular 3D interpretation. These differences in interpretation should be reflected in the codon description. For example, the description of (B) should include three separate codon strings rather than just one for the silhouette. Thus the silhouette (A) = ⟨2002⟩ whereas (B) is more correctly depicted as ⟨[2][000][2]⟩, with the two [2] being the "ears" of the head [000]. In this case the transformation from A to B is a simple restructuring of the string. Other cases with similar silhouettes will not be so simple. Yet, just as 3D shapes constrain the 2D codon descriptors and vice versa, so will there be constraints on the transformation of strings of type B into those of type A (and vice versa). Here is an exciting but difficult area for future study.

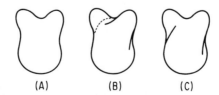

(A)   (B)   (C)

FIG. 8.   Internal contours may drastically alter the 3D interpretation as well as the codon description.

9. SUMMARY

Codons are simple primitives for describing planar curves. They thus are principally image-based descriptors. Yet they have the power to capture important information about the 3D world, such as making part boundaries explicit. The codon description is highly redundant (useful for error-correction). This redundancy can be viewed as a constraint on the number of possible codon strings. For smooth closed strings that represent the bounding contour (silhouette) of many smooth 3D objects, the constraints are so strong that sequences containing 6 elements yield only 33 generic shapes as compared with a possible number of 15,625 combinations. An intriguing and important question for image understanding is to explore the constraints on the possible 3D configurations that can project into these 33 generic 2D shapes.

APPENDIX I: A BINARY MAPPING FOR CODON STRINGS[2]

1. Mapping Rule

Five basic codon types would normally require at least three bits for a binary encoding. However, there are sufficient constraints on codon joins that the 0^- and 0^+ codons can be distinguished, provided at least one member of the string is not a type 0 codon. By inspecting Tables 1 or 2, we see that if a type 0 codon follows a 1^- codon, then it must be an 0^+, whereas if the type 0 follows a 1^+ or 2 type codon, then it must be an 0^-. Similarly if a type 0 precedes a 1^- or 2, it must be type 0^-, but if it precedes a 1^+ codon, then it is type 0^+. Because adjacent type 0 codons must have the same sign, the designation of the 0 codon type will be completely specified by its neighbors. This redundancy is also reflected in the number of legal codon pairs, which is thirteen and can be mapped into 4 bits or 2 bits per codon.

Our mapping scheme utilizes the constraint that between every minima there is at least one maxima (provided the positive minima of 0^+ are noted). Thus, given the location of a minima in a binary string we only need to encode the position and number of inflections in relation to the maxima. (This was the basis for the codon definitions.) Let "1" represent an inflection and "ϕ" represent no inflection. Then the mapping rule will be as follows:

CODON TYPE		BINARY CODE
0^-	→	$\phi\phi$
1^+	→	$\phi 1$
1^-	→	1ϕ
2	→	11

Note that in this mapping, the position of both the maximum and minimum is implicit. Namely the minima lie at the beginning and end of a binary pair whereas the maximum lies between the pair. This property will be seen to be useful in depicting figure-ground reversals where maxima and minima exchange places. The

---

[2] This mapping and its properties were first noted by Chris Fitch and Steve Schad in WR's class, "Natural Computation" in the Fall of 1983.

exchange can be brought about simply by phase shifting the starting point on a string by one element.

2. Mirror Transform

A mirror transform in a codon string occurs most frequently when a shape is symmetric. The rule for effecting a mirror transform is to read the string backwards and change the signs of the 1^+ and 1^- codons (see [4]). The binary rule is simpler: "Read the string backwards."

EXAMPLE.

ORIGINAL STRING	1^+	2	1^-	1^+	0	1^-
BINARY MAPPING	01	11	10	01	00	10
REVERSAL BINARY	01	00	10	01	11	10
MIRROR STRING	1^+	0	1^-	1^+	2	1^-

Note that the mirror codon is simply the original read backwards with the signs changed.

3. Lock–Key or Figure–Ground Transform

The basic idea underlying a figure–ground reversal is that the maxima and minima must be exchanged. This can be accomplished by rotating the binary string by one element. However, because a figure–ground exchange also entails a reversal in the direction of traversing the curve, the order of the binary string must also be reversed. Hence the figure–ground rule is: "Rotate the binary string by one element and read the string backwards."

EXAMPLE.

ORIGINAL STRING (FIGURE)	1 +	2	1^-	1^+	0	1^-
BINARY MAPPING	01	11	10	01	00	10
ROTATE ONE ELEMENT	00	11	11	00	10	01
REVERSED BINARY	10	01	00	11	11	00
COMPLEMENTARY STRING (GROUND)	1^-	1^+	0	2	2	0

APPENDIX II: NUMBERS OF POSSIBLE OPEN, SMOOTH CODON STRINGS

1. Strategy of Proof

An upper bound on the number of legal codon strings with smooth joins, but which are not closed, will be obtained by induction. First we will determine the number of possible strings of length $N + 1$ given the number of strings of length N. This relation will then lead to an obvious sequential pattern for even and odd Ns of low numbers. The sequence will be bounded by $5 \cdot 7^{(N-1)/2}$.

2. Two Types of Strings

Referring to Table 1, we note that a codon string may be extended in only two ways: (a) by adding either a 0^-, 1^-, or 2 or (b) by adding either a 0^+ or 1^+. If the string ends in a 0^-, 1^+, or 2, then there are three choices, namely (a), for the addition, but if the string ends in a 0^+ or 1^-, then there are only two choices, namely (b). Let us designate the 0^-, 1^+, and 2 codons as type A and the 0^+, 1^- as type B. (A and B simply specify whether the head of the codon has positive or negative curvature, respectively.) Then if there are A_N strings of length N ending in 0^-, 1^+, or 2, there will be $3A_N$ possible strings of length $N + 1$ that are constructed from these A_N codons. Similarly there will be $2B_N$ possible strings of length $N + 1$ constructed from these B_N codons. The total number $\Sigma(N + 1)$ of strings of length $N + 1$ will then be

$$\Sigma(N + 1) = 3A_N + 2B_N. \tag{1}$$

Let us now consider a string of length N ending in a type A codon ($0^-, 1^-, 2$). How did each of these codon types arise from the string of length $N - 1$? Again referring to Table 1, we see that the next-to-last codon must have been either an 0^-, 1^+, or 2. Thus we have two instances of type A (namely $0^-, 2$) and one instance of type B (namely 1^+). The number of A_N codon strings is then simply

$$A_N = 2A_{N-1} + B_{N-1}. \tag{2}$$

Similarly, we find that the last type B codon in a string (namely $0^+, 1^-$) must be preceded by either an 0^+, which is type B, or a 1^-, which is type A. Hence we have

$$B_N = A_{N-1} + B_{N-1} \tag{3}$$

We now can solve for A_N and B_N in terms of Σ. But first note that adding (2) and (3) gives us the relation

$$A_N + B_N = 3A_{N-1} + 2B_{N-1} = \Sigma(N) \tag{4a}$$

or

$$B_N = \Sigma(N) - A_N. \tag{4b}$$

Now if the right-hand terms of (4b) are replaced by the appropriate forms of Eqs. (1) and (2), we find that

$$B_N = \Sigma(N - 1). \tag{5a}$$

Thus from (4a),

$$A_N = \Sigma(N) - \Sigma(N - 1). \tag{5b}$$

Finally, by substitution in (1) and changing the index by one, we obtain

$$\Sigma(N) = 3\Sigma(N - 1) - \Sigma(N - 2). \tag{6}$$

These totals for N are given in column 3 of Table 3.

3. Upper Bound

An upper bound on these totals can be set by making the negative right-hand term of Eq. (6) smaller and then approximating the sums by the positive term. For example, by algebraic manipulation, the negative term can be reduced to $\Sigma(N - 4)$, giving

$$\Sigma(N) = 7 \cdot \Sigma(N - 2) - \Sigma(N - 4). \tag{7}$$

An upper bound on the possible number of open codon strings is thus $7 \cdot \Sigma(N - 2)$. We then observe the following pattern:

	CORRECT
$\Sigma(3) = 7 \cdot 5 \quad\quad = 35$	34
$\Sigma(4) = 7 \cdot 13 \quad\quad = 91$	89
$\Sigma(5) = 7 \cdot 7 \cdot 5 \ = 245$	233
$\Sigma(6) = 7 \cdot 7 \cdot 13 = 637$	610
$\vdots$	

Note that for all odd sums the factor other than 7 is 5, whereas for the even sums, the factor is 13. Thus if N is odd, $\Sigma_{\text{odd}} < 5 \cdot 7^{(N-1)/2}$ whereas if N is even, $\Sigma_{\text{even}} < 13 \cdot 7^{(N-2)/2}$. Now note that 13 may be approximated by $5 \cdot 7^{1/2}$, or more especially $13 < 5 \cdot 7^{1/2}$. Thus the factor 13 may be replaced to yield the single equation for the upper bound on Σ,

$$\Sigma(N) < 5 \cdot 7^{(N-1)/2}. \tag{8}$$

APPENDIX III: NUMBER OF SMOOTH CLOSED CODON STRINGS

1. Strategy of Proof

We will use the binary representation presented in Appendix I. Furthermore, we will count only the basic closed shapes without regard to whether figure or ground is specified. The counting proceeds by constructing a binomial tree, subject to three constraining rules:

(i) The sum of the 1s must be even.

(ii) There must be an even number of adjacent binary ϕs in any sequence.

(iii) Only the $1111\ldots$, string can end in a 1.

The first rule says that the total number of inflections in a closed string must be even (or zero). If there were an odd number of inflections then the string cannot close on itself because the sign of curvature at the beginning and end of the string would be different.

The second rule follows indirectly from the first. A type 2 codon is represented by "11" because it has two inflections. Thus taking all "2"s from the string will still leave an even number of "1"s. For each remaining "1" there will be an equal number of ϕs. This number will be even. The total number of ϕs in the binary string remains even because all other ϕs in the binary string will come from the type 0 codon, which is represented by a pair of binary ϕs. The requirement that there must be an even number of adjacent ϕs follows from the legal joins shown in Table 1. For example, a $1\phi11$ sequence, corresponding to a 1^-2 string is illegal. The third digit must be a ϕ, changing the string to a 1^-1^+, etc.

TABLE 4

Tree Structure of Binary Codon Strings of Length N

STRING POSITION (or LEVEL, N)	BINARY TREE	LEGAL POSSIBILITIES
0	$\binom{1}{1}$	—
1	$\phi \quad \text{- - - - - - -} \quad 1$ $\phi \text{- - - - - - - -} \quad 1$	—
2	$\phi\text{- -} \quad 1 \qquad \phi \text{- - -} 1.$ $\phi \quad \text{- } 1 \qquad \phi.\text{- - -} \quad 1$	3
3	$\phi \text{. } 1 \quad \phi \quad 1 \qquad \phi. \text{. } 1 \quad \phi \quad 1$ $\phi \text{ `1} \quad \phi \quad 1 \qquad \phi \quad \text{`1.} \quad \phi \quad 1$	5
4	$\phi\,1 \quad \phi\,1 \quad \phi\,1 \quad \phi\,1 \quad \phi\,1 \quad \phi.\,1 \quad \phi\,1 \quad \phi\,1$ $\phi\,1 \quad \phi\,1 \quad \phi\,1 \quad \phi\,1 \quad \phi\,1 \quad \phi.\,1 \quad \phi\,1 \quad \phi\,1$ $\quad (w) \quad (y) \quad (x) \qquad (w)$	9

The third rule simply forces the end position in the string to be a zero to prevent duplication of strings. The exception is a codon string made up only of type "2" codons, which must be included in the count. Otherwise the string is rotated to remove a final binary "1".

2. The Construction

We wish to count all possibilities for the binary ϕ and 1 in any position of the string of codon length N. This will be accomplished by constructing a tree, with two binary positions added at each new level, N, of the tree. The binary positions, of course, represent the five basic codons plus the constraint that allows both the 0^- and 0^+ codons to be represented by the binary pair $\phi\phi$ (see Appendix I).

Table 4 shows the construction of the binary tree. The tree is initiated by the pair of 1s in the first row at level 0. These pairs of 1s then branch to a pair of 0s and 1s at level 1, corresponding to a single codon.

At this level the possible legal binary pairs according to our rules would be $\phi\phi$ and 11, corresponding to the type 0 and 2 codons. However neither of these single codons can close on itself without introducing a maxima. Hence the first legal *closed* binary sequences begin at level 2.

Reading down from the top through level 2 (and ignoring the initializing 1s), we have only three possibilities: $\phi\phi\phi\phi$, 11ϕ, ϕ, and 1111 (see Fig. 5). The sequences $\phi\phi11$ and $1\phi\phi1$ are illegal because a sequence cannot end in a "1" unless all members of the sequence are "1" (rule (iii)). Hence there are only three possible closed strings made of two codons.

Moving to the third level, we now need explore only those branchings (and cross-branchings) that end in ϕ. There are five legal strings obtained by directly moving down the branches without crossing over. These are $\phi\phi\phi\phi\phi\phi$, $\phi\phi1\phi1$,

$11\phi\phi\phi$, $1111\phi\phi$, and 111111. However, note that the second and third strings are simply a rotation of one another and hence are duplicates. Indeed, any right-branching sequence from a $\phi\phi$ to a 11 on the left side of the tree must be duplicated on the right side of the tree, because a simple leftward rotation of the binary string can move the 11 pair into the first position. The initial pair 11 will now correspond to the 11 pair at level one on the right side of the tree, and the preceding pair of binary $\phi\phi$s will have moved into the last position, corresponding to the $\phi\phi$s at the highest level being considered. Hence all direct strings on the left side of the tree can be ignored in the direct string count, with the exception of the sequence $\phi\phi\phi\phi\ldots$, consisting solely of binary ϕs. Thus, the number of legal "direct" strings constructed by moving down the tree without "crossovers" (dashed lines) will be

$$\text{Number of direct strings: } = 2 + 2^{N-2}. \tag{9}$$

3. Crossover Strings

The above count does not include "crossings" between branches similar to those indicated by the dashed lines. Given that a "crossing" is made at one level, we are then required by rule (ii) to cross back at the next or later level in such a manner that the number of adjacent ϕs is even, and such that the string ends in ϕ. Thus the first crossing $1\phi\phi1$ is illegal because it ends in a "1." However this sequence can be extended at level 3 into a legal string, namely $1\phi\phi1\phi\phi$. (Note that the other crossing $1\phi11\phi\phi$ is illegal because there is a single "ϕ.") We thus see that there are no legal crossover strings of codon length two, and only one of codon length three, namely $1\phi\phi1\phi\phi$.

Moving to level four, we may continue to use the $1\phi\phi1$ crossover as a "header." Now a 11 at level three may be used to extend the string, for we have a pair of binary ϕs available at level four. This gives us the two crossover strings ending in columns "y" and "z," as indicated in the last row of Table 4. In addition, we may now also create a new crossover header, namely $1\phi\phi\phi1$, which becomes legal because of the binary ϕs available at level four. This new sequence, $1\phi\phi\phi1\phi\phi$ ends in column "x." By considering crossovers on the left side of the tree we have thus added three more strings of codon length four.

Now consider the right-half of the tree. At level two, we may add another crossover at the "1" followed by a period. Crossing over here and back again at level three, we obtain the following sequence ending in column (w): $111\phi\phi1\phi\phi$. But this sequence is the mirror transform of a previous string found by an earlier crossover to the left side of the tree, namely $1\phi\phi111\phi\phi$. (The mirror transform is the same string read in reverse, and in this case rotated by two to place the two binary ϕs at the end.) It should be obvious that the symmetry of the crossover header, namely $1\phi\ldots\phi1$, allows one to read it backwards to get the same result. Hence all crossovers on the right half of the tree will be the "mirrors" of strings obtained on the left half.

We are now in a position to count the crossover strings. At each new level, we add one string of the form $1\phi\phi\ldots\phi1\phi\phi$. This sequence doubles at each successive level, giving us 2^{N-3} possible strings from the first possible crossover, 2^{N-4} from the second, etc.:

$$\text{Number of crossover strings} := \sum_{J=3}^{N} 2^{N-J}. \tag{10}$$

4. Final Count

Adding the counts for the direct (9) and crossover (10) strings, we obtain

$$\text{Number of closed strings:} = 2 + 2^{N-2} + \sum_{J=3}^{N} 2^{N-J}. \tag{11}$$

By algebraic manipulation, it can be shown that the above reduces to

$$\text{Number of closed strings:} = 2^{N-1} + 1 \quad (N \geq 2). \tag{12}$$

ACKNOWLEDGMENTS

This report describes research done at the Department of Psychology and the Artificial Intelligence Laboratory of the Massachusetts Institute of Technology. Support for this work is provided by AFOSR under a grant for Image Understanding, contract F49620-83-C-0135. William Gilson helped with the preparation of the manuscript. The comments of Aaron Bobick and John Rubin were appreciated. Chris Fitch and Steve Schad broke the combination that made Appendix III possible.

REFERENCES

1. G. Agin, *Representation and Description of Curved Objects*, Stanford A.I. Memo No. 173, Stanford Univ., 1974.
2. T. O. Binford, Unusual perception by computer, in *IEEE Conference on Systems and Control*, December, Miami, 1972.
3. D. Hoffman, *Representing Shapes for Visual Recognition*, Ph.D. thesis, MIT, Cambridge, Mass., 1983.
4. D. Hoffman and W. Richards, Representing smooth plane curves for visual recognition: Implications for Figure–Ground Reversal, in *Proceedings of the American Association for Artificial Intelligence*, pp. 5–8, 1982.
5. D. D. Hoffman and W. Richards, Parts of recognition, *Cognition*, in press; MIT A.I. Memo No. 714, 1984.
6. D. A. Huffman, Impossible objects as nonsense sentences, in *Machine Intelligence*, Vol. 6 (B. Meltzer and D. Michie, Eds.), Edinburgh Univ. Press, Edinburgh, 1971.
7. J. Koenderink and A. Van Doorn, The shape of smooth objects and the way contours end, *Perception*, 11 (1982), 129–137.
8. D. Marr, Analysis of occluding contour, *Proc. R. Soc. London Ser. B*, 197, 1977, 441–475.
9. D. Marr, Early processing of visual information, *Philos. Trans. R. Soc. London*, 275, 1976, 483–524.
10. D. Marr, *Vision: A Computational Investigation into the Human Representation and Processing of Visual Information*, Freeman, San Francisco, 1982.
11. W. Richards, J. Rubin and D. D. Hoffman, Equation counting and the interpretation of sensory data, *Perception*, 11, 1983, 557–576.
12. J. M. Rubin and W. A. Richards, Color vision and image intensities: When are changes material? *Biol. Cybern.*, 45, 1982, 215–226.
13. K. A. Stevens, Visual interpretation of surface contours, *Artif. Intell.*, 17, 1983, 47–73.
14. W. Turton, *A Conchological Dictionary of the British Islands*, (frontispiece), printed for John Booth, London, (1819). [This early reference was kindly pointed out to us by J. F. W. McOmie.]
15. D. Waltz, Understanding line drawings of scenes with shadows, in *The Psychology of Computer Vision* (P. Winston, Ed.), McGraw–Hill, New York, 1975.

Environment-Centered and Viewer-Centered Perception of Surface Orientation

H. A. SEDGWICK AND S. LEVY

Schnurmacher Institute for Vision Research, State University of New York,
State College of Optometry, New York, New York 10010

Received March 20, 1985

This paper reports two experiments that compared human observers' ability to perceive the environment-centered orientation of surfaces with their ability to perceive the viewer-centered orientation of surfaces. Computer-generated perspective representations of rectangular grids at various orientations were viewed monocularly from a stationary viewpoint. Observers were found to be substantially less variable when attempting to match the environment-centered orientation of a surface than when attempting to match its viewer-centered orientation. This finding is taken to be consistent with the proposal that environment-centered orientation is perceived directly from the perspective structure of the optic array rather than being derived from a prior processing stage in which viewer-centered orientation is represented. It was also found, however, that observers' settings under instructions to match the environment-centered orientation of a surface tended to deviate somewhat in the direction of its viewer-centered orientation, which suggests that environment-centered perception is not entirely independent of viewer-centered variables. © 1985 Academic Press, Inc.

1. INTRODUCTION

What do we perceive when we perceive our environment? Phrased in terms of computer vision rather than human perception, this question might be: What internal representation of the environment should we use when we design a computer system to perceive environmental schemes? As Marr [8] has pointed out, our choice of a representation is a crucial step in the design of such a system. The most effective representation to use is far from obvious; many widely divergent types of representation are currently being investigated.

One strategy is to look to the human visual system as an example of a design that works. If we had a deeper understanding of the human perception of the environment we might have a clearer idea of the sort of representations that would be most effective in the design of computer vision systems. Gibson [3] has argued that the essential foundations of visual perception exist independently of any particular perceiving organism (or, we could add, mechanism), in the systematic relations that exist between the structure of the environment and the structure of the light, termed by Gibson the *optic array*, that is reflected from the environment to a potential point of observation. If we could understand how one organism makes use of these relations, which Gibson refers to as *available information*, then we should be able to design other systems that use the same relations.

A few years ago Marr [8, 9] clearly articulated an idea about space perception that had been around in one form or another for a long time before, and he helped to draw attention to the idea by giving it a distinctive name. The name is the "$2\frac{1}{2}$-D sketch," and the idea is that the visual processing of spatial information procedes through a sort of half-way house in which 3-D information about the layout of surfaces in the environment has been extracted from the structure of the light reaching the eye but has not yet been organized into meaningful, recognizable objects. Marr characterized this half-way house as a *viewer-centered representation*, because he believed that at this relatively early stage of processing of spatial information the layout of every surface would be represented internally in terms of its spatial relation to the point of observation. Thus, the location of every point on a surface would be represented by its distance from the eye, and the orientation of every point on a surface would be represented by the surface's orientation with respect to the line of regard at that point. According to Marr's view, later stages of representation that were independent of the viewer, such as what Marr called object-centered representation, would be derived from the viewer-centered representation.

One may agree with Marr's emphasis on the perception of surface layout (an emphasis also found in Gibson [2]) while questioning the prominent position he gives to the viewer-centered representation. An alternative to the use Marr makes of the viewer-centered representation is based on what one of us has called an *environment-centered representation* of spatial layout [13]. In an environment-centered representation the spatial layout of surfaces is specified in terms of their relation to the fixed framework of the environment. For example, the orientation of a surface is specified by its angular relation to another environmental surface, such as the horizontal ground plane.

This distinction between viewer-centered and environment-centered representations of spatial layout is only a generalization to other aspects of spatial layout—such as size, shape, and location—of a distinction introduced years ago by Gibson and Cornsweet [4] between *optical slant*, which is the slant of a surface with respect to the line of regard, and *geographical slant*, which is the slant of the surface with respect to the fixed reference surfaces of the environment. In this paper we concentrate on that original distinction, centering our discussion on the perception of surface orientation.

The viewer-centered and the environment-centered representations of surface orientation differ in some ways that might make the latter more advantageous to a vision system. Considering the viewer-centered representation of surface orientation, we can see that a flat extended surface, like the ground plane, has not one but many orientations. As the line of regard sweeps along the surface from near to far the angle that it makes with the surface continually changes so that the orientation of every point on the surface has a different value. Also, we can see that whenever the observer moves the orientation to the line of regard of every point on the surface changes so that as the observer moves around in the environment this representation must be continually updated. The environment-centered orientation of a flat surface, on the other hand, is the same at every location on the surface, and remains unchanged, or invariant, when the observer moves. Thus, it would seem that considerable economies might be achieved by a visual system that could dispense with the viewer-centered representation and proceed directly to the sparser and more stable environment-centered representation.

The suggestion that information for spatial layout is first in viewer-centered form gains support, however, from some analyses of the available visual information for surface orientation. For example, as Gibson [2] first pointed out and as Purdy [10] demonstrated mathematically, there is a one-to-one relation between a surface's orientation with respect to the line of regard at a given location and the gradient of texture density, as defined by Purdy, at that location.

If all of the available information for surface orientation specified orientation with respect to the line of regard, then it might seem necessary that the visual system first register viewer-centered orientation. This, however, is not the case. One source of visual information that directly specifies environment-centered surface orientation is what one of us [13] has referred to as the *perspective structure of the optic array*, which is the set of all vanishing points and all horizons in the optic array (this is an extension of the concept of the "ghost image," which is simply the set of all vanishing points in the optic array, that was introduced by Hay [5]; the perspective structure of the optic array is also quite close in structure to the Gaussian sphere representation of orientation that has been used in some recent research [1, 6, 7]). There is a set of simple relations by which the perspective structure of the optic array directly specifies the environment-centered orientation of every visible straight edge and flat surface in the environment. For example, the relative environment-centered orientation of two environmental surfaces is equal to the angle in the optic array between their horizons. Although vanishing points and horizons are rarely explicitly present in the optic array, they are often implicitly specified by other structures, so that it makes sense to think of the optic array from a normal environment as making available to the visual system an *implicit perspective structure*. Both the specification of the implicit perspective structure of the optic array and the information that this structure makes available concerning the orientation of surfaces, as well as their scale, shape, and location, are discussed in detail in Sedgwick [12–14].

The existence of available information that directly specifies environment-centered orientation makes it possible to postulate [13] that a visual system might directly register environment-centered surface orientation without having to pass through a stage of viewer-centered representation. The present paper reports a series of empirical studies investigating this hypothesis in human observers.

2. EXPERIMENT I

Consideration of the perspective structure of the optic array shows that there is potential information on the basis of which human observers could perceive environment-centered surface orientation directly, without the need to derive it from a prior viewer-centered representation. Do they in fact do so? To obtain some empirical evidence relevant to this question, we conducted an experiment in which we compared the ability of observers to perceive environment-centered surface orientation with their ability to perceive viewer-centered surface orientation.

Although the experimental literature on the human perception of surface orientation is very extensive (see [14] for a review), little attention has been paid to the distinction between environment-centered and viewer-centered orientation. Gibson and Cornsweet [4] made this distinction clearly, but in subsequent research the distinction has been generally ignored. Experimentally, these two potential frameworks for surface orientation are usually confounded, often by using a stimulus display in which the environment-centered orientation of the experimental surface is the same as its viewer-centered orientation.

In our experiment each observer viewed the representations of two rectangular surfaces, one of which was located 22.5° above the other. One of the surfaces was slanted around a horizontal axis in the frontal plane, and the observer's task was to rotate the other surface around its horizontal axis until its orientation matched that of the first surface. Because of the difference in elevation between the two surfaces, the correct match in terms of environment-centered orientation differed by 22.5° from the correct match in terms of viewer-centered orientation. In one condition observers were given instructions that required them to base their matches on environment-centered orientation, and in another condition they were required to base their matches on viewer-centered orientation. We could then compare their performance on these two conditions.

Because of our interest in the potential use of the perspective structure of the optic array to directly perceive environment-centered orientation, we chose in this experiment to use static, monocularly viewed displays in which the information for surface slant was supplied by linear perspective.

The stimulus used in the experiment was a line representation of a rectangle divided into square boxes. The rectangle was 20 boxes wide and 10 boxes high. For each slant angle and elevation used in the experiment, the appropriate projection of the stimulus rectangle was generated by computer and displayed on a high-resolution display oscilloscope. A photographic slide was then made from the oscilloscope screen of each projected rectangle. During the experiment these slides were rear-projected onto a 129 by 129 cm screen. The observer sat on the opposite side of the screen and viewed the slides with head held stationary by a chin and forehead rest and with an eye patch covering the non-dominant eye (as determined by a pointing task). The viewing eye was located 70 cm from the center of the rear projection screen. The distance of the slide projectors from the other side of the rear projection screen was adjusted so that the stimulus rectangle subtended 20 by 10° when it was at eye level and in the frontal plane.

Three slide projectors, arranged vertically, were used in the experiment: the upper, middle, and lower projectors were mounted, respectively, 29 cm above, at, and 29 cm below the observer's eye level. Each of the slide projectors was mounted with its optical axis perpendicular to the projection screen so that all of the slides were projected without distortion. On a given trial either the upper or lower projector was used to display the projection of a slanted rectangle; this was the standard that the observer attempted to match.

The middle slide projector held a circular carousel containing 80 slides representing the rectangle in all slants from 0 to 180° in 2.25° steps. The observer held a remote control that allowed this carousel to be moved forward or backward at the rate of about one slide per second. Because the projections of the rectangle from 180 to 360° were identical to its projections from 0 to 180°, the rectangle could be made to rotate "continuously" (i.e., in 2.25° steps) in either direction. The observer was required to adjust the projected slant of this comparison rectangle until it matched the slant of the standard rectangle. Each trial started with the projected comparison rectangle horizontal, so that the observer was viewing it edge-on, and continued until the observer was satisfied that a correct match had been made.

Each observer made matches on 16 trials, divided into 2 blocks of 8. Four different slants of the standard rectangle were used—45, 67.5, 112.5, and 135°, measured from the horizontal; angles smaller than 90° indicate that the upper half of the rectangle was slanted away from the observer. Each of the four standard slants was displayed at two elevations—22.5° above and 22.5° below the observer's eye level. These eight trials were arranged randomly within each block of trials.

For one block of trials the observer was given instructions indicating that environment-centered slant should be matched, and for the other block of trials the instructions indicated that viewer-centered slant should be matched. Half of the observers made environment-centered matches first, and the other half of the observers made viewer-centered matches first. The instructions given to the observers did not actually use the terms "environment-centered" and "viewer-centered." Instead, the environment-centered match was described as one in which both rectangles made the same angle with the horizontal, and the viewer-centered match was described as one in which both rectangles made the same angle with the observer's line of sight to the center of each rectangle. Diagrams were used to illustrate these two types of matches, and these diagrams remained available to the observer throughout the experiment. The instructions requested observers to base their matches on their perceptual impressions and to not try to cognitively figure out the correct settings.

No attempt was made to fool observers into believing that they were looking at actual slanted rectangles, but efforts were made to bring out the 3-dimensional quality of the displays by minimizing perceptual information for their actual 2-dimensionality. At the outset of the experiment observers were told that they would be looking at computer-generated slides of slanted rectangles and were shown, as an illustration of what was being pictured, a 3-dimensional model of two slanted rectangles mounted one above the other. During each experimental trial the room lights were turned off. The slide projectors themselves were enclosed so that no extraneous light escaped from them. Each slide showed the stimulus rectangle as white lines on a black background, and neutral density filters were placed in front of the apertures through which the slides were projected to reduce the intensity of each rectangle to a level that was comfortably visible but not brightly luminous. A black screen was placed 6.5 cm in front of the observer with a circular hole cut in it that limited the observer's view to an 80° wide circular area of the projection screen. Thus during each trial the observer saw two mildly luminous figures floating in a dark space in which nothing else was visible (it was possible with an effort, however, to make out the very dimly visible surface of the projection screen itself, which was faintly illuminated by light scattered from the projected slides). Under these conditions the display gave a strong 3-dimensional impression; observers had no difficulty in perceiving the projected figures as rectangles slanted in depth.

Data were obtained from 16 paid observers, most of whom were students and all of whom were naive as to the theoretical constructs and hypotheses behind the experiment.

Figure 1 shows the correct settings of the comparison rectangle for one setting of the standard rectangle as a function of the instructions and of the elevation of the standard. As the left half of the figure shows, the (environment-centered) angle to which the comparison rectangle should be set under environment-centered instructions is simply equal to the setting of the standard rectangle and thus should be the same for the upper and lower elevations of the standard. On the other hand, as the right side of the figure shows, under viewer-centered instructions the correct setting of the comparison rectangle varies with the elevation of the standard rectangle. When the standard is positioned 22.5° above eye level, the comparison should be set to an angle, that is (in environment-centered terms), 22.5° less than the angle to which the standard rectangle is set. This difference between the angles of the

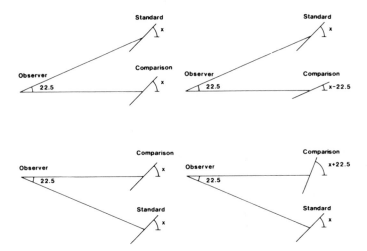

FIG. 1. Examples of correct matches under environment-centered instructions (left side) and viewer-centered instructions (right side). The diagrams, which are not drawn to scale, show the standard and comparison rectangles as seen from the side.

comparison and the standard rectangle is a function only of the angular elevation of the standard relative to the comparison; the difference remains constant as the slant of the standard is changed. Similarly, when the standard is positioned 22.5° below eye level, the comparison should be set to an angle that is a constant 22.5° greater than the angle of the standard.

The actual results, averaged across observers, are shown in Fig. 2. The axes of the graph are labelled in environment-centered angles. The solid lines in the figure indicate where observers settings would be if they had been able to make correct

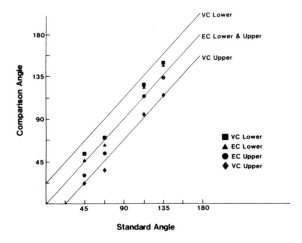

FIG. 2. Averaged results for Experiment I.

matches according to their instructions, with the center line showing the correct settings of the comparison, under environment-centered instructions, for both the upper (EC UPPER) and lower (EC LOWER) positions of the standard, and with the lower and upper lines showing the correct settings, under viewer-centered instructions, for the upper (VC UPPER) and lower (VC LOWER) positions of the standard, respectively.

An examination of Fig. 2 shows that the subjects' settings did vary, in the appropriate directions, as a function of instructions; the VC LOWER settings are consistently higher than the EC LOWER settings and the VC UPPER settings are consistently lower than the EC UPPER settings—differences that are statistically significant ($p < 0.05$ and $p < 0.01$, respectively, using a non-parametric chi-2 "goodness of fit" test). Clearly, observers are capable of responding, when requested to do so, in either viewer-centered or environment-centered terms.

Figure 2 also shows a result that we had not expected: The observers' settings under environment-centered instructions vary as a function of the elevation of the standard rectangle, with the EC LOWER settings being consistently higher than the EC UPPER settings. This difference is highly significant statistically ($p < 0.001$ using a non-parametric chi-2 "goodness of fit" test), and we shall pursue it at length below. A companion effect, in which the separations between actual VC LOWER and VC UPPER settings are less, on the average, than the separations between the correct values for those conditions, may also be observed in Fig. 2.

Another apparently systematic effect may be seen in Fig. 2. All of the data points for angles less than 90° appear to be shifted down somewhat, while all of the data points for angles greater than 90° appear to be shifted up somewhat. Because 90° is the vertical, this means that all of the data points show a constant error in which they are shifted away from the vertical, toward the horizontal. As a later study, not reported here, shows, this constant error is simply due to having every trial begin with the comparison rectangle in a horizontal orientation.

Our main interest in this experiment was in comparing performance under environment-centered instructions with performance under viewer-centered instructions. We have seen that both types of instructions produce constant errors in the observers' average settings. Another measure of performance is the variability of the observers' settings. Figure 3 shows the standard deviations of the settings, under both types of instructions, for each angle and elevation of the standard. It can be seen that variability was consistently substantially higher for the viewer-centered instructions than for the environment-centered instructions ($p < 0.01$ using the non-parametric, Wilcoxen matched-pairs test). This result suggests that matching viewer-centered surface orientations may have been a considerably more difficult task for our observers than matching environment-centered surface orientation; this suggestion was supported by the spontaneous comments of several of our observers.

We take the greater difficulty of following viewer-centered as compared with environment-centered instructions, suggested by the greater variability in the former condition, as being consistent with, although not proving, our hypothesis that environment-centered surface orientation is obtained directly from the optic array without first having to pass through a stage in which it is represented as viewer-centered surface orientation.

Concerning our finding that observers' settings under environment-centered instructions varied with the elevation of the standard, two possible explanations

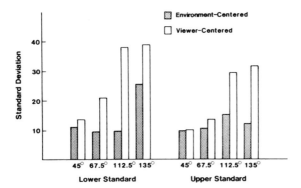

FIG. 3.   Standard deviations for Experiment I.

suggest themselves. The more interesting one is that observers' perceptions of environment-centered surface orientation are somewhat influenced by the surface's viewer-centered orientation. This would lead to the observers' actual settings under environment-centered instructions being located somewhere between the correct settings for those instructions and the correct settings for viewer-centered instructions. Thus when the position of the standard is below eye level, the angular setting of the comparison would be somewhat too high, and when the position of the standard is above eye level, the angular setting of the comparison would be somewhat too low. This of course is just what we found.

Another, less interesting, explanation of these results is possible, however. The shape of the standard rectangle's projection on the screen varied with its elevation. For example, for a 45° angle, the standard's projection becomes more compressed vertically as the standard is raised above eye level and becomes less compressed vertically as the standard is lowered below eye level. The projection of the comparison rectangle, on the other hand, always remains at eye level but becomes more compressed vertically as the angle of the comparison is decreased below 45° and becomes less compressed vertically as the angle of the comparison is increased above 45°. Similarly, potentially congruent changes occur in the projective convergence of the standard and comparison rectangles. Thus it is possible that the different settings we found for the upper and lower positions of the standard, under environment-centered instructions, occurred because our observers' settings were influenced by a tendency to match the projective shapes of the standard and the comparison. (One could match either compression or convergence exactly but both together could be matched only approximately.)

3. EXPERIMENT II

We carried out a second experiment in an attempt to determine whether the effect of the elevation of the standard on observers' settings that we found under environment-centered instructions was due to the influence of viewer-centered orientation or to a tendency to match projective shapes. We reasoned that we could distinguish between these two possibilities by leaving the viewer-centered orientation of the standard rectangle unchanged while changing the standard's projective shape

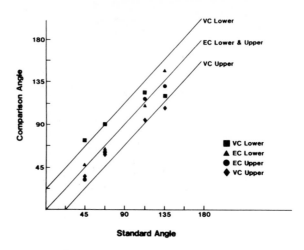

FIG. 4.   Averaged results for Experiment II.

so that the projective shape of the comparison rectangle could no longer be made to even approximately match it. This change should have eliminated the effect of elevation of the standard if it was due to projective matching, but should not have altered the effect if it was due to the influence of viewer-centered orientation.

We changed the projective shape of the standard by rotating the standard rectangle through 45° in the frontal plane before slanting it, around its new horizontal axis, away from the frontal plane. The convergence and compression produced by the projective transformation then acted along different axes of the standard and comparison rectangles and so produced projected shapes that were substantially different no matter what the angular setting of the comparison was.

One other change that we made in our second experiment was to somewhat expand our environment-centered and viewer-centered instructions to the observers in a further attempt to ensure that they clearly understood what they were being asked to do in both conditions.

Apart from the expansion of the instructions and the changed projective shape of the standard, the second experiment was an exact replication of the first. Again we used 16 paid observers, all of whom were students.

The results of the second experiment are shown in Figs. 4 and 5. It can be seen that they are quite similar to the results of the first experiment. Once again, as Fig. 4 shows, the observers' settings vary consistently in the appropriate directions as a function of instructions with their VC LOWER settings being significantly higher than their EC LOWER settings ($p < 0.025$) and with their VC UPPER settings being significantly lower than their EC UPPER settings ($p < 0.01$). Also, as Fig. 5 demonstrates, the settings made under viewer-centered instructions are once again significantly more variable than the settings made under environment-centered instructions ($p < 0.01$).

Of most interest in the results of the second experiment is the observation, which can be made in Fig. 4, that under environment-centered instructions there remains a substantial and highly significant difference between the matches made to the upper

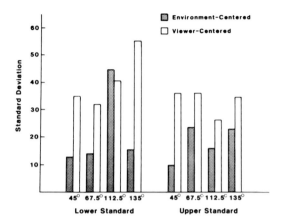

FIG. 5.   Standard deviations for Experiment II.

and lower position of the standard rectangle ($p < 0.001$). Because we have greatly reduced the possibility of projective shape matching in this experiment, we take this result as an indication that this difference here, and probably in the first experiment as well, is due to the influence of viewer-centered orientation on the perception of environment-centered orientation.

In comparing the results of our two experiments, it can be seen that the settings made in the second experiment were generally more variable than those made in the first experiment. A possible source of this greater variability was suggested by remarks made by some of our observers in the second experiment, who commented that the standard rectangle occasionally appeared to reverse its orientation in depth, i.e., the upper half of the rectangle would suddenly appear to switch from being in front of the frontal plane to being behind it, or vice versa. Examination of the observer's settings supported these remarks by showing that in some instances a setting was much closer to the reversed orientation of the surface than to its projectively specified orientation (e.g., closer to 45° than to 135°). Such large departures from the correct values, even though only occurring occasionally, would clearly have a large effect on the measured variability of the settings. Why these reversals occur is not clear to us. They would not be predicted from the available perspective information and so must arise from some other aspect of our stimulus display, presumably one that is related to the oblique orientation of the standard rectangle in the second experiment.

In a rough attempt to estimate the effects of such perceptual reversals on our data, we classified every setting as either a reversal or a non-reversal, depending on whether it was closer to the correct orientation of the surface or to its reversed orientation (which we took to be the reflection around the frontal plane of the correct orientation), and we then recalculated our averages and standard deviations omitting all of the settings classified as reversals. This recalculation had little effect on the results of the first experiment, in which only 3% of the settings were classified as reversals, but it did reduce the variability of the settings in the second experiment, in which 12.5% of the settings were classified as reversals, to levels similar to those found in our first experiment.

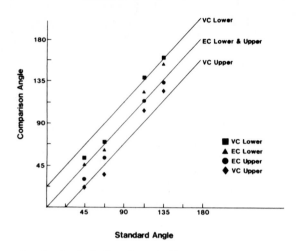

FIG. 6.   Results for Experiment I with reversal data removed.

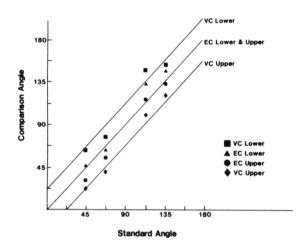

FIG. 7.   Results for Experiment II with reversal data removed.

As shown in Figs. 6 and 7, our recalculations also result in an even greater similarity between the average settings of our first and second experiments, thus further supporting our conclusion that a tendency toward projective matching was not a significant factor in producing the results obtained in either experiment.

4. CONCLUSIONS

The results of both of our studies show that human observers are capable of doing a fairly good job of matching the orientation of two surfaces according to either their viewer-centered orientation or their environment-centered orientation. Observers, however, generally find environment-centered matches easier to make than viewer-centered matches, as is indicated both by their spontaneous remarks and by their settings, which are substantially less variable for environment-centered than for viewer-centered orientation.

We take these results to be at least consistent with the hypothesis that human observers obtain environment-centered surface orientation directly from the available visual information, such as the perspective structure of the optic array, rather than deriving it from an earlier viewer-centered representation.

Clearly, other explanations of this result are possible. It could be, for instance, that a viewer-centered representation does exist as a prior stage but that this stage is not readily available to perception, perhaps because the observer is less often called upon to make judgments on the basis of it. Nevertheless, it seems to us that our interpretation is the most parsimonious. If an intermediate stage is to be postulated, there should be some reason for doing so, and neither our theoretical analysis of the available information nor our empirical data concerning the actual use of such information provides such a reason.

More generally, our present results are consistent with earlier results [11] showing that relative sizes of objects can be perceived, using available information based on objects' relations with the terrestial horizon, independently of any need to perceive the observer's distance from the objects. Together, these results help to build some support for the hypothesis that human visual perception may involve a comprehensive, environment-centered registration of spatial layout, including information for the size, shape, location, and orientation of surfaces, that is obtained directly from the available information in the optic array rather than from some intermediate viewer-centered representation.

Observers do, of course, have access to some viewer-centered information about their environments. Such information is clearly essential for some activities in which the observer interacts with the environment. Viewer-centered information could either be registered in parallel with environment-centered information or could be derived, as needed, from environment-centered information.

These hypotheses must be tempered, however, by our finding that an observer's perception of the environment-centered orientation of a surface is influenced by its viewer-centered orientation. This finding suggests that one's environment-centered perceptions may never be fully independent of one's own position in the environment. Whether this lack of complete independence arises from a low-level failure to register the necessary features of the optic array with sufficient accuracy, from a use of "algorithms" that are too simplified or only approximate the mathematically correct ones, from genuine interactions with independently derived viewer-centered information, or from some other cause, remains to be determined.

ACKNOWLEDGMENTS

This research was supported in part by NEI Training Grant T35-EY-07079. We are grateful for the assistance of T. Ruggiero-Corliss in some of our data gathering and analysis.

REFERENCES

1. S. T. Barnard, Interpreting perspective images. *Artif. Intell.* **21**, 1983, 435–462.
2. J. J. Gibson, *The Perception of the Visual World*, Houghton Mifflin, Boston, 1950.
3. J. J. Gibson, Ecological optics, *Vision Res.* **1**, 1961, 253–262.
4. J. J. Gibson and J. Cornsweet, The perceived slant of visual surfaces—Optical and geographical, *J. Exp. Psych.* **44**, 1952, 11–15.

5. J. C. Hay, The ghost image: A tool for the analysis of the visual stimulus, in *Perception: Essays in Honor of James J. Gibson* (R. B. MacLeod & H. L. Pick, Jr., Eds.), Cornell Univ. Press, Ithaca, N.Y., 1974.

6. J. R. Kender, A computational paradigm for deriving local surface orientation from local textural properties, *IEEE Workshop on Computer Vision*, pp. 143–152, 1982.

7. M. J. Magee and J. K. Aggarwal, Determining vanishing points from perspective images, *Comput. Vision Graphics Image Process.* **26**, 1984, 256–267.

8. D. Marr, Representing visual information, in *Computer Vision Systems* (A. R. Hanson and E. M. Riseman, Eds.), Academic Press, New York, 1978.

9. D. Marr, *Vision*, Freeman, San Francisco, 1982.

10. W. C. Purdy, *The Hypothesis of Psychophysical Correspondence in Space Perception*, General Electric Technical Information Series R60ELC56, Schenectady, N.Y., 1960.

11. H. A. Sedgwick, *The Visible Horizon: A Potential Source of Visual Information for the Perception of Size and Distance*, Doctoral dissertation, Cornell University, 1973.

12. H. A. Sedgwick, The geometry of spatial layout in pictorial representation, in *The Perception of Pictures I: Alberti's Window: The Projective Model of Pictorial Information*, (M. A. Hagen, Ed.), Academic Press, New York, 1980.

13. H. A. Sedgwick, Environment-centered representation of spatial layout: Available visual information from texture and perspective, in *Human and Machine Vision*, (J. Beck, B. Hope, and A. Rosenfeld, Eds.), Academic Press, New York, 1983.

14. H. A. Sedgwick, Space perception, in *Handbook of Perception and Human Performance*, (K. Boff, L. Kaufman, and J. Thomas, Eds.), Wiley, New York, in press.

Perception of Organization in a Random Stimulus

BEVERLY J. SMITH

University of Victoria, Victoria, Canada*

Received March 13, 1985

This paper describes an experimental test of the role of perceptual organization in the perception and reproduction of a visual stimulus. A perceptually random stimulus was presented to subjects who were to reproduce it. A procedure of serial reproductions was used and the perceptual organization inherent in the subjects' reproductions was quantified by a psychophysical scaling procedure. The prediction of increased organization in successive reproductions was confirmed. When there was little or no perceptual organization in the stimulus (as in the random stimulus), subjects imposed perceptual organization on the sensory input. When there was perceptual organization inherent in the stimulus, subjects perceived it and further emphasized the organization in their reproductions. Of particular interest was the investigation of the distinction between perceptual organization as a characteristic of the sensory input and perceptual organization as a characteristic of the processing operations of the visual system acting on the sensory input. © 1985 Academic Press, Inc.

The central hypothesis explored in this research is that perceptual organization determines the perception of a stimulus field and that this process of organization is evident in the characteristics of the reproduction of the stimulus field. Of particular interest here is the issue concerning the nature of the organization of the stimulus; that is, to what extent is the organization of the visual field the result of processing operations of the visual system acting on the stimulus or the result of physical characteristics inherent in the stimulus.

In order to investigate these issues of perceptual organization, a perceptually random stimulus was presented to subjects. Their task was to reproduce the stimulus from memory.

The target stimulus was an isotropic, i.e., uniform density distribution of dots (see Fig. 1) . The target stimulus was determined by a quasi-random process. The sheet of paper was divided into a 9×9 grid and each of the resulting 81 squares was itself divided into a 10×10 grid. A single dot was placed in each of the 81 squares; the position in the square was determined by a random number pair corresponding to a position in the 10×10 grid. This process yielded a target stimulus that was virtually patternless. A purely random process of distributing dots on the paper would result in clusters or groups of dots. The restriction of uniform density minimizes this.

A perceptually random stimulus was necessary in order to investigate the extent to which perceptual organization is a characteristic of the processing operations of the visual processing system acting on the sensory input under conditions where there is virtually no inherent organization in the stimulus.

The reproduction procedure involved cascading subjects' reproductions in such a manner that (1) each subject made only one reproduction of the stimulus with no appreciable delay and (2) the reproduction of one subject became the target for the

*Current address: Interact Research & Development Corporation, 4252 Commerce Circle, Victoria, Canada V8Z 4M2.

FIG. 1.   Random target stimulus for the first subject (S_1) in each cascade.

next subject. That is, the first subject in a cascade viewed the random dot target that was prepared by the experimenter and was asked to reproduce it. This was the only reproduction that he/she made. The next subject viewed the previous subject's reproduction as his/her target and reproduced it. This procedure, in which each subject reproduced the previous subject's reproduction, was done five times and constituted a single cascade.

Based on the Gestalt assertions that the human visual system imposes perceptual organization on the sensory input, it was predicted that each subject's reproduction would be more organized than the target stimulus he/she viewed. Therefore, in a single cascade there should be a substantial increase in organization from the original target of random dots to the final subject's reproduction. By cascading subjects, small increments of organization that a subject makes in a single reproduction will be detected and amplified through successive reproductions.

Method

Subjects. Sixty undergraduates volunteered to be subjects.

Stimuli and apparatus. The target stimulus for the first subject in each of twelve cascades was a 12″ × 12″ sheet of paper with a uniform distribution of random dots.

Procedure. Subjects were seen individually and shown a target stimulus. They were asked to study the dots carefully because the sheet would be taken away and they would have to reproduce them as accurately as possible. The first subject in each of 12 cascades was shown the target sheet of 81 random dots. They were then asked to reproduce the target. (Two sheets of paper and a carbon were used in order to obtain a duplicate copy.) When the subjects had finished their reproduction they were asked how they remembered where the dots were. It was known from pilot work that subjects typically reported remembering the dots in various patterns. Therefore, they were asked to connect the dots in the carbon copy of their reproductions to indicate those patterns. When this was completed, subjects were shown their target stimulus and were asked to indicate those patterns in the target which they had shown in the reproduction. Finally, the subject was shown a copy of the target stimulus which had the individual dots numbered, and he/she was asked to assign numbers to the dots in their carbon reproduction which corresponded to the dots in the target. In doing

FIG. 2. Cascade A (one of 12 cascades): S_1's reproduction of Fig. 1, also S_2's target.

this subjects identified which dots in the target they had remembered and reproduced. This part of the procedure allowed certain patterns and dots to be traced
throughout successive reproductions in a cascade.

Results

A psychophysical scaling technique was used to quantify the perceptual organization in the subjects' reproduction. The scale of perceptual organization was represented as an actual line on a table along which subjects placed the actual stimuli.
Exactly where on the scale a stimulus was placed indicated how much perceptual
organization it contained. The relative positions of the stimuli along the scale were
measured after the subject had finished [1, 2].

Twenty-four additional subjects were recruited and each was asked to scale 3 of
the 12 cascades, one cascade at a time, along a scale of perceptual organization. A
single cascade consisted of six stimuli—the random target and five serial reproductions. Figures 1–6 illustrate one of the cascades in reduced form.

Each cascade was scaled by six subjects. The amount of agreement among the
subjects' estimates of the perceptual organization inherent in each stimulus was
determined by the use of analysis of variance for estimating reliability [3].

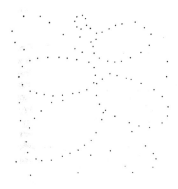

FIG. 3. Cascade A: S_2's reproduction of Fig. 2, also S_3's target.

FIG. 4. Cascade A: S_3's reproduction of Fig. 3, also S_4's target.

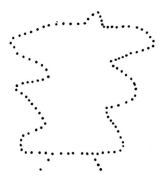

FIG. 5. Cascade A: S_4's reproduction of Fig. 4, also S_5's target.

FIG. 6. Cascade A: S_5's reproduction of Fig. 5.

The reliability coefficients (measured by the intraclass correlation coefficient) for the 12 cascades were high; they ranged from $R = 0.89$ to 0.99. This indicates that the subjects' estimates of the amount of perceptual organization in the stimuli are consistent.

In order to examine whether perceptual organization was imposed on the isotropic stimulus and whether successive reproductions showed an increase in perceptual organization, linear trend tests were conducted on the average perceptual organization estimates of each stimulus in each cascade. The F values ranged from

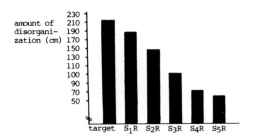

FIG. 7.   Mean perceptual organization ratings for stimulus reproductions, across all cascades. (N.B. A low rating in centimeters indicates high perceptual organization.)

$F(1, 25) = 123.06$ to 509.1, all of which are, of course, significant, $p < 0.0001$. The mean scores for each stimulus across all cascades are shown in Fig. 7.

Discussion

The predictions of increased organization were confirmed. By viewing the subjects' reproductions in a cascade and by examining the results of tests for linear trend, it is clear that perceptual organization is increased in successive reproductions. Thus, the organizational processes operating in the visual system impose organization on sensory input as well as perceive organizational properties inherent in the input.

In a review of visual information processing Cooper [4] raises the issue regarding the locus of perceptual organization effects. This issue concerns whether organizational properties are inherent in the physical stimulus or whether they result from the processing operations acting on the visual information; or indeed whether they result from some interaction between the visual information and visual processing system. In this experiment the issue is partially addressed by using a perceptually random stimulus at the beginning of each cascade. Under these circumstances the organizational properties of the stimulus and the processing system are separated. Any organization occurring in a cascade that is started with a random stimulus must be due to organization imposed on the sensory input as there is no organization inherent in the input. The strongest support for the perceptual randomness of the initial stimulus (i.e., Fig. 1) comes from the finding that the 12 cascades originating from it all resulted in very different patterns. Given the opportunity to trace patterns throughout a cascade by the procedure of numbering the dots, it is evident that when subjects impose organizational properties into their reproduction these properties are detected by subsequent subjects. Therefore, it is assumed that if there were any obvious, inherent patterns in the initial stimulus subjects would have detected and reproduced them. This would have resulted in much more similarity among the cascades than is found. Therefore, it is assumed that the initial stimulus had no perceptually salient patterns or organization.

ACKNOWLEDGEMENT

The author would like to thank Professor Alex Bavelas for many fruitful discussions.

REFERENCES

1. J. B. Bavelas and B. J. Smith, A method for scaling verbal disqualification, *Hum. Comm. Res.*, **8**, 1982, 214–227.
2. E. S. Lee, *A Test of Two Minimax Models for Predicting the Scaling of Partitions of Stimulus Sets*, Doctoral dissertation, University of Victoria, 1977.
3. B. J. Winer, *Statistical Principles in Experimental Design*, 2nd. ed., McGraw–Hill, New York, 1971.
4. L. A. Cooper, Recent themes in visual information processing: A selected overview, in *Attention and Performance VIII* (R. S. Nickerson, Ed.), Erlbaum, Hillsdale, N.J., 1980.

Autonomous Scene Description with Range Imagery

DAVID R. SMITH AND TAKEO KANADE*

Department of Computer Science, Carnegie–Mellon University, Pittsburgh, Pennsylvania 15213

Received February 10, 1985

This paper presents a program to produce object-centered 3-dimensional descriptions starting from point-wise 3D range data obtained by a light-stripe rangefinder. A careful geometrical analysis shows that contours which appear in light-stripe range images can be classified into eight types, each with different characteristics in occluding vs occluded and different camera/illuminator relationships. Starting with detecting these contours in the iconic range image, the descriptions are generated moving up the hierarchy of contour, surface, object, to scene. We use conical and cylindrical surfaces as primitives. In this process, we exploit the fact that coherent relationships, such as symmetry, collinearity, and being coaxial, which are present among lower-level elements in the hierarchy allow us to hypothesize upper-level elements. The resultant descriptions are used for matching and recognizing objects. The analysis program has been applied to complex scenes containing cups, pans, and toy shovels.
© 1985 Academic Press, Inc.

1. INTRODUCTION

The research presented in this paper aims at producing object-centered 3-dimensional descriptions starting from point-wise 3D range data obtained by a light-stripe range finder. While most of the initial work in range data analysis was on generating object descriptions of simple objects: representation of snakes and dolls made of cylindrical parts by means of generalized cylinders [1, 8] or representation of polyhedra by planes [11, 9], recent work seems to be more concerned about efficient matching of objects with 3D models [3, 4]. Our emphasis in this paper, however, is data-driven bottom–up autonomous processing, generating object descriptions from complicated scenes without referring to specific pre-stored object models.

Starting from the iconic range data, the descriptions are generated moving up the hierarchy of contour, surface, object, to scene. We use conical and cylindrical surfaces as primitives. While a top–down verification process is important, the bottom–up process for producing plausible, natural, object-level descriptions is at least as crucial in order to realize general vision systems [7, 2] as the task world becomes larger and less contrived. Our approach to the problem is to exploit the fact that coherent relationships, such as symmetry, collinearity, and being coaxial, that are present among lower-level elements in the hierarchy allow us to hypothesize upper-level elements. This is justified because those coherent relationships do not usually occur accidentally [6]. For example, if the same surfaces with the same relationships appear across two scenes, they tend to be grouped into one object; if one cylinder's axis intersects with another one's, like the relationship between the

*This research was sponsored by the Defense Advanced Research Projects Agency (DOD), ARPA Order 3597, monitored by the Air Force Avionics Laboratory under Contract F33615-81-K-1539. The views and conclusions contained in this document are those of the authors and should not be interpreted as representing the official policies, either expressed or implied, of the Defense Advanced Research Projects Agency or the U.S. Government.

243

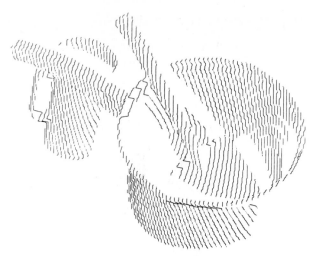

FIG. 1.   Light-stripe image of a scene.

handle and body of a pan, they tend to belong to the same object. These coherencies must be present because they have been inherited through the hierarchy from the scene level down to the iconic range-data level. Our task is to trace and exploit these coherent relationships reversely for autonomous generation of object descriptions.

We focused our effort on the use of occluding contours, which can be extracted quite reliably from the light-stripe range data. First, contours are extracted, segmented, and classified. From the coherencies among them, such as parallelism, surfaces are hypothesized. These are represented as conic surfaces (pipes, cones, and planes). The surface hypotheses are confirmed or refuted by their ability to account for observed surface area. Hypotheses of surface groups are formed by examining coherencies among the verified surfaces, such as axis intersections. Finally, such surface groupings from multiple scenes are compared. If a similar structure repeatedly occurs, it is identified as an object. The succeeding sections of this paper follow these steps in order.

2. TAXONOMY OF CONTOURS IN LIGHT-STRIPE IMAGES

The range images for this work were produced by a light-stripe rangefinder, which consists of an illuminator projecting a sheet of light into the scene and a camera that detects amount of deflection in the light stripe on each scan line. Triangulation produces surface-point positions in three dimensions. A range image is shown in Fig. 1, which is a composite of the camera's views of the light stripes, using every tenth stripe.

The parallax between illuminator and camera makes ranging feasible, but it also causes occlusions which are difficult to interpret. Figure 2 shows the geometry in light-stripe imaging which includes a circular object A and the background B. It explains how contours are generated which bound a surface against either another surface or a region which cannot be measured. Object A cast a deep shadow region *umbra*, which cannot be seen from either the illuminator or the camera. It also casts

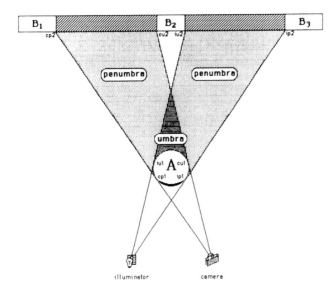

FIG. 2.   Generation of contours with a light-stripe rangefinder.

two half-shadow regions, *penumbras*, which might be seen from either the illuminator or the camera, but not both. No data can be recorded for a surface which lies in either an umbra or a penumbra.

Occlusions occur at the four combinations where the line of sight, either from the illuminator or the camera, is tangential to the surface of the foreground object A: that is, $ip1$-$ip2$, $iu1$-$iu2$, $cp1$-$cp2$, and $cu1$-$cu2$. Here, the first point of each pair forms the occluding contour and the second the occluded contour; therefore there are eight types of contours in the light-stripe range imagery. This analysis points out a few interesting points. First, previous researchers have dealt only with the simple occlusions involving $cp1$-$cp2$ and $ip1$-$ip2$, by converting to three dimensions and drawing rays from the illuminator and camera. It can be shown that this can be done without resorting to 3-dimensional geometry, by exploiting information in the raw deflection image. Second, interpretation of the occlusions $iu1$-$iu2$ and $cu1$-$cu2$ provides information about the object, even though the occluding contour is not recorded. This is especially true and useful when we can assume cylindrical objects, because the totally visible region (from $cp1$ to $ip1$) is fairly small, and expanding the known part to the region from $iu1$ to $cu1$ will greatly increase the accuracy in reconstructing the cylindrical shape.[1]

Figure 3 shows the contours detected in the image of Fig. 1: (a) shows all the contour points, (b) shows the occluding points, and (c) and (d) show the penumbral and umbral occluded points, respectively. The occluding contours are directly useful for shape cues, while the occluded contours provide indirect information [10].

---

[1] Incidentally, this point suggests that the light-stripe range data be taken *with* the background, as opposed to the conventional way in which the background is blacked out by a black carpet or curtain.

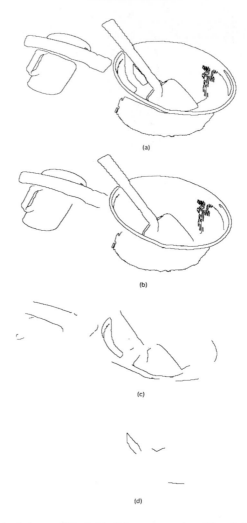

FIG. 3. Contours in the image of Fig. 1: (a) all the contour points; (b) occluding points; (c) penumbral occluded points; (d) umbral occluded points.

3. CONTOUR ANALYSIS

3.1. Segmentations

For an extracted contour, local curvatures along it are calculated. The contour is segmented into pieces at the peaks of the curvature value, expecting that the segment between peaks can be described simply. Figure 4 illustrates an example of contour segmentation. The lower part of the figure is a plot of curvature vs position on the contour, traced clockwise around the shovel handle. In this case, the contour has been divided into three segments at the cross-marked positions. The result of segmentation for the whole occluding contours is shown in Fig. 5a.

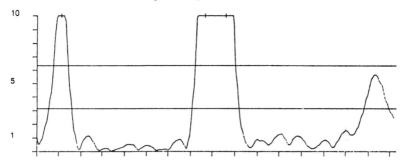

Marks are at 3 segmentation points

Thu Feb 9 21:56:06 1984 Curvature, global mean & significance
occluding contour 2 curv.mean ≈ 3.2, signif. ≈ 6.3 h = 15

FIG. 4.   Segmenting a contour. The upper is the contour of the shovel handle, and the graph is a plot of curvature vs position on the contour traced clockwise. The curve is segmented at the tip of the left peak, and on the shoulders of the peak in the middle. The line at 3.2 is the mean curvature for all contour points in the image. The threshold for peak significance is twice the mean (upper line). A more fortuitous choice would have segmented at the right peak, where the handle tapers into the shovel blade at lower right.

3.2. Segment Classification

Each contour segment is now classified into one of the four shape categories: *straight*, *circle*, *plane*, and *space*. For this, first a straight line is fit by least-squares. If the error residual is low, it is classfied as a line. Otherwise, a plane is fit. If the plane does not fit well, the contour is classified as a (nonplanar) space curve. If the plane fits well, a circle is fit to decide whether it should be declared a circle. Figures 5b and c show the results of classification of the occluding contour segments of our scene.

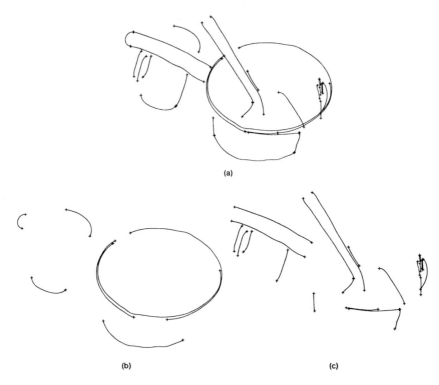

(a)

(b)   (c)

FIG. 5.   Results of contour segmentation and classification: (a) all contours with marks at the segment end points; (b) circular contour segments; (c) straight contour segments. Short segments are suppressed.

4. SURFACE ANALYSIS

Once the contours have been analyzed, they are examined to find what they can tell about the surfaces in the scene. This proceeds in three steps. First, contour segments are grouped (using coherent relationships among them) into ensembles which suggest various primitive surface shapes. Second, specific surface types and equations are proposed for the contour groups together with their spatial extent. Finally, the surface hypotheses are verified in the range image data.

4.1. Contour Groups

We seek binary coherence relationships between contours which suggest surface shapes. The relations sought depend upon the shapes of the surfaces, and include:

- Straight vs straight
  - Parallel
  - Antiparallel
  - Perpendicular
  - Collinear
  - Coplanar
  - Opposed

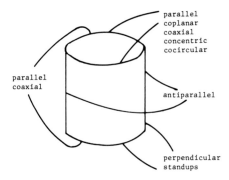

FIG. 6. The group type CONE and the relationships involved for it. All of the segments and relationships are not necessary to suggest the group.

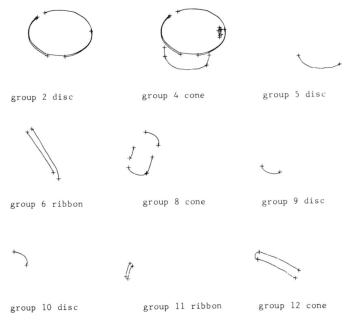

FIG. 7. The result of the contour grouping for Fig. 5a. There are gaps in the numbering because one group may be subsumed in a later hypothesis, as the binary relations involving different contours are examined. Group 2 is formed by a set of cocircular contours, and suggests a (nonexistent) disc. Group 4 suggests the frustrum of a cone. It was formed because the bottom circular contour was coaxial with the top ones, while the straight sides extended between top and bottom. Groups 8 and 12 were aggregated in the same way, although group 12 lacks a bottom. Groups 5, 9, and 10 are discs suggested by lone circular contours. Groups 6 and 11 are ribbons. The ribbon classification avoids too-early commitment to shape, since there are no cross-contours to indicate whether the surface is curved. Group 6 lacks the cross-contour because the contour at the end was discarded as unreliable because it was too short.

- Straight vs circle
  - ○ Perpendicular
  - ○ Stands-up
- Circle vs circle
  - ○ Parallel
  - ○ Coaxial
  - ○ Concentric
  - ○ Cocircular

Contours sharing appropriate combinations of these relations are aggregated into contour groups. Each contour group suggests a surface, and is classified as one of the following types:

- Cone (including cylinder)
- Ribbon
- Disc
- Plane,

As an example, Fig. 6 shows what kind of relationships are involved for the group type cone. The result of the contour grouping for our example scene is shown in Fig. 7, whose caption explains the details of individual groups.

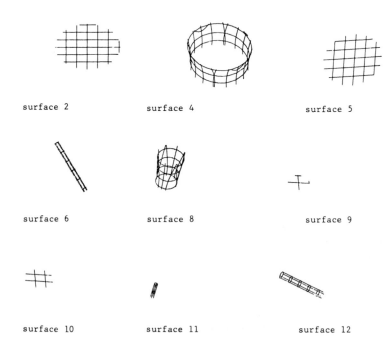

surface 2   surface 4   surface 5

surface 6   surface 8   surface 9

surface 10   surface 11   surface 12

FIG. 8.   Surfaces proposed by the contour groups in Fig. 7. Surfaces 4 and 8 are internally represented as rings cut from quadric surfaces, but are symbolically classed as (frustums of) cones. Surfaces 6 and 11, derived from ribbon contour groups, are seen to be cylinders.

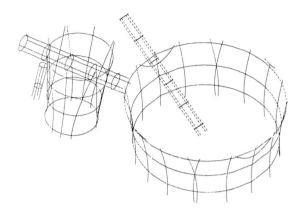

FIG. 9.   Accepted surfaces from Figure 8.

4.2. Surface Proposal

Each surface group proposed is converted to a surface equation together with the limits in its spatial extent. Fig. 8 shows the surface proposals generated from the corresponding contour groups of Fig. 7.

4.3. Surface Verification

The surface hypotheses are checked by going back to the range image and determining if each hypothesis can account for enough surface area in the scene. This involves a test of position and surface normal in 3-space for each pixel. The pixels which pass this test are summed according to the area which they individually represent in the scene. Based on this test, the proposed surfaces are either accepted or rejected as missing. For example, proposed surface 2 (top of the pan opening) is rejected, because no real surface exists at the proposed position. The surfaces which are accepted are shown together in Fig. 9.

TABLE 1

	Plane/disc	
Plane/disc	Coplanar Coextent Gap	Axis-in-plane Stands up
Cone/cylinder	Axis-in-plane Stands up	Coconical Coextent Gap Intersecting-axes Interior-intersection

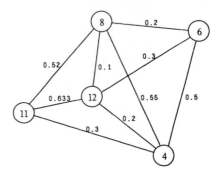

FIG. 10.   Relationship graph for surfaces.

5. OBJECT ANALYSIS

Surfaces are grouped into objects in a similar manner as contour grouping, but in this case based on coherent relationships among surfaces. In addition to the obvious (strong) relationship of shared contours (i.e, connectivity), we have considered the relationships shown in Table 1. These relationships are examined between pairs of surfaces and their evidence is weighted by their strength and importance. The results are summarized as a graph, such as shown in Fig. 10, in which the nodes are the surfaces and the arcs carry the weights of relationships. The surface groups with stronger relationships are shown in Fig. 11. For example, the cup body and handle are strongly grouped together because:

• The axes are nearly parallel.

• But the handle axis does tip in a little, and its extension intersects the extension of the body axis.

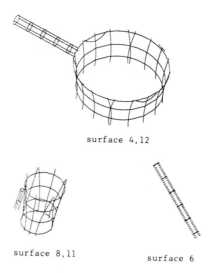

surface 4,12

surface 8,11   surface 6

FIG. 11.   Objects in the scene: surface groupings.

- The surfaces are close together.
- The surfaces oppose each other for the whole length of the handle.
- In the image, the surfaces have a path to bleed together.

However, grouping at this level should not be considered final, because surfaces not belonging to the same object can exhibit strong accidental alignments. In the example scene, the shovel handle has a fairly strong relationship with the pan body, since their axes intersect and the shovel is inside the pan. These are both accidental alignments. Without other knowledge, it is not possible to tell whether they belong to the same object. One way to resolve this problem is to combine information from different scenes, which will be discussed next.

6. MULTIPLE SCENE ANALYSIS

Figure 12 shows a different scene and its processing results. Note that the round-handled cup is also included in this scene, with a view angle which is opposite

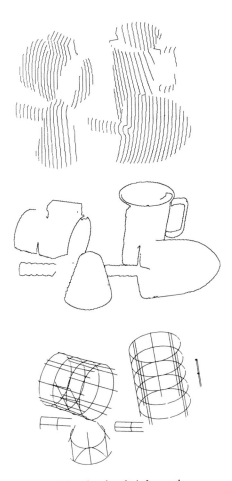

FIG. 12. Results of analysis for another scene.

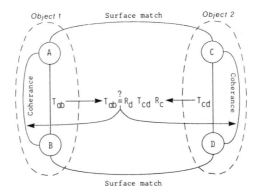

FIG. 13.   Matching surface pairs from different images.

to that in the previous scene. The extracted surface components and their relationships, however, are the same as in the previous scene.

In this way, if a group of same surfaces can be identified in several different
scenes, holding the same relative positions and orientations, one can assert that they
are part of a common object. Relating objects from different scenes is a matching
problem, illustrated in Fig. 13. Suppose object 1 comprising surfaces a and b from
scene 1 matches object 2 comprising c and d from scene 2. Then two conditions
must be met:

• A surface from object 1 matches a surface from object 2. This is called the
surface match.

• If the surfaces a and b are to match surfaces c and d respectively, then the
placement and orientation of b with respect to a must match the placement and
orientation of d with respect to c. This is called the *transform match*.

The transform match gets its name from the transform which maps the local
coordinate system of b into the coordinate system of a. This must match the
transform mapping the coordinate system of d into that of c.

To solve the transform match in a general manner is not a straightforward
calculation of coordinate transformation matrices for three reasons. First, when the
component surfaces include some symmetry, such as in cylinders and cones, then
placing the coordinate frame is not unique. Therefore, the computed transforms may
appear different even for the same geometrical situation. Second, the objects may
have parts connected by linear or rotational articulations, such as scissors. We need
a method of representing, calculating, and comparing transforms which accommo-
dates objects with articulations. Finally, due to the measurement errors, the calculated transforms will not be exactly the same even when they should be. Thus a
method is required which can tell whether the transform is approximately the same.
This is especially important for the cases of objects including articulations, because
element-by-element comparison does not work. Smith [12] and Tomita and Kanade
[13] discuss these three problems in more detail, and present partial solutions. A
technique of merging descriptions from image sequences has been developed also in
[5] for the domain of aerial photo interpretation.

7. SUMMARY

This paper has described a method for 3D range-data analysis, which uses coherencies among contours, surfaces, and scenes to generate object descriptions. Specifically, the following points have been discussed:

• Taxonomy of contours in light-stripe images. This helps us to understand what causes each contour; whether it occludes or is occluded. The detection can be done with the initial deflection image, prior to conversion to three dimensions.

• Explicit use of the hierarchy of contour, surface, object and scene to analyze range-data imagery.

• Development of a method for utilizing coherent relations among lower-level elements as shape cues to aid extraction of higher-level elements.

• Data-driven autonomous generation of object descriptions without specific prestored models.

We plan to further develop and implement a systematic method of combining images of different scenes to obtain consistent descriptions of objects.

ACKNOWLEDGMENTS

The light-stripe rangefinder images used in this research were provided by Dr. T. Oshima, Electrotechnical Laboratory, Japan. We thank Martial Hebert, Martin Herman, and Fumiaki Tomita for useful discussions.

REFERENCES

1. G. J. Agin and T. O. Binford, Computer description of curved objects, in *Proc. 3rd Int. Joint Conf. Artificial Intelligence*, pp. 629–640, 1973.
2. T. O. Binford, Survey of model-based image analysis system, *Robotics Res.* **1**, No. 1 (1982), 18–64.
3. R. C. Bolles, P. Horaud, and M. J. Hannah, 3DPO: A three-dimensional part orientation system, in *Proc. 8th Int. Joint Conf. Artificial Intelligence*, Karlsruhe, W. Germany, August 1983.
4. O. D. Faugeras and M. Hebert, A 3-D recognition and positioning algorithm using geometrical matching between primitive surfaces, in *Proc. 8th Int. Joint Conf. Artificial Intelligence*, Karlsruhe, W. Germany, 1983.
5. M. Herman, T. Kanade, and S. Kuroe, Incremental acquisition of a three-dimensional scene model from images, *IEEE Trans. Pattern Anal. Mach. Intell.* **PAMI-6**, No. 3 (1984).
6. T. Kanade, Recovery of the three-dimensional shape of an object from a single view, *Artificial Intelligence* **17** (1981), 409–460.
7. D. G. Lowe and T. O. Binford, The perceptual organization of visual images: Segmentation as a basis for recognition, *Proc. DARPA Image Understanding Workshop*, pp. 203–209, June 1983.
8. R. Nevatia and T. O. Binford, Structured descriptions of complex objects, *Proc. 3rd Int. Joint Conf. Artificial Intelligence*, pp. 641–647. Stanford, Calif., 1973.
9. R. J. Popplestone, C. M. Brown, A. P. Ambler, and G. F. Crawford, Forming models of plane-and-cylinder faceted bodies from light stripes, in *Proc. 4th Int. Joint Conf. Artificial Intelligence*, Tbilsi, Georgia, USSR, 1975.
10. S. A. Shafer, *Shadow Geometry and Occluding Contours of Generalized Cylinders*, Ph.D. Thesis, Carnegie–Mellon University, May 1983.
11. Y. Shirai and M. Suwa, Recognition of polyhedrons with a range finder, *Proc. 2nd Int. Joint Conf. Artificial Intelligence*, pp. 80–87, 1971.
12. D. R. Smith, *Autonomous Scene Descriptions with Range Imagery*, Ph.D. thesis, Dept. of Computer Science, Carnegie–Mellon University, in preparation, 1985.
13. F. Tomita and T. Kanade, A 3D vision system: Generating and matching shape descriptions in range images, *Preprints of the Second International Symposium of Robotics Research*, Kyoto, Japan, Aug. 20–23, 1984.

Intelligible Encoding of ASL Image Sequences at Extremely Low Information Rates

GEORGE SPERLING, MICHAEL LANDY, YOAV COHEN, AND M. PAVEL*

Human Information Processing Laboratory, Psychology Department,
New York University, New York

Received June 17, 1985; accepted July 2, 1985

American Sign Language (ASL) is a gestural language used by the hearing impaired. This paper describes experimental tests with deaf subjects that compared the most effective known methods of creating extremely compressed ASL images. The minimum requirements for intelligibility were determined for three basically different kinds of transformations: (1) gray-scale transformations that subsample the images in space and time; (2) two-level intensity quantization that converts the gray scale image into a black-and-white approximation; (3) transformations that convert the images into black and white outline drawings (*cartoons*). In Experiment 1, five subjects made quality ratings of 81 kinds of images that varied in spatial resolution, frame rate, and type of transformation. The most promising image size was 96 × 64 pixels (height × width). The 17 most promising image transformations were selected for formal intelligibility testing: 38 deaf subjects viewed 87 ASL sequences 1–2 s long of each transformation. The most effective code for gray-scale images is an analog raster code, which can produce images with 0.86 *normalized intelligibility* (I) at a bandwidth of 2,880 Hz and therefore is transmittable on ordinary 3 KHz telephone circuits. For the binary images, a number of coding schemes are described and compared, the most efficient being an extension of the quadtree method, here termed *binquad coding* which yielded $I = 0.68$ at 7,500 bits per second (bps). For cartoons, an even more efficient *polygonal transformation*, which approximates an outline by connected straight line segments, is proposed, together with a *vectorgraph* code yielding, for example, $I = 0.56$ at 3,900 bps and $I = 0.70$ at 6,000 bps. Polygonally transformed cartoons offer the possibility of telephonic ASL communication at 4,800 bps. Several combinations of binary image transformations and encoding schemes offer $I > 80\%$ at 9,600 bps. © 1985 Academic Press, Inc.

1. INTRODUCTION AND OVERVIEW

1.1. Purposes

American Sign Language (ASL) is a manual form of communication used primarily among and with the deaf and hard of hearing. This paper describes our investigations into the ultimate limits of low-bandwidth methods for the transmission of American Sign Language images. Our purpose is twofold. First, we are interested in learning more about the perceptual structure of ASL as representative of natural, dynamic sources of visual information. What kinds of visual cues embedded in ASL images can be used to comprehend those images? What is the relative importance of the various cues? What are the limits of intelligibility? Second, this research leads to the specification of the minimum requirements for devices to

*George Sperling, and Michael Landy are with the Human Information Processing Laboratory, Department of Psychology, New York University, 6 Washington Place, Room 980, New York, NY 10003. M. Pavel is with the Department of Psychology, Stanford University, Stanford, CA 94305. Yoav Cohen is with the National Institute for Testing and Evaluation, Jerusalem, Israel.

communicate ASL through limited capacity channels: the existing telephone net-work, and such other networks as may come to fruition.

The transmission limits through the public switched telephone network are a passband of 300 to 2,800 Hz for analog signals and about 4,800 bits per second (bps) for digital signals ([1, p. 430 ff]). The analog limit is inherent in the present design and construction of the system. The digital limit is less well established since it depends critically on the properties of the noise and nonlinear distortion in the system and on the codes used to overcome it. To build a *sign telephone* that would permit speakers of ASL to communicate by means of dynamic visual images transmitted over the present public telephone network would require analog encoding of ASL images at 3 kHz, or digital encoding at bit rates of 4,800 bps.

1.2. ASL

Hearing people who learn to sign ASL are often surprised to discover that ASL is a *language* comparable, except in modality, to spoken languages. ASL has a large vocabulary of *signs* (which function as words), a complex grammar, and the ability to express a wide range of concepts and ideas. Experimental studies [2, 3] show that ASL signers can communicate stories about daily events at about the same rate as speakers of English. Since ASL is a living language used by a large and cohesive social community, it share the traits of any such language, including local dialects, slang, and historical language growth.

American Sign Language, like other sign languages (e.g., Danish Sign Language, Japanese Sign Language, Signed English, etc.), uses movements of the hands and arms, along with facial expressions, to express ideas. Signs in ASL have been described by specifying a number of basic parameters. These include: the configuration of each hand; the orientation of the hands, hand arrangements, and contacting region; the place of articulation; and the pattern of movement [3–5]. ASL differs from most spoken languages in that space and movement are used in the grammatical process. Thus, rather than combine a series of sequential morphemes or affixes as in spoken languages, ASL allows modifiers to be incorporated into a sign. The use of space is also important in the grammar of ASL. For example, the subject and object of transitive verbs in ASL are indicated by assigning locations in space to these objects. References to these objects can then be incorporated into verbs and other signs by referring to these spatial locations in the use of the sign. In ASL, facial expressions can serve to indicate emphasis, the topic of conversation, imperatives, and questions.

1.3. Other Forms of Visual Language

1.3.1. Finger Spelling

In finger spelling, the hand is formed into a position that represents a letter, and words are spelled out letter-by-letter much as in Morse code. Finger spelling typically proceeds at rates of 3 to 10 characters per second and is used to supplement ASL by providing representations for words (usually names of places and persons) for which no ASL sign exists. Some schools for the deaf use finger spelling as their primary language medium, but it is much slower than ASL [6].

1.3.2. Signed English

American Sign Language has no particular relation to the spoken English language, any more than it has to, say, German or Chinese. ASL is merely the sign language in use in America and is, in fact, totally different from and incomprehensible to users of the sign language in use in England. For the literal translation of spoken English into manual communication, signed English is sometimes used. English nouns, verbs, and other important words are translated into ASL equivalents; function words, prefixes, and suffixes are finger-spelled; English word order is retained.

1.3.3. Speech Reading

Lip reading, or speech reading as it is now called, relies on visual cues provided by the lips, tongue (when visible), cheeks, jaw, and even the throat. Speech reading is seldom adequate by itself as a language medium. It is most useful in combination with acoustic speech (for persons who retain some residual hearing) and in combination with finger-spelling or ASL (for the profoundly deaf). Because of the large number of persons who suffer hearing loss in later life, speech reading is an important supplement to English communication.

1.3.4. Teletypewriter

The teletypewriter, which transmits a typed sequence of alphanumeric characters, is a medium for communication via written language. Presently, there is no commonly accepted written form of ASL (see [7]), so written telecommunication between deaf persons in the USA is in English. The extraordinary lack of facility with English among the congenitally deaf (as contrasted to those with acquired deafness) has been amply documented [8]. However, the teletypewriter is essential in the absence of alternatives for telecommunication, and it is useful for communication between the hearing and the deaf. Unfortunately teletypewriter communication relative to ASL is even more inefficient than the teletypewriter communication relative to spoken English. For many, perhaps most congenitally deaf persons, English (the TTY language) is a late-acquired second language in which communication is difficult.

1.4. Matching Communication Channels to the Requirements of Different Language Forms

For most congenitally deaf persons, ASL telecommunication would be the most useful form because it is both the normal and the fastest means of communication. ASL involves both hands and arms, the upper body and the face. Finger spelling involves just one hand. When this hand is large in the image (i.e., close to the camera), finger spelling requires less spatial but more temporal resolution than ASL. Speech reading involves the mouth and lower part of the face [9] but also the cheeks [10]. It requires good resolution of low-contrast detail that is not required for ASL or finger spelling. Ideally, an image representation that is adequate for ASL would also be adequate for finger spelling and speech reading. However, *optimal* codes for these language forms differ somewhat ([11, p. 2000]).

High resolution video telecommunication systems (such as the abortive American Picturephone and British Viewphone) would have been more than adequate for all forms of visual communication. Such systems have great appeal to the deaf. Their disadvantage is their high price, which is proportional to their bandwidth (about 1

MHz for picturephone compared to 3 kHz for the telephone). A picture (television at 4 MHz) literally is worth a thousand words (telephone at 3 kHz). High-bandwidth interpersonal communication systems survive today only as local networks within a few specialized institutions (e.g., [12]). The solution, obviously, is bandwidth compression.

2. EARLY STUDIES OF COMPRESSED ASL

2.1. Television Experiments: Postage Stamp Study

The ASL bandwidth compression problem was first formulated in 1978 by Sperling [13] who observed "In the development of video communication devices, it is notable that basic studies of the bandwidth (channel capacity) requirements for manual-visual communication have not yet been conducted" (p. 113). Unable to persuade anyone else to work on measuring minimum ASL bandwidths (although he did succeed in enlisting K. Knowlton to initiate research on a related problem—see below), Sperling set out to determine bandwidths for ASL with the only equipment then available to him, ordinary television recording and playback apparatus.

2.1.1. Raster Scan

Television uses a raster-scan principle. That is, the 2-dimensional image is represented as a *frame* consisting of a series of 525 horizontal raster lines. The odd numbered lines (counting from the top) are painted first, beginning at the upper left (Field 1) and then the even numbered lines are painted (Field 2). Together, the two *interlaced* fields comprise the frame. In American TV, there are 30 frames per second, equivalent to 60 fields or 15,750 lines per second. Bandwidth refers to the number of alternating light/dark cycles that can be represented along the total length of all the lines painted in one second. For example, 263 cycles per horizontal

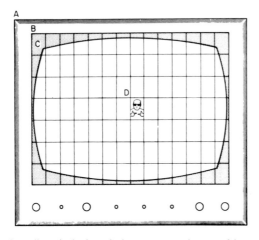

FIG. 1. "Postage Stamp" method of producing raster-scan images of known bandwidth: (A) TV monitor; (B) raster area shared by 7 × 14 = 98 postage stamps (calibrated at 2.0 ± 0.1 MHz.); (C) visible area of raster; (D) one postage stamp illustrating one dynamic ASL transmission. Area (D) approximately the minimal bandwidth (21 kHz) determined by Sperling [13] to retain 90% of intelligibility.

line (representing a vertically oriented grid) would yield 4,142,250 cycles per second, or 4.14 MHz, a typical value. This value approximately equates horizontal with vertical resolution because, if alternate raster *lines* were painted black and then white (representing a horizontal grid), there would be $525/2 = 262.5$ vertical light/dark cycles. The television system used by Sperling [11, 13] included a recording camera, video tape recorder, and playback monitor that were found to have a net bandwidth of 2.0 ± 0.1 MHz.

The principle of bandwidth-compression measurements is exemplified by photographing a sheet of stamps on the TV raster. The total bandwidth of the picture is shared by all the stamps (Fig. 1) and thus the bandwidth allocated to each stamp is easily calculated. In principle, each postage-stamp sized area can carry an independent ASL conversation. By determining the intelligibility of the transmission as a function of the number of simultaneous conversations sharing the screen, intelligibility as a function of bandwidth is determined for this particular raster image transformation.

2.1.2. Spatial Subsampling: Procedure and Results

The actual procedure involves photographing a signer (Fig. 2) signing intelligibility test materials (e.g., isolated nouns, short sentences, finger-spelled names), and then determining the ability of viewers to interpret these video-recorded communications as a function of the screen area (bandwidth) allocated to them. Sperling [11, 13] found that intelligibility was quite high for pictures that used bandwidths of 21 kHz or more but fell off rapidly below 21 kHz. The apparatus did not produce interlace, so the display consisted of 60 frames per second. We now know (Sect. 5.2.3) that, for dynamic gray-scale images of isolated ASL signs, reduction of the frame rate to 15 frames per second does not appreciably impair intelligibility. Thus, Sperling's [13] minimum bandwidth estimates immediately can be reduced fourfold to 5 kHz.

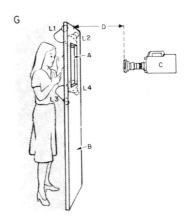

FIG. 2. Method of recording ASL intelligibility test materials. The signer stands behind an aperture (A), 12×18 in (30.5×45.7 cm) cut in a screen (B), and in front of a black curtain (G). Four lights ($L_1 \ldots L_4$) are arranged to facilitate the discrimination of the hands from the face and body from the point of view of the recording camera (C), a TV or 16 mm motion camera, each at 30 frames per second, at a distance $D \approx 10$ ft (3m) away from the signer.

2.2. Further Television Experiments

Postage-stamp experiments revealed the minimum spatial resolution needed to interpret ASL and finger spelling. Pearson, who had already built a high-bandwidth video communication system for use by the deaf [14], initiated an investigation of various temporal and intensity parameters in dynamic raster-scan images of deaf communication.

2.2.1. Intensity Subsampling

With respect to subsampling intensity (reducing the number of gray levels) "no problems were encountered down to 3 bits/pel [8 intensity levels]" ([Pearson, 15, p. 1990]). Further reductions in intensity resolution did impair performance but even with just two intensity levels (binary quantized intensity) "finger-spelling was achieved... with only a few repeat requests. Overall, the impression was formed that deaf communication is remarkably tolerant of PCM quantization distortion."

2.2.2. Combinations of Subsampled Dimensions

British television normally presents 50 frames (100 fields) per second. Pearson investigated temporal subsampling by repeating fields. Performance began to deteriorate when new fields occurred less often than 17 per second, "was still possible with difficulty" at 12.5 per second, and was "very difficult" at 10 per second ([15, p. 1990]). Pearson also investigated the time to completion of various communication tasks in which subjects used video communication systems that combined various impairments of spatial, temporal, and intensity resolution. He concluded that "just-comfortable communication can be achieved at around 100k bits/s and just-possible communication at around 5 k bits/s" (p. 1986).

2.3. Sensing Finger Positions

Because finger spelling and sign language seem to depend critically on finger location, it has occurred to several investigators that communication might be mediated by sensors that simply transmitted finger and hand location (e.g., [16]). The sensor information could be used to manipulate an artificial hand (perhaps embodied in a computer program) or be communicated directly in a dynamic 2D display of sensor position.

2.3.1. Point-Light Experiments

The simplest 2D displays of sensor position are provided by simply displaying points of light attached to the fingers. These can be produced by miniature lights attached to the body as in Johansson's classic experiments [17, 18] or by reflecting papers attached to gloves worn by the signing subject. Poizner, Bellugi, and Lutes-Driscoll [19] experimentally determined the lexical and motion aspects of ASL signs that were conveyed by 9 point-lights (attached to the head and to each shoulder, elbow, wrist, and index finger). Tartter and Knowlton's [20] signers used 27 point-lights (13 on each hand and one on the nose) and were apparently able to conduct a brief demonstration conversation in ASL. These sensor methods seem to require low information rates—all that needs to be transmitted from frame to frame is the (usually small) change in position of two dozen sensors. However, the empirical determinations of actual intelligibility and of actual information rates have yet to be carried out.

2.4. Early Image-Processing Studies

Having apparently determined the bandwidth limitations of raster codes, and demonstrated the feasibility of transmitting coded finger-location information, the next step was to apply more elaborate image-processing methods to dynamic ASL images. Three laboratories approached this problem simultaneously, each producing a conference report in the summer of 1982 that was published in 1983.

Pearson and Six [21] continued the investigation of binary images: two-level intensity quantization and outline cartoons. Their best results were with images of 50×50 pixels, with two-level intensity quantization, and with 12.5 frames per second. With subsequent run-length encoding and a further recoding of the runs by a 3-dimensional Huffman code, "readable" transmission of a sign language sentence was achieved at 6,800 bps.

Abramatic, Letellier, Nadler [22] used an edge extraction method based on Gaussian-filtered Laplacian operators (see Sect. 3.3.2) to generate dynamic cartoons of signers on images of 256×256 pixels. The images appear to be quite intelligible but the authors give neither bit rates nor intelligibility measures.

Sperling, Pavel, Cohen, Landy, and Schwartz [23] explored a variety of binary and gray-scale image transformations of ASL on a 96×64 pixel grid. They produced apparently intelligible ASL demonstration sequences with the following image transformations (bit rates are based on ten fps and, for binary images, hierarchical encoding): a gray-scale code (block truncation [24]) at 37,000 bps; two-level intensity quantization at 9,000 bps; and numerous cartoon drawings based on a variety of edge-masks and variants of Gaussian-filtered Laplacians (which worked better than edge masks). Cartoons based on zero-crossings [25] produced good images with 6% blackened pixels (20,000 bps); images based on intensifying the minima of a Gaussian-filtered Laplacian (6% blackened pixels, 13,000 bps) looked even better than comparable zero-crossing sequences.

2.5. What More Is Needed?

While the early studies began the determination of bandwidth and information limits for ASL communication, it was not clear that actual minimum bandwidths had been attained. Furthermore, two things were urgently needed: (1) A comparison in a comparable setting of the various proposed methods. (2) Objective measures of performance, such as intelligibility test scores and/or task completion times, to indicate the potential utility for communication of the proposed methods. It is precisely these problems to which the present study is addressed. The goal is to determine the intelligibility versus bandwidth tradeoffs for the known techniques of image compression, with the aim of describing methods for communicating ASL through the existing telephone network.

The organization of the remainder of the paper is as follows. First we survey the techniques for *image transformation* that are applicable to the problem of compression of sign-language images. We then describe three experiments that we performed to test intelligibility of processed sign-language images. Next, we describe methods for *image coding* to compress the code used to describe the transformed images. The transformations and codes mostly involve previously available techniques, and some new techniques developed in our laboratory. Lastly, applying these coding-compression methods to our stimuli enables us to evaluate the tradeoffs between the bandwidth or information rate and the measured intelligibility.

3. COMPRESSION TECHNIQUES

3.1. Overview of a Low-Bandwidth Video Communication System

The image transformations in a low bandwidth, digital, video communication system are illustrated in Fig. 3. The subject is photographed by a video camera which converts the optical array into an analog raster representation of the subject. Alternatively, as in the simulation of this system in our Experiments 2 and 3, the subject is photographed by a 16 mm motion picture camera (operating at 30 frames per second), and the developed film images are projected and "photographed" at leisure by the video camera.

The analog raster is converted into a digital raster and then passed on to a computer by a "frame grabber," a component of an image processor. The digitized raster is represented in the computer's memory as an $m \times n$ array of pixels with full gray scale. From this array, a new digital $m' \times n'$ representation (in the example of Fig. 3, a cartoon) is produced by means of an *image transformation*. The transformed image is represented more compactly by an *image code* (a hierarchical code is illustrated as the tree structure in Fig. 3).

The image code can be further compressed by means of a general code optimizer, such as a Huffman code [26], which is illustrated in Fig. 3 as a conversion table that gives the optimal output bit pattern for each input bit pattern. In fact, the image codes considered in this paper are already so compressed that Huffman codes usually produce further decreases of only a few percent in the length of the message, and therefore they will not be considered further.

A modem converts the optimized image code into a format that is efficiently transmitted on a telephone line. Designing modem codes to overcome the noise and

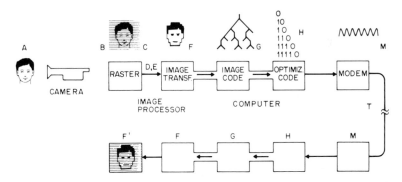

FIG. 3.   Information transformations in a digital, low-bandwidth video communication system. Camera transforms optical array (A) into analog raster (B); image processor digitizes it (C) converting it into a computer-readable format (D); computer represents the image as an $m \times n$ array in memory (E), and performs an *image transformation* (e.g., binary intensity-quantized image, F); the image is *recoded* (e.g., by a hierarchical code G which may span several images; this code may be further optimized (e.g., by a Huffman code, H); a *modem* converts the Huffmanized bit stream into a code (M) for transmission (T) through the switched telephone network Decoding proceeds in reverse order up to the level of the transformed image (F) which is converted to raster representation (F') for viewing on a display monitor. In this scheme, information is lost between A and B but most critically in the transformation from E to F, hence no inverse transformation beyond F' is possible.

bandwidth limitations of telephone circuits is a specialized technology all in itself and will not be treated further here.

At the receiver, the transformations proceed in the reverse order up to the point of the transformed image. At this point, further inverse transformation generally is not possible because information has been irretrievably lost, and the receiver views the transformed image, usually as represented by a raster scan.

There is some information loss inherent in the conversion from optic array to raster—spatial, temporal, color, and depth resolution are reduced. Conceptually, however, the main information reduction comes in the image transformation from the $m \times n$ gray scale image to the $m' \times n'$ transformed image. Subsequent image codes considered here are lossless and invertible. For the purpose of evaluating communication systems, therefore, it is necessary only to test subjects' ability to perceive transformed images (F in Fig. 3). If the image code, optimizing code, or modem had introduced significant further losses, it would have been necessary to evaluate the effects of these losses on intelligibility by testing subjects with the fully coded and decoded transmissions (F' in Fig. 3).

3.2. Grey-Scale Image Compression

3.2.1. The Focus of Existing Technology

3.2.1.1. *Compression.* The image-compression methods in common use, when applied to gray-scale images, yield another gray-scale image, ideally identical or very similar to the original. Thus, they are here termed compression methods rather than transformations to emphasize the lack of transformation.

Digital image-compression techniques have developed substantially in recent years [27–29] under the impetus of low-bandwidth television schemes for satellite communication, aerial mapping and other image data banks, tele-conferencing, and so forth. In general, compression schemes attempt the maximal compression of a highly sampled gray scale image compatible with a minimally distorted final image. The distortion criteria most often used are whether the distortion can be perceived at all, whether the distortion is mildly unpleasant or unaesthetic, and most often in terms of average mean squared error. Typically, these schemes begin with images of 512×512 pixels, 8 bits per pixel, 30 frames per second. Their success is measured in the number of bits per pixel needed for the compressed form of the images.

Representative image compression methods include: (a) predictive image coding, such as differential pulse code modulation [30]; (b) transform image coding techniques which first apply a transform such as the Fourier or discrete cosine transform and then quantize [31]; (c) hybrid transform/predictive image coding which applies a transform in one dimension and uses predictive coding of the transform components along another [32]; and (d) frame replenishment methods (for multi-frame television images) which attempt to segregate the images into changing and stationary components [33, 34].

These compression techniques range in efficiency from 2 or 3 bits per pixel to a lower bound of about 0.125 bit/pixel [29, 34]. A television-quality image contains 512×512 pixels/frame $\times$ 8 intensity bits/pixel $\times$ 30 frames/s $= 60 \times 10^6$ bit/s or 7.5×10^6 pixels/s. At 0.125 bits per pixel, the bit rate would exceed the nominal telephone circuit capacity of 10^4 bit/s by a factor of more than 100. Unfortunately, these compression techniques, which were developed for "oversampled" (512×512)

TV images, fare poorly with the less finely sampled images described here. For example, the block truncation coding method [24, 35] retains approximately constant compression (about 0.6 bits per pixel) for the increasingly coarsely sampled images, but the drop in intelligibility and image quality is precipitous.

3.2.1.2. *Evaluation.* Images are evaluated by objective and subjective methods. Objective methods of image evaluation that fail to consider the human perceptual system (such as computing the mean square difference between the original and compressed images) cannot even be applied to the images (such as cartoons) being investigated. Binary-intensity transformations can only be evaluated perceptually. The subjective and aesthetic standards traditionally used to evaluate compressed images are appropriate for much better images and for purposes other than communication, which can proceed with distorted, unaesthetic images. Evaluation of images for communication requires objective measures of intelligibility. Thus, neither the methods of measuring image quality nor the digital compression techniques developed for almost perfect reproduction of television-quality images are appropriate for our needs.

While our previous research [23] strongly suggests that gray scale, *digital* image coding methods would fail to provide the extreme compression required, in order to establish a baseline for the usefulness of these methods, we have incorporated two gray-scale procedures into our experiments.

3.2.2. Undersampling

We tested gray-scale images that were undersampled in space and in time, but not intensity, as undersampling in intensity ultimately results in binary images, described below. In the space domain, the following image sizes were investigated, given in terms of number of pixels in height × width: 96 × 64, 48 × 32, 24 × 16. In the time domain, the following frame rates, given in terms of new frames per second, with no interleave, were investigated: 30, 15, 10 fps. Undersampling in space had previously been investigated by Sperling [13], and selected combinations of undersampled space, time, and intensity had been studied by Pearson [15], but some important new space–time sampling combinations are first measured here.

3.2.2.1. *Variable temporal resolution: Frame repeating, frame interpolation.* To create variable resolution stimuli, we begin with the base stimuli derived from photographic movie images. These were taken at 30 frames per second (fps). Each frame was digitized at a spatial resolution of 512 × 512; it was cropped and reduced by a factor of 4 (vertically and horizontally) to 96 × 64 pixels, with 8 bits of nominal luminance resolution per pixel. The effective luminance resolution is 7 + bits, due to the camera and other system noise [36]. Stimuli with lower temporal resolution are created by repeating frames. A 15 fps stimulus repeats every odd-numbered frame in the original 30 fps sequence, substituting the repeated frame for the subsequent even-numbered frame. The reduced sequence still is produced as a standard television signal at 30 frames per second, but only 15 of these frames contain new information, hence our designation 15 fps. For 10 fps, every third frame of the original sequence occurs three times, and the other frames are omitted. We also investigated a condition here called *frame interpolation*, which contained 15 new frames per second with an interpolated frame produced between each successive pair

of these frames by averaging the pixel values in the previous and following frame
[34, 37].

   3.2.2.2. *Variable spatial resolution: Subsampling and frame enlargement.*   Spatial
resolution is varied by pixel averaging. From the full-resolution 96 × 64 pixel image,
a 48 × 32 half-resolution image is created by averaging 2 × 2 groups of pixels in the
full image. This yields a new image with one quarter as many pixels in which each
dimension is halved. All images (full and reduced) were presented at the same screen
size. Reduced frames were enlarged by pixel interpolation to the original size but,

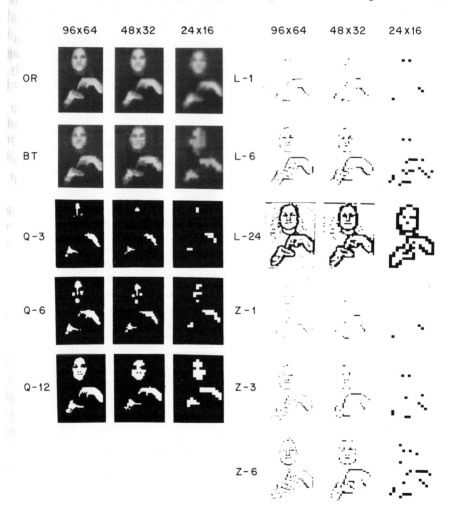

FIG. 4.   Image transformations judged for quality in Experiment 1. The pixel resolution is given at the
top of each column. All images were viewed at the same size, images of reduced resolution were
subsampled and then magnified. All image sequences were viewed at 15 and at 30 fps. OR, grey-scale
"original"; BT, block truncation; Q-i, binary intensity-quantization, i% white pixels; L-i, dark side
Laplacian, i% black pixels; Z-i, zero-crossing, i% black pixels.

obviously, with only half the original resolution. Examples of reduced spatial-resolution stimuli are given in Fig. 4, top row. The frame enlargement method uses a pixel interpolation algorithm as follows.

Let $x(i, j)$ represent the luminance value of a pixel (i, j) in the reduced, parent, image. Let $y(k, l)$ represent the luminance of a pixel in the enlarged, child, image. And let m, an integer, represent the magnification factor. Some child pixels $y(k, l)$ are copied directly, without alteration, from the parent image, specifically pixels for which $d_k = k \bmod m = 0$ and $d_l = l \bmod m = 0$. Such a pixel is the *direct* child of $x(i, j)$, where $i = k/m$ and $j = l/m$. *Indirect* children of $x(i, j)$ lie within the square (with corners C_q) formed by the direct children of $x(i, j)$, $x(i + 1, j)$, $x(i, j + 1)$, and $x(i + 1, j + 1)$; that is, within $C_1 = y(mi, mj)$, $C_2 = y(m(i + 1), mj)$, $C_3 = y(mi, m(j + 1))$, and $C_4 = y(m(i + 1), m(j + 1))$. The luminance value $y(k, l)$ of an indirect child is determined by a weighted average of the luminances of the four corners:

$$y(k, l) = \left[\frac{m - d_k}{m}\right] \times \left[\frac{m - d_l}{m}\right] \times C_1$$
$$+ \left[\frac{d_k}{m}\right] \times \left[\frac{m - d_l}{m}\right] \times C_2$$
$$+ \left[\frac{m - d_k}{m}\right] \times \left[\frac{d_l}{m}\right] \times C_3$$
$$+ \left[\frac{d_k}{m}\right] \times \left[\frac{d_l}{m}\right] \times C_4.$$

For example, for $m = 2$, each parent point must ultimately reproduce four times by means of one direct and nine indirect children in the enlargement. Table 1 shows the weightings of four parent points (arranged on the corners of a square) to a direct child (a) and three indirect children (b), (c), (d). These parent points, in other combinations of course, are involved in the computation of many other children in the image.

TABLE 1

Weights for Pixel Interpolation in a
2 × Enlargement

(a)	1.0 0.0	(b)	0.5 0.5
	0.0 0.0		0.0 0.0
(c)	0.5 0.0	(d)	0.25 0.25
	0.5 0.0		0.25 0.25

Note. Block (a) represents the direct child; blocks (b), (c), (d) represent the indirect children; entries represent the spatial weights assigned to the luminances of the four corners (C_q, adjacent direct children). See text for details.

More complicated subsampling and enlargement schemes were tried but did not provide discriminably better images with the ASL image sequences.

3.2.3. Block Truncation (BT)

The *block truncation* method [24, 35] was chosen as representative of extreme gray scale compression schemes because of its efficiency and simplicity. BT produces compressed images that average about 0.65 bits per pixel on our images which nominally contain 8 bits per pixel. We describe the BT algorithm briefly, and direct the reader to Mitchell and Delp [24] for a full description.

In its simplest form, BT acts by dividing an image into a number of smaller nonoverlapping subimages, on which it acts independently. Our images were divided into 4×4 subblocks. Each subblock is described by its means pixel value μ, the variance of pixel values contained in that block σ^2, and a single bit for each pixel denoting whether that pixel is above or below the subblock mean. The compressed image is then reconstructed as follows. Let the number of pixels in the block be k (in our case, 16), and the number of pixels above the mean be q. Then the pixel luminance values for that subblock are set to $\mu + \sigma\sqrt{(k-q)/q}$ for pixels whose luminance value was above the mean, and to $\mu - \sigma\sqrt{q/(k-q)}$ if it was below the mean.

The BT algorithm includes several heuristics to allow for further savings in bit rate. First, the μ and σ values are quantized differently. As only seven bits are allotted for the combination of μ and σ, when σ is large, fewer bits are used for μ. Second, for very small values of σ, the bit map is not transmitted, and the image is reconstructed as a uniform block of value μ. Lastly, for low values of σ, only half of the bit map is transmitted, and the other pixel positions are interpolated. The net result of this is a bit rate of approximately 0.65 bits per pixel for BT as applied to our 96×64 pixel base stimuli. Sample BT images are shown in Fig. 4.

This BT method achieves compression rates that are nearly as good as even more complicated gray scale methods (such as [34]), is easy to program, and lends itself to a real-time hardware implementation. When applied to our undersampled images, the distortion inherent in BT compression is quite visible, but it still yields comprehensible images.

3.3. Binary Image Transformations

The gray-scale methods are intended to convey a transformed image that is physically and visually similar to the source image. On the other hand, we are primarily concerned with intelligibility, and not with appearance, so substantial distortions of the original image may indeed be tolerable. Sperling *et al.* [23] demonstrated a number of binary image transformations that appeared to yield intelligible ASL, as did Pearson and Six [21] and Abramatic, Letellier, and Nadler [22]. Our strategy will be to survey a broad sampling of these transformations in a preliminary study, and to subject the most promising transformations to formal intelligibility tests.

3.3.1. Binary Intensity Quantization

The only stimuli we have used which vary luminance sampling reduce the eight luminance bits per pixel to a single bit. This is accomplished by applying an intensity threshold to each image in a sequence. If the pixel gray scale value exceeds the intensity threshold it is intensified to value 255 (white); if not, it is set to value 0 (black). The intensity threshold is set between 0 and 255 so as to produce the desired fraction of white pixels.

A separate intensity threshold value (variable threshold) was computed for each frame of the sequence to maintain a constant percentage of intensified pixels. This results in an image code of a nearly the same length for different images. We discovered later that a constant percent of intensified pixels is not quite as clean as applying a single intensity threshold to an entire sequence of images. In our images, the hands and face are the objects most likely to be intensified. In the variable threshold procedure, when the hands are obscured or out of the frame, this causes previously unintensified pixels in the background, the hair, and in other parts of the image to become intensified. When the hands reappear, these parts are again set to zero. resulting in a kind of pixel flicker. Whether this flicker impairs or enhances intelligibility is not known. Examples of thresholded images with three different percentages of pixels above threshold are shown in Fig. 4.

3.3.2. Edge Enhancement and Detection

A number of the most promising image transformations used in our work involve edge detection. There are a large number of schemes for edge detection (for reviews see [38, 39]). In general, the techniques for edge detection break down into the following categories: linear filters followed by a nonlinearity (such as a threshold), optimal edge detectors including statistical techniques and edge fitting schemes, and sequential techniques which use heuristics to follow a given edge once it is found.

The first category comprises such edge enhancement and detection techniques as high-pass filtering, directional derivatives, and gradient computations. A number of these techniques were explored with our ASL images, including those of Prewitt [40], Roberts [41], Sobel (in [42]), Kirsch [43], Abdou [38], Kasvand [44], Eberlein and Weszka [45], Robinson [46], and Marr and Hildreth [25]. A few edge fitting schemes were also investigated, including those of Abdou [38] and Shaw [47].

In applying this wide variety of edge operators to the ASL images, the intent was to find edge operators which met two criteria: "important" edges in the image are retained (such as the outline of the fingers and face), and low noise susceptibility. The first criterion implied that the edge enhancement operator be optimized for a particular scale of edges, or in other words, it should be a bandpass filter with a peak at a particular spatial frequency optimal for the communication task. The low noise susceptibility is needed to avoid the production of spurious edges that distract from the communication. This made it unsuitable to use adaptive thresholds after edge enhancement, since such techniques tend to become noise sensitive in nearly uniform image areas. It also required a modification of the Marr and Hildreth [25] technique, because their zero crossings operator yields noisy edge images (see below).

3.3.2.1. *Edge enhancement operators.* There were two forms of edge-detected images used in the experiments, and both were derived from edge-enhancement techniques. The first step in creating all of the edge-detected images was to filter the images with a convolution mask that represents a linear, bandpass filter. For the first experiment, the mask used is shown in Fig. 5a.

In many edge-enhancement/edge-detection schemes, the linear bandpass filter is an approximation to the Laplacian ($\partial^2 I/\partial x^2 + \partial^2 I/\partial y^2$) of the image. The

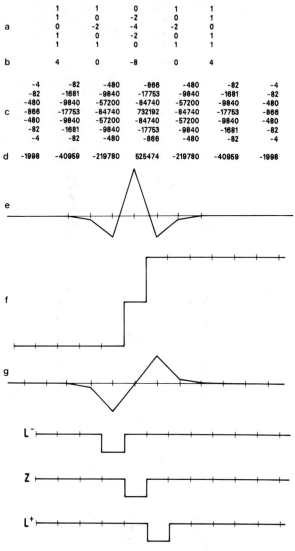

FIG. 5. Edge-detection convolution masks and their effects: (a) The 5 × 5 mask used in Experiment 1 as a simple approximation to a Gaussian-smoothed Laplacian. The values in the rows and columns represent the values of the convolution operator at the corresponding x, y locations. (b) The projection of mask (a) onto the x axis—its response to a vertical line. (c) The 7 × 7 mask used in Experiment 2 to better approximate a Gaussian-smoothed Laplacian (shown in opposite sign of (a)). Mask (c) is efficiently derived as a difference of Gaussians (*dog*) from separable 1-dimensional Gaussian masks. (d) Line response of (c). (e) Graphic representation of (d). (f) A steplike edge representing a 1-dimensional boundary. (g) Response of (c) to edge (f). (L-) A pixel blackened at the minimum of (g), the dark side Laplacian transformation with black pixels at the dark side of edges. (Z) A pixel blackened at the zero crossing of (g), the zero-crossing transformation. (L+) A pixel blackened at the maximum of (g).

Laplacian is an isotropic operator which enhances edges of any orientation. It was proposed by Mach [48, 49] as an operator in human edge detection. A Gaussian-smoothed Laplacian (a Laplacian of a Gaussian distribution) approximates the center-surround receptive fields of neurons in the retina and lateral geniculate nucleus, early in the human (and other) visual systems (for review see [50]). The use of a Gaussian-smoothed Laplacian in computer image processing was proposed by Marr and Hildreth [25].

The Gaussian-smoothed Laplacian is the composition of a Laplacian operator with a Gaussian blur function, (the $\nabla^2 G$ operator described by Marr and Hildreth [25]). Marr and Hildreth, in their discussion of this operator, observe that this operator is very well approximated by a Difference Of Gaussians (or *dog*) function, where the two Gaussians have variances which differ by a factor of 1.6. The 2-dimensional Gaussian operator is separable in x and y. Therefore, it is possible to compute Gaussians by convolving separately by rows and columns, rather than using a 2-dimensional mask. Thus, it is possible to approximate a $\nabla^2 G$ operator using four one-dimensional convolutions, rather than one 2-dimensional convolution. For the larger mask sizes required to best approximate the $\nabla^2 G$ operator, the 1-dimensional procedure is substantially faster than the usual convolution with a 2-dimensional mask, and is the method employed in this study.

In Experiment 2, the difference of Gaussians approximation was used for edge enhancement. The convolution mask was 7×7 (Fig. 5c), and taking advantage of the separability property, only four 7×1 convolutions are performed rather than one 7×7 convolution. We use two Gaussians which differ in standard deviation by a factor of 1.6. The standard deviation of the smaller, central Gaussian is 0.6 pixels, which we determined to yield results which appeared both most pleasing to the eye, and most similar to the mask convolutions of Experiment 1. The response to a line stimulus of this operator is shown in Figs. 5d, e, and its response to a slightly graded edge in Fig. 5g.

3.3.2.2. *Edge location.* We used two techniques for deriving binary images from these edge-enhanced images: thresholding and zero-crossing detection. As depicted in Fig. 5g, when an edge is filtered by a Gaussian-smoothed Laplacian, the output contains a positive peak on one side and a negative peak on the other side of the edge. There are three potential places where one might indicate the edge in the image: at the negative peak, at the zero crossing, and at the positive peak (L-, Z, L+, respectively, in Fig. 5g). Marr and Hildreth [25] suggested that the zero crossing is the best place to indicate. On the other hand, we have found that the images derived from zero crossings look rather noisy, and that placing the edges at the negative peaks yields the most informative-appearing images [23]. Letellier *et al.* [51] confirm this observation. Pearson and Robinson [52] propose that object boundaries in 3-dimensional space produce dark-appearing edges because object boundaries frequently are oriented tangentially to the line of sight and therefore reflect less light to the eye. The negative peak of the Laplacian would tend to find these dark edges and thereby L- would indicate object boundaries.

In Experiment 1, both zero crossing and negative peak thresholding transformations were used. The basic 96×64 gray scale images were convolved (filtered) with the mask of Fig. 5a, resulting in a new value for each pixel. To produce *dark side Laplacian* images, the $i\%$ of the most negative values were painted black, where $i = 1.5, 6, 24$. Examples are shown in Fig. 4, L-1, L-6, and L-24.

For zero crossings, the same mask (Fig. 5a) as for dark side Laplacians was applied, but now the threshold was applied to an estimate of the slope of the zero crossing. In the filtered images, zero crossings separate regions of positive and negative pixel values. Essentially, the slope of the zero crossing was approximated by taking the difference between abutting positive and negative pixels. Candidate zero crossing are indicated according to the magnitude of the slope of the zero crossing (as opposed to the magnitude of the adjacent peak used to determine L-). The magnitude thresholds for zero crossings where chosen so that 1.5, 3, and 6% of the pixels were painted black, yielding the images illustrated in Fig. 4, rows Z-1, Z-3, Z-6. Note that zero crossings (along with the thresholded smoothed Laplacians) are represented as black edges on a white background, which appeared much more natural to our observers than the reverse.

4. EXPERIMENT 1. RATINGS OF 81 IMAGE TRANSFORMATIONS

There are many image-processing techniques, each with its own particular type of image distortion. Evaluating these transformations involves a very large parameter space. The first experiment uses an efficient rating method to reduce this vast space to something more manageable for subsequent intelligibility studies. Three classes of parameters were varied: spatial resolution, temporal resolution, and type of image transformation (which subsumes variations in luminance resolution). Because these parameters can be independently varied to modify an image, they act multiplicatively to determine the number of possible image types.

4.1. Method

4.1.1. Equipment

The stimuli for Experiment 1 were recorded originally by a 16 mm motion camera operating at 30 fps. The developed images were projected and viewed by a JVC S-100U video camera whose output fed a Grinnell GMR 27-30 image processor which digitized the individual frames. Stimuli for subsequent experiments were recorded directly onto a video cassette using a Beta I format VCR (Sony SLO-323). A Sony video motion analyzer (Sony SUM-1010) was used to transmit the cassette-recorded images a single frame at a time to the Grinnell image processor. Images were digitized to a spatial resolution of 480 × 512 pixels, with 8 bits of luminance information per pixel, and transferred to a computer.

The digitized frames were further processed using a VAX-11/750 computer system with the HIPS image-processing system [53, 54] operating under the UNIX operating system [55]. The VAX system includes a high-speed interface to the Grinnell for image input and output, and a slow-speed parallel interface (a DR11-C) for the control of peripheral equipment. This DR11-C allows the system to advance the Sony Video Motion Analyzer after an image has been digitized, and it controls the Betamax VCR to coordinate it with output from the image processor in recording stimulus cassettes. The computer-produced stimulus tapes were presented to subjects using the Betamax recorder and a Conrac monitor (Model QQA14). (In Experiments 2 and 3, where the equipment was transported to schools for the deaf, a Koyo monitor (Model TMC-9M) was used. In these experiments, a cardboard hood was used around the monitor in order to eliminate glare and to maintain a fixed viewing distance of 56 cm.)

4.1.2. Stimuli

The signer was situated behind a screen with a 12×18 in $(30.5 \times 45.7$ cm) aperture, which allowed the upper body and head to be seen from the camera, approximately 10 ft (3m) away (see Fig. 2). There was a black curtain behind the signer, and the signer wore dark clothing and had dark hair. These are typical conditions for ASL interpreters; the hands and face are highlighted and extraneous visual information is minimized.

In Experiment 1, only two ASL messages were used, each was subjected to all 81 transformations. The ASL sign *"owe"* was produced by Ellen Roth, a native ASL signer. A sentence consisting of the signs "(in the) *summer* (the) *Greek grandfather eats chicken"* was signed by Nancy Frishberg, a linguist and professional ASL interpreter. The sign *"owe"* consists of two parts, first with the hands near the face, the second with the hands in front of the body. The sentence was signed rapidly as in normal discourse and involved a variety of finger and hand movements made in various locations, particularly fine finger movements in front of the face, visual stimuli that pose the greatest challenge to an image reproduction system.

4.1.3. Image Transformations

The two *original stimuli* were modified by a number of image transformations that were fully described above. All transformations were applied to both base stimuli. The actual combinations were as follows:

Image transformations: (1) original; (2) block truncation; (3, 4, 5) binary intensity quantization (12%, 6%, 3%, white pixels); (6, 7, 8) thresholded dark side Laplacians (24%, 6%, 1.5% black pixels); (9, 10, 11) thresholded dark side Laplacians (24%, 6%, 1.5%) with frame interpolation; (12, 13, 14) zero crossings (6%, 3%, 1.5%).

Spatial resolutions: 96×64, 48×32, 24×16 pixels.

Temporal resolutions: 30, 15, 10 (new) fps, and 15 (new) fps with frame interpolation (15i). The full range of combinations is shown in Table 2.

4.1.4. Task

Subjects were shown the 162 stimuli and were requested to make two judgements for each stimulus. First, they were to judge the "intelligibility" of the stimulus on a six-point rating scale [0 = "completely illegible" ... 5 = "nice and clear"]. Second, they were to judge how "pleasant" [0 = "obnoxious" ... 5 = "very pleasing"] the stimuli were, and the extent to which they would "be willing to use such a transformed image for actual communication." Both judgements were made on the same six-point scale.

4.1.5. Subjects

Five subjects took part in this experiment; they included members of the laboratory who were familiar with ASL, and a deaf person not connected with the laboratory.

4.2. Results

Subjects used a somewhat wider range of the intelligibility rating scale than the pleasantness scale. The intelligibility and pleasantness judgements were highly

TABLE 2

Stimuli for Experiment 1

$\left\{\begin{array}{c}\text{Image} \\ \text{transform} \\ \text{(density)}\end{array}\right\} \times$	$\left\{\begin{array}{c}\text{Spatial} \\ \text{resolution} \\ \text{(pixels)}\end{array}\right\} \times$	$\left\{\begin{array}{c}\text{Temporal} \\ \text{resolution} \\ \text{(fps)}\end{array}\right\}$	Number of conditions
Gray-scale stimuli			
$\left\{\begin{array}{c}\text{OR} \\ \text{BT}\end{array}\right\} \times$	$\left\{\begin{array}{c}96 \\ 48 \\ 24\end{array}\right\} \times$	$\left\{\begin{array}{c}30 \\ 15 \\ 15i \\ 10\end{array}\right\}$	24
Binary stimuli			
Binary intensity quantization (Q)			
$\left\{\begin{array}{c}12 \\ 6 \\ 3\end{array}\right\} \times$	$\left\{\begin{array}{c}96 \\ 48 \\ 24\end{array}\right\} \times$	$\left\{\begin{array}{c}30 \\ 15\end{array}\right\}$	18
Thresholded dark side laplacians (L)			
$\left\{\begin{array}{c}24 \\ 6 \\ 1.5\end{array}\right\} \times$	$\left\{\begin{array}{c}96 \\ 48 \\ 24\end{array}\right\} \times$	$\left\{\begin{array}{c}30 \\ 15\end{array}\right\}$	18
Interpolated dark side laplacians			
$\left\{\begin{array}{c}24 \\ 6 \\ 1.5\end{array}\right\} \times 96 \times 15i$			3
Zero crossings (Z)			
$\left\{\begin{array}{c}6 \\ 3 \\ 1.5\end{array}\right\} \times$	$\left\{\begin{array}{c}96 \\ 48 \\ 24\end{array}\right\} \times$	$\left\{\begin{array}{c}30 \\ 15\end{array}\right\}$	18
Total			81

Note. Combinations of image transformations, spatial resolutions, and temporal resolutions investigated by the rating method.

correlated ($r = 0.92$). No systematic differences between the two ratings were noted. Therefore, in discussing the results of this experiment, it is sufficient to consider the intelligibility judgements.

The results of Experiment 1 are shown in Fig. 6, which displays the mean judged intelligibility (for the 5 subjects and two ASL messages) as a function of the bit rate for each of the 81 conditions. The bit rates are actual rates derived from coding algorithms which are discussed fully in Section 7. (Binary-intensity image bit rates are based on quadtree coding; BT rates are inherent in the BT transformation process. Bit rates for spatially subsampled originals are based on a nominal rate of 3 bits per pixel, based on Pearson's [15], p. 1990] observation that there is no impairment when full gray scale is reduced to 3 bits. In our experience, there is little savings in gray scale coding methods compared to the savings in undersampling, and since we will not be concerned with digital codes for undersampled gray scale images, great precision in bit rate estimation is unnecessary.)

Figure 6 shows quite clearly the obvious tradeoff between intelligibility and information content that has been found in all previous studies. A desired result

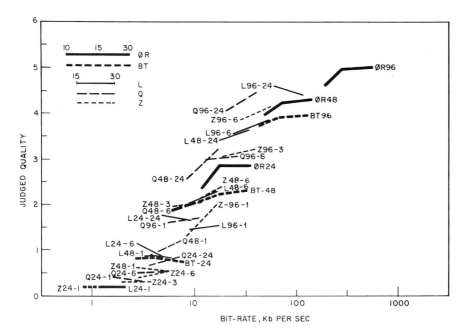

FIG. 6.   Quality judgments as a function of bit rate for the 81 combinations of image transformations used in Experiment 1 and described in Table 2. In the curve labels, single letters (L, Q, Z) refer to binary images; double letters (OR, BT) to gray-scale images; see Fig. 4 for notation. The first number after the transformation code (96, 48, 24) refers to the vertical resolution in pixels; the number after the dash refers to the percent of black pixels in L and Z images, and to white pixels in Q images. Three frame rates (10, 15, 30 fps) are represented from left-to-right along the curves for gray-scale images; two rates (15, 30) for binary images. See Section 7 for details of the bit-rate computations.

would be a method offering a high intelligibility at a low bit rate—a point in the upper-left corner of Fig. 6. As is evident from Fig. 6, there is not a great amount of scatter among the methods: More bandwidth, in terms of better spatial, temporal, or intensity resolution produces higher ratings. Nevertheless, the representation of the data in Fig. 6 indicates many other, more useful results, considered below.

4.2.1.1. *Temporal resolution.*   For gray scale images, there is no loss in intelligibility rating when frame rate is reduced from 30 to 15 fps, although additional reduction to 10 fps does produce a loss. For binary images, there is, on the average, some loss in reducing frame rate from 30 to 15 fps. There was very little difference in ratings for stimuli using frame interpolation compared to those using frame repetition (all at 15 fps). The results shown in Fig. 6 in fact average all 15 fps and interpolated 15 fps conditions.

4.2.1.2. *Spatial resolution.*   Without exception, for the range of image sizes under consideration here, spatial resolution has a major effect on judged intelligibility. The 96 × 64 denser images (gray scale, binary intensity with higher percentages of intensified pixels) are rated highly intelligible; the 24 × 16 sparser images are less than unintelligible, they are completely unrecognizable.

4.2.1.3. *Density of intensified/darkened points.* For the percentage ranges of intensified or darkened points investigated here, without exception, the larger the percentages, the higher the rated intelligibility. By interpolation, it can be seen that L96 and Z96 are rated similarly at comparable densities; Q96 is rated slightly lower but more than compensates by permitting more efficient coding.

4.2.1.4. *Interactions and comparisons between transformations.* It is noteworthy that high density, high resolution, binary transformations (L96-24, Q96-24) are rated almost as intelligible as original gray scale images (OR96) and approximately equal to the middle-sized original, OR48, which receives astonishingly good ratings. These original images are remarkably tolerant of spatial subsampling. The smallest original image OR24 is equalled or surpassed by only middle-sized images (Q48-24, L48-24), and is the only small-sized image to receive ratings that suggest it might be intelligible.

Among the binary transformations, the best prospects for a communication system are offered by the high-density images of all three transformations (Q96, L96, Z96). With the possible exception of L48-24, and Q48-24, the ratings and bit rates of the smaller binary images are not sufficiently promising to warrant further testing. The next step, obviously, is to obtain objective measures of intelligibility.

5. EXPERIMENT 2. INTELLIGIBILITY TESTS OF 12 IMAGE TRANSFORMATIONS

Experiment 1 indicated several image-transformations that seemed to promise high intelligibility at low information rates. For practical reasons, it is not possible to conduct an intelligibility test with more than about a dozen conditions. The problem, therefore, is to choose the conditions that, together, offer the most useful set of data. Some criteria to be satisfied are: (1) It must be possible to compare the three binary intensity transformations (binary intensity quantization Q, dark side

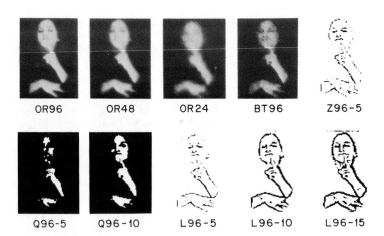

FIG. 7. Image transformations whose intelligibility was tested in Experiment 2. The letters refer to the transformation (see caption of Fig. 4); the numbers after the letters indicate the vertical resolution in pixels; and the numbers after the dash indicate the smaller of the percent of white or black pixels.

TABLE 3a

Intelligibility Test Items for Experiment 2. Twelve Groups of ASL Signs Balanced for Difficulty[a]

1	animal	world	our	accident	hospital	friday	pour
2	criticize	think	because	boss	apple	girl	emphasize
3	penny	week	short	punish	noon	preach	red
4	machine	wife	improve	flag	football	tempt	wolf
5	sorry	suffer	lousy	tree	bread	behind	daily
6	eye	cop	uncle	sit	secret	screwdriver	guilty
7	paper	understand	yesterday	letter	sergeant	summer	boring
8	deaf	finish	plan	ugly	tobacco	train	relax
9	dontwant	mother	bear	jump	disbelieve	talk	good
10	wrestling	leave	believe	love	school	read	follow
11	start	cheese	color	past/ago	pregnant	owe	telegraph
12	home	flower	member	country	challenge	kill	pay

[a] Three practice signs preceded each group: tomato, egg, mouse.

TABLE 3b

Greco-Latin Experimental Design

T1	2B	1A	3C	8H	7I	10L	6J	12F	9G	11K	4D	5E
T2	1D	2C	4A	7J	8E	9F	5H	11L	10K	12G	3B	7I
T3	8K	7F	5L	10A	9B	4I	12C	2E	3H	1J	6G	11D
T4	12I	11H	9J	2G	1L	7A	4K	5C	8B	6D	10E	3F
T5	5F	6K	8G	11B	12A	1H	9D	3J	2I	4E	7L	10C
T6	9H	10I	12E	3L	4G	5D	1F	7B	6C	8A	11J	2K
T7	4C	3D	1B	6E	5J	12K	8I	10G	11F	9L	2A	7H
T8	6L	5G	7K	12D	11C	2J	10B	4H	1E	3I	8F	9A
T9	10J	9E	11I	4F	3K	6B	2L	8D	5A	7C	12H	1G
T10	11E	12J	10H	1K	2F	8C	3G	6A	7D	5B	9I	4L
T11	3A	4B	2D	5I	6H	11G	7E	9K	12L	10F	1C	8J
T12	7G	8L	6F	9C	10D	3E	11A	1I	4J	2H	5K	12B

Note. Each row (T1, ..., T12) indicates the contents of a stimulus tape viewed by two subjects. The initial numeral in each entry indicates the stimulus group (Table 3a); the letter indicates the image transformation (Table 3c).

Laplacian L, and zero crossings, Z) at the same image size, frame rate, and black/white density. (2) At least one binary image transformation must be studied over a range of 3 black/white densities. (3) At least one transformation must be studied over a range of 3 frame rates. (4) At least one transformations must be studied over a range of 3 spatial resolutions (image "sizes"). (5) There must be sufficient data to make it possible to relate these digital transformations to the earlier analog data of Sperling [11, 13]. (6) The set of conditions should include the best candidates for a communication system.

Twelve transformations that met these criteria were chosen for intelligibility testing (Fig. 7 and Table 3c). The gray scale images provide a range against which to judge the binary techniques, and provide a baseline for comparing the present study to earlier studies [11, 13] that used ASL sentences and finger-spelling as well as isolated ASL signs.

TABLE 3c

Intelligibility of the Image Transformations as Determined in Experiment 2, and Bit Rates as Determined in Section 7

	Transformation	% correct	Confidence: 90% interval	Normalized intelligibility	Judged quality	bps ×1000	Bits per pixel
A	OR96	0.869	[0.825, 0.908]	1	4.95	276.5	3
B	30OR48	0.827	[0.778, 0.871]	0.952	4.3	138.2	3
C	OR48	0.863	[0.818, 0.903]	0.993	4.25	69.1	3
D	10OR-48	0.804	[0.752, 0.851]	0.925	3.95	46.1	3
E	OR24	0.744	[0.668, 0.796]	0.856	2.85	17.3	3
F	BT96	0.821	[0.771, 0.866]	0.945	3.9	63.0	0.683
G	L96-15	0.792	[0.740, 0.840]	0.911	4.25*	24.5	0.266
H	L96-10	0.792	[0.740, 0.840]	0.911	3.92*	19.5	0.211
I	L96-5	0.702	[0.644, 0.757]	0.808	3.17*	14.3	0.155
J	Z96-5	0.673	[0.614, 0.730]	0.774	3.61*	18.5	0.201
K	Q96-10	0.714	[0.657, 0.768]	0.822	3.37*	9.4	0.102
L	Q96-5	0.589	[0.528, 0.649]	0.678	2.74*	7.5	0.081

Note. Stimulus transformations: OR = untransformed grey-scale *OR*iginal, BT = *B*lock *T*runcation code, L − *i* = dark side, Gaussian-filtered *L*aplacian with *i*% black pixels, Z − 5 = *Z*ero crossings with 5% black pixels, Q − *i* = two-level intensity *Q*uantization with *i*% white pixels; 96 = 96 × 64 pixels, 48 = 48 × 32 pixels, 24 = 24 × 16 pixels; 30 = 30 new frames per second (fps), 10 = 10 fps, all other stimuli are 15 fps. Intelligibility is mean percent correct transcriptions of ASL signs. The 90% confidence interval is determined from ANOVA of arcsin-transformed data. Judged quality is derived from ratings in Experiment 1; an * indicates an interpolated value.

5.1. Methods

5.1.1. Equipment

The equipment used to record, process, and present the stimuli was described in Experiment 1.

5.1.2. Intelligibility Test

The construction of intelligibility test materials was a formidable task undertaken with the assistance of Dr. Nancy Frishberg, a linguist specializing in ASL. The intelligibility items were constructed with the following properties:

(a) The test items were common, isolated ASL signs with little dialectic variation and unambiguously interpretable by our entire population of subjects. We used isolated single signs, rather than phrases or sentences, to simplify the scoring procedures (since ASL does not follow English grammar or sentence structure, and subjects recorded their responses in English).

(b) The test included signs for which the primary cues involve a wide range of physical aspects of ASL, i.e., signs that are perceived on the basis of hand shape, of movement, of location, signs that involve one hand and signs that require both hands, signs that involve single and multiple movements, and so on. The list of signs included most of the basic sign parameters as described in Stokoe notation [5], including all locations, most handshapes, and a variety of types of movement. The proportions of hand arrangements reflect those found in ASL.

(c) The test included a wide visual range of signs, signs performed in all the various areas of the viewing aperture, signs in which the hands are in front of the face, in front of the body, occluding each other, and so on.

(d) The test included a number of minimal pairs—i.e., pairs of signs that differ only in a single feature such as hand shape, or type of movement. The observation of which distinctions between minimal pairs are lost gives specific information about deficiencies in an image transformation.

(e) The test included a range of easy and hard items so that it could make distinctions between high bandwidth as well as between low bandwidth image transformations.

The initial version of the intelligibility test contained over 300 items; 150 of these were filmed, and on the basis of studies not described in this paper (e.g., [56]), many more signs were eliminated for a variety of reasons. At the time of Experiment 2, the number of signs had been reduced to 87, and the difficulty level of all of these was known quite accurately. This enabled us to make groups of signs, balanced for difficulty, although this feature of the experiment was not critical because the experimental design required all signs to be viewed in all conditions. The list of signs is given in Table 3a.

5.1.3. Stimuli

The stimuli in Experiments 2 and 3 were derived from the intelligibility test items described above. This stimulus base, consisting of 87 single isolated signs, was signed by Ellen Roth, a native signer. Ms. Roth is a congenitally deaf person who was brought up in a signing environment with American Sign Language (ASL) as her primary language. To minimize the number of parameters that guided perception, only the hand and arm motions were used in signing, without the facial expressions that would normally accompany the signs. This yielded stimuli which some deaf subjects found somewhat unusual. In another measure taken to eliminate cues extraneous to ASL, the signer began and ended each sign with the arms folded in the same resting position.

The isolated signs were videotaped using the configuration shown in Fig. 2. Signs were digitized to a resolution of 480 × 512 pixels, 256 gray levels (i.e., 8 bits per pixel), and 30 fps. The images were then reduced in size by a factor of 4 in both x and y (by pixel averaging), and cropped to include only the aperture within which the signer was visible. This yielded our stimulus base. The 87 base stimuli were 96 × 64 pixels, 8 bits of luminance resolution per pixel, and 30 fps. These reduced and cropped stimuli are highly intelligible; the accuracy of reporting these base stimuli is quite typical of much higher-resolution television images (e.g., [11]). The base stimuli were reduced to 96 × 64 pixels for reasons of economy. Thereby it was possible to keep most of the base stimuli on-line simultaneously, allowing for much more efficient generation of the transformed stimuli and stimulus tapes.

5.1.4. Gray-Scale Image Reductions and Transformations

Twelve stimulus transformations are used in this study, including six gray scale transformations, and six binary-intensity transformations. As before, all of these transformations start with our *base stimuli*, which are the reduced and cropped originals, sampled at 96 × 64 pixels, 30 fps, and 8 bits per pixel.

The first group of stimulus transformations are the *image reductions*. These five transformations manipulate the spatial and temporal sampling of the base stimuli. The temporal sampling is reduced by repeating frames, as in Experiment 1. The spatial sampling is reduced by pixel averaging and, as before, the undersampled images are then restored to the size of the base stimuli. The five transformations specifically designed to explore reductions in spatial and/or in temporal sampling are:

(1) The 96 × 64 base stimuli at 15 fps (OR96).

(2–4) The base stimuli *spatially* reduced by a factor of 2 and displayed at 30, 15, and 10 fps (30OR48, OR48, and 10OR48).

(5) The base stimuli reduced by a factor of 4 and displayed at 15 fps (OR24).

The sixth image transformation included in the study is the same block truncation transformation used in Experiment 1 with a spatial resolution of 96 × 64 pixels, and with 15 fps (BT96).

5.1.5. Binary-Intensity Image Transformations

Six binary-intensity image transformations were used: Binary intensity quantization with the proportion of black pixels being fixed at 5% and 10% (Q96-5, Q96-10); darkside Gaussian-smoothed Laplacians with thresholds at 5%, 10%, and 15% (L96-5, L96-10, L96-15); and zero crossings with 5% of the pixels classified as an edge (Z96-5).

5.1.6. Greco-Latin Experimental Design

In order to avoid contaminating the intelligibility data with possible memory and bias effects, we are forced to show a given ASL sign only once to each subject. Therefore, a sign is only viewed by a given subject under one of the twelve transformation conditions. In order to have the same sign appear in each of the twelve transformation conditions (again, in order to balance the experimental design), the sign will have to be shown to a different subject for each transformation, so that at least twelve subjects are needed for a fully balanced viewing. Similarly, it seemed desirable that the order in which signs and transformations occurred within a session should be balanced. If a given sign appeared early in the session for some subjects, it should appear later for other. If a pair of signs appeared in the order *AB* for one subject, they should appear as *BA* (with possible intervening signs) for another subject. Finally, in order that subjects be optimally prepared to receive each stimulus, stimuli with the same transformation are run as a block (a *condition*) preceded by practice trials.

The constraints of fully balanced conditions and balanced order for conditions and for stimuli can be satisfied by a 12×12 Greco-Latin square [57]. The stimuli were blocked into twelve groups of equal number. Each block was processed by a different image transformation. A particular subject viewed the twelve blocks in a particular order, as indicated by a given row of the Greco-Latin square in Table 3b. The twelve rows of the square yield different *forms* for the experiment. Each entry in Table 3b specifies the stimulus group and image transformation for a condition. Two subjects were assigned to each form (row) of 12 conditions.

Three signs (tomato, egg, mouse) were presented in the beginning of every block in the experiment, under the same transformation condition as the block which followed, allowing the subjects to become familiar with the transformation condition before responses were required. The actual signs used, along with a representation of the Greco-Latin square, are given in Tables 3a and 3b.

5.1.7. Sequence of Trials

For each form, the Greco-Latin square design dictates the order in which blocks of trials are presented. Each block consists of three practice signs followed by the seven signs of that block, all ten of which have been processed by the same transformation condition (as controlled by the Greco-Latin square). The twelve blocks, including practice signs, are recorded on a video cassette. Every sign is preceded by a label displayed on the monitor, either "PRACTICE" for the practice signs, or "STIMULUS NNN" for each stimulus, where "NNN" is the ordinal position of that stimulus in the entire form, corresponding to the position on the answer sheet where the English gloss of the sign is to be written. Additionally, each new block is also indicated with a label. A few seconds of blank space are included between every stimulus and every label to allow the subjects sufficient time to write their responses before looking up for the next sign.

The portable video cassette recorder and a small (14×18 cm) monitor were used to run subjects at Public School 47, a New York high school for the deaf and hard of hearing. We discovered that the students did not know English well enough to write English equivalents of common ASL signs, so the subjects were adults: the teachers and friends whom they recruited, and who were paid for their time. Subjects first filled out a brief questionnaire inquiring about their exposure to ASL, and then viewed a videotape of a native signer describing the task in ASL. This was followed by six practice signs, which were not included in the experiment. Subjects were then allowed to clarify their understanding of the task by signing with the experimenter. Each subject was given a printed form on which to write responses. The subject then viewed the prerecorded stimuli, and wrote responses on the printed form. No feedback was given.

5.1.8. Subjects

There were 24 subjects in this experiment. They were all fluent in ASL and also had English skills. The ages ranged from 22 to 68 years old, with an average age of 50, and an average of 39 years of ASL experience. All subjects were either born deaf, or became deaf before the age of 6. Two subjects had deaf parents, the rest had hearing parents.

5.2. Results

5.2.1. Scoring

A sign/response scoring form was first prepared which gave the allowable responses to each sign. For any given videotaped sign there were several English responses which were considered correct. There were several reasons for this. First, for any given ASL sign, there are a number of appropriate English translations. Also, given the historical changes in ASL, a given sign may be interpreted differently by older ASL speakers. Lastly, a small number of signs were rendered sufficiently ambiguously that two different interpretations could be considered to be correct.

The written answer forms were scored by a hearing person who was fluent in ASL. All subjects were judged by the same, consistent criterion defined by the sign/response form. Among the residual scoring problems: poor spelling, with mistakes quite different than those typically made by hearing persons (i.e., they do not produce near homonyms); only part of a compound sign being correctly identified (scored as *incorrect*); marking answers in the wrong position on the page. The necessity of looking away from the screen to mark responses, combined with the fact that trials were not self-initiated, was a source of difficulty.

5.2.2. Design Balance

The response data were subjected to an analysis of variance in order to determine the success of the experimental design, and to gauge the effectiveness of the image transformation in controlling intelligibility. (For statistical issues concerning the analysis of Greco-Latin square designs see [57].) The data for a given cell are the percent correct in a single stimulus block. Because this is a statistic in which the mean and variance are highly correlated, we first applied an arcsin transformation to the data before performing the analysis. The analysis under the conservative test for repeated measures designs shows the image transformation to be a significant source of variance ($p < 0.01$); the stimulus block also is significant ($p < 0.05$). Neither the ordinal position of the stimulus block nor the residual between cell variances are statistically significant. The form viewed by the subjects is not significant. In other words, response accuracy was controlled entirely by the image transformation and the stimulus block. The nonzero block effect implies that we were not entirely successful in balancing the stimulus blocks for difficulty, despite the previous study [56]. However, blocks were completely balanced over subjects and transformations so differences in block difficulty should cancel when evaluating image transformations.

5.2.3. Comparison of Twelve Image Transformations

The results of the experiment are summarized in Fig. 8 and Table 3c. All 12 transformations are quite intelligible, but the gray-scale image sequences are generally more intelligible than the black-and-white cartoon transformations. We consider first temporal and spatial resolution of gray scale images, and then the other transformations.

5.2.3.1. *Subsampling time and space.* Three frame rates (produced by frame repetition) were tested: 30, 15, and 10 new fps. Although 10 fps tended to yield slightly lower intelligibility than 15 or 30 fps, the differences between the three rates were not statistically significant. With these isolated ASL signs, which now have been investigated in many contexts, we usually do find that there is some decrement between 15 and 10 fps, and that intelligibility drops precipitously below 10 fps.

With respect to spatial resolution, diminishing image size from 96 × 64 to 24 × 16 lowers intelligibility only by 13%. Even the quarter-resolution gray-scale images are more intelligible than many of the cartoons. The high intelligibility of 24 × 16 images, which look very impoverished, is quite extraordinary, but is quite consistent with earlier results obtained with cropped television displays [13].

To compare spatial resolution in television displays (based on bandwidth) with resolution in computer displays (based on pixels) requires Shannon's theorem [58]: $C = 2W$, where C is the capacity (number of pixel samples per second), and W is bandwidth. Although Sperling's television data were obtained at 60 fps, we know

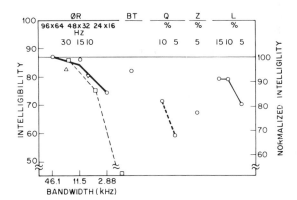

FIG. 8. Intelligibility (left ordinate) and normalized intelligibility (right ordinate) as determined in Experiment 2 for the transformations illustrated in Fig. 7. Image transformations are indicated on top line; spatial resolution (when different from 96 × 64) is indicated on next row; frame rates (when different from 15 fps) are indicated under "Hz"; the percent of white pixels under Q; and the percent of black pixels under Z and L. The abscissa indicates the equivalent bandwidth of subsampled gray-scale originals. Also shown for comparison (as a dashed line connecting open squares) are data from Sperling [11], for which an equivalent frame rate of 15 fps is assumed (see text).

from the temporal resolution results just described above that 15—or perhaps even 10 fps—would have yielded equivalent intelligibility. For the purposes of comparison, Sperling's intelligibility data obtained with triplets of isolated ASL signs also are graphed in Fig. 8 (conservatively assuming 15 fps).

5.2.3.2. *Implications for telephone transmission of ASL.* From Fig. 8, it is self-evident that the two methods (digital, analog) of producing images of low spatial resolution give completely consistent results. What is most significant in Fig. 8 are the implications of the results for the transmission of images via television-like raster scans. The 24 × 16 gray scale image at 15 fps achieved an intelligibility of 0.744, which was 86% of control intelligibility (measured with 96 × 64 images). A 24 × 16 image contains only 384 pixels; 15 frames contain only 5,760 pixels, which could be transmitted with a raster scan of bandwidth 2,880 Hz, well within the telephone network's capability. Simple subsampling of ASL image sequences in space and time is sufficient to reduce them to intelligible telephone transmittability, not by digital coding but by analog raster scans. One solution to the problem of transmitting ASL over telephone networks would be to use raster scans. There are many possibilities for improvement that come readily to mind, but the present results demonstrate the sufficiency of the analog raster. Digital coding schemes for gray scale images will be considered (and rejected) in Section 7.3.

The only other gray scale method tested here is block truncation coding, which yields images comparable to the untransformed images at half spatial sampling. The block truncation coding method is a very efficient method in terms of minimum bandwidth requirements for relatively high quality gray scale images, and appears to have minimal effects in terms of lowered image intelligibility. Its "cost-effectiveness" in terms of its code length versus intelligibility is considered in the Section 8.1.

5.2.3.3. *Binary images.* The more nearly equal are the proportions of black and white pixels in binary images, the more information the images may potentially contain. (The upper bound on information is $I(p) = p \log p + (1 - p)\log(1 - p)$, where p is the proportion of black pixels.) Three levels of p were tested with dark side Laplacian images. Not surprisingly, they show a significant effect of p on intelligibility. For example, the dark side Laplacian images at $p = 10\%$ were substantially more intelligible than those at $p = 5\%$, although the effect appears to saturate between 10% and 15%. The intelligibility of binary-quantized-intensity images also appears to benefit from a more equal distribution of pixels of both colors, although the data are insufficient to suggest what the optimum p might be. (The data of Experiment 1 in Fig. 6 suggest it might be considerably closer to 0.5.)

Three different binary image transformations can be compared at $p = 5\%$. Binary intensity quantization, in which pixels are used to fill areas of the same color, fares considerably worse than either zero crossings or dark side Laplacians in which pixels outline, but do not fill, areas. The two cartoon transformations (Z5, L5) were equally intelligible, to the precision afforded by our experiment. The bottom line, the cost-effectiveness of binary images for communication is considered in Section 8.

5.2.3.4. *Interpretation of intelligibility.* The testing procedure involves an open form. That is, subjects are given a blank sheet of paper on which to denote their responses. Thus, if a subject were to apply a guesssing strategy, the expected level of chance performance is effectively zero. The performance of our subjects on the most difficult image transformation, the 5% binary intensity quantization, is 0.59 (68% of base stimulus intelligibility)—a quite respectable performance. At the other end of the range, intelligibility of the base stimuli at 15 fps was 0.87, which is quite significantly below 1.00. The base stimuli are nearly identical to the initial videotapes we created, although somewhat reduced in size, and yet our subjects still miss approximately one sign out of eight. This is typical of such tests [11, 13]. Mistakes are due to unfamiliarity with an ASL sign, inattention, and to confusion with a visually similar (minimal pair) sign. In the context of normal conversation, most of these errors would disappear. While we have not carried out task completion studies, which are a more functional test of a communication system, the levels of intelligibility observed here suggest that other indices of performance would reflect the high observed intelligibilities.

5.2.3.5. *Comparison of judgements (Experiment 1) and intelligibilities (Experiment 2).* Not all 12 conditions that were tested in Experiment 2 were among the 81 tested in Experiment 1. To obtain ratings for comparison, it was necessary to interpolate in five cases (see Table 3c). This done, the correlation between the subjective ratings (Experiment 1) and the objective scores (Experiment 2) turns out to be $r = 0.848$, an impressive vindication of the rating procedure. The most significant instance of disagreement between the ratings and the intelligibility scores occurs with the 24×16 pixel gray scale images which look terrible but are surprisingly intelligible. It is precisely such instances that ultimately necessitate formal performance tests.

6. EXPERIMENT 3. POLYGONAL APPROXIMATIONS

Experiment 2 demonstrated that substantial manipulations of image quality were possible without greatly reducing image intelligibility. Here we explore further degradations in image quality with the aim of further reducing the acceptable information rate. Experiment 3 investigates images that require substantially lower bandwidth than those of Experiment 2, and includes conditions that potentially fall within the capabilities of the current telephone network and modem technology.

The edge-detected cartoon images used in Experiment 2 bear a certain resemblance to pen-and-ink line drawings. These images are further transformed by approximating the edge regions in the image with a series of straight line segments. This results in a new set of image transformations called *polygonal transformations*. In this section, the polygonal image transformation is described, and results of intelligibility tests with deaf subjects are given. In the following section, the *vectorgraph code* used to compress the code for polygonal images is discussed, and vectorgraph compression is compared to various compression methods for the images of Experiment 2.

6.1. Methods

6.1.1. Equipment

The equipment used to record, process, and present the stimuli is the same as for Experiment 2.

6.1.2. Stimuli

The base stimuli used in this experiment are a subset of those used in Experiment 2. There were a few stimuli used in Experiment 2 which were nearly unrecognizable in all transformations conditions, being reported correctly by only one or two of the 24 subjects who saw them under the various transformations. (These difficulties arose because the sign was signed poorly, because the sign was ambiguous, or because it was uncommon.) In Experiment 3, the seven poorest signs from Experiment 2 were discarded, leaving a total of 77 base stimuli (see Table 4). The same three practice signs were used as in Experiment 1.

There were seven transformation conditions in Experiment 3. Two transformation conditions were replications of those used in Experiment 2, in order to be able to reasonably compare the results, especially given the slightly reduced set of base stimuli used. These two repeated conditions were the 96 × 64 base stimuli at 15 fps (condition OR96 of the previous experiment), and the edge detected cartoon involving a *dog* with a threshold of 5% (condition L96-5). The L96-5 transformation served as the input to the five polygonal transformations, described below.

6.1.2.1. *Thinning and categorization.* The polygonal image transformation consists of two main components. The first component takes an edge-detected binary image, breaks it up into separate connected edge regions, and thins these regions so that they are only one pixel wide. The second component takes this thinned image and approximates it as a series of straight line segments (polygonal splines). The thinning process, illustrated in Figs. 9, 10, further distorts the image, maintaining all edge regions (or "brush strokes" in the pen-and-ink drawing analogy), but distorting the exact content of those regions. The benefit, as we shall see in the next section, is a substantially lower information rate. The polygonal image transformation is more fully described in Landy and Cohen [59], which also reviews other work on thinning and splining techniques used both for pattern recognition and for image compression.

The thinning and categorization algorithm used here is an extension of the thinning and point categorization techniques described by Sakai *et al.* [60]. The binary image is thinned, and the points which remain are categorized as being either *endpoints*, *multiple branch points*, or simply *portions of an arc*. The subsequent tracing and approximation algorithm becomes simpler if the input image has as few pixels as possible. Therefore, Sakai *et al.*'s method was extended to delete almost every pixel it could without changing the 8-connectivity of the image. The insistence that the thinning process remove as many edge pixels as possible makes it easier to trace the remaining pixels, minimizing the possibility that a given edge pixel (termed an *edgel*) has more than one potential follower along the curve.

After thinning and categorizing the edge regions, the resulting curves are traced to yield a graph representation of the image. Any given edgel in the thinned image has a corresponding vertex in the graph representation, and arcs represent neighbor relations. By itself, this procedure of representing a thinned image by tracing the sequences of neighboring black pixels is known as a *chain code* [61], and has been suggested as a compression scheme [62–65]. In the current work, however, the chain-coded image will be further processed by a splining technique.

6.1.2.2. *Splining.* Some further definitions are required at this point. The thinning or chaining process results in a graph of edgels as vertices and neighbor relations connecting these vertices. A subset of these edgels are chosen as *knots* for the subsequent splining process. These edgels are used to anchor the polygonal approximation process, and include the endpoints and multiple branch points. The input to the approximation process (the result of the tracing) is a set of knots, and

TABLE 4a

Intelligibility Test Items for Experiment 3. Seven Groups of ASL Signs Balanced for Difficulty[a]

1	deaf	world	plan	hospital	jump	because	flag	summer	noon	bread	sergeant
2	dontwant	color	week	good	train	past/ago	boring	read	cheese	pour	tempt
3	love	home	eye	paper	improve	football	bear	yesterday	finish	challenge	tree
4	understand	friday	uncle	letter	criticize	accident	penny	pay	suffer	emphasize	ugly
5	flower	believe	punish	sorry	secret	animal	wife	short	disbelieve	follow	guilty
6	think	our	machine	wrestling	boss	girl	country	behind	pregnant	sit	owe
7	start	mother	member	leave	cop	daily	lousy	apple	school	kill	talk

[a] Three practice signs preceded each group: tomato, egg, mouse.

TABLE 4b

Greco-Latin Experimental Design

T1	2G	5D	3E	1A	4B	6C	7F
T2	5B	3F	4A	6D	7C	2E	1G
T3	6F	2A	5C	7E	3G	1B	4B
T4	1C	6G	2D	4F	5E	7A	3B
T5	7D	1E	6B	3C	2F	4G	5A
T6	4E	7B	1F	5G	6A	3D	2C
T7	3A	4C	7G	2B	1D	5F	6E

Note. Each row (T1,.....T12) indicates the contents of a stimulus tape viewed by two subjects. The initial numeral in each entry indicates the stimulus group (Table 4a); the letter indicates the image transformation (Table 4c).

TABLE 4c

Intelligibility of the Image Transformations as Determined in Experiment 3, and Bit Rates as Determined in Section 7

	Transformation	% Correct	Confidence: 90% interval	Normalized intelligibility	bps ×1000	Bits per pixel
A	OR96	0.916	[0.873, 0.951]	1	276.5	3
B	L96-5	0.792	[0.733, 0.846]	0.865	14.3	0.155
C	P96	0.747	[0.684, 0.805]	0.816	8.9	0.097
D	10P96	0.636	[0.568, 0.702]	0.695	6.0	0.097
E	P48	0.675	[0.608, 0.738]	0.738	7.8	0.084
F	10P48	0.566	[0.496, 0.634]	0.617	5.2	0.084
G	7P48	0.513	[0.443, 0.582]	0.560	3.9	0.084

Note. Stimulus transformations: OR = untransformed grey-scale *OR*iginal, L-5 = dark side, Gaussian-filtered *L*aplacian with 5% black pixels, P = *P*olygonal outlines. 96 = 96 × 64, 48 = 48 × 32 pixels; 10 = 10 new frames per second (fps), 7 = 7 fps, all other stimuli are 15 fps. Intelligibility is mean percent correct transcriptions of ASL signs. The 90% confidence interval is determined from ANOVA of arcsin-transformed data.

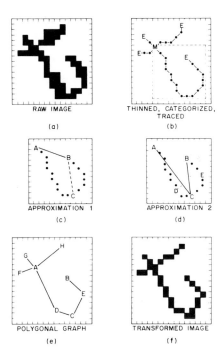

FIG. 9. Generating a polygonal transformation: (a) A portion of a cartoon generated by $L96$-5 (dark side Laplacian, 5% black), the input image. (b) After thinning, categorizing, and tracing. (M) is a *multiple branch point*, (E) is an *endpoint*. Panels (c) and (d) refer only to the subarea enclosed in dashes. (c) The first approximation ($A - B$) fails because point C is too far away. (d) The second approximation incorporates point C but fails because points D and E are too far. (e) The third approximation incorporates points D and E, and satisfies the distance criterion. (f) The polygonally transformed image derived from the polygonal graph (e).

arcs between these knots, which are the sequences of edgels from the thinned image which connect these knots. In the interest of minimizing the resulting code, it is useful to reduce the number of arcs. Thus, when a few lines converge in an image, the tracing algorithm will choose a single multiple branch point among the several in the resulting clump of edgels as the *attractant* knot for incoming arcs. The tracing includes only those neighbor relations needed to connect the incoming arcs to that knot. In the following process, each arc between knots will be approximated with a series of straight line segments.

Figure 9 illustrates a concrete example of the thinning, categorization, and splining processes. Figure 9a shows a single connected edge region (black edges on a white background). The result of the thinning, categorizing, and tracing process on this image is given in Fig. 9b. Despite the sizes of the clusters of edgels in the original edge image, the thinning and categorizing process results in only one multiple branch point and four arcs (each leading to an endpoint in this example).

The final process in the polygonal image transformation approximates each arc with a sequence of one or more straight line segments. The algorithm used here is similar to that described by Ramer [66]. The algorithm starts with an arc leading

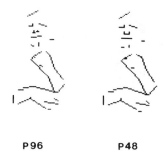

P 96   P 48

Fig. 10.   Polygonally transformed ASL images derived from L96-5. (P96) The full resolution image based on a 96 × 64 pixel grid. (P48) A half-resolution image derived from L96-5, reduced to 48 × 32 (to reduce code length) and then magnified for viewing to 96 × 64.

from knot A to knot B, and a parameter that expresses the maximum error tolerated by the approximation. The algorithm begins by attempting to use line segment $\overline{AB}$ as an approximation to the arc from A to B. The point on this arc, C, which is the greatest distance from the line segment $\overline{AB}$ is found. If the Euclidean distance from C to line segment $\overline{AB}$ is within the error criterion, the segment $\overline{AB}$ is used to approximate the curve from A to B. If the error criterion is exceeded, the algorithm then considers the two line segments $\overline{AC}$ and $\overline{CB}$ as the approximation, treating point C as a *cut point*, and recursively examines $\overline{AC}$ and $\overline{CB}$ in a similar fashion, stopping when all line segments fall within the error criterion.

The splining algorithm is illustrated in Fig. 9c, which shows a portion of Fig. 9b from the branch point to an end point. The knots which terminate this arc are labeled A and B. The algorithm first finds the point on the arc which is the greatest distance from the line segment $\overline{AB}$. The point C is found, and is added as a cutpoint since the distance from C to $\overline{AB}$ (in this case, the length of $\overline{BC}$) is above criterion. In Fig. 9d the process continues, and points D and E are added as cutpoints. At this point, all segments meet the criterion (which in our work has been set to a distance of 1.5 pixels). The resulting line-segment graph is illustrated in Fig. 9e, and the reconstructed polygonal image is shown in Fig. 9f.

The end result of the polygonal approximation as applied to the edge detected image of Fig. 7 (L96-5) is shown in Fig. 10a. The L96-5 image was thinned and categorized. Before splining, a cleaning operation was applied to the thinned image which deleted any connected groups of black pixels containing only 1 or 2 pixels. The resulting image was traced, splined, and the resulting polygonal graph is reconstructed as the image in Fig. 10a. This polygonal approximation transformation is termed a *full* polygonal transformations, since it uses the full 96 × 64 spatial resolution of the edge image to which it is applied. The full polygonal transformation was tested at 15 and at 10 resulting in two of the conditions of Experiment 3 (P96 and 10P96).

The final set of transformations studied in Experiment 3 involve a polygonal transformation which uses the full 96 × 64 image to compute the polygonal graph, but displays the resultant graph with a resolution of only 48 × 32. The idea was that once the polygonal graph was achieved based upon the 96 × 64 sampled edge image, it might not be critical if the endpoints of the line segments were reconstructed with less precision. This *half-resolution* polygonal transformation is achieved by taking the graph structure achieved by the full polygonal transformation (resolved on a 96 × 64 grid) and deleting the least significant bit. This results in an image very similar to the full polygonal approximation, but one in which the knots and cut points are jiggled slightly from their original positions. The half-resolution polygonal transformation has a halved sampling rate in each spatial dimension. Figure 10b shows an example of the half-resolution polygonal transformation. The half-resolution polygonal transformation was displayed at 15, 10, and 7.5 fps, yielding the final three conditions in Experiment 3 (P48, 10P48, 7P48).

In summary, the polygonal intelligibility tests included seven image transformations: the base stimuli, at 15 fps (OR96); 5% dark side Laplacian images (L96-5); full-resolution polygonal stimuli at 15 and 10 fps (P96 and 10P96); and half-resolution polygonal stimuli at 15, 10, and 7.5 fps (P48, 10P48, and 7P48). A Greco-Latin square design was used, similar to that used in Experiment 2. The seven conditions and 77 base stimuli resulted in 11 signs per block and 7 blocks of signs (see Table 4).

6.1.3. Presentation

The presentation of the stimuli was similar to that used in Experiment 2. Subjects were given the same televised instructions as before, and filled out a blank form with their answers. The stimuli were presented in blocks by condition, preceded by three practice signs as before, each transformed in the manner of stimuli of the following block.

6.1.4. Subjects

There were 14 subjects in this study, 2 subjects per form of the test. The subjects ages ranged from 16 to 79; all used ASL as their principle mode of communication. Three were native signers. All subjects were either born deaf, or became deaf by the age of 12.

6.2. Results

6.2.1. Scoring

Responses were scored as in Experiment 2.

6.2.2. Design Balance

As in Experiment 2, in order to evaluate the results and to evaluate the effectiveness of the design, the data were subjected to an analysis of variance. As before, the arcsin transformation and the conservative test for repeated measures design [57] was applied. The transformation condition is highly significant ($p < 0.001$). The stimulus block (group of 7 signs) is significant under the normal test ($p < 0.001$), but is not significant under the conservative test. It was slightly disappointing to find that, even by using the results of Experiment 2, we did not succeed in equating the difficulty of all the stimulus blocks. However, because of the completely counterbalanced Greco-Latin design, the residual inequality of block difficulty should not affect any of the conclusions. The ordinal positions, subject group, and residual variances were not statistically significant.

6.2.3. Comparison of the Methods

The results are summarized in Table 4. As one might expect, discarding the most difficult signs used in Experiment 2 raised the overall scores in Experiment 3 (compare Tables 3c and 4c). Intelligibility of the original gray scale base stimuli (OR96) increased from 87% to 92%, and the dark side Laplacian L96-5 intelligibility increased from 70% to 79%. For purposes of comparison, in both Experiments 2 and 3 (Tables 3c and 4c), each intelligibility score is normalized by dividing it by the score on the control condition (OR96) to yield *normalized intelligibility*.

It is apparent that there is a loss of intelligibility for the polygonal transformation conditions as compared with the previous conditions we have employed, and yet it is surprising how well subjects interpret these exceedingly impoverished images. For polygonally transformed images, the loss of intelligibility from reduced temporal resolution is greater than from reduced spatial resolution. Compare the drop of intelligibility from the full-resolution 15 fps (82%) to full-resolution 10 fps (70%) with the drop from full-resolution 15 fps (82%) to half-resolution 15 fps (74%). Temporal subsampling was more deleterious than spatial subsampling despite the fact that the spatial resolution was reduced to 0.25 (i.e., 0.5 resolution reduction in both x and y), and temporal resolution was reduced to 0.67 (15 to 10 fps). The apparent disparity in how spatial and temporal subsampling affect human observers is only partially mirrored by the the actual bits per second (bps) rates we have achieved in coding these images, indicating that the observers are sensitive to the form of *information* contained in the image sequences (see Sect. 8.3).

7. COMPRESSED CODES FOR ASL IMAGE SEQUENCES

7.1. Efficient Codes for Binary Images

This section introduces new techniques for errorless encoding and compression of binary images and compares them with existing methods. Discussion is restricted to the errorless case in order that the intelligibility results reported above be applicable to the encoded and reconstructed images. For cartoon images, a number of *hierarchical* methods for image coding have been tested, some of which are quite efficient. For a fuller treatment of these hierarchical coding methods, including comparisons with standard compression methods for binary images, see Cohen, Landy, and Pavel [67].

7.1.1. Two-Dimensional Hierarchical Image Codes

7.1.1.1. *Quadtree code* (*QT*). In a hierarchical description of an image, the data structure is that of a tree. Nodes nearer to the root of the tree describe large subareas of the image; further from the root, nodes describe smaller portions of the image. The best-known hierarchical representation is the *quadtree* code. In this code, the root of the tree denotes the entire image, which is assumed to be square. Every node, including the root, describes a square portion of the image. The children of a node each represent the four quadrants created by splitting the subimage represented by the parent into four equal pieces.

In pattern recognition and other applications, the tree structure is used as a dynamic data structure for the fast computation of various image algorithms. For compression, the application of the hierarchy is much simpler. It is used merely to

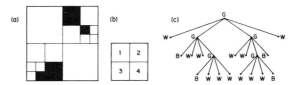

FIG. 11.   An example of a simple binary image and its quadtree code: (a) The image. (b) The order of labeling quadrants. (c) The hierarchical description (quadtree) generated by the code. The tree is read from the top down and from left-to-right within branches of a common node. Each node represents a particular subimage; the top node (root) represents the entire image. Because the entire image is not uniform black or white, the root is labeled *G* (gray). Each *G* node is subdivided into four branches (children) representing the four quadrant subimages in the order (b). Thus the first child is (*W*) white, the second child is *G*, and therefore further subdivided into *B*, *W*, *W*, *G*, and so on. See text for details.

represent the image itself. Thus, hierarchical coding algorithms seek to compute the minimal tree that describes a given image or sequence of images. The tree is rooted, ordered, and labeled. That is, the root represents the particular image under consideration. Any given node represents a particular portion of the image, determined by the node's exact position (order) in the tree. The label for the node specifies the color of the subimage: either uniform black, uniform white, or nonuniform (which is referred to as gray).

Consider a simple example. Figure 11 shows a simple binary image and the quadtree that describes the image. It is assumed that the size of the image being described is known in advance. To interpret the tree, it is examined in a top-down fashion. The root is labeled *G*, for gray, which means that the image is not a uniform color. Therefore the image is split into four equal subimages, each of which corresponds to one of the children of the root (according to an agreed upon ordering, given in Fig. 11b). The labeling and splitting processes continue in a recursive fashion. For example, the first child represents the upper-left quadrant of the image, which is uniformly white. Hence, this child is labeled *W*, for white, and is a leaf of the tree since it need not be split further. In contrast, the second child represents the upper-right quadrant of the image which is nonuniform. It is labeled *G* and subdivided further.

In order to use a hierarchical code, one needs to specify the manner in which the tree is to be converted to a binary representation and transmitted. The labels of the nodes in the tree are transmitted in a depth-first traversal of the tree (top-to-bottom, left-to-right). The receiver knows at any given point what node is about to be received, and what subimage will be described by that node, simply as a consequence of the information it has already received. It remains only to choose a binary code for each node label. In the most general case, the binary code for the labels is:

$$G = 0$$
$$B = 10$$
$$W = 11.$$

In many instances, it is possible to decrease the number of bits used to represent the labels. For example, if we are about to send the description for a node describing a single pixel (i.e., a subimage of size 1×1), then such a subimage can only be black or white, since it can not longer be subdivided. Thus, the potential alphabet for this particular node is reduced, and we can save by using the subcode

$$B = 0$$
$$W = 1$$

for such leaves. Where the potential alphabet of symbols at a given point is reduced, this scheme eliminates redundancy in the coding scheme. Comparable savings are possible in several special situations with QT coding, and even more often with the more complicated hierarchical coding schemes described below (see [67] for details).

The quadtree scheme is a particular exemplar of a more general technique, referred to as hierarchical coding. As in the case of the QT code, a hierarchical code hierarchically subdivides the image until the smallest subimages are uniform in color. A hierarchical code yields a rooted, labeled, ordered tree structure describing the image. Any given node in the tree denotes a particular subimage, and the label associated with that node either gives the color of that subimage (if it is uniform), or specifies that it is nonuniform and that a *cut* is to be made. The various hierarchical methods differ in the type and number of cuts that are possible.

7.1.1.2. *Binary tree codes* (*BT*). In binary tree codes, each nonuniform subimage is cut into two equal pieces, rather than the four quadrants used by quadtrees. The tree structure derived from binary trees has only two children for each parent node. The cut can either be in the horizontal or vertical direction. The vertical and horizontal cuts are made in a particular order, based on the *dominance* of either the vertical or horizontal cut. For horizontal dominance, if the entire image is nonuniform, then the top node will be labeled G, and the image will be cut horizontally. The top and bottom halves, if nonuniform, will then be labeled gray and cut vertically. The cuts continue, until unformity is reached, always alternating horizontal with vertical. Because of this assumed order for the type of cut to be made, the receiver need only know that a node is nonuniform in order to know how it is to be cut, since the distance of that node from the root of the tree will specify the cut.

7.1.1.3. *Adaptive hierarchical codes* (*AHC*). In some binary tree codes, the node label itself further specifies what kind of cut is to be made. These methods are referred to as *adaptive*, because the coding method can adapt the cutting sequence to best suit the content of the image. The first adaptive method considered here is *adaptive hierarchical coding*. In this extension of the BT method, vertical and horizontal cuts are not strictly alternated. Rather, the algorithm determines which order of cuts yields the minimum length of code. The node label for nonuniform nodes now specifies not only that the subimage is nonuniform, but also whether it is to be cut vertically or horizontally. The number of letters in the alphabet has increased by one, and the adaptive binary codes are necessarily longer. In the general case there are four possibilities:

$$00 = B = \text{black}$$
$$01 = W = \text{white}$$
$$10 = V = \text{vertical cut}$$
$$11 = H = \text{horizontal cut.}$$

The advantage of AHC is that it can, through clever use of the cuts, adapt its tree structure to yield the minimum number of nodes. If an area of the image is filled

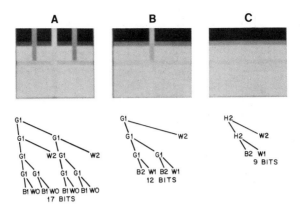

FIG. 12. A simple image (horizontal black bar) and its representation by three hierarchical codes, the level of grey indicates the level of cut: (a) binary tree code with vertical dominance, (b) binary tree code with horizontal dominance, (c) adaptive hierarchical code. The letters indicate the labeling of the subimage; the adjacent digit indicates the number of bits in the code for that letter.

primarily with long vertical uniform regions, then the tree will use fewer horizontal cuts to describe that region. AHC computes the tree that produces the minimum length binary representation—the most efficient AHC code—over all possible ways of cutting the image.

A comparison of binary tree codes BT and an adaptive hierarchical code AHC is illustrated in Fig. 12. Figure 12a shows a simple image and a representation of the cuts made in that image by BT with vertical dominance. In Fig. 12b, the same image is processed by BT with horizontal dominance. Lastly, in Fig. 12c this image is processed by AHC. Beneath each image a representation is given of the tree structure used to represent the image, and an indication of the number of bits used to code each node (taking into account all possible redundancy elimination). AHC, since it takes most effective advantage of the characteristics of the image, is most efficient. This is true both in terms of the number of nodes in the coding tree, and in terms of the number of bits in the binary representation of that tree. A further example of these methods is given in Fig. 13, which shows one cartoon frame as it is partitioned by QT, BT with horizontal dominance, and AHC. The efficient, adaptive nature of the cuts made by AHC is self-evident.

7.1.2. Three-Dimensional Codes

The hierarchical coding methods described so far all operate in two dimensions. Given a sequence of image frames, such as the ASL stimuli, these codes process each frame separately; no attempt is made to take advantage of the similarity of successive frames. Three-dimensional hierarchical codes involve the same hierarchical decomposition of the image, but take advantage of the third dimension, time. For these codes, the to-be-coded array has three dimensions: row, column, and frame. The cuts used to partition the image sequence are planes slicing through this 3-dimensional block, horizontally, vertically, or temporally.

7.1.2.1. *Oct-tree code (OT).* OT is the simplest 3D code; it is the obvious extension of quadtrees to three dimensions. (Note: OT is not to be confused with the octrees of Meagher [68].) In OT, a perfect cubic image sequence is required (number

a   b   c

FIG. 13. The description of an ASL image by three different 2-dimensional hierarchical codes: (a) quadtree; (b) binary tree with horizontal dominance; (c) adaptive hierarchical code. (Cuts are shown in gray.)

of rows, columns, and frames all identical), with sides a power of two. The algorithm proceeds identically to that of quadtrees, except that the subimages are cubic, and if nonuniform, they are subdivided into octants. This yields a tree where each interior node has eight children, hence the name oct-tree. The possible node labels are still G, W, and B, and all other aspects of the algorithm are analogous to the QT method.

7.1.2.2. *Three-dimensional adaptive hierarchical codes (3D-AHC).* The OT algorithm does not take full advantage of the image characteristics in three dimensions, just as the QT algorithm cannot adapt to particular image characteristics in two dimensions. In 2D, nonoptimality led to the development of the AHC method. The analogous development in 3D is termed 3-dimensional adaptive hierarchical coding, 3D-AHC. 3D-AHC is similar to (2D) AHC, except that the subimages are 3-dimensional rectangular parallelepipeds instead of simply rectangles. In 3D-AHC, there are three possible cuts, horizontal, vertical, and temporal, and the alphabet in the unconstrained case consists of five possible node names: B, W, H, V, and T. As the number dimensions in the subimage whose size is greater than one diminishes, that is, as each dimension is eventually cut a sufficient number of times so that no further cuts in that dimension are possible, then the size of the alphabet decreases. Each time the alphabet decreases, the binary representation of the alphabet is updated in order to reflect the decrease and to minimize the binary code. The 3D-AHC algorithm is the most complicated of the methods described here.

7.1.2.3. *Binquad code (BQ).* BQ, the last 3D code considered here, is a hybrid between QT and 3D-AHC. Recall that the impetus for extending the codes to 3D was to take advantage of the image areas that remain constant over time. Otherwise stated, it is useful to note and take advantage of stationarity in portions of the image sequence. A stationary area in 3-dimensional image sequence is a set of elongated uniform 2D image areas, where the elongation is in time dimension. To take advantage of elongated 2D uniformities, the BQ method treats the temporal dimension differently from the spatial dimension. At any given point, two possible partitions of the image are considered, a spatial cut or a temporal cut. The spatial cut is identical to the quadtree cut extended across time. The temporal cut is the binary temporal cut of the 3D-AHC method. Any interior node of the coding tree can have two or four children, and is labeled T (for temporal cut) or S (for spatial cut), respectively. The two cuts are chosen adaptively as in AHC and 3D-AHC so as to minimize the length of the binary representation of the coding tree.

7.1.3. Implementation of Hierarchical Codes

All of the hierarchical codes are feasible to implement. Any hierarchical code can be implemented on a serial computer to yield linear time and space complexity (in the number of pixels), although the more complicated methods (e.g., 3D-AHC) are slower to compute than the simpler methods (e.g., QT). The computations involved in hierarchical codes also lend themselves to parallel (i.e., hardware) implementations. Finally, the restrictions to square or cubic images, power of two dimension size, and binary cuts, are all unnecessary; they were included to simplify the exposition. For example, if a dimension were not a power of two, the algorithms could proceed in the identical fashion as long as the transmitter and receiver of the code both knew the image size and the rules for where cuts were to be made. Similarly, one could easily extend the algorithms to make ternary cuts instead of binary cuts.

One important practical extension of the methods is needed to deal with the nonsquare 96×64 ASL images. As described above, each code yields a *tree* that describes the entire image. The concept of tree can be extended to include the possibility of an *ordered forest* of trees describing the image. For example, this might correspond to transmitting only the lower portions of the tree and skipping the top few levels. The transmitter and receiver would mutually assume that the top levels of the tree consisted entirely of a particular known sequence of uniform and nonuniform nodes. The 96×64 ASL stimuli cannot be handled by the simple power of two schemes described above. Therefore, the images are divided into six 32×32 subimages, and the codes applied to each subimage separately. The receiver of such a code already knows the partitioning and the order in which the six partitions are to be transmitted, and the image reconstruction continues apace. In the 3D-AHC and BQ methods, a restriction is placed on the extent of the time dimension considered by the algorithm. The 3D-AHC code uses 16 frames, the BQ code uses either 2, 4, 8, or 16 frames at a time.

7.2. Compressive Coding of Polygonal Image Sequences

A variety of edge-detected images had been shown in Experiment 2 to be usefully intelligible. The polygonal transformations were designed to take advantage of the redundancy inherent in the line-drawing-like quality of these images. The *polygonal graph* which results from the polygonal transformations lends itself to efficient coding. The nodes of this graph are the knots and the cut points derived by the transformation. The arcs are the straight line segments which connect the nodes. The coding scheme employed here, *vectorgraph coding*, describes the graph by coding a traversal of the graph, much as a computer plotter would draw the line image by following the line segments one by one, occasionally lifting its pen and moving to draw another set of segments. Vectorgraph coding is described fully in Landy and Cohen [59].

7.2.1.1. *Vectorgraph: Symbolic code.* In vectorgraph coding, the first task is to compute a traversal of the polygonal graph. This traversal covers a single graph component (set of connected lines) at a time, and continues on in a component-by-component fashion. For a given component, the traversal begins with an arbitrarily chosen endpoint (or multiple branch point, if no endpoints are available). The algorithm then traverses the graph component segment by segment, never retracing any segment. When a node is reached such that all of the outgoing segments have already been traversed, the algorithm goes back to a previously visited node (always a multiple branch point), not all of whose outgoing arcs have been traversed, and continues the traversal from there. This process continues until all arcs of a component have been traversed, and then repeats for all components of the graph.

The end result of the traversal process is a symbolic code for the graph. The code consists of a sequence of commands which describe the traversal, much like commands for a computer plotter. Four commands are required. First, an *initial point command* (or I command) describes the first node visited in a component, giving the x and y coordinates of that point. Next, a *continue command* (C) is used to describe the traversal of a single line segment; it gives the coordinates of the endpoint of that line segment. Within a component, a *back-to command* (B) is used to return to a previously visited point (with the "pen up") in order to continue tracing through this component. Finally, an *end of image command* (E) is used to mark the end of a single image frame.

An example of this process is illustrated in Fig. 14. The polygonal graph in Fig. 14a is traced beginning with endpoint G, and continues through nodes A, D, C, and E to reach endpoint B. The traversal then goes back to node A twice in order to traverse the arcs to F and H, resulting in the traversal path of Fig. 14b. The symbolic code which represents this traversal is given in Fig. 14c. The B instructions refer to a numbering of the I and C points that depends on the particular traversal path.

7.2.1.2. *Vectorgraph: Binary code.* In order to compute an information rate for image sequences, the binary representation of the symbolic coding must be specified. The most efficient binary code depends on the statistics of the images to be coded, including the number of graph components, the number and variety of vectors to be drawn, and the resolution of the images. The polygonal images used here contain 30–40 vectors and 15–20 components per frame. The vectorgraph code has been found to be highly efficient for these images.

As with the symbolic code, the binary code comprises a series of commands; each command includes a command code and optional command arguments. The following mapping is used for the command symbols:

$$\{I, C, B, E\} \Rightarrow \{01, 1, 001, 000\},$$

which is the Huffman code [26] for these four symbols.

The I command requires a description of the coordinates of the nodes which begins the next component. A two-tiered arrangement is used, describing the node either using absolute coordinates, or coordinates relative to the previously drawn point (from the previously traversed component). An absolute coordinate requires 13 bits (7 for row, 6 for column) to specify a point in the 96×64 full polygonal images. A relative vector uses 8 bits, 4 for the row and 4 for the column. This allows the relative vector mode to be used for nodes inside a 16×16 square centered on the previously drawn point. Generally this square is centered on the previous point, but if that point is too close to an edge of the picture, the square is moved over so as to be entirely contained within the picture, thereby maximizing the use of relative vectors. One extra bit is used to distinguish between absolute and relative cases, and

(a) POLYGONAL GRAPH

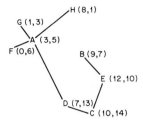

(b) SPANNING PATH

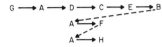

(c) VECTORGRAPH CODE

POINT	CODE TYPE	CODE BITS	MODE	MODE BITS	ADDRESS	ADDRESS BITS
0	I	2	ABS	1	1,3	13
1	C	1	VECT 1	2	3,5	4
2	C	1	VECT 2	1	7,13	8
3	C	1	VECT 2	1	10,14	8
4	C	1	VECT 2	1	12,10	8
5	C	1	VECT 2	1	9,7	8
6	B	3	NA	NA	1	3
7	C	1	VECT 2	1	0,6	8
8	B	3	NA	NA	1	3
9	C	1	VECT 2	1	8,1	8
10	E	3	NA	NA	NA	NA

FIG. 14.   The vectorgraph code for polygonal transformations: (a) The polygonal graph representing the image (see Fig. 9e). (b) A spanning path that describes the order of coding arcs. (c) The vectorgraph code for the polygonal graph (a) spanned by path (b). ABS is absolute x, y specification of the origin of the graph; VECT1 is a short vector; VECT2 is a medium length vector; NA indicates "not applicable" for retraces and endpoints.

the trees are output in such a way as to maximize the use of the relative vectors, since they use fewer bits.

The C points use a similar scheme as I points except with three tiers. The codes for the three C modes are

    00—absolute coordinates (13 bits follow)

      1—(medium length) relative vectors (8 bits follow)

    01—short relative vectors (4 bits follow).

Medium length relative vectors are the most common, and are given the shortest code. Short relative vectors are used for line segments contained in a 4×4 square centered on the previously visited point. The medium length vectors are used for line segments contained in a 16×17 square centered on the previously visited point (larger than for I points, because the points reachable by short vectors can be excluded).

The code for *B* points contains the *number of the previously described point* in the present component to which the algorithm must return. For this number, we have used the following coding schemes, based on the number of points in the component which have already been visited and to which a return can be made:

Number of Points	Method
1	No code is required
2	1 Bit
3–4	2 Bits
5–8	3 Bits
> 8	3 Bit shift code [69]

Referring again to Fig. 14c, note that the modes used and number of bits required for each command are given.

The vectorgraph code described thus far pertains to the full polygonal images. For the half polygonal images, the polygonal graph utilizes a 48×32 spatial resolution. For these images, a similar scheme is used, except the following substitutions are made: the absolute coordinates only require 11 bits (6 for the row, 5 for the column), and the relative modes for *I* and *C* commands use the same number of bits but, given the subsampling, they effectively double their reach, resulting in a greater use of the relative modes. Thus, in the half-polygonal images, savings are made (1) because two bits are saved in each absolute coordinate and (2) because the relative vector and short vector modes are used more frequently.

7.3. Coding of Grey-Scale Images

There were six gray-scale transformation methods in Experiment 2. Five of these were based on spatial and temporal subsampling of the base stimuli, and the last was block truncation coding. We now estimate the bit rates and bandwidths needed for gray-scale images.

The analog coding of gray-scale image sequences has been considered above (Sect. 5.2.3.2); by Shannon's sampling theorem [58] the analog bandwidth is simply $0.5 \times$ *number of pixels transmitted per second* (see Fig. 8). Unless gray scale images are intelligently image-processed (not merely subsampled), the bit rates for digital coding are so high that gray-scale images are not competitive with other transformations. Therefore, we have not actually programmed gray-scale codes, but merely estimated their efficiency. For the variously sampled versions of the base stimuli, there are a number of ways one can estimate bit rates. (1) The simplest would be to compute the product of the number of bits per pixel, the number of rows, columns, and frames per second. This would yield the number of bits per second required to transmit the image exactly as it is stored in the computer. (2) Alternatively, this amount can be reduced by computing the effective number of bits per pixel, taking into account the inherent noise in the video system (from video camera, digitizer, and monitor), and the effective dynamic range of the system. This calculation [36] reduces the number of bits per pixel from eight to seven, as measured for the equipment used in our experiments. (3) One can consider the savings that lossless coding schemes might provide when applied to these seven-bits-per-pixel images. Our experience suggests that little would be gained in this. We have applied adaptive Huffman coding [26] and run-length coding [69] to our gray scale images, and have only arrived at savings of a few percent. (4) Based on Pearson's [15] and our own observations, little is lost perceptually until the gray scale is reduced to less than 8 levels; therefore we conservatively value each pixel at three bits. The estimate of bit rate is thus three times the number of rows, columns, and frames per second. The results in bit rates were given in Table 3c.

For block truncation image transformations, the bit rate calculation is inherent in the transformation itself [24]. For each given block as reconstructed in the stimuli used in our experiment, a known number of bits needs to be transmitted. The BT method is quite efficient. We have applied the BT method to all of our base stimuli in order to create the stimuli used in Experiment 2. The average bit rate achieved over these 84 image sequences is given in Table 3c.

7.4. Comparisons of the Compressive Coding Results

7.4.1. Binary Images

In Cohen et al. [67] hierarchical methods for coding binary images are described in more detail, and more compression results are discussed. These analyses include discussion of worst case coding and expected compression from random images. None of the hierarchical codes considered above can be applied directly to 96×64 images; all images need to be partitioned into suitable subareas. Here, the hierarchical codes are used to represent an image (or image sequence) as a forest of coding trees, each tree representing a subarea of the image. The hierarchical codes and subareas ($X \times Y \times T$) were

QT, BT, AHC	32×32
OT	$16 \times 16 \times 16$
3D-AHC	$32 \times 32 \times 16$
BQ	$32 \times 32 \times (2, 4, 8, \text{ and } 16)$

Figure 15 illustrates the compression achieved by the hierarchical coding algorithm as applied to the cartoon and to the binary-quantized intensity stimuli of Experiment 2. The bit rate achieved by each code is plotted as a function of image transformation. Clearly, BQ code (16 frames deep; BINQUAD in Fig. 15a) and 3D-AHC (also 16 frames deep) are the most efficient codes, regardless of the type of binary image. (The actual bit rates achieved by BQ16 coding of the images of Experiment 2 are given in Table 3c.) Figure 15a also shows that the 5% binary-intensity quantization transformation (Q96-5) yields the shortest code of any of the image transformations. Binary intensity quantization produces images with large uniform areas, more so in the 5% images than with higher densities; these large areas are very efficiently coded by hierarchical codes.

The edge-detection cartoon images have a larger number of thin lines than binary-intensity quantized images, requiring the codes to construct deeper coding trees, and therefore cartoons require more bits per frame. The comparison between the codes is made especially clear in Fig. 15a. The consistency of operation of the hierarchical methods is clear, as the ordering from best to worst method is preserved

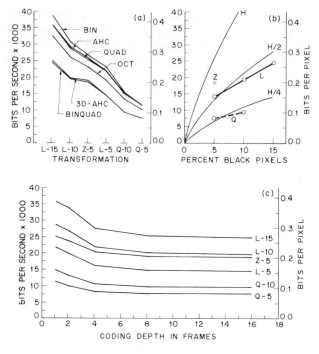

FIG. 15. The efficiency of image codes compared on representative ASL sequences: (a) The average code length in bits per second required to code six ASL image transformations, all at 15 fps. See Fig. 4 for key to transformations. The right-hand ordinates give the average bits per pixel (all images 96 × 64). The curve parameter indicates the code (see text for details). Two-dimensional codes: (BIN) binary tree code; (AHC) adaptive hierarchical code; (QUAD) quadtree code; (OCT) oct-tree code; (3D-AHC) 3-dimensional adaptive hierarchical code; (BINQUAD) binquad code. (b) The efficiency of three optimally coded transformations (Z, L, Q) as a function of the percent of black or white pixels (whichever is smaller). For comparison, the theoretical minimum code length required to code a completely random picture with the same percent of black pixels (the information limit) is indicated by the curve H, showing that binquad-coded Q-transformed images use about $H/4$, and L images about $H/2$ bits per pixel. (c) The efficiency of 3-dimensional binquad code as a function of the coding depth in frames for six ASL image transformations.

across the various cartoon types and other binary-intensity coded images. Also, although adaptivity in the method appears ineffective in the 2-dimensional case, where AHC lags slightly behind QT, in three-dimensions adaptivity is quite efficient. The hybrid method, BQ, is slightly more efficient than 3D-AHC.

The expected compression efficiency of hierarchical methods for random images shows a U-shaped dependence on the proportion of the two colors. As one might expect, from the definition of information ($H = -p \log p - (1 - p)\log(1 - p)$), code length as a function of the fraction p of black pixels is an inverted-U function that increases monotonically as p increases from 0 to 0.5, and then decreases symmetrically thereafter. The computation of H is illustrated in Fig. 15b; H is a lower bound for any binary image when pixel correlations are ignored. For comparison, $H(p)/2$ and $H(p)/4$ also are shown. The efficiency of coding the various images can be gauged by noting that dark side Laplacian cartoons with densities of 5%, 10%, and 15% (L96-5, L96-10, L96-15) are coded with an efficiency of approximately $H/2$, whereas the binary intensity quantized images of 5% and 10% (Q96-5, Q96-10) are coded with an efficiency of approximately $H/4$. (These results are for binquad coding.) These results show the advantage of taking uniform regions into account, binary intensity quantized images having large uniform regions.

From Fig. 15a, it was evident that the 3-dimensional coding methods (binquad BQ16 and 3D adaptive hierarchical coding 3D-AHC) were consistently superior to the 2-dimensional methods across all images. These 3D methods both used 16 frames. There are problems with coding image sequences 16 frames deep. First, the devices which do the compression and the receiving both need to buffer 16 frames of data at a time. More importantly, the algorithm cannot complete and begin transmitting until the 16th frame has been digitized. Assuming a sampling rate of 15 fps, this means there would be at least a one-second delay inherent in the transmission. In voice conversations, such long delays are quite damaging to interactive conversation. How much depth of coding is actually needed in the time dimension? We investigate this question with BQ16, which was consistently the best method.

Figure 15c shows the coding efficiency of binquad code as the depth of coding is varied from 16, 8, 4, 2, to 1 frame. Both the bits per second at 15 fps, and the bits per pixel are shown for five types of binary images. At a depth of 1 frame, the binquad method is identical to the quadtree method. The major gain in 3D coding of these image sequences is made in the first four frames, with little further improvement between 4 and 16 frames. Therefore, most of the advantage of 3D coding could be gained with transmission delays of 0.25 to 0.5 s; not optimal, but tolerable.

7.4.2. Polygonal Images

The results of applying the vectorgraph coding method to all the full and half polygonal images of Experiment 3 were given in Table 4c. The various vectorgraph-coded cartoons used between 0.54 and 0.62 of the code length of the hierarchically coded cartoon from which they derived (L96-5, a negative Laplacian on a grid 96×64 with 5% black pixels and 15 fps). When the vectorgraph-code and 3D binquad code are compared on precisely the same image (P96, a full resolution polygonal representation of L96-5), the vectorgraph code requires 0.77 the code length of the depth-16 hierarchical code. The knowledge that a cartoon is polygonally constructed can be used to code it more efficiently by a single-frame code than by the most efficient 16-frame deep hierarchical code (BQ).

8. THE TRADEOFFS BETWEEN INTELLIGIBILITY AND BITS PER SECOND

The main intelligibility results are given in Fig. 16, which shows normalized intelligibility versus bits per second for 17 different image transformations (two transformations are repeated). Normalized intelligibility is the measured intelligibility of the test signs divided by their intelligibility in the untransformed, control condition (OR96). The reason for considering normalized intelligibility is that the ASL sign set for the polygonal transformations (Experiment 3) eliminated some ambiguous signs that had been used in Experiment 2, and therefore yielded slightly higher control-test scores. Normalized intelligibility scoring makes the intelligibility measurements in the two experiments comparable. (The two control conditions (Experiments 2, 3) are designated as OR96 and OR'96, respectively, in Fig. 16.) For

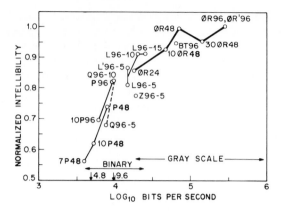

Fig. 16. The intelligibility versus information rate trade-off. Normalized intelligibility (measured intelligibility divided by intelligibility of the *OR*96 control condition) as a function of $\log_{10}$ bits per second required to (optimally) code the various transformed ASL images. The curve labels indicate image transformations (see Figs. 4 and 10 for the keys). An initial number (7, 10, 30) preceding the transformation key indicates the frame rate; when not otherwise designated, the frame rate is 15 fps. Connected points represent the same transformation, they differ only in frame rate or spatial resolution. *P* transforms, *L'*96-5, and *OR'*96 were determined in Experiment 3, all other points were determined in Experiment 2. On the abscissa, 4.8 and 9.6 indicate 4,800 and 9,600 bps, respectively.

reference, 4,800 and 9,600 bps are marked on the abscissa. The obvious conclusions are that more bits per second produced more intelligibility, and that the gray scale codes required more bits per second than did the binary codes.

Evaluating the significance of normalized intelligibility scores is an essential ingredient in evaluating the trade-off between intelligibility and information rate. To estimate the cost of reduced intelligibility in practical situations, one would ideally like to know task completion times for ASL communication tasks under various levels of intelligibility. Unfortunately, only data for acoustic communication systems are available. Task completion can proceed at 95% of the normal rate over noisy acoustic channels at S/N levels judged " useless" by subjects [70]. Sentence intelligibility has been determined under the same noisy conditions as auditory intelligibility (measured on isolated words drawn from 1000-word sets). Sentences have the advantages of lexical and semantic context; a normalized intelligibility for isolated words of 56% (the lowest for any of our image tranformations) corresponds to a sentence intelligibility of about 90% [71]. The reproduction of isolated words, drawn from a large or unspecified vocabulary as in our studies, is one of the most demanding tests of a communication system. Lexical constraints on ASL may be weaker than in spoken English [3, 11], but even the poorest image sequences considered here would be expected to yield good sentence intelligibility in normal conversation. Below, we consider in more detail the tradeoffs between intelligibility vs information rate for the various image transformations.

8.1. Grey-Scale Images (BT, OR)

Two gray-scale procedures were investigated: block-truncation (BT) and space–time subsampling (OR). BT96, a 96 × 64 image required 63,000 bps and produced about the same intelligibility as the 48 × 32 subsampled gray-scale original or the dark side Laplacian cartoon (L96-10 and L96-15). Since the complex BT code produced no intelligibility or bit rate advantage over the much simpler subsampled image (OR48), BT will not be further considered here. Even OR48 is expensive in terms of bps. It obviously is better matched to analog transmission than to digital transmission. As an analog signal (Sect. 5.2.3.1), OR48 requires a bandwidth of 11,520 Hz. The most subsampled gray scale image OR24 (24 × 16, 15 fps), has a normalized intelligibility of 86% and requires a bandwidth of only 2,880 Hz. This image obviously could be used for successful ASL communication, could be transmitted by simple raster scan, and could utilize standard switched network facilities, as they typically offer a minimum bandwidth of about 2,700 Hz. Of all the image transformations considered here, this is the most obvious candidate for telecommunication by use of existing facilities.

The extremely subsampled image, OR24, is an image that looks worse than it is. For example, in Experiment 1, it was rated as appearing to be slightly less intelligible than Q96-6 (96 × 64, binary intensity coded, 6% white pixels) and much less intelligible than Z96-6 and L96-6 (zero crossing and dark side Laplacian cartoons). Objectively, however, OR24 is more intelligible than Q96-10 (Fig. 16) which, with 10% white pixels yields even more intelligible images than than does Q96-6 which, with 6% pixels, exceeded OR24 in quality ratings. Similarly, OR24 is more intelligible than Z96-5 and as intelligible as L96-5, both of which were *rated* much higher.

Comparisons of rating data (Experiment 1) and intelligibility data (Experiments 2, 3) raise an important practical question not fully answered here: All other things being equal, will experienced users learn to prefer the images that yield the greatest intelligibility? Over the full set of images, the preference for intelligibility (or bit rate) is readily manifest. Rated intelligibility and rated pleasantness were very highly correlated ($r = 0.92$). And, rated intelligibility correlated 0.85 with objectively measured intelligibility. But in comparing images that are of roughly similar intelligibility, other factors were important. The conclusion, nevertheless, stands. In spite of its blurred appearance, the 24 × 16 15-fps gray-scale image has high intelligibility, is easily transmitted using ordinary raster scan technology, and is the premier candidate for communication of ASL on the existing telephone network.

8.2. Binary Intensity-Quantized Images (Q)

Two Q images were fully tested: Q96-5 and Q96-10, both at 15 fps. It is clear that the increased intelligibility of Q96-10 over Q96-5 is obtained at a relatively small increase in information rate (7,500 to 9,400 bps). Because of their low information rates, binary intensity quantized images are obvious candidates for ASL communication on the switched network. We did not pursue further our search for optimal parameters for Q images because it appeared to us that the outline drawings (cartoons) would be more profitable. Exploratory studies using Q transformations were also conducted by Pearson and Six [21] who used 50 × 50 pixel images at 12.5 fps and Pearson [72] who studied 64 × 60 images at 12.5 fps. For transmissions which were judged to be not always intelligible, they found bit rates (6,500 and 10,000 bps) very comparable to those reported above.

The conclusion about Q transformations is that the lower limit of usable ASL images is in the 5,000 to 10,000 bps range. While a better choice of parameters than 96 × 64 pixels, 10% white pixels, and 15 fps (e.g., lower spatial resolution, larger percent white pixels, slightly slower frame rate) may bring the bps rate down slightly below the rates tested here (7,500 to 9,400 bps) without a corresponding decrease in intelligibility, it does not appear that great improvements will be possible. The problem is that the best hierarchical codes for Q are extremely efficient, and bit rates do not tend to decrease unless information is correspondingly decreased; the information loss ultimately is reflected in lowered intelligibility scores. (See, for example, the trade-off between spatial resolution and frame rate in the comparison between the P96 and P48 polygonal transformations below, and the bps cost of the percent of white pixels being closer to 0.5 in Fig. 15b.)

8.3. Cartoon Images (L, Z, P)

Three kinds of cartoon images were investigated and are represented in Fig. 16: zero crossings (Z), dark side Laplacians (L), and polygonally transformed images (P). Information rates for Z and L images were computed using binquad code; vectorgraph code was used for polygonally coded images.

The Z images were not quite as intelligible as comparable L images and did not lend themselves to the same wide variation in the fraction of blackened pixels as did the L images, so only Z96-5 was tested. Within L images, normalized intelligibility is directly related to bit rate. (The two slightly different scores for L96-5 represent performances for the different subjects and slightly different stimuli used in Experiments 2 and 3.)

The polygonally transformed images (P, based on L96-5) offer a range of normalized intelligibilities: P96, a full resolution, 15 fps image, is almost equal in intelligibility to L96-5; 7P48, a half-resolution 7 fps image, has very marginal 56% normalized intelligibility. An interesting observation from Fig. 16 is that full resolution polygonally transformed images (P96) are slightly more intelligible than half-resolution images (P48) even when their bit rates are matched. Put another way: To preserve intelligibility of polygonally transformed images, reduce frame rate not spatial resolution. Generally the polygonal images offer intelligibility at bit rates below those accessible to other binary images. For example, Q96-5, lies below the P48 and P96 curves indicating that at low bit rates, polygonal images are somewhat more intelligible than Q images.

Several of the cartoon images fall in the 4,800 to 9,600 bps range that is so common in current technology. At the low end of this range, 7P48, 10P48, and 10P96 (at 3,900, 5,200, and 6,000 bps) present the possibility of noisy but marginally possible ASL communication on a digital 4,800 bps circuit. The full polygonal (P96) and the binary intensity-quantized image (Q96-10) require only 8,900 and 9,400 bps (both at 15 fps). Other images, not intelligibility tested, but likely (from the results of Experiment 1) to fall in this bps and intelligibility range would be reduced-size cartoons, e.g., L48-24. In conclusion, only polygonally transformed images have demonstrated usable intelligibility at digital communication rates of 4,800 bps; at 9,600 bps, many alternatives are possible, both cartoons and binary intensity-coded images.

8.4. Overview: The Limits of Intelligible ASL Communication

8.4.1. Intelligibility Versus Bit Rate

The overall conclusions from the intelligibility versus bit rate tradeoff in Fig. 16 are that the bit rate is by far the major determinant of intelligibility, and that the

TABLE 5

Information Requirements for ASL Communication

	≈ B & W TV	I > 90%	I > 60%
Gray-scale	46,000 Hz OR 96	11,500 Hz OR 48	2,880 Hz OR 24 6,000 bps 10P96
Cartoon	—	25,000 bps L96-15	5,200 bps 10P48
Binary quantized intensity	—	9,400 bps Q96-10	

Note. Determined by the type of image at three levels of quality: Images subjectively comparable to black and white TV; eminently useable images, normalized intelligibility (I) greater than 90%; and marginally adequate images for ASL communication. (All images sequences are 15 fps except 10P which are 10 fps; pixel dimensions are indicated as follows: $96 = 96 \times 64$, $48 = 48 \times 32$, $24 = 24 \times 16$.)

kind of image transformation has only a small, second-order effect for the extremely efficient transformation and codes studied here. It is quite remarkable that such vastly different image transformations can have nearly equal intelligibilities when their bit rates are matched. See, for example, three images represented in the center of Fig. 16: L96-5, a cartoon, Q96-10, a binary intensity-quantized image, and OR24, a subsampled gray-scale image. All these have approximately the same bit rate, and they have the same intelligibility.

The subjective quality of the images represented in Fig. 16 is not adequately described by their intelligibility because even low-quality images can be quite intelligible. Humans are amazing in their ability to extract information from noise. Table 5 combines the information from Fig. 6 (quality ratings) and Fig. 16 (intelligibility) to arrive at a rough indication of the subjective quality of some of the image transformations and their bit-rate requirements. Higher quality images, for example, convey more than merely ASL, the convey nuances of facial expression, lip movements, details of apparel, and so on. Only the OR96, 15 fps original images have a quality typical of black and white TV. These head and shoulders gray scale images fit comfortably into a 46,000 Hz channel. Several images are of lower quality, but quite acceptable to users and perfectly adequate to communicate ASL without appreciable loss. Typical representatives of these are (all 15 fps) OR48 (bandwidth of 11.5 kHz), Q96-24 (19,500 bps) and L96-15 (25,000 bps). Minimal usable images, such 10P48 (5,200 bps) have already been discussed extensively above.

To evaluate the images, there are at present no alternatives to human judgement and measures of human performance. There certainly are no algorithms that would enable one to compute that a cartoon, a binary intensity-quantized, and a subsampled gray-scale image were all equally useful representations of the original. Furthermore, the occasional divergences between quality judgments and objective measures

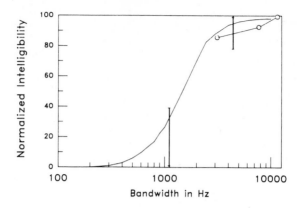

FIG. 17. Comparison of the bandwidth–intelligibility trade-off for acoustically coded speech and raster-coded ASL. The smooth ogival curve is taken from speech intelligibility data reported by French and Steinberg [78]. The three connected open circles represent ASL grey-scale data (OR96, OR48, OR24, all 15 fps) from Experiment 2. The vertical bars represent the performance of the middle 75% of subjects in Sperling's [11] ASL television experiment, assuming an effective frame rate of 15 fps.

of performances show that image quality is a multidimensional quantity. For predicting performance, performance measures are necessary.

8.4.2. Comparison of Visual and Auditory Communication Requirements

It used to be believed that a picture is worth a thousands words. This belief was instantiated in the design of television and telephones: 4,000,000 Hz was allocated to a television channel and only about 3,000 Hz to a telephone channel. Even the American Picturephone and the English Viewphone systems [73–77] which showed only head and shoulders views, required bandwidths of about 1,000,000 Hz.

What is the current status of the picture : word ratio? Figure 17 shows auditory intelligibility data obtained by French and Steinberg [78] on the effect of bandwidth (cutoff frequency) upon the intelligibility of auditory words. For comparison, the data of Experiment 2 with OR24 and OR48 are shown, together with the data of Sperling [13] recomputed, assuming 15 fps (see Sect. 5.2.3). The astounding conclusion is that the picture–word ratio has shrunk almost precisely to unity for analog-encoded signals! Acoustically-coded speech and raster-coded sign language require the same bandwidth, well within the range of subject variability.

Any particular value of the picture–word ratio (for ASL versus speech) is only temporary; the required channel capacities obviously depend on available techniques and thus are a function of time. Digitally encoded speech is intelligible at bit rates of about 2400 bsp [79], and digitally reconstructed speech is judged to be marginally useful at 300 to 600 bsps (e.g., [80]). The lowest bit rates for speech are based on source encoding—they assume profound knowledge of the vocal apparatus and of speech signals. The source constraints of ASL (the anatomy of the joints, the linguistic constraints of ASL) could, in principle, also be employed to produce more efficient image codes. For the moment, therefore, the picture-word ratio for *digitally* encoded language is greater than one, perhaps as large as ten.

8.4.3. Implications for Communication Systems

The most significant result vis-a-vis communication systems in general is that vastly different transformations yield intelligible ASL images. Whether viewers wish to communicate in ASL by cartoons, binary intensity-quantized images, or blurred gray-scale images is a matter of convenience and availability. For any size channel, different codes can serve different visual purposes, and the decision about which code to use can be made at the initiation of each conversation, or even changed during the conversation to better express one meaning or another. As computing power becomes more affordable, viewers can add additional codes. For example, Sperling [11] noted that, because finger spelling proceeds faster than ASL, a code for finger spelling might use finer temporal resolution than a code for ASL. For speechreading (lipreading), "the ability to resolve the shape of the lips and to see the teeth and the tongue through the lips is important to speechreaders. Thus, a specialized code for speechreading requires better contrast resolution but less spatial resolution than do codes for ASL and finger spelling" [11, p. 2000]. Some of these notions have been implemented in a communication device that uses different codes for graphic and for dynamic head and shoulders views [81]. In the future, whatever the available channel capacity, we may expect to see a multiplicity of visual codes, each designed to optimize the utility of the channel for the purpose at hand.

ACKNOWLEDGMENTS

The work on the image processing of American Sign Language was supported by National Science Foundation, Science and Technology to Aid the Handicapped Grant No. PFR-80171189. The preparation of this article was supported by the NSF and by USAF, Life Sciences Directorate, Grant AFOSR 80-0279. Special thanks to August Vanderbeek whose knowledge of ASL, rapport with the deaf community, and hard work were an essential ingredient of these studies. We appreciate the help we have received by many persons in the deaf community and schools for the deaf, including Dr. Jerome Schein, Director of the Deafness Research and Training Center at NYU; the staff of Public School 47, and especially Mrs. O'Shay, Mr. Jeff Rothchild, and Ms. Pakula; Mr. Ziev of the New York Society for the Deaf; and Ms. Solomon of the Hebrew Association of the Deaf. Dr. Nancy Frishberg provided essential guidance in the construction of the intelligibility test materials. We would like to thank our patient deaf signers, Ellen Roth and Alec Naimen. We also thank O. R. Mitchell, who made available his computer programs for block truncation coding. Finally, we wish to acknowledge the skillful technical assistance of Thomas Riedl and Robert Picardi.

REFERENCES

1. Technical Staff, Bell Labs, *Engineering and Operations in the Bell System*, Bell Telephone Laboratories, 1977.
2. U. Bellugi and S. A. Fischer, A comparison of sign language and spoken language, *Cognition* 1, 1972, 173–200.
3. E. Klima and U. Bellugi, *The Signs of Language*, Harvard Univ. Press, Cambridge, Mass., 1979.
4. E. L. Cohen, L. Namir, and M. Schlesinger, *A New Dictionary of Sign Language*, Mouton, The Hague, The Netherlands, 1977.
5. W. C. Stokoe, D. C. Casterline, and G. C. Groneberg, *A Dictionary of American Sign Language on Linguistic Principles*, Gallaudet College Press, Washington, D.C., 1965.
6. H. Bornstein, Sign language in the education of the deaf, in *Sign Language of the Deaf* (I. M. Schlesinger and L. Namir, Eds.), pp. 333–361, Academic Press, New York, 1978.

7. G. Sperling, Future prospects in language and communications for the congenitally deaf, in *Deaf Children: Developmental Perspectives* (L. Liben, Ed.), pp. 103–114, Academic Press, New York, 1978.

8. H. G. Furth, *Thinking without Language: Psychological Implications of Deafness*, Free Press, New York, 1966.

9. J. Jeffers and M. Barley, *Speechreading (Lipreading)*, Thomas, Springfield, Ill., 1971.

10. J. S. Scheinberg, Analysis of speechreading cues using an interleaved technique, *J. Commun. Disorders* 13, 1980, 489–492.

11. G. Sperling, Video transmission of American Sign Language and finger spelling: Present and projected bandwidth requirements, *IEEE Trans. Commun.* COM-29, 1981, 1993–2002.

12. D. E. Pearson, An experimental visual telephone for the deaf, *Television-J. Roy. TV Soc.* 16, 1978, 6–10.

13. G. Sperling, Bandwidth requirements for video transmission of American Sign Language and finger spelling, *Science (Washington, D.C.)* 210, 1980, 797–799.

14. D. E. Pearson and J. P. Sumner, An experimental visual telephone system for the deaf, *J. Roy. Television Soc.* 16, 1976, 2–6.

15. D. E. Pearson, Visual communication systems for the deaf, *IEEE Trans. Commun.* 29, 1981, 1986–1992.

16. H. Poizner, E. S. Klima, U. Bellugi, and R.B. Livingstone, Motion analysis of grammatical processes in a visual gestural language, in *Motion: Representation and Perception*, pp. 148–171, Assoc. Comput. Mach., New York, 1983.

17. G. Johansson, Visual analysis of biological motion and a model for its analysis, *Percept. Psychophys.* 14, 1973, 201–211.

18. G. Johansson, Visual motion perception, *Sci. Amer.* 232, 1975, 76–88.

19. H. Poizner, U. Bellugi, and V. Lutes-Driscoll, Perception of American Sign Language in dynamic point-light displays, *J. Exp. Psychol.: Human Percept. Perform.* 7, 1981, 430–440.

20. V. C. Tartter and K. C. Knowlton, Perceiving sign language from an array of 27 moving spots, *Nature* 289, 1981, 676–678.

21. D. E. Pearson and H. Six, Low data-rate moving-image transmission for deaf communication, *Int. Conf. Electron. Image Process.*, July 1982, pp. 204–210.

22. J. F. Abramatic, P. H. Letellier, and M. Nadler, A narrow-band video communication system for the transmission of sign language over ordinary telephone lines, in *Image Sequence Processing and Dynamic Scene Analysis* (T. S. Huang, Ed.), pp. 314–336, Springer-Verlag, New York, 1983.

23. G. Sperling, M. Pavel, Y. Cohen, M. S. Landy, and B. J. Schwartz, Image processing in perception and cognition, in *Physical and Biological Processing of Images* (O. J. Braddick and A. C. Sleigh, Eds.), Rank Prize Funds International Symposium at the Royal Society of London, London, England, Springer Series in Information Sciences, Vol. 11, pp. 359–378, Springer-Verlag, Berlin, 1983.

24. O. R. Mitchell and E. J. Delp, Multilevel graphics representation using block truncation coding, *Proc. IEEE* 68, 1980, 868–873.

25. D. Marr and E. Hildreth, Theory of edge detection, *Proc. Roy. Soc. London. Ser. B* 207, 1980, 187–217.

26. D. A. Huffman, A method for the construction of minimum redundancy codes, *Proc. IRE* 40, 1952, 1098–1101.

27. R. H. Stafford, *Digital Television*, Wiley, New York, 1980.

28. W. K. Pratt, *Digital Image Processing*, Wiley, New York, 1978.

29. W. K. Pratt (Ed.), *Image Transmission Techniques*, Academic Press, New York, 1979.

30. H. G. Musmann, Predictive image coding, in *Image Transmission Techniques* (W. K. Pratt, Ed.), pp. 73–112, Academic Press, New York, 1979.

31. A. G. Tescher, Transform image coding, in *Image Transmission Techniques* (W. K. Pratt, Ed.), pp. 113–155, Academic Press, New York, 1979.

32. J. A. Roese, Hybrid transform/predictive image coding, in *Image Transmission Techniques* (W. K. Pratt, Ed.), pp. 157–187, Academic Press, New York, 1979.

33. B. G. Haskell, Frame replenishment coding of television, in *Image Transmission Techniques* (W. K. Pratt, Ed.), pp. 189–217, Academic Press, New York, 1979.

34. J. R. Jain, and A. K. Jain, Displacement measurement and its application in interframe image coding, *IEEE Trans. Commun.* COM-29, 1981, 1799–1808.

35. D. J. Healy and O. R. Mitchell, Digital video bandwidth compression using block truncation coding, *IEEE Trans. Commun.* **COM-29**, 1981, 1809–1817.
36. Y. Cohen, *Measurement of Visual Noise*, Technical report, Human Information Processing Laboratory, New York University, Feb. 1982.
37. A. N. Netravali and J. D. Robbins, Motion compensated television coding: Some new results, *Bell Syst. Tech. J.* **59**, 1980, 1735–1745.
38. I. Abdou, *Methods of Edge Detection*, University of Southern California, Image Processing Institute Report No. 830, 1978.
39. L. S. Davis. A survey of edge detection techniques, *Comput. Graphics Image Process.* **4**, 1975, 248–270.
40. J. M. S. Prewitt, Object enhancement and extraction, in *Picture Processing and Psychopictorics* (B. S. Lipkin and A. Rosenfeld, Eds.), pp. 75–149, Academic Press, New York, 1970.
41. L. G. Roberts, machines perception of three-dimensional solids, in *Optical and Electrooptical Information Processing* (J. T. Tippett, *et al.*, Eds.), pp. 159–197, MIT Press, Cambridge, Mass., 1965.
42. R. O. Duda and P. E. Hart, *Pattern Classification and Scene Analysis*, Wiley, New York, 1973.
43. R. Kirsch, Computer determination of the constituent structure of biological images, *Comput. Biomed. Res.* **4**, 1971, 315–328.
44. T. Kasvand, Iterative edge detection, *Comput. Graphics Image Process.* **4**, 1975, 279–286.
45. R. B. Eberlein and J. S. Weszka, Mixtures of derivative operators as edge detectors, *Comput. Graphics Image Process.* **4**, 1975, 180–183.
46. G. S. Robinson, Edge detection by compass gradient masks, *Comput. Graphics Image Process.* **6**, 1977, 492–501.
47. G. B. Shaw, Local and regional edge detectors: Some comparisons, *Comput. Graphics Image Process.* **9**, 1979, 135–149.
48. E. Mach, Uber die physiologische Wirkung raumlich vertheilter Lichtreize, IV, *Sitzungsber. Math. Naturwiss. Kl. Kais. Akad. Wiss.* **57**, 1868, 11–19.
49. F. Ratliff, *Mach Bands: Quantitative Studies on Neural Networks in the Retina*, Holden–Day, San Francisco, 1965.
50. C. Enroth-Cugell and J. G. Robson, Functional characteristics and diversity of cat retinal ganglion cells, *Invest. Ophthalmol. Visual Sci.* **25**, 1984, 250–267.
51. P. Letellier, M. Nadler, and J.-F. Abramatic, The telesign project, *Proc. IEEE* **73**, 1985, 813–827.
52. D. E. Pearson and J. A. Robinson, Visual communication at very low data rates, *Proc. IEEE* **73**, 1985, 795–812.
53. M. S. Landy, Y. Cohen and G. Sperling, HIPS: Image processing under Unix. Software applications, *Behav. Res. Methods, Instrum. Comput.* **16**, 1984, 199–216.
54. M. S. Landy, Y. Cohen, and G. Sperling, HIPS: A Unix-based image processing system, *Comput. Vision Graphics Image Process.* **25**, 1984, 331–347.
55. D. M. Ritchie and K. Thompson, The UNIX time-sharing system, *Bell Syst. Tech. J.* **57**, 1978, 1905–1929.
56. M. Pavel, G. Sperling, T. Riedl, and A. Vanderbeek, *The limits of visual communication: The effect of signal-to-noise ratio on the perception of American Sign Language*. New York University, Department of Psychology. Mathematical Studies in Perception and Cognition, **85–4**, 1985.
57. B. J. Winer, *Statistical Principles in Experimental Design* (2nd ed.), McGraw–Hill, New York, 1971.
58. C. E. Shannon and W. Weaver, *The Mathematical Theory of Communication*, Univ. of Illinois Press, Urbana, 1949.
59. M. S. Landy and Y. Cohen, Vectorgraph coding: Efficient coding of line drawings, *Comput. Vision Graphics Image Process.* **30**, 1985, 331–344.
60. T. Sakai, M. Nagao, and H. Matsushima, Extraction of invariant picture substructures by computer, *Comput. Graphics Image Process.* **1**, 1972, 81–96.
61. H. Freeman, Computer processing of line-drawing images, *Comput. Surveys* **6**, 1974, 57–97.
62. P. Suetens, P. Dierckx, R. Piessens, and A. Oosterlinck, A semiautomatic digitization method and the use of spline functions in processing line drawings, *Comput. Graphics Image Process.* **15**, 1981, 390–400.
63. T. Pavlidis, Technique for optimal compaction of pictures and maps, *Comput. Graphics Image Process.* **3**, 1974, 215–224.
64. D. Proffitt and D. Rosen, Metrication errors and coding efficiency of chain-encoding schemes for the representation of lines and edges, *Comput. Graphics Image Process.* **10**, 1979, 318–332.

65. T. H. Morrin, Chain-link compression of arbitrary black-white images, *Comput. Graphics Image Process.* **5**, 1976, 172–189.

66. U. Ramer, An iterative procedure for the polygonal approximation of plane curves, *Comput. Graphics Image Process.* **1**, 1972, 244–256.

67. Y. Cohen, M. S. Landy, and M. Pavel, Hierarchical coding of binary images, *IEEE Trans. Pattern Anal. Mach. Intell.* **PAM-7**, 1985, 284–298.

68. D. Meagher, Geometric modeling using octree encoding, *Comput. Graphics Image Process.* **19**, 1982, 129–147.

69. R. C. Gonzalez and P. Wintz, *Digital Image Processing*, Addison–Wesley, Reading, Mass., 1977.

70. D. L. Richards, *Telecommunication by Speech*, Wiley, New York, 1973.

71. K. D. Kryter, *The Effects of Noise on Man*, Academic Press, New York, 1970.

72. D. E. Pearson, Evaluation of feature-extracted images for deaf communication, *Electron. Lett.* **19**, 629–631.

73. T. V. Crater, The picturephone system: Service standards, *Bell Syst. Tech. J.* **50**, 1971, 235–269.

74. I. Dorros, The picturephone system: The network, *Bell Syst. Tech. J.* **50**, 1971, 221–233.

75. G. A. Gerrard and J. E. Thompson, Experimental differential PCM encoder-decoder for viewphone signals, *Radio Electron. Eng.* **43**, 1973, 201.

76. C. F. J. Hillen, The face to face telephone, *Post Off. Telecommun. J.* **24**, 1972, 4–7.

77. D. E. Pearson, *Transmission and Display of Pictorial Information*, Wiley, New York, 1975.

78. N. R. French and J. C. Steinberg, Factors governing the intelligibility of speech sounds, *J. Acoust. Soc. Amer.* **19**, 1947, 90–119.

79. N. S. Jayant and P. Noll, *Digital Coding of Waveforms: Principles and Applications to Speech and Video*, Prentice–Hall, Englewood Cliffs, N.J., 1984.

80. S. Roucos, R. M. Schwartz, and J. Makhoul, Segmentable vocoder at 150 b/s, in *Proc. Int. Congress on Acoustics & Signal Processing*, Boston, Mass., 1983, pp. 61–64.

81. D. Anastassious, M. K. Brown, H. C. Jones, J. L. Mitchell, W. B. Pennebaker, and K. S. Pennington, Series/1-based videoconferencing system, *IBM Syst. J.* **22**, 1983, 97–110.

Preattentive Processing in Vision

ANNE TREISMAN

University of British Columbia, Vancouver, British Columbia, Canada

Received January 14, 1985

Visual analysis appears to be functionally divided between an early preattentive level of processing at which simple features are coded spatially in parallel and a later stage at which focused attention is required to conjoin the separate features into coherent objects. Evidence supporting this dichotomy comes from behavioral studies of visual search, from differences in the ease of texture segregation, from reports of illusory conjunctions when attention is overloaded, from subjects' ability to identify simple features correctly even when they mislocate them, and from the substantial benefit of pre-cuing the location of a relevant item when the task requires that features be conjoined but not when simple features are sufficient. Some further studies of search have revealed a striking asymmetry between several pairs of stimuli which differ in the presence or absence of a single part or property. The asymmetry depends solely on which of the pair is allocated the role of target and which is replicated to form the background items. It suggests that search for the *presence* of a visual primitive is automatic and parallel, whereas search for the *absence* of the same feature is serial and requires focused attention. The search asymmetry can be used as an additional diagnostic to help define the functional features extracted by the visual system. © 1985 Academic Press, Inc.

Psychologists, perhaps other scientists too, tend to like dichotomies. We should, I suppose, be suspicious of this preference for simplification, but there does seem to be a striking one in the visual system, at least as a first approximation. Some discriminations appear to be made automatically, without attention and spatially in parallel across the visual field. Other visual operations require focused attention and can be performed only serially. These two kinds of visual processing have been attributed to different levels, originally by Neisser in 1967 [11]. He distinguished a stage at which simple features are preattentively registered, which determines texture segregation and figure ground grouping, from a second stage at which objects with their complex combinations of features are identified. In computational vision, a similar distinction has been drawn by a number of people, for example, between Marr's primal sketch and his model-based recognition [10], or between Barrow and Tenenbaum's intrinsic images [1], again followed by model-based recognition. This dichotomy is one starting point for the research that I will describe.

Another is the accumulating evidence, both physiological and psychological, that early stages of visual processing are analytic, that is, that they decompose the physical array of light along a number of separate dimensions. These seem to be mapped into different areas in the brain, each of which is specialized to analyze a different property; for example, neural units selectively responsive to particular orientations are found in one area, those responsive to stereo depth in another, those to color, movement, and so on in yet other functionally separate areas [6, 22, 4]. Differences in processing time may supplement differences in localization as evidence for specialized analysis. Thus, in humans, one can measure on the scalp evoked responses which pool the activity from populations of cells in different areas of the brain. By varying the discriminations required by the task and showing

313

different evoked response latencies, one can infer that some properties are extracted before others [13]. One can also demonstrate adaptation which is selective to particular properties. If one stares at a waterfall and then looks at the bank, it appears to flow in the opposite direction. This may reflect selective adaptation of detectors for a particular direction of movement, which respond independently of what is moving. The bank looks very different from the water in color and texture, but it still shows the aftereffects of movement. Finally, one can attend selectively to different attributes. For example, a speeded classification task in which cards must be sorted on the basis of color shows little interference from irrelevant variations in shape ([5]; see also [15] for a more detailed review of psychological evidence for feature analysis).

If we accept that there is some kind of early decomposition along different dimensions, we are confronted with two different problems for psychological research. One is to define which features or properties are the basic elements or visual primitives in this language of early vision. The second concerns how they are put together again into the correct combinations to form the coherent world that we perceive. I have been interested in both these questions. I will focus on two kinds of psychological evidence about early visual processing. The first is texture segregation. This is likely to reflect early stages of analysis because it is a prerequisite for figure ground separation which sets up the candidates for subsequent object recognition. The other source of evidence is visual search. Subjects are asked to look for a particular target in displays containing varying numbers of distractor items. If the target is defined by a simple visual feature, detection appears to result from parallel processing; the target "pops out" of the display regardless of how many distractors surround it. The spatially parallel processing suggests that the task depends on early vision, before the stage at which attention becomes involved. I will start with a brief discussion of evidence from texture segregation, and then devote most of the paper to some recent research using visual search to explore the nature and the limits of preattentive processing.

Texture segregation and grouping appear to reflect what Julesz [7] described as immediate, effortless perception, without scrutiny, of distinct areas in the visual field, the initial "parsing" of the world into the objects and backgrounds that may later be identified. Some time ago, Beck [2] showed that texture segregation is easy when it is based on simple properties such as color (a red area will segregate clearly from a green area); brightness (a dark area will segregate from a light one); and line orientation (an area containing tilted Ts segregates well from an area containing vertical Ts). However, if two areas differ only in line arrangements (one contains Ts and the other Ls), the boundary is much more difficult to detect. Beck suggested that texture segregation depends on features that are easily discriminable with peripheral vision and with distributed attention. More recently, Beck [3] also suggested that texture segregation results from a computation of local *differences*, which is performed automatically across the visual field. Any discontinuity where adjacent elements differ in one or more features sets up a boundary between adjacent regions.

Our experiments have confirmed that segregation is easy when areas differ in simple properties like shape and color (Figs. 1a and b), [16]. However, a boundary which is defined solely by a conjunction of properties (e.g., green triangles and red circles on the left and red triangles and green circles on the right), is much harder to find (Fig. 1c). Latencies to decide whether the boundary is vertical or horizontal are

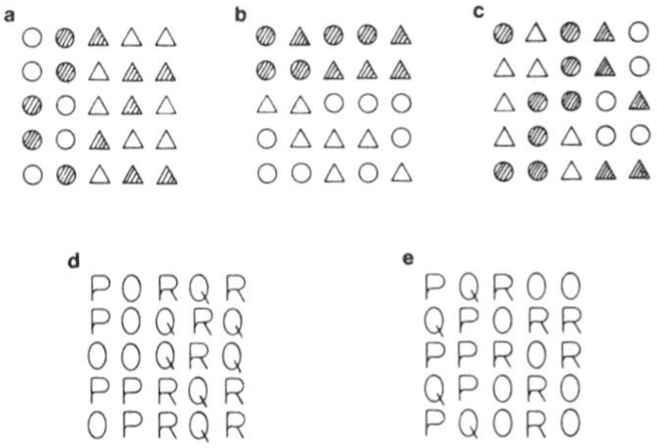

a
```
○ ⊘ ▲ △ △
○ ⊘ △ ▲ △
⊘ ○ △ ▲ △
⊘ ○ ▲ ▲ △
○ ⊘ △ ▲ ▲
```
b
```
⊘ △ ⊘ ⊘ ▲
⊘ ⊘ △ ▲ △
△ △ ○ ○ ○
○ △ △ △ ○
○ ○ △ ○ △
```
c
```
⊘ △ ⊘ ▲ ○
△ △ ⊘ ▲ ○
△ ⊘ ⊘ ○ △
△ ⊘ △ ○ ○
⊘ ⊘ △ ▲ ▲
```

d
```
P O R Q R
P O Q R Q
O O Q R Q
P P R Q R
O P R Q R
```
e
```
P Q R O O
Q P O R R
P P R O R
Q P O R O
P Q O R O
```

FIG. 1.   Examples of easy and of difficult texture segregation: (a) salient vertical boundary between circles (curved shapes) on left and triangles (straight and angular shapes) on right; (b) salient horizontal boundary between red shapes above and green shapes below; (c) no salient boundary between conjunctions of green triangles and red circles on left and green circles and red triangles on right; (d) salient vertical boundary between letters without diagonal line on left and letters with diagonal line on right; (e) no salient boundary between *P*s and *Q*s on left and *R*s and *O*s on right.

much slower than when either shape alone or color alone are sufficient to divide the display into discrete areas. Similar results hold with parts of shapes as well as with values on different dimensions. Segregation is easy, for example, when the boundary divides *P*s and *O*s from *R*s and *Q*s (Fig. 1d). The letters on one side have a diagonal slash whereas those on the other side do not. If the areas mix *P*s with *Q*s and *R*s with *O*s (Fig. 1e), there is no single distinguishing element, and texture segregation is again much harder. Some of our results, however, seem to conflict with Beck's suggestion that local differences are computed automatically, and that texture segregation depends on the detection of local boundaries only. For instance, if you look quickly at Fig. 2a you may miss the two odd items. On the other hand, if you look at their local contexts alone (Figs. 2b and c) without the surrounding groups, the odd ones are immediately salient. The "masking" effect depends on the presence elsewhere of other elements sharing the locally distinctive property; unique elements

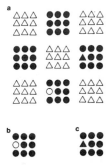

FIG. 2.   (a) Preattentive "masking" of locally salient items by the presence of their locally distinctive properties elsewhere in the display. Unless attention is directed to the relevant group, the odd items are likely to be missed. (b) and (c) the same items are immediately obvious when attention is restricted to their local context.

FIG. 3. Three groups are perceptually salient when defined by different features of shape in (a) and of color in (b), but the central group may be camouflaged preattentively, as in (c), when it shares one feature (color) with the group to the left and another feature (shape) with the group to the right.

are not masked in the same way. I ran an experiment showing that subjects scan each group serially when the locally different property is present elsewhere, but not when it is unique in the whole display [14]. The result seems inconsistent with the idea that local discontinuities are automatically detected.

Another demonstration may also cast doubt on the local processing suggestion: In Figs. 3a and b the immediate impression is of three different types of element, but if one looks quickly at Fig. 3c without focusing attention on the central column, one tends to see two groups rather than three. The central group shares one property with the group on the left and one property with the group on the right. When texture segregation depends only on preattentive processing, it seems to occur within a color representation or within a shape representation, but not within a global representation which combines both color and shape. If attention is distributed over the whole display, the central group is absorbed either into the white group or into the circles. At the preattentive level the white circles appear to have no independent and separate existence [14]. For Neisser [11], Beck [3], Marr [10], and Julesz [8], I believe that the spatially parallel, preattentive representation or primal sketch is a single representation, a global map showing the boundaries formed by any number of simple properties. For Julesz [8] the visual primitives that mediate texture segregation (which he calls "textons") include conjunctions of different dimensional values, such as "a vertical elongated red blob in a blue surround." The experiments I have described perhaps cast some doubt on these views, and suggest instead that several different representations may be set up preattentively within each dimension separately, and that they are accurately combined only at a later stage through focused attention. This view is more consistent with Barrow and Tenenbaum's idea [1] of separate intrinsic images, and with the modular organization that physiologists describe. Clearly the information from the different feature maps must be pooled before it reaches conscious awareness. Perhaps Beck's observations relate more to this level of integrated response of which we are subjectively aware; in this sense, his results are not necessarily incompatible with mine. However, when we overload or divert attention, the earlier stages of spatially parallel analysis seem to occur within separate representations for different dimensions.

The remainder of this paper will be concerned with visual search. If a single blue letter is embedded in a display of brown and green letters of other colors, it "pops out." Detection appears to be spatially parallel. There is no need to check each of the brown and green letters before the blue one can be found. Similarly, if a single curved letter (e.g., "S") is presented in a display of straight or angular letters (e.g., "X" and "T"), it is also immediately salient. But if the task is to find a target which conjoins two properties (e.g., green and T), each of which is present in other distractors (e.g., green "X"s and brown "T"s), the search is much more difficult.

Latencies increase linearly with the number of distractors, as if attention had to be focused on each item in turn [16]. The slope relating search time to display size (number of distractors) is twice as steep on trials where the target is absent as on trials where it is present, which suggests a serial self-terminating search. The area or visual angle of the display has little effect, provided that acuity limits are not exceeded. Kraus and I have shown more recently that linear search functions are also obtained with very brief displays in which eye movements would be ineffective. The serial scan appears to depend on movements of the "mind's eye" rather than (or as well as) movements of the physical eyes.

As a tentative conclusion, I suggest that parallel pop-out may be diagnostic of the presence of a unique feature which is analyzed in early vision. To link this idea with the hypothesis of multiple feature maps, we might hypothesize that pop-out occurs when the target produces activity in a separate feature map, which is unaffected by the distractors. The strategy would be to consult the particular feature map that uniquely responds to the target and, if there is any activity present, to respond "yes." Thus, when looking for a red target, you check the map for red and see if there is any activity there. On the other hand, if you are looking for a conjunction of properties, such as green and T among green distractors and T distractors, there is no uniquely activated feature map. Each item must be located and checked individually.

The role of attention can be tested more directly by giving subjects a cue in advance, which tells them where the target will occur if it is present at all. Now if attention is needed to detect conjunction targets, the precue should eliminate the serial checking phase. On the other hand, with targets defined by a single feature, the cue should have very little effect: separate features are registered in parallel anyway. We used displays like those in Fig. 4a containing shapes that varied in shape, size, color, and whether they were outline or filled. The target was defined either by a conjunction of properties, for example, a large brown outline triangle, or by a single property like red or large or outline. We precued the location at which the target

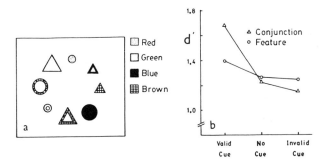

FIG. 4. (a) Example of a display of multi-dimensional stimuli used either for feature search or for conjunction search. The feature target for this display might be a red item and the conjunction target might be a large brown outline triangle. An advance cue, consisting of a bar marker outside the display pointing at the location to be occupied by one of the eight items, was given on most trials. (b) Mean accuracy (expressed as the signal detection measure d') in the different cue conditions for feature and for conjunction targets.

would occur if it was present at all, by flashing a pointer to that location 100 ms before presenting the display. The precue was valid on 75% of the trials on which the target occurred. It was invalid on 25% of trials: in these cases the target occurred somewhere other than cued location. On invalid trials attention would be directed to the wrong location rather than distributed across the whole display. An invalid cue should therefore give rise to costs rather than benefits relative to the condition with no cue. On 25% of trials no advance information was given about the target location, although a temporal warning signal was given to equate the general level of preparation. We matched the accuracy of performance for feature targets and for conjunction targets by presenting the display for a longer duration for the conjunction targets (though never more than 150 ms, to minimize the effect of eye movements). The question we asked was whether the effect of the cue would be greater for conjunction than for feature targets. Figure 4b shows the results: for conjunction targets, there was a substantial benefit from a valid cue, while for feature targets the cue had very little effect. In fact the whole improvement for feature targets with the valid cue was due to better detection of the small size target when it was precued. Small targets were missed more often when they were in invalid locations. Thus there appears to be little effect of attention when a target is defined by a single property, but there is a large effect of knowing where to attend when the target is defined by a conjunction of properties.

If attention is necessary for conjoining features, we should predict errors of conjunction when attention is divided or overloaded. The preattentive levels of early vision would represent only the presence of various features and not their interrelations. We briefly presented displays which contained a row of three colored letters in the middle and two black digits at each end of the array (see Fig. 5a; Treisman and Schmidt [18]). In order to ensure that attention would not be focused on any single letter, subjects were asked to report first the digits, and then any colored letters that they were reasonably sure they had seen. Subjects reported almost as many "illusory conjunctions" in which the color of one letter was recombined with the shape of another as they did correct conjunctions. Some of these conjunction errors were made with high confidence and appeared to be genuine perceptual illusions. Does the occurrence of illusory conjunctions of shape

FIG. 5. (a) Example of displays used to demonstrate the occurrence of illusory conjunctions when attention cannot be focused on each letter in turn. If solid letters were blue, outline letters green and speckled red, then subjects, given this display, might report, for example, a blue T or a red X. (b) Example of displays used to investigate possible similarity constraints on illusory conjunctions. Subjects were as likely to attribute the color of the large filled triangle to the small outline circle as to attribute to it the color of the small outline triangle (or even of another small outline circle, when two were included in the display).

and color depend on how similar the stimuli are on other dimensions? For example, are subjects more likely to switch colors between two small outline triangles, because they are the same shape, size and style, than to switch colors between a small, blue, outline circle and a large, red, filled triangle (see Fig. 5b)? If the color is represented in a wholistic, analog form which preserves the quantity and the spatial distribution of the color as well as the hue, saturation, and lightness, one might expect fewer exchanges to occur when they would violate these constraints. In fact, it seems that subjects are quite happy to fill in, for example, whatever amount of blue is necessary to represent the shape, size, and style they have coded as belonging with it. It is as if, when attention is overloaded or divided, the presence of one or more values on each dimension is coded separately and categorically; the codes are then combined, whether correctly or incorrectly, and consciously experienced in whatever form fits the set of specified codes. If the color blue is assigned to a large, filled triangle, then the amount and the spatial distribution of the blue will be appropriate to that set of descriptions.

The final evidence suggesting that features are preattentively detected without being conjoined whereas conjunctions require attention comes from an analysis of interdependencies between the accuracy of target identification and the accuracy of target localization. If we do conjoin only by attending to an object, we should be forced to locate a conjunction target in order to identify it correctly, whereas this would not be necessary for a feature target. Subjects were shown displays like those in Fig. 6 and were asked both to identify the target and to say where it was [16]. In the feature task, they had to decide on each trial whether there was an orange letter or an H. In the conjunction task they had to decide whether there was a blue O or a red X. We analyzed the conditional probability that the identity was correct given that the location was wrong. We expected this probability to be above chance for feature targets, and it was. Thus subjects could sometimes tell correctly that there was an orange letter in the display while mislocating it by two or more squares. For conjunction targets, on the other hand, correct identification was completely dependent on correct localization, as it should be if attention must be focused on a location in order correctly to combine the features it contains.

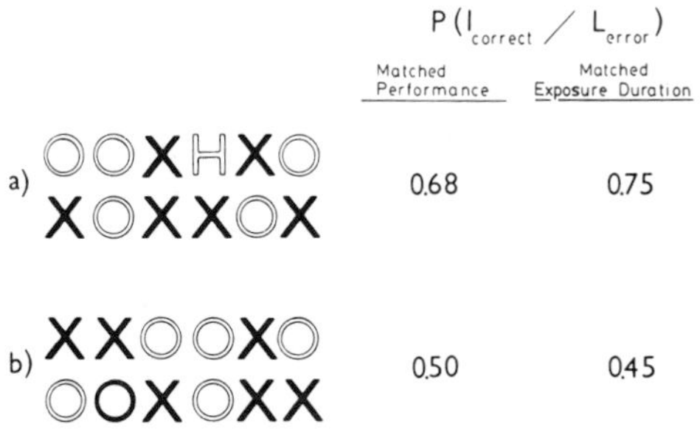

$$P\left(I_{correct} \Big/ L_{error}\right)$$

	Matched Performance	Matched Exposure Duration
a) OOXHXO XOXXOX	0.68	0.75
b) XXOOXO OOXOXX	0.50	0.45

FIG. 6. Examples of displays used to investigate the dependence of accurate identification on accurate localization. (a) The target was either an H or an orange letter (among red and blue distractors). Forced choice identification was significantly better than chance even when the target was mislocalized by more than one position in any direction. (b) The target was either a red O or a blue X (among blue O and red X distractors). These targets differ from the distractors only in the way their properties are conjoined. Forced choice identification was at chance when localization was incorrect.

It seems, then, that information about features can be "free-floating" or inde-terminate in location, but information about conjunctions is available only through accurate localization. If attention is over-loaded, free-floating features may recom-bine at random when their associations were originally arbitrary. In a natural scene, of course, many conjunctions are ruled out by our prior knowledge. We seldom come across blue bananas or furry eggs. There are top-down constraints which may prevent us from seeing too many conjunction illusions in everyday life.

The remainder of this paper will describe our current attempts, so far unpub-lished, to discover more about the features that form the functional elements in the language of early vision. The visual system is likely to have developed ways of detecting structure in the real world, the regularities that are non-accidental because they are caused by physical objects. Surfaces in the real world tend to be homoge-neous rather than randomly colored or textured; lines, curves, or boundaries are continuous; edges are often parallel; texture gradients change smoothly within objects and discontinuously between objects or between object and ground. Witkin and Tenenbaum [21] suggest that vision scientists should look for "an alphabet soup of descriptive chunks that are almost certain to have some fairly direct semantic interpretation." The experiments I have described so far used uncontroversial properties like orientation and color which are almost certain to be separately coded. I used these to identify a set of behavioral "symptoms" that these features are likely to show in perceptual tasks. They mediate effortless texture segregation; they allow "pop-out" or parallel search when a single feature is present to define the target; they may recombine to form illusory conjunctions; they can be identified without being accurately localized. We can now try to use symptoms from this feature syndrome both to define more precisely the features we have already classified, such as orientation, and also to discover or diagnose new features which are more theoretically controversial. For example, we can use behavioral tests to help de-termine whether closure is a perceptual feature or not.

In the next experiment, I used the different pattern of results expected in feature and in conjunction search to explore how the visual system codes orientation. Is the same representation formed for the orientation of solid lines and for the orientation of dot pairs, or are there different codes for orientation depending on the nature of the carrier? Marr [10] suggested that vision "goes symbolic" at an early stage; that orientation, for example, is coded abstractly as the orientation of a "virtual" line whose ends can be marked by any kind of discontinuity or change in intensity. If that is the case, the same symbolic code may be used by the visual system to represent the orientation of dot pairs and of lines. We have seen that orientation is separable from color. The question now is whether orientation is integral with the substance that carries it or whether it is also separable from its carrier.

The test we devised was to look for evidence of conjunction problems in a search task, which would suggest that the visual system uses interchangeable codes for line orientation and dot orientation. Subjects searched in one condition for a target line tilted right among distractor lines that were tilted left (see Fig. 7a). In another condition they searched for a tilted line amongst dot pairs that were tilted in the same direction (see Fig. 7b). In both conditions the target "popped out" regardless of the number of distractors (see Figs. 8a and b). Thus we have evidence that both the orientation of lines and the difference between lines and dot pairs are preatten-tively discriminable, separate features. In the critical condition, the target was

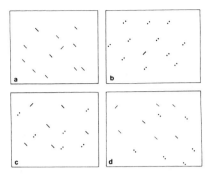

FIG. 7. Examples of displays used to test the nature of the code used for orientation. In (a) and (b) the target differs from the distractors in a single feature (line orientation and line versus dot, respectively); in (c) the target differs only in the conjunction of orientation with carrier (line versus dot). (d) Control condition to see whether mixed line and dot displays are inherently more difficult. In each case the target is a line tilted to the right.

defined by the conjunction of an orientation and a carrier; subjects searched for a tilted line among dot pairs tilted in the same direction and lines tilted in the opposite direction (see Fig. 7c). If the same representation is used for the orientation of dot pairs and of lines, we would expect search to be serial, as in fact it appears to be (see Fig. 8c). A control condition, using both dots and lines but with the target line orientation unique did not show the same effect of display size (see Figs. 7d and 8d), so the difficulty of the conjunction condition does not simply reflect the fact that the mixture of dots and lines is confusing.

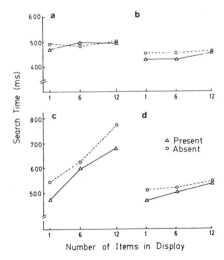

FIG. 8. Search times to decide whether the target was present or absent in displays like those shown in Figs. 7a to d: (a) Line orientation; (b) line versus dots; (c) conjunction; (d) control. The target pops out in every case except the conjunction search, where the latency appears to reflect serial item by item checking at the rate of about 20 ms per item.

The result is consistent with Marr's suggestion that orientation is coded abstractly, in the sense that a common representation is used for the orientation of dot pairs and of target lines. However, this abstraction could still be implemented by cells with oriented receptive fields, like those described by Hubel and Wiesel [6]. The activity from the two dots would be pooled if both fell within a receptive field and could activate the cell in the same way as an oriented line. In order to test this possibility, we will repeat the experiment using black and white dot pairs on a grey background to see whether orientation is abstracted even if the two dots contrast in opposite directions from the background. Simple cells would not respond to dot pairs of opposite contrast; their effects would cancel out. But Marr's place-markers should be established in the same way as for two black dots.

We looked next at other possible visual primitives. I have suggested that pop-out may be mediated by activity in separate feature maps. The idea is that we access directly a pooled response for each feature map—for example, a map for red, a map for vertical, a map for movement to the right. The pooled response would tell us whether there is activity in a given map, and perhaps also how much activity there is, but it would not tell us where it is, nor how it is arranged spatially, nor how it relates to activity in other maps. We can think of the visual system coding a certain number of simple and useful properties (not too many one hopes), which are separately detected and represented in orderly arrays. The properties may be ordered systematically across a stack of maps, coding continuously changing orientations in one 3-dimensional cube, color in another, the direction of movement in another. These maps, the physiologists tell us, are usually spatiotopic [4]; they do preserve spatial relations. However, the spatial information may not be directly accessible in parallel. In particular, the spatial information which links one map to another may be accessed only through a serial scan. In Fig. 9, I show the serial scan as controlled through links to a single master map of locations, in which the presence of any discontinuities in intensity or color is registered without specifying what the discontinuities are. Focused attention acts through this master map, simultaneously selecting, through its links to all the separate feature maps all the features that are currently present in the selected location. This would be one mode of perceptual processing—the focused attention mode, which automatically retrieves and conjoins all features currently in the spatially limited attention spotlight, and does this serially for each object in turn.

In addition, I suggest that, independently of attention, each feature map also directly signals the presence of its particular feature, but without specifying where it is. There could be some kind of pooled signal conveying the information that, for example, red is present in the scene, in small or large amounts, at any given moment. The pooled response loses position information; it is equivalent to a simple form of Hough transform. It may tell us how much red is present, provide a means of linking separate areas sharing the same color, and also help to direct attention to the locations in the master map that are linked to a currently salient or relevant feature.

This is certainly a crude framework, but it does predict an interesting phenomenon. There should be a marked asymmetry between search for the *presence* of a feature and search for the *absence* of the same feature. Beck [3] reports such an asymmetry for long lines in a background of short lines and for complete triangles in a background of incomplete triangles compared to the inverse displays. He attributes the asymmetries to differences in discriminability in peripheral vision with distrib-

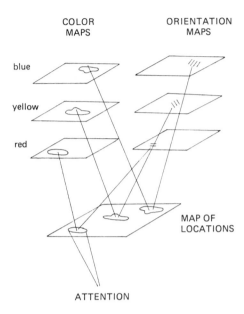

COLOR
MAPS

ORIENTATION
MAPS

blue

yellow

red

MAP OF
LOCATIONS

ATTENTION

FIG. 9.   General framework relating hypothesized feature maps within and across dimensions to a master map of locations, through which focused attention serially conjoins the properties of different objects in the scene.

uted attention—a kind of masking by neighboring stimuli which affects shorter more than longer lines. The prediction can be derived more directly from the framework proposed above. Suppose that the target has feature "χ" and the distractors do not. For example, the target is a circle with a vertical slash across it and the distractors are regular circles. Now in order to decide whether the target is present, one could simply check categorically whether there is activity in a feature map for a straight line (or for vertical orientation, or for any other feature that characterizes the slash but not the circles). Now suppose that all the distractors have the feature "χ" and the target does not; in this case, there is no feature map which will tell one whether the target is present or not. The only difference between the effects of displays containing the target and displays without it would be a slight reduction in activity in the feature maps coding the slash when the target was present compared to when it was absent. So when the target was the circle without the slash, subjects might be forced to scan serially with focused attention in order to find the one circle that did not have a slash. On the other hand, if the target was the single circle with the slash, its presence would be signalled by the presence of activity in the relevant feature map or maps. We tested this prediction [19], using circles with and without slashes as a clear example of feature presence or absence (see Fig. 10). As predicted, we found a very large asymmetry, shown in Fig. 11. Search appears to be serial for the circle without a slash among circles with slashes, while search is parallel for the circle with a slash among circles without. Notice that this is a somewhat strange and counter-intuitive prediction, because the same discrimination between the same two stimuli is involved in each case. One might think that the only relevant factor would be how

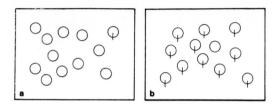

FIG. 10. Examples of displays used to test the efficiency of search for a target defined by the presence or by the absence of a single feature. The target in (a) is a circle with an intersecting vertical line. The target in (b) is a circle without an intersecting line.

discriminable the circle with a slash is from a circle without a slash; but in fact, performance looks completely different in the two cases. The result is consistent with the idea of a pooled signal conveying the presence but not the absence of a distinctive feature.

We can now apply this test to other hypothetical features to see which pop out when they are present but not when they are absent. Note that the primitives extracted by the visual system need not (and in fact are unlikely to) correspond to the simple dimensions defined by physicists. The relevant features are those that best characterize objects and surfaces in the real world. These may be relational or "emergent" features, created by the combinations or arrangements of components. They would nevertheless be directly coded by specialized functional detectors at the preattentive level (see [12]). We tried a number of different candidates. We did find

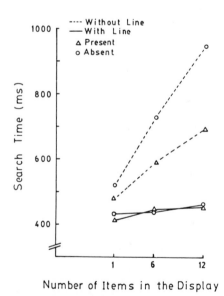

Number of Items in the Display

FIG. 11. Search times for displays like those shown in Fig. 10. Search appears to be parallel for the presence of the intersecting line and serial for its absence.

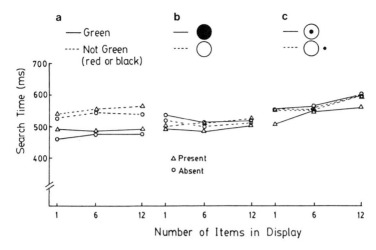

FIG. 12. Search times for targets defined by (a) color (green vs not green), (b) filled vs outline shape, and (c) inside vs outside dot. In each case the roles of targets and distractors were reversed in the paired condition. Search appeared to be unaffected (or hardly affected) by the number of distractors in all these tasks, suggesting that all six targets are characterized by a preattentively detectable feature which is absent from the distractors.

pop-out for filled versus outline circles (see Fig. 12a); however, we also found it for outline versus filled circles. No asymmetry was present, suggesting that both are coded preattentively as visual primitives. We found pop-out for blue among green distractors and also for green among blue (see Fig. 12b). Again, both colors are presumably coded as separate features. We tested the supposedly more abstract property of "inside" versus "outside." Ullman [20] has suggested that this distinc-

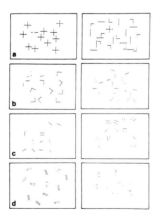

FIG. 13. Examples of displays used to test search for targets defined by the arrangement or number of straight lines: (a) The target was in one case a plus and in the other case a separate line; (b) the target was in one case a right angle and in the other two separated orthogonal lines; (c) the target was in one case a pair of parallel lines and in the other a single line; (d) the target was in one case a pair of parallel lines and in the other a pair of converging lines.

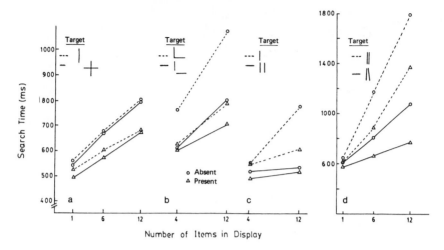

FIG. 14.   Search times for displays like those shown in Fig. 13. None of the targets appears to "pop out" of the displays, except the pair of parallel lines among separate single lines: (a) intersection; (b) juncture; (c) number (one vs two); (d) parallel vs converging.

tion is difficult to extract computationally; however, it appears not to be hard for people, at least in the form in which we tested it. We used a circle containing a central dot contrasting with a circle with one dot at the same distance from the circumference but outside the circle. Both targets popped out independently of display size (see Fig. 12c). However, the uniformity of the container shapes may make this a special case of the inside–outside distinction—one which possesses an additional emergent feature. The bull's eye pattern might even be innately coded as part of a facial recognition system. A better test of the inside–outside discrimination would use varied shapes as containers and various dot positions within the shapes. We are now exploring this version of the inside–outside distinction.

Next we tried some features which may characterize line arrangements. The first was intersection, using displays such as those in Fig. 13a. Notice that the stimuli without intersections shared as many other properties with the intersecting lines (the plus) as possible; in particular we removed the cue of global size which could have been used if the only stimuli were a plus and an "L" or "T" with lines of the same length as the plus. We did not find pop-out for intersection (see Fig. 14a). There was no asymmetry in search latencies and search appeared to be serial in both cases. Julesz and Bergen [9] suggested that intersection is a preattentive feature (or "texton"). However, texture discrimination in their displays could have been mediated by the global outline of the shapes; the pluses were more compact than the "L"s and this may have been preattentively detected.

Another potential feature formed by the arrangement of lines is juncture. If two lines are joined to form a right angle, as opposed to separated (see Fig. 13b), would either the joined or the separate pairs pop out as a target among distractors? The answer is no: we did find an asymmetry, but neither target popped out. The joined lines gave slower search rates than the unjoined lines, but in both cases there was a substantial effect of the number of distractors (see Fig. 14b). Next, we looked at

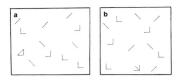

FIG. 15.   Examples of displays used to test search for a triangle in (a) and an arrow in (b). The triangle pops out of the display while the arrow, for many subjects, appears to require serial search.

Julesz's suggestion [8] that the preattentive system can "count" or discriminate numbers at least up to four or five. The two stimuli we tested were a single line versus a pair of parallel lines (see Fig. 13c). We found a clear asymmetry (see Fig. 14c). The pair of lines pops out in a background of single lines, but the single line does not when embedded among pairs. It seems, unlikely, however, that the discrimination depends on counting, since the number one should be as discriminable from two as two is from one. It is possible that the pair of lines creates another "emergent" feature; two possible candidates might be parallelism and a form of "closure" in the sense of a partly enclosed space. The single lines possess no emergent feature relative to the paired lines and search is therefore serial. Finally, to distinguish whether the pairs pop out because they are parallel or because they form a partly enclosed area, we tested search with pairs of lines that were either parallel or converging (see Fig. 13d). Neither type of target popped out, although there was an asymmetry (see Fig. 14d). Serial search for the converging lines was faster than serial search for the parallel lines.

Closure is an interesting and controversial feature. Most subjects show good pop-out for a triangle in a background of angles and lines, but not for an arrow, made up of the same component lines ([17]; see Fig. 15). The triangle contains an enclosed space surrounded by a connected contour, and we attributed the parallel detection to the presence of this emergent feature, which is absent both from the angles and lines and from the arrows. Julesz (personal communication) suggested as an alternative possibility that triangle pop-out is mediated by the absence of line ends or terminators rather than by closure. The arrow, on the other hand, has three terminators and therefore differs less than the triangle from the right angle and line distractors, which each have two. Julesz and Bergen [9] tested texture segregation with stimuli like those in Fig. 16 and found no salient preattentive boundary, despite the presence of closure on one side of the display. Clearly, further experiments were needed.

The test we devised was to use circles with and without gaps [19]. The gaps produce line ends which are absent from closed circles. Subjects were asked to search for a target that was either a complete circle in a background of circles with gaps or a circle with a gap in a background of complete circles. We varied discriminability by making the gap larger or smaller, so that it was $\frac{1}{8}$, $\frac{1}{4}$, or $\frac{1}{2}$ the circumference. We predicted that if closure is a feature, it should mediate good pop-out for the complete circle targets. Similarly if line ends are features, we predict pop-out for the circles with gaps. Figure 17 shows examples of all the displays. The results were very clear and quite unexpected. There was a large asymmetry in search latencies (see Fig. 18): circles with gaps pop out and closed circles do not. Another interesting point to note is that there was no effect of discriminability when the target was the circle with

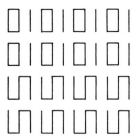

FIG. 16. Example of stimuli used by Julesz and Bergen [9] to test texture segregation based on closure. The boundary is not immediately apparent, suggesting that closure is not preattentively detected.

a gap. Either line ends are present or they are not; their separation does not matter (once they are above the acuity threshold). On the other hand, if the target is a connected circle, the size of the gap makes a large difference. The asymmetry suggests that performance is controlled by a different feature in the two different target conditions. If subjects are looking for a closed circle, the degree of closure matters; if they are looking for terminators, their presence is determined categorically. Julesz was right that closure, in the sense of a connected contour with no gap, is not (by this test) a categorically detected feature at the preattentive level. On the other hand, the absence of terminators does not allow pop-out, so Julesz's explanation for our triangle data was probably wrong. Triangles must have some other distinctive feature differentiating them from angles and lines; or perhaps they have closure by a different definition, where it means not connectedness but some sort of "blobness" or convex surround, where the closure can vary in degree (Rosenfeld, personal communication). The circles with gaps are closed (by this definition) to different degrees. Like the completely closed target, they activate the feature map for closure when they are the distractors, but they do so quantitatively less than the complete closed circle.

Another controversial feature is curvature. Neurophysiologists have not yet reported cells which respond selectively to curvature, but they may not have looked

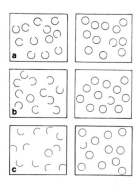

FIG. 17. Examples of displays used to test search for targets defined either by a connected contour (closure) in the displays on the left, or by a gap (line ends) in the displays on the right; (a), (b), and (c) differ in the size of the gap.

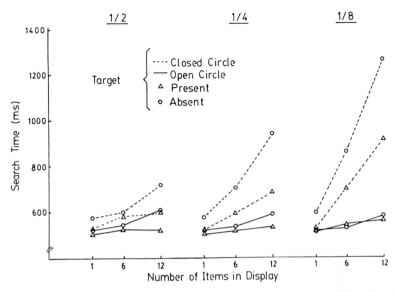

FIG. 18. Search times for complete circles and for circles with gaps in displays like those shown in Fig. 17. The size of the gap was half the circumference, or one quarter, or one eighth. The closed circle appears in each case to require serial search, although the rate varies with gap size, while the open circle with a gap usually pops out.

systematically for them. Behaviorally, we can ask whether curves pop out of straight line distractors, or whether straight lines pop out of curves. It is sometimes suggested that curves are coded as conjunctions of straight lines with changing orientations. If this were correct, they should not pop out of lines in mixed orientations like those in Fig. 19. But in fact, these displays gave another surprising result. There was a large asymmetry which favored curves as the visual primitives, rather than straight lines

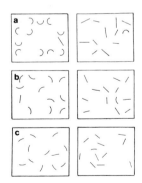

FIG. 19. Examples of displays used to test search for a straight line and for a curved line. The curves in (a)–(c) differ in degree of curvature and therefore in discriminability from the straight line targets or distractors. The target in the displays on the left is a straight line and the target in the displays on the right is a curved line.

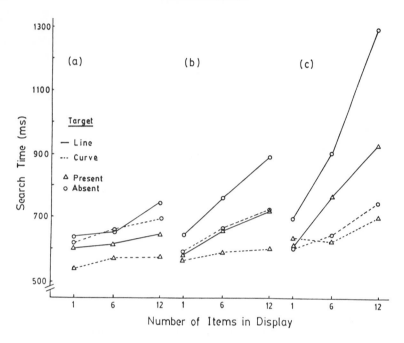

FIG. 20.   Search times for displays like those shown in Fig. 19. Curved targets appear to pop out of displays of straight lines, but straight line targets require serial checking to find them in displays of curved lines. Conditions (a)–(c) differ in the degree of curvature of the curves.

(see Fig. 20). Again there was a large effect of discriminability (in this case the degree of curvature) when the target was a straight line, but much less when the target was a curve. If we apply the presence/absence diagnostic for visual primitives, then we would have to infer that straightness is coded not as a positive feature, preattentively detected by the visual system, but simply as the absence of curvature. In other words, it might be the neutral point on the curvature dimension, while curves (or departures from straightness) are what the nervous system detects.

Line orientation is an obvious candidate for a visual primitive, and we showed earlier that it can mediate pop-out. In this case, there is considerable physiological evidence for early coding [6]. Beck [2] showed long ago that orientation mediates easy texture segregation. We would therefore expect pop-out for any target and distractor pair that activate differently tuned orientation channels, and we would not expect any search asymmetry. We tested subjects with vertical targets among tilted lines and tilted targets among vertical lines (see Fig. 21a) and again obtained a surprising result (see Fig. 22a). The tilted line pops out, and the vertical line does not. Again, the presence/absence logic would suggest that the tilted lines have a feature that is preattentively coded and the vertical lines do not. Perhaps vertical, like straight, is coded as a neutral point on the orientation dimension, simply as the absence of tilt.

Perhaps, however, another explanation is possible. Rather than the target being the one item that is identified, perhaps the visual system encodes the whole display,

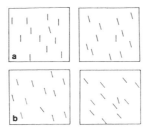

FIG. 21.   Examples of displays used to test search for a target line differing from the distractor lines in orientation. (a) The target is a tilted line among vertical distractors on the left and a vertical line among tilted distractors on the right. (b) The target is a line that is more tilted than the distractors on the left and less tilted than the distractors on the right.

so that the ease or difficulty of search is determined more by the nature of the distractors than by the nature of the target. It may be the fact that all the distractors are vertical and not the fact that the target is tilted that makes the tilted target easier to detect. Similarly, the displays with the curved target could be easy because all the distractors are straight lines rather than because the target is a curved line. We tested this account of the orientation results by trying a search task which did not involve vertical lines. All the lines were tilted and the target was either more or less tilted than the distractors (see Fig. 21b). Neither of these conditions should give pop-out if parallel processing depends on the distractors being vertical; but in fact they both do

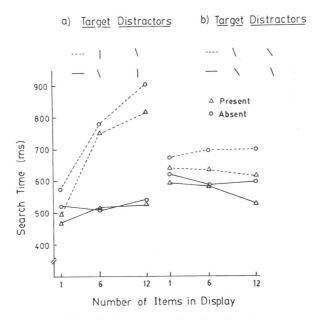

FIG. 22.   Search times for displays like those shown in Fig. 21. (a) The tilted target appears to pop out of displays of vertical lines, but the vertical target among tilted distractors does not. (b) Both the more tilted and the less tilted target pop out of tilted distractors.

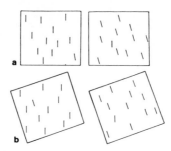

FIG. 23. Examples of displays used to test search for vertical or tilted targets in displays (a) with a vertical frame, or (b) with a tilted frame. The target is a tilted line in the displays on the left and a vertical line in the displays on the right.

(see Fig. 22b). The difficulty, therefore, does seem to arise when the target has the standard value rather than when the distractors do not.

Can we further define the nature of this standard value in the case of orientation? Is it vertical on the retina, or vertical with respect to the surrounding framework, which was a vertical and horizontal aperture in the tachistoscope? We tested this by putting an additional outline frame, which was either vertical or tilted, around the displays (see Fig. 23b). If the difficulty arises when the target matches the frame, we would expect the tilted target to be difficult to find in the tilted frame. On the other hand, if the difficulty arises when the target is vertical on the retina, the frame should make no difference. The results showed a large effect of the frame (see Fig. 24); there may in addition have been an effect of retinal (or gravitational) vertical, which reduced the effect of the frame, but the main difficulty in both cases arose when the target orientation matched the frame. The relevant codes determining performance seem, then, to be relative ones rather than those activating a particular subset of physiological feature detectors. Search is controlled by further operations relating different populations of feature detectors, and not by a single cell shouting! We certainly suspected this; pop-out in search cannot be used as a psychological electrode inserted in single cells of the various visual areas. We are exploring the perceptual properties that are extracted from patterns of activity across different populations of cells, the functional codes that are presumably produced by combining the responses of many units.

Very briefly, what conclusions seem to emerge from these search experiments? I think they are consistent with the idea that early visual analysis results in separate maps for separate properties, and that these maps pool their activity across locations, allowing rapid access to information about the presence of a target, when it is the only item characterized by a particular preattentively detectable feature. Second, the pop-out test has so far uncovered rather few such features, which, I think, is encouraging. We would not want to assume that there are hundreds of visual primitives, each of which is separately represented in a map in the brain. Color, brightness, line ends or terminators, blobness or closure (in the sense of convexity), tilt and curvature appear to be among the visual primitives, whereas our data cast some doubt on other candidates such as intersection, juncture, number and connectedness. Several properties seem to be coded relative to one or more neutral

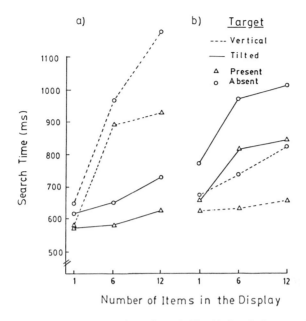

FIG. 24. Search times for displays like those shown in Fig. 23. Search times are slower when the target orientation matches the frame rather than when the target orientation is vertical. (a) Frame vertical. (b) Frame tilted.

points; deviations are signalled whereas the standard is not; we code curved not straight, and tilted not vertical. Finally, coding may be relative rather than absolute, as suggested by the frame effect on the vertical and tilted targets. The main contribution of this research may be to add some converging operations to other psychological methods of exploring early preattentive vision and of deciphering the elementary codes of perception.

ACKNOWLEDGMENTS

This research was supported by a grant from the National Scientific and Engineering Research Council of Canada. The author holds a fellowship from the Canadian Institute of Advanced Research. Thanks are due to Daniel Kahneman for helpful criticism and suggestions, and to Hilary Schmidt, Janet Souther, and Stephen Gormican who collaborated in running many of the experiments. Requests for reprints should be addressed to Anne Treisman, Department of Psychology, University of British Columbia, 2136 West Mall, Vancouver, British Columbia, Canada V6T 1Y7.

REFERENCES

1. H. G. Barrow and J. M. Tenenbaum, Recovering intrinsic scene characteristics from images, in *Computer Vision Systems* (A. Hanson and E. Riseman, Eds.), Academic Press, New York, 1978.
2. J. Beck, Perceptual grouping produced by line figures, *Percept. Psychophys.* **2**, 1967, 491–495.
3. J. Beck, Textural segmentation, in *Organization and Representation in Perception* (J. Beck, Ed.), Erlbaum, Hillsdale, N.J., 1982.
4. A. Cowey, Cortical maps and visual perception, The Grindley Memorial Lecture, *Q. J. Exp. Psych.* **31**, 1979, 1–17.

5. W. R. Garner, *The Processing of Information and Structure*, Erlbaum, Potomac, Md., 1974.
6. D. H. Hubel and T. N. Wiesel, Receptive fields and functional characteristics of monkey striate cortex, *J. Physiol.* **195**, 1968, 215–243.
7. B. Julesz, Experiments in the visual perception of texture, *Sci. Amer.* **232**, 1975, 34–43.
8. B. Julesz, Toward an axiomatic theory of preattentive vision, in *Dynamic Aspects of Neocortical Function* (G. Edelman, M. Cowan, and E. Gall, Eds.), Wiley, New York, 1984.
9. B. Julesz and J. R. Bergen, Textons, the fundamental elements in preattentive vision and perception of textures, *Bell Syst. Tech. J.* **62**, 1983, 1619–1645.
10. D. Marr, *Vision: A Computational Investigation into the Human Representation and Processing of Visual Information*, Freeman, San Francisco, 1982.
11. U. Neisser, *Cognitive Psychology*, Appleton–Century–Crofts, New York, 1967.
12. J. R. Pomerantz, L. C. Sager and R. G. Stoever (1977). Perception of wholes and their component parts: Some configural superiority effects, *J. Exp. Psychol. Human Percept. Perform.* **3**, 1977, 422–435.
13. V. L. Towle, M. R. Harter, and F. H. Previc, Binocular interaction of orientation and spatial frequency channels: Evoked potentials and observer sensitivity, *Percept. Psychophys.* **27**, 1980, 351–360.
14. A. Treisman, Perceptual grouping and attention in visual search for features and for objects, *J. Exp. Psychol. Human Percept. Perform.* **8**, 1982, 194–214.
15. A. Treisman, Properties, parts, and objects, *Handbook of Perception and Human Performance* (K. Boff, L. Kaufman, and J. Thomas, Eds.), Wiley, New York, 1985.
16. A. Treisman and G. Gelade, A feature integration theory of attention, *Cognit. Psychol.* **12**, 1980, 97–136.
17. A. Treisman and R. Paterson, Emergent features, attention and object perception. *J. Exp. Psychol. Human Percept. Perform.* **10**, 1984, 12–31.
18. A. Treisman and H. Schmidt, Illusory conjunctions in the perception of objects, *Cognit. Psychol.* **14**, 1982, 107–141.
19. A. Treisman and J. Souther, Search asymmetry: A diagnostic for preattentive processing of separable features. *J. Exp. Psychol. General*, 1985, in press.
20. S. Ullman, Visual routines, *Cognition* **18**, 1984, 97–159.
21. A. P. Witkin and J. M. Tenenbaum, On the role of structure in vision, in *Human and Machine Vision* (J. Beck, B. Hope, and A. Rosenfeld, Eds.), Academic Press, New York, 1983.
22. S. M. Zeki, The mapping of visual functions in the cerebral cortex, in *Brain Mechanisms of Sensation* (Y. Katsuki, R. Norgren, and M. Sato, Eds.), Wiley, New York, 1981.

Early Orientation Selection: Tangent Fields and the Dimensionality of Their Support

Computer Vision and Robotics Laboratory, Department of Electrical Engineering,
McGill University, Montréal, Québec, Canada

Received May 7, 1985; revised May 15, 1985

Orientation selection is the inference of orientation information out of images. It is one of
the foundations on which other visual structures are built, since it must precede the formation
of contours out of pointillist data and surfaces out of surface markings. We take a differential
geometric view in defining orientation selection, and develop algorithms for actually doing it.
The goal of these algorithms is formulated in mathematical terms as the inference of a vector
field of tangents (to the contours), and the algorithms are studied in both abstract and
computational forms. They are formulated as matching problems, and algorithms for solving
them are reduced to biologically plausible terms. We show that two different matching
problems are necessary, the first for 1-dimensional contours (which we refer to as Type I
processes) and the second for 2-dimensional flows (or Type II processes). We conjecture that
this difference is reflected in the response properties of "simple" and "complex" cells,
respectively, and predict several other psychophysical phenomena. © 1985 Academic Press, Inc.

CONTENTS. 1. *Introduction*. 1.1. Occluding contours and surface markings. 1.2. The fox and
the forest. 1.3. Two structural classes. 2. *The Framework*. 2.1. Generalization of the framework.
3. *Static and Dynamic Flows*. 4. *Tangents, Vector Fields, and the Recovery of Contours*. 5.
Outline of a Model for Orientation Selection. 6. *Dot Patterns and the Geometry of Orientation
Selection*. 7. *A Model for Early Orientation Selection and Grouping*. 7.1. What is a curve? 7.2.
Estimating the tangent. 7.3. Orientation estimation for straight lines. 7.4. The curvature
constraint. 8. *Response Matching Problems and Functional Minimization*. 8.1. From functional
minimization to cooperative network. 9. *Results of the Orientation Selection Algorithm*. 10.
Predictions. 10.1. Prediction 1: The size/spacing constraint. 10.2. Prediction 2: Dot positioning
effects. 11. *From contours to hair patterns*. 12. *Type I and Type II Processes*. 13. *Estimating
Tangents in Type II Patterns*. 14. *The Difference Between Type I and Type II Processes*. 14.1.
Vector fields and flows. 14.2. The dimensionality difference between Type I and Type II
processes. 15. *Psychophysical Predictions for Type II Patterns*. 15.1. Prediction 3: Orientation
change sensitivity in Type II patterns. 16. *Simple and Complex Cells*. 17. *Conclusions*. 18.
References

1. INTRODUCTION

Function within our visual systems has evolved to reflect, at least in part, ecologically relevant aspects of the structure of the physical world. Perhaps the most salient of these structures is orientation, whose importance is underlined by the fact that a major fraction of the visual systems in primates are somehow involved in analyzing it. Orientation is clearly essential for inferring contours, as they arise from creases, occlusions, and any number of other distinct physical situations. It also plays an intimate role in inferring (descriptions of) other kinds of physical structures. We therefore begin this paper with an examination of physical structures rich in orientation information—including flow patterns such as wheat fields and hair coverings as well as contours—and note how their structure is reflected in images. Our immediate goal is to discover whether these physical structures map into

335

HUMAN AND MACHINE VISION II

Copyright © 1985 by Academic Press, Inc.
All rights of reproduction in any form reserved.
ISBN 0-12-597345-5

well-defined classes of image structure. If so, then they provide viable candidates to be inferred out of images and, once available, interpreted [36].

Given this background, the majority of the paper is concerned with developing and establishing the plausibility of a model for early orientation selection. The development begins along mathematical lines, with a consideration of how contours can be built up from more local elements—arrangements of tangents—and how abstract ideas from functional minimization and variational theory can be used to develop an algorithm for actually accomplishing the inference of tangents. Thus the model differs from most previous ones, in the sense that the concentration is not on so-called *line detectors*, but rather on a mathematical abstraction of what it means to actually detect lines and contours.

To establish the model's plausibility, we show how it leads to new psychophysical predictions, all of which have been confirmed, and to a novel conjecture about how the computations that it requires might be reduced to physiological terms.

1.1 Occluding Contours and Surface Markings

Contours and flow patterns are abstractions of some of the most prevalent structures in the physical world. Contours are produced every time an occlusion takes place between coherent objects. They are also produced by well-defined highlights cast from surface creases and other such physical events. Flow patterns, such as the hair on one's head or the surface markings on the skin of an apple, are also ubiquitous and can offer powerful clues about 3-dimensional shapes. But flow patterns arise from physical situations of a fundamentally different structure than distinct contours, as the following example shows.

1.2. The Fox and the Forest

Imagine a fox chasing a rabbit through the forest. The fox will focus its eyes on the rabbit, trying to keep most of it in full view. The fox must be sensitive to small changes in the path of the rabbit, or the rabbit could affect evasive manoeuvres. This is analogous to contour inferencing, in the sense that the fox must infer the rabbit's path through space/time.

Now consider the forest, which we shall suppose to be a dense collection of grasses and trees. As the fox runs the image cast by the forest will change, with the grasses and trees going into and out of occlusion relationships. This variability and unpredictability will be further complicated by changes in lighting and cast shadows. No matter how important the structure of the forest is, there is no way for the fox to accurately infer it in detail. Particular objects project into the fox's image for only a short time before another object obscures them. Unlike the rabbit, the forest is more like a waterfall flowing past him. The fox must make do by observing only gross changes. These two events, the rabbit and the forest, define two conceptually different optical flow problems for the fox engaged in a chase [30].

1.3. Two Structural Classes

We are now in a position to relate the metaphor of the fox and the forest to the opening examples of contours and surface markings. From now on we shall consider only spatial patterns.[1] Like the path swept out by stable highlights on the rabbit,

---

[1] The full extension of this to space/time, or optical flow, will be dealt with in a subsequent paper.

occluding contours are usually well defined *almost everywhere*. However, like the forest or a waterfall, the pattern of hair on one's head is well defined *almost nowhere* in relative terms. Each hair passes into and out of occlusion relationships with neighboring hairs so rapidly that no clear hair contours are seen: rather the impression is one of a *flow* pattern supported primarily by occasional highlights.

Both types of pattern are rich in orientation structure, but they differ in spatial support. We take this difference to be fundamental for both computational and mathematical reasons. There is a precise sense in which contours are 1-dimensional entities, while hair patterns and (the static projection of) waterfalls are 2-dimensional. Consider, in particular, an infinitesimal neighborhood in the plane. The contours with which we shall be concerned will cover only a small portion of this neighborhood as they pass through it; in fact, a 1-dimensional subneighborhood.[2] The flow of a waterfall, however, will cover the entire neighborhood with "locally parallel" entities; i.e., with entities that are pointing in roughly the same orientation.

Precisely what these entities are will become clear shortly, as will their basic computational differences. But the following example may illustrate the differences more intuitively. Consider a family of 1-dimensional surface contours, such as the pin-stripes on a shirt. Pinstripes are well defined almost everywhere, except possibly in a neighborhood around shirt creases (or self-occlusions). Now, let the pinstripes become more dense, say by smoothly decreasing the distance between them. As they become dense enough to completely cover the shirt, with no intervening space, they will completely cover the shirt: in any image of them the indication of orientation will be gone.

The difference with a hair pattern can now be stated: the image support of the hairs is given by occasional cast shadows and highlights. While the hairs cover the surface completely, the image of its orientation structure does not. Somehow the orientation structure in areas where the hairs are occluded or where there are no highlights will have to be filled in by our visual systems.

In summary, while both contours and flows provide examples of orientation structure, there is a basic difference between them: their dimensionality. But this is just the beginning. As we now show, such differences are indicative of different functional roles in recovering structure from images. For example contours (of discontinuities) delimit image areas, while flows are defined over image areas. Such distinctions are reminiscent of "edge" and "region" differences in classical computer vision, and can be expressed within a framework of partial differential equations. This framework can be specialized for the recovery of orientation-based structure and generalized to allow the integration of other kinds of structure, as follows.

2. THE FRAMEWORK

The way in which occluding contours and hair patterns relate to the physical world leads to another conceptual difference between them: Occluding contours arise when surfaces intersect projectively; they give rise to *inter-surface constraints*. Hair patterns, on the other hand, provide information about the particular surface on which they lie: they give rise to *intra-surface constraints*. This difference is fundamental to the processes that must put various sources of information together.

---

[2] We shall not be considering either fractal curves or space filling curves in this paper.

The difference can be captured metaphorically by differential equations whose solution is governed by two distinct classes of constraints:[3] the differential operator, which constrains how the solution varies over its domain, and the boundary conditions, which constrain the solution value at certain points in the domain. Note that, for 2-dimensional differential equations, such as Laplace's equation, the differential operator is an *infinitesimal* function of two variables, while the boundary condition is given by, say, the values along a 1-dimensional contour. To be more specific, recall that Laplace's equation is

$$\Delta u(x, y) = 0,$$

where Δ denotes the differential operator $(\partial^2/\partial x^2 + \partial^2/\partial y^2)$. If Ω is an open neighborhood, then a well-defined problem would be to: Find u in Ω from prescribed values of Δu in Ω and of u on $\delta\Omega$, the boundary of Ω. Such problems are known as *Dirichlet problems*. Within Ω, u is completely determined by the constraints provided by Laplace's equation and by the value of u along the boundary $\delta\Omega$.

Infinitesimally such differential operators represent the kind of constraint available from flow patterns; while the boundary conditions resemble 1-dimensional contours. In terms of our previous examples, the Laplacian corresponds to the orientation information provided by an infinitesimal "piece" of a waterfall, while the boundary condition corresponds to its bounding contour. Boundary conditions can also be specified within the domain of support Ω, as is the case with surface contours and certain highlights.

The above example is, of course, metaphorical. We do not intend to say that waterfalls are Laplacians. Rather, it is the abstract mathematical form that concerns us, and it is not limited to waterfalls. Other sources of static intra-surface constraint come from monocular shape cues, such as shape-from-shading [6, 18]: from binocular stereo disparities [16, 9, 24], and so on. Intra-surface cues only hold for particular surfaces, when coordinates are imposed on them, they are 2-dimensional. However, the values of these intra-surface cues undergo an abrupt transition as the projected image passes through a jump from one surface to another. Similar arguments hold for transitions in lighting, say from an illuminated area to one in a cast shadow [13]. Note that all of these transitions lie along 1-dimensional contours; they are topologically different from the intra-surface cues. The 1-dimensional contours can be viewed as the boundary conditions that constrain the area over which the other, 2-dimensional constraints can be integrated.

2.1. Generalization of the Framework

The framework provided by inter- and intra-surface information, or, in different terms, by differential equations, holds not only for the features described here, but for abstractions over them. Contours arising from abrupt changes in, say, a flow or hair pattern could provide the boundary constraint to a higher-level process. This could correspond to a physical situation in which the underlying surface changed orientation abruptly, but the surface markings *smoothed* it over somewhat. Thus

---

[3]A third class of constraint is also needed, which delimits the domain of the operator, but which we shall not consider in this paper. Its effects are often linked to the other boundary conditions.

issues of how to differentiate flows become as important as the flows themselves. As we shall show, the inference of a flow field may even smooth over a discontinuity (Sect. 15)! In motion, or optical flow, even more such cases arise. For it is here that the fox had to detect abrupt changes in the flow of the rabbit from smooth ones. These changes, of course, relate to the rabbit's acceleration.

It is important to stress that the *difference between the constraints is in their dimensionality*, not in the fact that they correspond to intra- and inter-surface information. While this is often the case, it is not necessarily always so, as in the case of well-defined linear surface markings or highlights. Although these are *intra-surface* events, they do arise from *inter-light-source* arrangements. But they still serve nicely as boundary conditions.

3. STATIC AND DYNAMIC FLOWS

We are about ready to launch into the body of the paper, although one caveat is necessary. For the remainder of the paper we shall concentrate on static images, understanding completely that this is an idealization for biological vision systems. Natural systems respond to images both as functions of space and of time [2]. However, these systems do have a response in normal spatial frequency and low temporal frequency ranges; this is what we are studying. The extension to more dynamic image flows is in progress [30].

4. TANGENTS, VECTOR FIELDS, AND THE RECOVERY OF CONTOURS

Since orientation selection plays such an intimate role in contour recovery, we begin with the fundamental question: *what is a contour?* It is from the answer to this question that a definition of orientation selection can be obtained.

According to differential geometry, a contour is a locus of points that satisfies a given (but perhaps unknown) functional relationship. Smooth contours arise when the function is differentiable. In such cases we locally require that the tangent, or the direction in which the contour is going as it passes through each point, must be known as well. Therefore we propose that: *Orientation selection is the process of inferring (a representation of) these tangents.* The particular representation that we adopt is one of vector fields, or a collection of unit length "needles" arranged over a 2-dimensional, planar region. That is, a vector field is a mapping that assigns a vector to each point in the region. Each of these unit vectors points in a direction that is tangent to the contour at that point.

A physical example often helps to motivate the idea of a vector field. Consider a particle of dust moving in a dust storm. Clearly it sweeps out a curve through space such that, at every point, the velocity is given by a vector at that point. The length of this vector is proportional to the speed of the particle, and its orientation indicates the direction in which it is going just as it passes through that point. The velocity vector is always tangent to the path of the particle; the tangents at every point along a curve are an arrangement of vectors in $\Re^2$. Such an assignment of vectors to points in the plane is a vector field. The naturalness of this choice as a representation for contour inferencing will become clear shortly.

5. OUTLINE OF A MODEL FOR ORIENTATION SELECTION

We propose a specific computational model for orientation selection that is motivated by the differential geometry of contours. It consists of two distinct stages, the first of which amounts to orientation selection, or the inference of a vector field of tangents, and the second of which is one of curve synthesis, or the formation of integrals through this vector field. Since this second stage is a global one, it is not unrelated to computations of shear and compression in the vector field as well.

We concentrate on the first stage of the model; for a discussion of how to find integral curves through such vector fields, as well as how they could relate to the processes by which objects are physically formed, see Kass and Witkin [11].

While the overall goal of inferring a tangent field is not sufficiently constrained by the differential geometry to lead to an algorithm, the consideration of physiological evidence suggests that there are actually two conceptual steps to this first stage. The first of these steps is one of measurement, or the acquisition of information carrying signals about orientation information. We formulate this stage as a series of convolutions that model known receptive field structures. While this first step is quite standard, the next one is not. The second step is one of interpretation of these convolution values, and we show that it cannot be done by the most commonly applied algorithm: namely, select the maximal response. Rather, more complex interactions are required, and these are formulated into what we refer to as a *response matching problem*. While this leads to an abstract formulation in optimization terms, we next sketch how this formulation can be reduced to a cooperative network, and demonstrate that the network works. A much more detailed presentation of the network and its properties is in Parent and Zucker [17].

The real scientific test of any model is in its predictions, however, and several of these are discussed. The first two relate to the convolutions that provide the initial measurements, and predictions about curvature sensitivity and density are shown to be consistent with human psychophysics. The third class of predictions leads to functional speculations about how the structure of our visual systems reflects the structure of the world. It leads to what we refer to as the *Type I* and *Type II* distinctions. The numerals here refer to the dimensionality of support of the tangent fields.

Throughout the discussion, however, it is important to remember that orientation selection in particular, and grouping in general, are complex processes. There is a wonderful diversity in what appears, on the surface, to require only one process [35]. Throughout the entire paper we shall only be talking about early orientation selection. In order to delimit when it might be active, we shall require some control over sample image patterns.

6. DOT PATTERNS AND THE GEOMETRY OF ORIENTATION SELECTION

The problem of orientation selection is inextricably connected to many aspects of early vision. There are first-order applications in which it may be thought of being applied directly to image information, such as the recovery of linear surface markings, and second-order applications in which it can be applied to the result of local processes of intensity discontinuity detection. How, then, can orientation selection be studied in isolation? Our answer to this question consists in finding a class of patterns that captures the essential geometry of orientation selection without the added complication of the interconnections with other processes. Arrangements of dots provide just such a class of patterns, as we shall now explain.

Suppose a process of discontinuity detection has operated upon an image. Three qualifiers are necessary to characterize the output: (i) the spatial positions (in, say, retinal coordinates); (ii) the value at that position; and (iii) the process responsible for producing it. Note that point (i) is common to every orientation selection process; the arrangement of positions that define the contour. Since we are concentrating on early orientation selection, as was alluded to above, it is further convenient to assume that the positions are represented in a pointillist fashion—that is, as an array of dots. Note that the intensity values associated with these dots will not be considered here; they correspond to the information produced by the process (point (ii) above), nor will the particulars of the process. Rather, we shall assume that one composite process is responsible for conveying the (high contrast) dot patterns back to the orientation selective machinery (see Zucker and Hummel, [32], for one physiologically motivated model of such a process). Details of this preliminary process, such as the fact that positive and negative contrast data are separated, change only the details of our model, not its substance. In summary, then, it is dot patterns that capture the geometry underlying orientation selection, and which permit its study (to a large extent) independently of contrast, size, and other complications. These other feature dimensions must still be investigated, however. For some preliminary research along these lines, see [34, 20].

While dot patterns may seem an unnecessary abstraction of more elementary notions such as a dark contour drawn on a light background, this is not the case. Since the contour will be sensed by an array of photoreceptors, its first representation will be pointillist; it will be an arrangement of dark points within a field of light ones. Orientation selection is the process of recovering this contour from the pointillist array. As the dots become slightly less dense, the task of orientation selection begins to resemble the task of perceptual grouping. One of the consequences of the model presented in the next section is that similar (in fact, identical) mechanisms are sufficient for a range of orientation selection and grouping tasks, but not for all. It is this difference, which is a function of both the size and the density of the dots, that in principle separates early processing from later processing.

7. A MODEL FOR EARLY ORIENTATION SELECTION AND GROUPING

Since our ultimate goal is the recovery of curves, any theory of orientation selection must begin with the definition of a curve. This, of course, raises issues of differential geometry, which we begin in the next section. Our goal is to provide the formal motivation for our model which consists of two distinct stages, the first one aimed at producing a local representation based on quantized measurements, and the second one actually recovering (a representation of) the contour. The stages are as follows:

Stage 1. Estimate a vector field of tangents. This is a spatial arrangement of unit *arrows* touching the contour at exactly one position and pointing in the direction that the curve is going as it passes through that point. The tangent can thus be interpreted as the best linear approximation to the contour at a point, an interpretation that motivates our decomposition of this first stage of the model into two steps:

Step 1. Perform measurements on a representation of the dot patterns. These measurements will turn out to be related to physiologically observed receptive field structures. But their interpretation is not unique, so we must:

Step 2. Interpret the results of the measurements. This step is formulated both abstractly as a functional minimization problem (the *response matching problem*), and concretely as a cooperative network that computes solutions to the problem. Physiologically this amounts to interactions between the various receptive fields.

Stage 2. Find integral curves through the vector field. The second stage of the model is based on the fact that the tangent is the first derivative of the contour. This suggests that contours can be recovered by a process of integration, which for our model is primarily a matter of numerical analysis and will not be treated in this paper.

These ideas will now be developed in more detail, both intuitively and formally. We concentrate, in this paper, on the two steps comprising the first stage.

7.1. What is a Curve?

The mathematical definition of a (parameterized, differentiable) curve is a differentiable map $\alpha: I \mapsto \Re^2$, where $I \subset \Re$ is an open interval, $I = (a, b)$. Here t is a parameter that runs along the curve, and for each $t \in I$ there corresponds a point $\mathbf{x}(t) = ((x(t), y(t))$ on the curve. The image set $\alpha(I) \in \Re^2$ is called the *trace* of α; it consists of just the points through which the curve passes. In the dot examples, all we are given is an aproximation to this trace; our task is to infer the curve from it.

The first derivative of the curve $\alpha'(t) = (x'(t), y'(t))$ at t is called the tangent vector to α at t. It indicates the direction in which the curve is going as it passes through t. *By the definition of a first derivative, the tangent gives the best linear approximation to the curve in the neighborhood of a point.* This observation will be important shortly when we try to estimate the tangents. Since we shall require such tangents to exist, we shall assume that our curves are (at least) piecewise C^1.[4] If the tangent vector is of unit length, $|\alpha'(t)| = 1$, then the parameter t measures *arc length* along the curve. Unit tangents are convenient for us, because our approach to orientation selection will estimate the direction of the tangent, not its length (which we shall take to be unity). It is further convenient because the derivative of the tangent $|\alpha''(t)|$, the second derivative of the curve, is the *curvature*. Viewing the tangent as the best linear approximation to the curve at t, the curvature measures how rapidly the curve is deviating from this linear approximation.

It is important to differentiate between the curve $\alpha(t)$, which is a map, and the *trace*$(\alpha(t))$, which is a set. *The reason that orientation selection is not altogether trivial is that, in the vision context, the given information consists entirely of discrete samples of the trace of the curve, not of the curve itself.* Our plan will be to use estimates of the tangent made from observations on the trace as a basis for inferring the curve. The next question, then, is what sort of measurement can provide information about the tangents, and how should it be represented.

7.2. Estimating the Tangent

Suppose that two points along the curve are given, $\alpha(t)$ and $\alpha(t + \delta)$. For δ close to zero, the two points will be *neighbors* along the curve, and the line joining them

---

[4] The issue of how to detect the breaks, or discontinuities, between the smooth curves relates to the tangent field and, hence, to how it is formed. We report some experiments on estimating human sensitivity to such breaks later in the paper.

will be an approximation to the tangent, $\alpha'(t)$. Since this is what we are after, the problem of estimating the tangent thus reduces to estimating the line joining nearby points. When the parameter t is discretized so that points lie a unit arc distance apart, the line connecting them will be a unit tangent. In actual vision applications, however, noise will be introduced by the sensors, by quantization, and so on. Therefore the formulation that we seek should allow some further degree of flexibility, as in the following re-statement of the problem: given the trace of the curve, match a template for a unit line segment (i.e., a unit tangent) with the trace of the curve; or find the unit line segment that agrees most closely with the trace samples in a neighborhood around each point. This is a mathematical problem, and it can be solved in many ways; what, for example, does "most closely" mean? These and other points must be settled, so additional motivation and constraint are required. We shall seek them in an abstraction of early visual physiology, in order to introduce a sense of biological plausibility into the model. As we show, this leads not only to a successful algorithm, but to new psychophysical predictions as well. It is these latter predictions that provide a kind of check on the biological plausibility; should any of them turn out to be false, the plausibility would be questionable.

7.2.1. Orientationally Selective Receptive Fields

Our principle biological constraint comes from orientationally selective receptive fields. Recall that receptive fields of cells in the visual system are methodologically defined by the class of stimuli that influence them. *Orientation selectivity* is a property that requires non-isotropic stimulus patterns, such as bars and lines, and indicates that the response is a function of the orientation of the stimulus.

The striate cortex, area 17, is the earliest location in the primate visual system at which any orientation selectivity can be evoked. When receptive fields here are mapped, some exhibit an elongated structure with well defined excitatory and inhibitory regions. We shall be particularly interested in the subclass of cells that Hubel and Wiesel [7] referred to as *simple cells*, or (some of) which Schiller *et al.* [21] referred to as S-cells. These cells exhibit receptive fields with a single, usually elongated center and antagonistic surrounds on either side. We shall model these as an elongated difference of Gaussians with the form shown in Fig. 1. Electrophysiologically it has been reported that these cells respond maximally to straight line stimuli with a given orientation and location; if either of these are varied, then the response drops. (We shall exhibit a precise model for this shortly.) More recently, Wilson [26] has estimated the properties of these cells psychophysically, and they agree with the model as well.

The first step of our model is a convolution of operators whose structure resembles the receptive field of certain simple cells against a dot pattern image. Although there are certainly non-linearities in the responses of cells such as these, within the first step of our model and for the class of stimuli that we are using we shall assume that they are linear. There is at least some physiological evidence for this [22], and non-linearities will be introduced by the second step of the algorithm. There is, moreover, recent psychophysical evidence that the task requires a contrast difference, which lends further support to the convolutions [20].

Another property that has been widely observed both electrophysiologically and psychophysically is that these receptive fields span a range of sizes. While this is usually explained by introducing a notion of "scale" according to which small

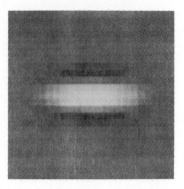

FIG. 1. A display of the operators used to model the first matching step. It is composed of a difference of two 2-dimensional Gaussians with 3 : 1 aspect ratio, and approximates the Gaussian envelope measured psychophysically.

receptive fields are sensitive to thin contours and large ones to wide contours, it will turn out that multiple size receptive fields are necessary for a more fundamental, though subtle, reason.

Although there is more to the behavior of orientationally selective cells than that listed above,[5] the above properties are sufficient for extracting the essentials: (i) the receptive field models a local line template and (ii) these templates are applied to (a representation of) the image data by a process of convolution. The templates are discrete, so orientation is quantized into explicit directions, and each of these can be interpreted as a model for a tangent to a putative contour passing through its spatial support. *Thus the receptive field templates both measure the presence of tangents and provide a medium within which they can be represented.* And the computational model is specified: define a collection of line-like templates of different orientations and sizes. Mathematically these can be specified by a collection of operators $S_x(\theta, \sigma)$, where θ indicates the orientation of the operator and σ its size. It is instructive to specify the operator at the vertical orientation, i.e., pointing along the y axis:

$$S_x(0, \sigma) = \left[c_1 G(x, \sigma) - c_2 G(x, 1.75\sigma) \right] \cdot G(y, 3\sigma) \qquad (OP)$$

where

$$G(x, \sigma) = \frac{1}{\sqrt{2\pi\sigma}} e^{-|x|^2/4\sigma}.$$

The constants were estimated by Wilson and Gelb [26].

Now, at each point in the image, perform a convolution of each of these templates against the image. In mathematical terms, if we interpret the $S_x(\theta, \sigma)$ as (non-orthoginal) basis functions, then the above procedure is tantamount to performing an L_2 match of the image against them. Although the amount of computation required for this match is enormous, it can be carried out completely in parallel. Presumably primate visual systems take full advantage of this parallelism.

[5] Such as contrast non-linearities, etc,; see Wilson and Gelb [26].

7.3. Orientation Estimation for Straight Lines

From a computational point of view, the matching scheme outlined in the previous section—convolutions against S_x basis functions—amounts to an initial local measurement of orientation information. But this measurement scheme is *not* sufficently powerful to *detect* contours in any but the simplest of circumstances. Detection requires processing subsequent to the measurement. Detection requires not only measurements, but a decision to determine what the measurements mean. Such decision processes are inherently non-linear. As long as the contours are perfectly straight and far apart (with respect to the width of the operator's spatial support), and as long as the operator is centered over the contour, this detection can be straightforward: since the convolution $S_x(\theta, \sigma)$ decreases monotonically with the difference in orientation between the operator and the contour, simply select the orientation at a point as that of the operator with the maximal response at that point. We shall call this scheme *straight maximum selection*, or *SMS*, since the selection of the maximal response at each position works only for straight lines. In symbols, for each x, let the tangent $\lambda(x)$ be given by

$$\lambda(x) = \max_{\theta} \{ S_x(\theta, \sigma) * I(x) \}. \qquad \text{(SMS)}$$

7.4. The Curvature Constraint

Now, assume the operator is still lying directly on the contour but suppose the contour is not straight within the spatial support of $S(\sigma)$. That is, let the contour curve. This introduces an inherent variation in response with the size of the operator that will totally disrupt the performance of (SMS). Somewhat surprisingly, this point is almost always missed in the literature, and slight variations on (SMS) are by far the most commonly expressed mechanisms for orientation selection.

There is one circumstance in which (SMS) is likely to work when the smallest operator is evaluated over thin contours. It will then cover only a discrete approximation to a "differential" element of the curve, which differential geometry tells us must be straight. The smallest operator thus defines the spatial precision of the vector field, and localizes the curve as precisely as possible within it. But larger operators will cover more of the curve. To illustrate how the response structure now differs from the straight case, consider an operator twice the smallest, unit size. This one covers about two unit tangent lengths. If the contour is straight, they will both be oriented identically, and the response profile will be the same as for the smallest one. However, if the contour curves, adjacent tangents will differ and the response will loose its monotonic structure.[6] Straight maximum selection cannot work.

But these response profiles—the variation in response as a function of orientation change—do contain the information necessary to generalize (SMS) into a scheme so that it can work. The key observation is that they contain information about curvature, or how the tangent changes direction within the spatial support of an operator. This information cannot be represented by the orientation at which the maximal response occurred—as it was for straight lines—but now requires information from all of the responses as a function of orientation at each point. We shall

---

[6] For graphs of how these responses change as a function of orientation change, see [29, 35].

refer to this function as the **response profile**:

$$R^S(\theta, \sigma), \qquad \theta = \theta_1, \theta_2, \ldots, \theta_N; \; \sigma = \sigma_1, \sigma_2, \ldots, \sigma_M,$$

denoting the response of the operator S, size σ, at orientation θ, where

$$R^S(\theta_i, \sigma_j) = S_x(\theta_i, \sigma_j) * I.$$

The response profiles are necessary for the generalization of straight maximum selection (SMS) into a full response matching strategy.

8. RESPONSE MATCHING PROBLEMS AND FUNCTIONAL MINIMIZATION

To generalize straight maximum selection, we shall shift our perspective to re-interpret what it was doing. Our immediate goal is to show that it worked because it was attempting to select a pattern which, if it were actually present, would give a response profile as close as possible (within the relevant universe of straight line segments) to the one actually measured. It is this matching of response profiles to known patterns with measured response profiles from unknown patterns that we refer to as a *response matching problem*.

The subsequent analysis is differential, so think in terms of small open neighborhoods around a point. We shall first indicate the structure of a response matching problem for estimating the tangent, then one for estimating curvature.

Suppose we are given an image I_{λ_1} of a straight line passing through the point x at orientation λ_1, say vertical. After convolutions against S, we would *expect* to get the response profile:

$$R^S_{\text{expected}}(\lambda_1 : \theta, \sigma) = \left\{ S(\theta, \sigma) * I_{\lambda_1}, \forall \theta, \forall \sigma \right\}.$$

Now, suppose we are given another image I_{λ_2} of a line passing through the same point but rotated one quantum in orientation. The convolution would now yield the *expected response profile*:

$$R^S_{\text{expected}}(\lambda_2; \theta, \sigma) = \left\{ S(\theta, \sigma) * I_{\lambda_2}, \forall \theta, \forall \theta \right\}.$$

which is just a shifted version of the previous one. Such *expected response profiles* could be obtained for all possible orientations of the line λ in images $I_{\lambda_1}, I_{\lambda_2}, \ldots, I_{\lambda_N}$. They signal what the perfect response profile would look like for all possible tangent patterns; i.e., for all distinct, quantized orientations of a straight line.

The above calculations can now be used to reformulate the selection process from one of selecting a maximal response to one of finding a "best" match, according to the following observation: Should any one of the line patterns λ_i, $i = 1, 2, \ldots, N$, be present in an image, then the result of the convolution should resemble one of the calculated response profiles $R^S_{\lambda_i}(\theta, \sigma)$. To be precise, suppose that we are given an image I_λ containing a line at an *unknown* orientation $\hat{\lambda}$. If we convolve the masks $S(\theta, \sigma)$ against I_λ the result will be an *observed response profile* $R^S_{\text{observed}}(\hat{\lambda}; \theta, \sigma)$. This is of the same form as the expected response profiles except that the unknown variable $\hat{\lambda}$ appears in it. Clearly $R^S_{\text{observed}}(\hat{\lambda}; \theta, \sigma)$ will match one of the

$R^S_{\text{expected}}(\lambda_i; \lambda, \sigma)$ most closely, and it is this value of λ_i that we should choose as the best instantiation of $\hat{\lambda}$. This is the line image which, if present, would give an expected response profile as close as possible to the one actually observed from the image with a line at an unknown orientation.

In symbols, then, we can formulate an abstract *response matching problem for inferring tangents to straight lines*:

Let a collection of expected response profiles $R^S_{\text{expected}}(\lambda_i; \mathbf{x}; \theta, \sigma)$ be given for a universe of primitive tangent patterns λ_i, $i = 1, 2, \ldots, P$ centered at position $\mathbf{x}$. Further, let an image $I_\lambda(\mathbf{x})$ which contains unknown tangent patterns $\hat{\lambda}(\mathbf{x})$ be given. The best estimate λ^* of $\hat{\lambda}(\mathbf{x})$ is the one that minimizes the norm difference between the expected and observed response profiles; i.e., the one that

$$\min_{\lambda_i} \left\| R^S_{\text{observed}}(\hat{\lambda}; \mathbf{x}; \theta, \sigma) - R^S_{\text{expected}}(\lambda_i; \mathbf{x}; \theta, \sigma) \right\| \tag{1}$$

at each position $\mathbf{x}$,

The estimation of (un-normalized) curvature at a point $\mathbf{x}$ can also be formulated as a response matching problem, but this time the expected responses must be built up from larger operators whose receptive field or spatial support covers (at least) two unit tangents. If we think of these tangents as λ_i and λ_j as the tangents located at neighboring positions $\mathbf{x}_i$ and $\mathbf{x}_j$, then we arrive at an analagous formulation to the one above: select λ^*_i and λ^*_j such that

$$\min_{\lambda_i, \lambda_j} \left\| R^{S_{\text{large}}}_{\text{observed}}(\hat{\lambda}, \hat{\lambda}'; \mathbf{x}; \theta, \sigma) - R^{S_{\text{large}}}_{\text{expected}}(\lambda_i, \lambda_j; \mathbf{x}; \theta, \sigma) \right\| \tag{2}$$

at each position $\mathbf{x}$.

8.1. From Functional Minimization To Cooperative Network

While the abstract formulation above is motivating, there are serious problems in trying to implement solutions to it directly. First, two tangents spanning three points are too local for accurately estimating curvature given discretization problems. Second, with larger neighborhoods the number of combinations of primitive tangents becomes overwhelming. Third, large operators will smooth over differences between local events, such as two nearby "c"-shaped curves or one "s"-shaped curve, so that inappropriate estimates will result. Finally, with large numbers of primitive patterns specified, the differences in the response profiles will become insignificant.

In general, the issue is how can we be guaranteed that a solution to minimization problem (1) above will be consistent with one from minimization problem (2) unless they are both solved simultaneously. Clearly the structure of the formulation must be used more directly in obtaining a solution. For example, recall that all of the convolutions and expected responses considered previously assume that the operator is centered on a piece of contour; responses from operators off the contour, but which overlap it to some extent at some orientation, will give responses also. These, too, must be dealt with.

A solution to these problems comes from realizing that variational and functional minimization problems can be solved using relaxation labeling techniques [8], and that the key to formulating a relaxation network consists in specifying the compatibility network. While the details here become significant, and are provided in [17], it is worthwhile to sketch a rough outline of the solution.

Associated with each possigle tangent λ at each positon $\mathbf{x}_i$ is a continuous variable[7] $p_i(\lambda)$. Neighboring tangents (in arbitrarily large neighborhoods) interact through compatibility functions $r_{i,j}(\lambda_i, \lambda_j)$ to maximize the support $S_i(\lambda_i)$ for tangent λ_i according to the formula:

$$S_i(\lambda_i) = \sum_{j, \lambda_j} r_{i,j}(\lambda_i, \lambda_j) p_j(\lambda_j)$$

where the above sum is taken over all tangent orientations λ_j at all positions $\mathbf{x}_j$ in the neighborhood of $\mathbf{x}_i$.

More precisely, the nature of the interaction is to modify the values of $p_i(\lambda)$ depending on how consistent λ at $\mathbf{x}_i$ is with its neighbors. A labeling is said to be consistent—in particular, solves a minimization problem like the ones sketched—when it maximizes all

$$\sum_{\lambda} S_i(\lambda) p_i(\lambda)$$

for all positions $\mathbf{x}_i$ and tangents λ simultaneously. The result is represented in the usual case by $p_i(\lambda*) = 1$, and $p_i(\lambda)$, $\lambda \neq \lambda^* = 0$. Appropriate formulae for accomplishing this iteratively are in [8].

What remains, then, is to specify the compatibility coefficients $r_{i,j}(\lambda_i, \lambda_j)$. As we have shown previously, tangents interact through curvature, or the change in the tangent's orientation as it is approached from either direction along a curve. Another way to characterize curvature is by the *osculating circle*, or the circle that just "kisses" the curve at a given point. We use the definition of an osculating circle to motivate the compatibility between two tangents: if a circle exists to which they are both tangent, then the tangents are said to be co-circular. Note that co-circularity is a function of both the orientation of the tangents and of their positions. It is a generalization of co-linearity in which the line is replaced by a circle. Compatibility is a simple function of co-circularity; it is one for co-circular tangents, and drops off smoothly with departure from co-circularity. The precise formulae and their derivations are in [17].

Co-circularity is a relation that can hold between putative tangents anywhere in an image. Their local neighborhood of interaction still remains to be specified. Here we use a notion of *curvature classes*, or a partitioning of an open neighborhood around each point into the discrete positions and orientations in which appropriate osculating circles can lie. Each curvature class amounts to an allowable estimate of curvature at each point. The resultant compatibilities are shown in Fig. 2 for the case of 7 curvature classes. The tangent being updated is the vertical one at the center of each display. These compatibilities generalize the earlier ones suggested on heuristic

---

[7]In biological terms, a firing rate.

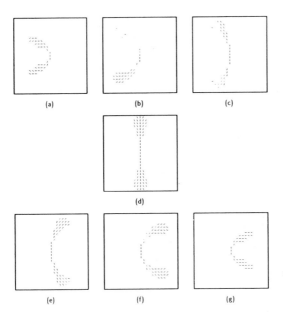

FIG. 2. The curvature classes and compatible tangent labels for the Type I process. Note how each of them contains a discrete approximation to a section of an osculating circle to the vertical tangent in the center of the displays (after Parent and Zucker [17]).

grounds by Zucker, Hummel, and Rosenfeld [33] which agree only for long straight lines that do not intersect or end. The current compatibilities extend them to curves.

9. RESULTS OF THE ORIENTATION SELECTION ALGORITHM

Now that we have formulated the orientation selection problem as two abstract steps, we must reduce those steps to realizable computations. The first step, the operator convolutions, only requires selecting discrete values for all of the parameters. We used a difference of two Gaussians, with a 3:1 aspect ratio and 1:1.75 ratio between central σ's, as suggested by Wilson and Gelb's [26] psychophysical data. Orientation (i.e., θ) was quantized into eight-directions, which is certainly too coarse for direct comparison with biological systems. The compatibilities for the relaxation process comprising the second step were the ones discussed above.

The result of applying this relaxation process to an image of a fingerprint is shown in Fig. 3. Note that the result is an arrangement of tangents that align exactly with the fingerprints, and whose orientation is consistent with theirs. This fingerprint pattern was chosen because it is more complex than the pure dot patterns that were used as motivation in the beginning of the paper. There are real variations in thickness, intensity, and contrast that have to be dealt with. The fact that the algorithm functions so robustly over this class of patterns suggests that it will work perfectly on pure dot patterns.

10. PREDICTIONS

The algorithm for orientation selection is necessarily abstract. It is derived primarily from the differential geometry of curves within the framework that visual

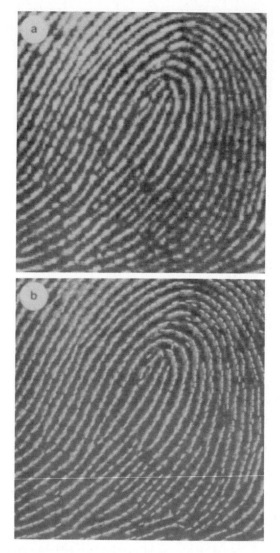

Fig. 3. An image of a fingerprint (a) and the computed tangent field (b). Each entry in the tangent field is a unit-length vector (with no difference between the head and the tail) pointing in one of 8 possible directions. The small amount of thickening at some orientations is due entirely to the coarse orientation quantization.

tasks this early are nicely formulated as matching problems. The algorithm works in a certain engineering sense. But does it have any psychophysical plausibility? Our goal in this section is to argue that it does. We shall simply sketch results, since they are all being expanded in separate papers.

The orientation selection algorithm has two steps; (i) convolutions with the oriented operators $S_x(\theta, \sigma)$, and (ii) the non-linear interpretation of these convolutions through relaxation matching. We shall concentrate on the first of these steps, since this is where the data for the response matching comes from. Should it be distorted, then we would expect the output of the response matching algorithm to be distorted. This is exactly what happens in the following two situations, both of which are designed to cause variations in the response solely with variations in the pattern. But it should be emphasized that the second processing step is also required, so that, e.g., the operator responses lying just off the contours are treated appropriately.

We shall now return to considering dot patterns as stimuli, because these will permit detailed control over the geometry of the patterns. Our particular goal is to vary the number and/or arrangement of dots that fall within the spatial support of the operators without varying the geometric structure of the patterns.

10.1. Prediction 1: The Size/Spacing Constraint

It takes two dots to define a line segment. It therefore follows that, for one of the operators $S_x(\theta, \sigma)$ to signal an oriented segment, there must be (at least) two properly oriented dots within the excitatory part of its spatial support (or receptive field).[8] Should this not be the case, then the operator will not signal the correct orientation. Perhaps the easiest way to check this is by varying the density of dots within a given pattern, leaving other structural aspects of the pattern identical. As long as two (or more) dots fall within the excitatory region, we would expect the percept to remain invariant.[9] However, as soon as the density falls below this level, so that there are less than two dots, we would expect the percept to change. For a given operator, moreover, this change should be abrupt. The prediction, to give it a first formulation, is that the percept should vary as a function of dot spacing.

But specifying spacing is not enough. Unless we also specify the size of the operators, one can be chosen to make the density take on any value. For dot patterns there is a natural manner in which the size of the operator can be chosen: by the size of the dots. For a given operator, dots that are much smaller than the excitatory center will have little effect, and those that are much larger will be canceled out by the inhibitory side lobes. There is a natural operator scale established by the size of the dots. The above prediction must be refined, then, to state that the percept should vary as a function of dot size and spacing.

We can use the Gaussian structure of the operators to quantitatively predict the function. By the above argument, the natural unit of distance is dot diameter. In the Gaussian context, take the excitatory center to be given by a Gaussian with $\sigma_{excitatory} = 1$ dot diameter. Since the other dimension is also given by a Gaussian weighting function, how far apart can two dots (with diameter $\sigma_{excitatory}$) be pushed before they no longer lie under significant support. That is, how does the integrated value of the Gaussian vary with the spacing between them? When the dots are 4.5 diameters apart, then the integrated Gaussian is about 96%. When they are 5 diameters apart, it is 99%, and more than 5 it is negligable. This means that, in the first case, when the dots are 4.5 diameters apart, there is something less than 4% of the Gaussian support left; for more than 5 diameters, there is essentially nothing. We thus have *a quantative prediction of the size/spacing constraint: the percept will*

---

[8] More precisely, there must be at least two more dots in the excitatory part than in the inhibitory part.

[9] Modulo perceived variations in density.

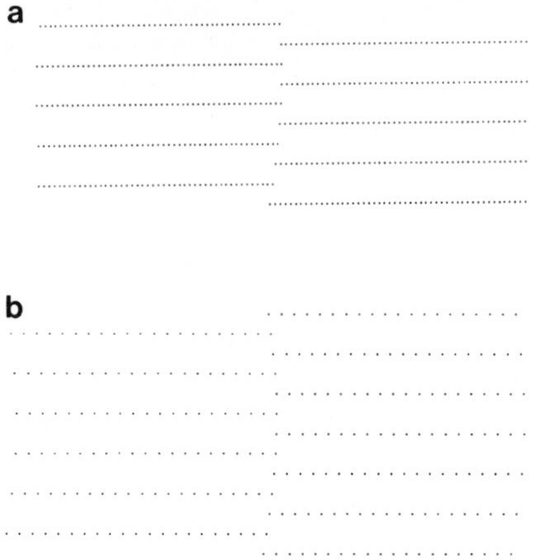

FIG. 4. A Kanizsa subjective edge drawn with dotted contours (a). For densely spaced dots, note the apparent difference in depth of the sides, and the brightness change along the edge. For sparse dots (b), however, note how these subjective effects disappear.

change at a spacing of 1 *dot*: 5 *spaces*. Below this point it should appear one way, and above it another.

This is precisely what occurs, although a specific class of patterns are necessary to reveal it. The requirement on these patterns is that they signal something different when the dots are grouped according to the above, early mechanism as compared with other, higher-level processes. We have discovered that patterns which contain *endpoints*, such as the Kanisza [10] subjective edge or the "sun illusion" work perfectly. When the dots are denser than the size/density constraint, they give rise to apparent "endpoint"; otherwise, they do not. See Fig. 4. These results are discussed in more detail in Zucker [35].

10.2. Prediction 2: Dot Positioning Effects

In our examination of the size/density constraint we varied the number of dots falling within the spatial support of an operator; we did not vary the geometry of the dots. In this next series of experiments we shall vary the positioning of the dots to determine the effects on operator responses. Now the geometry will be varying in a smooth way, and we would expect the percept to vary as well. However, as we now show, this happens only insofar as the structure of the receptive fields allows it.

Consider, to be specific, a dot pattern in which the dots are constrained to fall on the arms of a " ∧ ". How necessary is the *top dot* for defining the abrupt change in orientation? As we shift the dots along this pattern, so that the spacing[10] between them remains constant but their positions change, will there be a point at which the sharp wedge appears smoothly rounded at the top; i.e., will there be a point at which the " ∧ " will appear like a " ∩ " in the neighborhood of the top?[11]

---

[10]Assume that the density of dots is on the dense side of the size/spacing constraint, so that the above mechanism is plausible.

[11]When the experiments were actually performed, the angles of the "arms" remained constant, unlike these graphical symbols.

Many distinct lines of reasoning are possible to answer this question. The first might argue that the top corner will always be apparent, since the two arms of the "∧" are always well supported by other dots. This is not the case in practice, however; there is a point at which the "∧" appears like a "∩." How much shift is required, then? A second line of reasoning might suggest that any amount of shift is sufficent (provided it is beyond the limits of hyperacuity), because any of these would anchor the corner incorrectly. Or, one might argue, the dot must be shifted half of the inter-dot spacing, so that the pattern becomes symmetric and evenly curved on each side. Experimentally, neither of these holds either. Finally, our last line of reasoning is based on the model of orientation selection. It predicts that the dot must be moved far enough to properly inhibit the operators that signal the orientations on either side of the discontinuity; by the above geometric arguments demonstrating how dot size selects operators, one would have to predict a movement of one dot diameter. This is precisely what occurs in practice [Link and Zucker, in preparation; Link, in preparation]. Movements of $\frac{1}{4}$ or $\frac{1}{2}$ of a dot diameter cause no change.

11. FROM CONTOURS TO HAIR PATTERNS

The final test of the model comes from a class of patterns rich in orientation structure but possibly of a different sort than we have just considered. We shall now be concerned with the "flows" of waterfalls and surface markings discussed in the introductory sections. Recall that there we argued for basic structural and dimensionality differences. Our present goal is to use the model to determine whether in fact these differences exist.

In Fig. 5 we show an image of a fur pattern; in Fig. 6 we show the result of applying the algorithm to a window of it. Note that, although the predominant

FIG. 5.   An image of a fur pattern. Note that the impression is one of a flowing hair pattern.

FIG. 6. The tangent field resulting from the contour finding algorithm running on a sub-window of the fur image (Fig. 5). Note that the tangents, while indicating the correct orientation are sparse and incomplete.

orientations agree with the image pattern, they are sparse and short; it is not the dense arrangement of tangents that we would expect to underlie such patterns. Something else must be done.

12. TYPE I AND TYPE II PROCESSES

To analyze the differences between contours, such as those in the fingerprint pattern, and flows, such as the fur pattern above, we must return to basics and ask: what kinds of physical structure can give rise to what kinds of orientation structure. The most common examples cited are connected with (so-called) edge detection, or the detection of discontinuities in physical surface orientation, depth, or lighting. The salience of these physical events is manifest in the fact that they often result in intensity changes in images. It is important to realize, however, that while objects are coherent in the physical world, the ray properties of light and the arrangement of photoreceptors in our retinas destroy this coherence; rather, they result in pointillist arrays of values such as intensity discontinuities. The role of early orientation selection is to reconstruct contours through these points, contours which, when properly interpreted, will be the precursors to those which bound objects or separate light from shadows. We shall refer to the processes designed to recover patterns in this class as *Type I processes* and to the patterns themselves as *Type I patterns*.

The defining characteristics of Type I contours are that they are 1-dimensional and that they have extended and well-defined spatial support. While this notion will be made more precise shortly, to understand it intuitively just look around at any of the bounding contours in your immediate surround. Most will have clear definition almost everywhere (but not necessarily everywhere), and are quite extensive. Some may even form closed curves, although this is a point that in our view is utilized, if at all, by processes more abstract than those that we have considered. Other examples in this category come from extended highlights. This is the class of patterns that our orientation selection algorithm functioned on, so we can conclude that it is a Type I algorithm.

The physical genesis of Type I contours is that they arise from the topological intersection of 2-dimensional events; *inter-surface* occlusions; *inter-lightsource* shadows, or *inter-surface-orientation* highlights. Except for unlikely circumstances,[12] Type I contours will be 1-dimensional.

But there is another class of physical patterns rich in orientation structure that have a completely different sort of spatial support; these are more intuitively generated by *intra-surface* events such as surface markings. Consider, for example, a pattern of hair or fur [23] or a field of wheat. While these are clearly rich—even dense—in orientation information, their physical structure suffers a complexity totally unlike bounding contours. Instead of the photometry giving rise to well organized intensity events, now the photometry almost defies categorization. The image results from highlights and reflectance changes of objects (hairs) that are going into and out of occlusion relationships so often that almost no long contours are visible; rather, the impression is more one of a *flow* than of a contour. Because the subjective appearance of these *flow* patterns is so different from the Type I patterns above, we shall refer to them as *Type II patterns*; the processes that recognize and recover them are *Type II processes*. The fur image is archetypal Type II, and we have already seen that our Type I model of orientation selection does not work on it, which lends further support to the distinction. Our principle remaining goal is to formalize the difference between Type I and Type II patterns by developing a model for inferring Type II orientation structure.

13. ESTIMATING TANGENTS IN TYPE II PATTERNS

If we take a fingerprint contour as a Type I pattern, and a fur pattern as a Type II pattern, their structural difference is immediate. The first consists of single contours, densely supported and distinct. The other consists of "fragments" of contours (imaged hairs) distributed homogeneously over a surface. This difference must be incorporated into the orientation selection algorithm. Two possibilities are open. First, we could alter the initial convolutions. This is unsatisfactory since we would then have to develop another set of operators sufficent for initial orientation measurements.

Thus we are left with a second alternative, to modify the response matching and relaxation. Since the random nature of hair patterns can be shown to be equivalent to randomly skewing the positions of short hair perpendicularly to their axis of orientation, within the matching process *each response should be interpolated across several spatial positions perpendicular to the orientation of the opreator*. This will have the effect of spreading the orientation formerly associated with just one position to a small region of positions, so that "implicit contours" could then be said to exist. That is, *Type II patterns consist of dense families of implicit contours*. It is these implicit contours that give rise to the flows.

---

[12] I.e., those of measure 0.

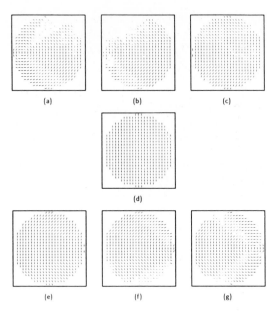

FIG. 7.   The compatibility relationships for fur, and, more generally, for flow patterns. Note that they consist not only of distinct osculating circles, but of laterally interpolated families of them.

The basic difference between the response matching problems for Type I and Type II patterns, then, is the alignment and density of the tangent fields orthogonal to the direction in which the tangents are aligned. Intuitively, some notion of "spreading" of tangents orthogonal to their orientation is required, and this can be accomplished by supporting putative tangents not only by others in the direction they are "pointing," but also skewed slightly to either side. The lateral interpolation can be seen within the new compatibilities shown in Fig. 7 for Type II patterns. The result of applying it to the fur image is shown in Fig. 8.

14. THE DIFFERENCE BETWEEN TYPE I AND TYPE II PROCESSES

The difference in the relaxation networks for Type I and Type II patterns gives additional insight into where the names come from. Since the first, Type I matching process takes place only along the curve, it is essentially a 1-dimensional process. The Type II process, however, which incorporates interpolation i the other direction, is essentially a 2-dimensional process. Within the discretely quantized grid, this difference is apparent when the compatibilities are compared. However, the difference can be expressed more elegantly within the language of dynamical systems and differential flows.

14.1. Vector Fields and Flows

Recalling that the tangent is the first derivative of a contour, it follows that vector fields are intimately associated with differential equations. For

$$x' = f(x)$$

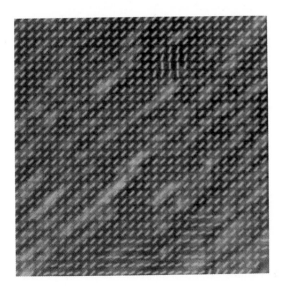

FIG. 8.   The result of running the relaxation process with the new compatibilities incorporating lateral interpolation on the sparse tangent field in Fig. 6. Note that now the tangent field is dense.

$f = \alpha'$ is a mapping from $S \subset \Re^2$ into $\Re^2$. The space S is an open subset of Eucledian space that we shall refer to as the *spatial support for the vector field*; it is the collection of points over which it is defined. Another way to think of this trajectory is as a map from $\Re \times S \mapsto S$ defined by $(t, x) \mapsto x_t$. The map $\phi_t : S \mapsto S$ that takes x into x_t is what is normally referred to as a *dynamical system*. These, too, are intimately connected with differential equations by

$$f(x) = \frac{d}{dt}\phi_t(x)\bigg|_{t=0}.$$

Thus, for $x \in S$, $f(x)$ is a vector in $\Re^2$ which one can think of as the tangent vector to the curve $t \mapsto \phi_t(x)$ at $t = 0$. $\phi_t(x)$ is the flow of all points over which the vector field is defined, starting with x and parameterized by t.

14.2. The Dimensionality Difference Between Type I and Type II Processes

With this background on differential flows, we are now in a position to precisely specify the dimensionality difference between Type I and Type II patterns. Mathematically, a Type I pattern is a flow along the spatial support S which is a 1-dimensional sub-manifold of $\Re^2$; in a Type II pattern, S is fully 2-dimenstional. Conceptually, in Type I patterns, the points flow along a contour; in Type II patterns, entire regions flow along "locally parallel" families of contours.

This is not to say that families of Type I contours cannot be arranged along the second dimension; they can. This is exactly what happened in the case of the fingerprint. But the kinds of patterns that they create are structurally different, as can be seen by running the Type II interpretation process in the fingerprint pattern;

FIG. 9. The tangent field computed with the Type II process for the fingerprint pattern. Note that now the tangent field is dense (only every sixth label vertically and horizontally is shown) and that they do not align with the specific print contours.

see Fig. 9. Note that now, although the tangents are oriented appropriately, they no longer align with the individual contours; rather, they cover the surface of the fingerprint uniformly.

15. PSYCHOPHYSICAL PREDICTIONS FOR TYPE II PATTERNS

To study human sensitivity to Type II patterns, it is convenient to have a dotted version of them. There is precisely such a class, known as random dot Moiré patterns (RDMPs), or Glass patterns [5]. Unlike those that we have been considering up till now, these have an orientation structure that is supported "randomly." There is no trace of a well-defined (albeit unknown) contour. Rather, there is a uniform distribution of short traces from a family of contours.

The structure of RDMPs becomes more clear when the mechanism for generating them is specified. It starts with a uniform distribution of random dots. A copy of this random dot pattern is then made. This copy is subjected to a transformation (such as a rotation, dilation, or vertical shift), and finally superimposed on the original. The result is striking for small transformations; see Fig. 10. The orientation structure imposed by the transformation is clear—in this case circular—although the pattern has a drastically different quality to it. Instead of consisting of clear, well-defined, 1-dimensional contours, now it consists of a 2-dimensional flow. *No contours are apparent running through it; just the impression of a flow.*

15.1. Prediction 3: Orientation Change Sensitivity in Type II Patterns

The additional lateral interpolation in Type II processing should effect human sensitivity to them and we can use RDMPs to study it. These differences are

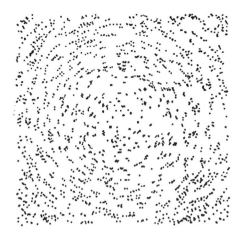

FIG. 10. A random dot Moiré (or Glass) pattern made with a circular transformation. Note how the impression is one of flow, and that no clear circular contours are apparent.

especially clear around discontinuities, as we show in the next figures. In Fig. 11, we show a parallel arrangement of Type I contours with a small orientation discontinuity horizontally through the center. These contours consist of pairs of dots at the correct orientation arranged randomly along the contour. Note that the horizontal discontinuity is immediately apparent. In Fig. 10b, however, we show the same dot pairs at the same orientation, but no longer constrained to lie along the straight contours; they can fall uniformly across the plane. The horizontal discontinuity is no longer apparent, and the display seems to change orientation smoothly from the top to the bottom. Larger differences in orientation are apparent both in arrangements of Type I patterns and in Type II patterns; see Fig. 12.

The reason why orientation discontinuities are smoothed over by the lateral interpolation is illustrated in Fig. 13. Further analysis and the effects of segment length (or number of overlays in RDMPs) are discussed in Link and Zucker [14].

The difference between the patterns in Fig. 11 can be used to illustrate the computational difference between them. Imagine applying the orientated operators in Fig. 1 to the top pattern in Fig. 11. It would give correct responses provided the lines did not get too close; at the point where the lines were really dense (less than 1 dot diameter apart) they would null the operators' response. The field would be essentially homogeneous. There is *no* way in which the operators could signal 2-dimensional versions of Type I patterns. In Type II patterns, however, the random skewing of dots allows the operators to function. The extra interpolation step, or the smearing introduced by the matching process, then allows the second dimension to be "filled in." This filling in accounts for a number of sensitivity differences in the perception of Type I and Type II patterns.

16. SIMPLE AND COMPLEX CELLS

The motivation for the first step of the orientation selection algorithm was based loosely on the physiologically observed performance of simple cells. These are cells that respond to, say, line stimuli as a function of both position and orientation. If

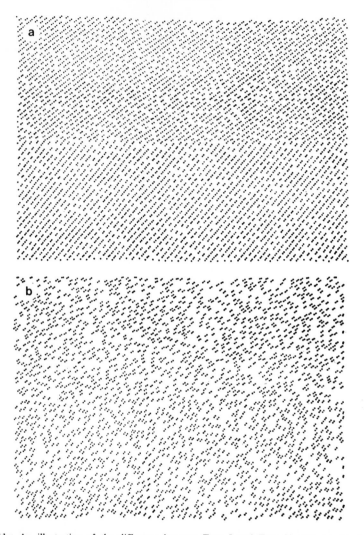

FIG. 11. An illustration of the difference between Type I and Type II patterns. (a) A pattern composed of parallel arrangements of Type I contours. The dots are in properly oriented pairs dropped randomly along the contours. There is a small orientation difference between the top half and the bottom half that is readily apparent. But the lines could not be moved much closer before the dots would interfere with one another along perpendicular directions. (b) A random dot Moiré pattern with the same orientation structure as the top pattern. Note that the line of orientation discontinuity is not visible.

either of these are varied from the maximal value, the response of the cell decreases. We are now in a position to re-examine this connection.

If we just consider the initial operator convolutions, then the above performance criteria hold. But it is significant to observe that when we add on the interactions between receptive fields necessary to implement the interpretation, they still hold. This is not, however, the case for Type II patterns and processes. In this latter

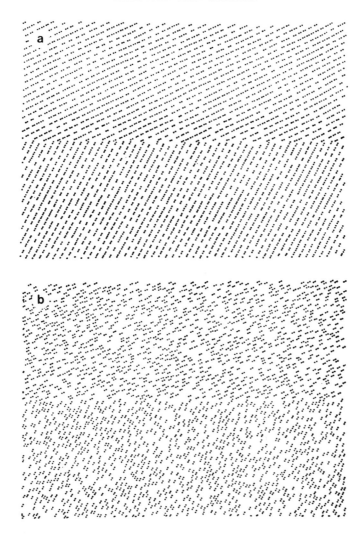

FIG. 12.   A pair of patterns identical to the previous ones, except that now the orientation difference is larger.

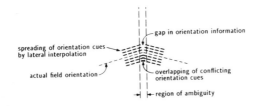

FIG. 13.   An illustration of how the lateral spreading of orientation information causes problems in the neighborhood of a discontinuity [14].

situation, since the match takes place over a 2-dimensional neighborhood rather than just point-to-point, different performance criteria emerge. The response will still drop off with changes in orientation, since this would alter the initial convolutions. However, it will *not* drop off with positon until this variation takes it out of the effective matching neighborhood! That is, if one were to perform what might be thought of as the equivalent to the electrophysiology on the Type II algorithm, orientation change sensitivity would be high but positonal sensitivity (within a range) low. This is precisely what Hubel and Wiesel [7] have observed for complex cells, and leads us to conjecture that, for some simple and complex cells, *simple cells are responsible for Type I processing and complex cells are responsible for Type II.* The fact that some Type I/simple cell processing preceeds Type II/complex cell processing is also consistent with the physiology, since a large number of complex cells receive input through what appear to be simple cells [4]. Also, none of the tangent field computations shown here required more than 4 iterations; i.e., more than 4 layers of interconnected simple and simple/complex cells. Hence there is more than ample "machinery" available in V1 and V2.

While the precise mapping onto physiology remains to be investigated, there is one class of predictions that would greatly accelerate it. According to the model, we predict that simple cells should only respond sparsely and occasionally to RDMPs and flow patterns. Simple cells near to the layers that receive the first innervation from the lateral geniculate nucleus should show the most responses, since these are providing the earliest orientation measurements, while those further along in the processing hierarchy should show less. It is these higher order cells that are presumably implementing something like the relaxation matching. Complex cells, on the other hand, should show strong responses to RDMPs and flow patterns.

17. CONCLUSIONS

How can contours be inferred from a collection of dots, or, more generally, from the intensity data available in biological vision systems? More generally, what is the role of contours in vision systems, and, more specifically, how is orientation connected with contour inference? The answers to these questions are all connected with the study of orientation selection, and they illustrate the scope of the investigation that we have begun.

Orientation selection was defined in abstract terms as the inference of a vector field of tangents. Since the tangent is the first derivative of a contour (at a point), this led to a 2-step algorithm for orientation selection: (1) try to estimate the tangent with a local measurement; and (2) since these measurements are ambiguous, interpret them. Both of these steps were given precise formulations as matching problems. The first match was further motivated by the rough structure of receptive fields early in vision. The second, called a response matching problem, amounted to a relaxation labeling network that can be thought of as excitatory and inhibitory interactions between the receptive field convolutions.

The algorithm worked, and, even more importantly, has led to a number of new psychophysical predictions about curvature sensitivity. But the emphasis in this paper was on orientation selection as an early process in vision. As such it should be syntactic, or data directed, and can provide only rough "first guesses" about significant orientation information. Another prediction, a size/spacing constraint, was confirmed psychophysically that seems to delimit when this syntactic processing could be reasonable. Heuristically it can be interpreted as defining conditions under which dotted lines are dense enough to function as solid ones. This heuristic was further supported by showing that densely dotted lines can trigger subjective figures and smooth curves, but sparse ones cannot. The size/density constraint is further connected to the model, because it constrains the operators that provide the initial orientation signals.

But not all patterns rich in orientation information can be handled by the contour detection process. Another class of patterns was uncovered that differ in a fundamental way. Waterfalls are an archetypal example of this class, in that they appear as dense flows rather than well-delimited families of contours. These flows arise from the fleeting highlights cast by the water, persist only briefly, and contain a random component. Random dot Moiré patterns model this class wonderfully, and we referred to them as Type II patterns. Type I patterns are the contours. The names, Type I and Type II, reflect the basic difference in dimensionality of the spatial support of the resultant tangent fields: Type I patterns are 1-dimensional, and Type II patterns are 2-dimensional. This dimensionality difference was reflected in the second matching step. It also leads to various sensitivity differences which have physiological counterparts. Thus we conjectured that Type I processes are supported by simple cells, and Type II processes by complex ones.

For orientation selection, one of the earliest and most general of the inverse problems comprising vision, the constraints necessary for a solution were derived from differential geometry. An algorithm for inferring oriented entities was developed that led, in examining its biological plausibility, to a number of predictions that have since been confirmed. Thus the paper began the cycle of theory, prediction, and confirmation in the context of orientation selection. Our next steps are to extend the theory into motion, or early optical flow. All indications are that analagous results will hold, and we remain excited about the shape of the predictions.

ACKNOWLEDGMENTS

An earlier version of this paper was presented at the Workshop on Human and Machine Vision held in Montreál, August, 1984. Research was sponsored by NSERC Grant A4470. The simulation was formulated with and implemented by Pierre Parent and the psychophysics were done with Norah Link. I thank them and Yvan Leclerc for comments on the manuscript.

REFERENCES

1. T. Binford, Inferrring surfaces from images, *Artif. Intell.* 1981.
2. D. Fleet, A. Jepson, and P. Hallett, *A Spatio-Temporal Model for Early Visual Processing.* RCBV-TR-84-1, Computer Science Dept., University of Toronto, 1984.
3. J. Gibson, *Perception of the Visual World*, Houghton Mifflin, New York, 1950.
4. C. Gilbert, Microcircuitry of the visual cortex, *Ann. Rev. Physiol.* 1983.
5. L. Glass, Moire effect from random dots, *Nature (London)* **243**, 1969, 578–580.
6. B. Horn, Obtaining shape from shading information, in *The Psychology of Computer Vision*, (P. Winston, Ed.), McGraw-Hill, New York, 1975.
7. D. Hubel and T. Wiesel, Functional architecture of macaque monkey visual cortex. *Proc. R. Soc. (London), Ser. B*, 1977, **198**, 1–59.
8. R. A. Hummell and S. W. Zucker, On the foundations of relaxation labeling processes, *IEEE Trans. Pattern Anal. Mach. Intell.* **PAMI-5**, 1983, 267–287.
9. B. Julesz, *Foundations of Cyclopean Perception*, Univ. of Chicago Press, Chicago, 1971.
10. G. Kanizsa, *Organization in Vision*, Praeger, New York, 1979.

11. M. Kass and A. Witkin, Analyzing oriented textures, in *Proc. Int. Joint Conference on Artificial Intelligence*, Los Angeles, 1985.
12. K. Koffka, *Principles of Gestalt Psychology*, Harcourt, Brace & World, New York, 1935.
13. Y. Leclerc and S. W. Zucker, The local structure of intensity discontinuities in one dimension, *Proc. 7ICPR*, Montreal, 1984.
14. N. Link and S. Zucker, *Sensitivity to Corners in Flow Patterns*, Technical Report 85-3, Computer Vision and Robotics Lab., McGill University, Montreal, 1985.
15. D. Marr, *Vision*, Freeman, San Francisco, 1982.
16. J. Mayhew and J. Frisby, Psychophysical and computational studies towards a theory of human stereopsis, *Artif. Intell.* **17**, 1981, 349–385.
17. P. Parent and S. Zucker, *Curvature Consistency and Curve Detection*, Technical Report 85-12R, Computer Vision and Robotics Lab., McGill University, Montreal, May, 1985.
18. A. Pentland, *Local Shading Analysis*, Tech. Note 272, SRI International, Palo Alto, Calif., 1982.
19. A. Pentland, Fractal-based description of natural scenes, in *Proc. Image Understanding Workshop*, 1983, pp. 184–192.
20. S. Pradzny, Some new phenomena in the perception of Glass patterns, draft, Schlumberger Palo Alto Research Center, 1985.
21. P. Schiller, B. Finlay, and S. Volman, Quantative studies of single-cell properties of monkey striate cortex. I. Spatiotemporal organization of receptive fields, *J. Neurophysiol.* **6**, 1976, 1288–1319.
22. R. Schumer and A. Movshon, Length summation in simple cells of cat striate cortex, *Vision Res.* **24**, 1984, 565–571.
23. K. Stevens, Computation of locally parallel structure. *Biol. Cybern.* **29**, 1978, 19–26.
24. D. Terzopoulos, Multilevel computational processes for visual surface reconstruction. *Computer Vision Graphics Image Process.* **24**, 1983, 52–96.
25. M. Wertheimer, Laws of organization in perceptual forms, *Psychol. Forsch.* **4**, 1923, 301–350; transl. in *A Source Book of Gestalt Psychology*, pp. 71–88, W. Ellis, Routledge & Kegan Paul, London, 1938.
26. H. Wilson and D. Gelb, Modified line-element theory for spatial-frequency and width discrimination, *J. Opt. Soc. Amer.* **A1**, 1984, 124–131.
27. A. Witkin and J. M. Tenenbaum, The role of structure in vision, in *Human and Machine Vision*, (J. Beck, B. Hope, and A. Rosenfeld, Eds.), Academic Press, New York, 1983.
28. S. W. Zucker, On the structure of texture, *Perception*, **5**, 1976, 419–436.
29. S. Zucker, *Early Orientation Selection and Grouping: Evidence for Type I and Type II Processes*, Technical Report 82-8, Department of Electrical Engineering, McGill University, August, 1982.
30. S. W. Zucker, *The Fox and the Forest: A Type I, Type II Constraint for Early Optical Flow*. Technical Report 83-11, McGill University, Montreal; presented at the *ACM Workshop on Motion: Representation and Control*, Toronto, 1983.
31. S. W. Zucker and R. A. Hummel, Toward a low-level description of dot clusters: labelling edge, interior, and noise points, *Comput. Graphics Image Process.* **9**, 1979, 213–233.
32. S. W. Zucker and R. A. Hummel, Receptive fields and the reconstruction of visual information, *Seventh International Conference on Pattern Recognition*, Montreal, July 1984.
33. S. W. Zucker, R. A. Hummel, and A. Rosenfeld, An application of relaxation labelling to line and curve enhancement, *IEEE Trans. Comput.* **C-26**, 1977, 393–403, 922–929.
34. S. Zucker, K. Stevens, and P. Sander, *Similarity, Proximity, and the Perceptual Grouping of Dots*, A.I. Memo 670, Artificial Intelligence Lab., MIT, April, 1982; *Percept. and Psychophys.* **34**, 1983, 513–522.
35. S. W. Zucker, Cooperative grouping and early orientation selection, in *Physical and Biological Processing of Images*, (O. Braddick and A. Sleigh, Eds.), Springer, New York, 1983.
36. S. W. Zucker, A. Rosenfeld, and L. S. Davis, General purpose models: Expectations about the unexpected, in *Adv. Papers Fourth International Joint Conference on Artificial Intelligence*, Vol. 2, Tblisi, USSR, September, 1975.

PERSPECTIVES IN COMPUTING